3x726

AT STAKE

Monsters and the Rhetoric of Fear

in Public Culture

EDWARD J. INGEBRETSEN

THE UNIVERSITY OF CHICAGO PRESS

CHICAGO AND LONDON

EDWARD J. INGEBRETSEN is associate professor of English and director of American studies at Georgetown University. He is the author of *Maps of Heaven, Maps of Hell: Religious Terror as Memory from the Puritans to Stephen King* and *Robert Frost's Star in a Stone Boat: A Grammar of Belief*.

The University of Chicago Press, Chicago 60637
The University of Chicago Press, Ltd., London
© 2001 by The University of Chicago
All rights reserved. Published 2001
Printed in the United States of America
10 09 08 07 06 05 04 03 02 01   1 2 3 4 5
ISBN: 0-226-38006-8 (cloth)
ISBN: 0-226-38007-6 (paper)

Library of Congress Cataloging-in-Publication Data
Ingebretsen, Ed.
    At stake : monsters and the rhetoric of fear in public culture / Edward J. Ingebretsen.
        p.   cm.
    Includes bibliographical references and index.
    ISBN 0-226-38006-8 (alk. paper)
    ISBN 0-226-38007-6 (pbk. : alk. paper)
    1. Monsters in mass media.   2. Mass media—United States.   3. Popular culture—United States. I. Title: Monsters and the rhetoric of fear in public culture. II. Title.
P96.M62 U655 2001
302.23'0973—dc21   2001001078

♾ The paper used in this publication meets the minimum requirements of the American National Standard for Information Sciences—Permanence of Paper for Printed Library Materials, ANSI Z39.48–1992.

CONTENTS

Dedicated to the memory of Fr. Leo Rock, S.J.,

magister spiritualis

who first taught me that monsters are only angels, coming upon us from our dark side. Be not afraid, they say; make your shadow your grace.

Thank you, Leo, and thank you to my brothers in the Society of Jesus.

ACKNOWLEDGMENTS

Those who gave
    Curtis Bryant, S.J.
    Michael Dolan
    Marc Fellman
    Mark Herlong
    Jason Juffras
    Christina Lorenz
    James Walsh, S.J.
    My students at Georgetown, Tromso, and Bergen

Those who read
    Laura Castor
    Richard Fusco
    Brian Colin Haines
    Elizabeth McKeown
    Ann Holden Ronning
    Mark Smith
    Martin Snyder
    Anne and Barry Weston
    Curt Withrow
    Jill and Stephen Wolfe

Friends in the dark time
    Rick Aldrich
    Ed Bodnar, S.J.
    John Breslin, S.J.
    Kevin and Paul Cahill
    Cecelia Cavanaugh
    Peter Church
    Greg Crist
    Gary Fisher

Leona Fisher
Michael Garanzini, S.J.
Tim Gilman
Paul Higgins
Theresa Keller
Tom Murphy
Nils Nissen
Patricia O'Connor
Orm Overland
Joe Petit
Ed Quinn
Sam Sara, S.J.
Mary Lee Settle
John Squiot
Margaret Stetz
Nick Street, *editor magnifico*
Patrick Terrian
Matthew Tinkcom
Kevin Wildes, S.J.
Janie, Ian, and Julia
Margaret, Peter, and the 'bits
the Counselors Four:
    Joe Dever, Jeff Resetarits, Michael Callahan, Scott Martin
My parents, always, and
Charles my brother, Yvonne and Carol, my sisters

Special thanks to Ken Pribanic, who found the angel warding the dead and brought him home.

And to Jay Kent Lorenz, who shares this.

Special thanks to Jean Olsen and the Norwegian-American Fulbright Association in Oslo; and to the Engelsk Institutt faculties at Tromso and Bergen; and to Tom Orange and the Georgetown English Department—the staff for technical help and the faculty for intellectual inspiration.

To Dr. Martin E. Marty, Dr. Jeffrey Jerome Cohen, and Dr. Jerry Cobb, S.J., for their careful reading of this text; and finally, to Doug Mitchell and Russell Harper at the University of Chicago Press, for the way they make hard things look easy.

Mythical creatures, cherubim combine attributes of several species, including . . . the strength of a bull, the swiftness of an eagle, and the wisdom of a human being.

Hershel Shanks, *Jerusalem: An Archeological Biography,* 47

Whoever fights monsters should see to it that in the process he does not become a monster. And when you look into an abyss, the abyss also looks into you.

Friedrich Nietszche, *Thus Spake Zarathustra*

St. Michael, the Archangel, defend us in battle, be our defense against the wickedness and snares of the devil. May God rebuke him, we humbly pray; and do thou, O Prince of the heavenly host, by the power of God, thrust into Hell Satan and the other evil spirits who prowl about the world for the ruin of souls. Amen.

Traditional

Prologue:
What the Angel Said

"Be not afraid."

It is a Christmas season close to the millennium. Plastic angels of all sizes fill store windows and float through malls. They have no genders, only wings; no clothes, only round, unformed flesh. Their gender has disappeared so that they might better serve a sex-obsessed yet body-phobic culture. These plastic *putti*—messengers of God, once alive with divine alarm—now flit through the air in the service of mammon, a different god entirely.[1] Once armed with flaming swords, angels are now mall chic for generic holiday shopping on the eve of the birth.[2]

Yet there is a messenger, instantly understood as otherworldly, whose divine credentials nonetheless seem suspect. That is, monsters, like angels, are ubiquitous in markets and cultural byways. From cinemas, bookstalls, and newspapers they issue reprisal and reproach, although coyly they offer invitation as well into a garden of fierce delights. While we might not always think of them in these terms, monsters are God-sent. Indeed, from time immemorial the monster was an "omen from the gods," who *like* the angelic visitor brought news of an often dread-ful kind.

Fear and dread, of course, are traditional markers of divinity. In this monsters are more like angels than not. On the other hand, angels, in the terror they inspire (see Titian's *Annunciation,* for example), are more akin to monsters than not. Indeed, a characteristic of all angelic visitations is that they are terrifying.[3] Scripture tells us that the ritual salutation of the angel is "Be not afraid!" The regularity of this greeting suggests that a bracing fear *should* mark the angel's visit, since it betokens mystery as well as grace; since the angel challenges as well as comforts. Rightly understood, then, monsters (dark angels, if you wish) are sacred—the one awe-ful and the other, awful. The monster might be said to be older than the angel, properly understood—its lineage of fabulous fright, the stone-making glance, lost in pre-Christian antiquity. (Even in Genesis it is the monster—the speaking and thus law-breaking serpent—who appears first. The angel only comes in at the last moment, apocalyptically, to announce the end of Eden.)

We are not, however, accustomed to our angels giving us a fright.[4] In that we cheapen them, as does *Forrest Gump,* where the angelic feather floating through the film intends us to read Gump's life as one of effortless revelation, "easy transcendence."[5] On the other hand, the monster encourages fear in a very direct way.[6] As Will Rockett writes in *Devouring Whirlwind,* citing William James, the "ancient saying that the first maker of the gods is fear receives voluminous corroboration from every age of religious history."[7] As an occasion of *pietas,* filial awe or awesome fear, one might say then that the monster's divinity is marked on the sly—a shadow of the fear inspired by God in every text in which He ever appeared, including the first. Remember that Eve and Adam, hearing God walk in the garden, "hid because they were afraid." The stories tell us true. We, children of those stories, know the fearful lesson of the angels firsthand. Those wings mark them as monstrous, the message they carried, awe-ful. One commentator notes the connection to the modern, intellectually underweight creature of the films: "And these mythic monsters are awe-inspiring. They play upon our fear and also our childlike awe."[8]

Why this initial meditation upon angels and monsters? Both derive from a religious cosmology which many sophisticated persons would declare to be tired and worn. Even swirling around the funeral of Matthew Shepard with wings made of sheets, angels bring intimations of this past. We separate angel and monster to our peril—first by domesticating the terror out of the angel, and second, by draining away the reverence due the monster. Either way we are left with cartoons—saccharine piety on the one hand, formula fright on the other. Stripped of their strangeness, angels have become pets of a sort, still subject to our control—guardian angels, as they are sentimentally called. It is part of our narcissistic religious fantasy that they hover nearby at moments of peril—a bridge crossing troubled waters, for example, or in some other figurative place of dreadful crossing (*trans-gressio,* to go across). Monsters, however, as traditions tell us, are also guardians, although with a slight change in emphasis. Like Cerberus, they guard bridges and gates, protecting human boundaries against those who think to test them by crossing out. Monsters warn by example: they are themselves terrible consequences.

Thus, in addition to their place in the markets and films, where we shop them as sentiment and cinematic thrill, angels and monsters bear an authority with ancient warrant. The language of religion—as the word itself suggests—is a binding, a holding together: the "attention paid to divine directives."[9] Somewhat cynically one could agree with William James that religion's unquestioned power to shape, bind, and control is judiciously guaranteed by the use of fear. This book argues that this suspect use of religious authority has not disappeared—an obvious conclusion, given the populations of winged creatures drifting through malls and theaters, and crowding boutiques. Similar conclusions can be reached by observing the darker creatures of dread crawling out of cinemas into tabloids and presidential address. Religious authority—or maybe its habit—has gone not away, but merely underground, hidden everywhere in full view as political commodity.[10]

And, of course, money figures in. Fright and scandal are the new form of worship, replacing piety and epiphany; a glut of goods exploits a hunger for God. Thus are angels and monsters retrieved from dusty religious basements for less than heavenly motives: the sacred and the scary sell. Marketed, angelic transcendence becomes little more than sentiment, feel-good shopping. An angel pinned to a lapel is an economic and civic statement as well as a theological memory. The angel cult drains pocketbooks while forming the "nice" person, thus dispensing with need for soul and interiority both.[11] More importantly, however, the angelizing of the civic boutique reflects a deep and insistent fear of the central mystery of the Christian imagination—the monstrous implications of a god who becomes mortal and who invites us to be god-like. Anxiety about what it all means takes us shopping at Christmas, not to church. That is, despite its vaunted systems of theology certain questions are unanswerable by Christian discourse, and these have central civic importance: Can the body possessed by the Divine ever be totally under human control? By way of analogy, in an era obsessed with safe sex, can *any* human intimacy be truly "safe"? Prompted by such anxieties the prepubescent bodies of mall-*putti* provide the safest bodies going.

The ubiquity of the monster in the last two decades is astonishing and practically unnoticed. It suggests a parallel to the obsession with angels, although in reverse form, as it were. If the plastic angel strips away the fiery sword and gives us Luke Skywalker's lightsaber, the monster likewise becomes an occasion of religion on the sly—sentimentalized fright, comfort rather than warning. And even that is evacuated of any real terror: "Learn to Hug Your Monster"—chirrups a new self-help book, while the "Monster in My Closet" doll is marketed to make you "feel better."[12] Anyone can become a nice angel; anyone can have a shadowy monster.

So maybe Engels was right, and maybe angels and monsters *are* partial evidence of what he called the "bunk" of religion.[13] Even today, for the many people who wouldn't give them a moment's thought, the language of angels and monsters serves as a formal emotional shorthand of civic possibility.[14] In effect, whether guarding the bridge or standing at the gates of the normal, angels teach us what we must love; from the other side, monsters teach us who or what we need to fear. To each, in differing ways, is entrusted the burden of warding civility. Beyond the limit of the human, as medieval maps attest, "that way monsters lie." Thus, the sacred and taboo derive strength from each other, as Utopia and Apocalypse, at first seemingly at odds, end up by completing each other. Monstrous bodies are the remarkable presences that appear as signs of civic omen, or trauma, and which demand interpretation: they offer a bit of each, apocalypse as well as utopia. These angels with flaming swords are divinities. They bring us news, and not always what we want to hear. Read Genesis. It's all there.

This particular moment has always seemed to me uncanny,
when the faceless image acquires a quasi-human personality,
and one is put in mind of the making of monsters.

Iris Murdoch, *A Severed Head,* 48

. . . the pleasure [of] monsters . . . the danger of monsters . . .
and their "promise."

Judith Halberstam, *Skin Shows: Gothic Horror*
and the Technology of Monsters, 85

. . . the Originall of all great, and lasting Societies, consisted not
in the mutuall good will men had towards each other, but in the
mutuall fear they had of each other.

Thomas Hobbes, *De Cive,* I.1.1

THINKING ABOUT MONSTERS

"The Monsters Next Door: What Made Them Do It?" *Time* magazine's cover question announced more than it asked.[1] True to the genre of the monster, however, it made two points: the monster is near, and the monster needs interpreting. But the cover failed to ask two important questions. How does one make a monster? What are the uses of monstrous persons in confirming the map of civility? The word "monster" brings with it into everyday use classical, pre-Christian echoes. From ancient times the monster—a child born with physical abnormalities—was an object of fear and wonder.[2] The unnatural birth was an omen from the gods, a remonstrance or rebuke to human communities for faults known and unknown. The monstrous birth was often abandoned or put to death. John Block Friedman cites Roman law dating from as early as 450 B.C.: "A father shall immediately put to death a son recently born, who is a monster, or has a form different from that of members of the human race."[3] In every age since, the monster has excited emotions ranging from fear and bewilderment to curiosity and reverence, even a desire for the strange and exotic.[4] In addition, while the child with two heads or no arms was portentous for the community, a *prodigium,* it was often a "providence" as well.[5] It was a boon, productive of gossip, financial exchange, and even of social cohesion. Thus, whether defined biologically as the "sport of nature" (*lusus naturae*); or socially, as deviant, abnormal or misfit; or religiously, as objectively disordered; and whether interpreted as a sign from the gods or an agent of the devil, monsters are occasions of dense exchange.[6] They are *monstra:* showings, and tellings—often of the bawdy kind, sometimes for money, always for moral trade.[7] Learning to read the various epistemologies and political significances of the monstrous body is central to this book.

At Stake explores the use of the word "monster" as metaphor and rubric in Gothic America: how, employed as a rhetoric of rebuke, the metaphor justifies a range of socially discounted but nonetheless tolerated behaviors—violences physical as well as rhetorical, social expressions of astonishment, scandal and insult, displays of sex as moral currency and economic exchange. Thus the paradox: On the one hand the monster is burdened with behaviors that are deemed to threaten society. On the other hand, the monster makes such incivilities possible, even justifies them or others in the name of the common good. I am concerned with how the scandal and reprisal invariably associated with monstrosity—its "show"— are staged pedagogically as explicit public preachment. Often this teaching is so successful that the violences condoned in such ceremonies are overlooked in the leering spectacle of their display.

In the main I shall confine my discussion to cases of public record, the *lingua monstra* of media, the casual drive-by vilification of failed humans that clutter vernacular discourse—newspaper, magazine, and tabloid accounts, radio talk shows and *cinéma vérité*. My primary focus will be a handful of persons deemed so terrible that they have been cordoned off as monsters, bringers of terrible news—for which, amazingly, we will pay much money to hear. Susan Smith, for example, killed her two children by drowning them. Another, Andrew Cunanan, was the presumptive killer of five persons, including a well-known fashion designer. Very little was known about either Smith or Cunanan, although as befits the monster, vast amounts were speculated as to both, their origins and consequences.[8] When the smoke cleared after his suicide, for example, it was the exotic detailing of Cunanan's (presumed) sexual life, rather than his criminality, that received the most media play. Cunanan had the misfortune of being swept into the representational gravity of Jeffrey Dahmer, whose (also presumed) sexual practices gave his story its enduring features. Susan Stewart observes that "the monster's sexuality takes on a separate life."[9] This was especially true in the Wagnerian cycle of another monster, Bill Clinton. (And when you think about it, there are similarities among these cases. Clinton's was a story about monstrous sex, or at least was monstrously *made* about sex.)[10]

For all the horror they inspire, monsters are obliquely sources of admiration (*ad mirare,* to wonder at) and amazement (Latin through Old English, to leave us in a-maze). Merely identifying the monster as terrible, as awful and perverse, is only one of the fearful ceremonies designed around them. Displaying the monster as desirable is of equal (though hidden) value. This may explain why the stories we tell about monsters are sexy, in literal ways—that is, the stories are *about sex,* however much this fact is disguised from view (sometimes the erotic charge is heightened by making the monster sexless or unsexy, at least in conventional ways—and thus, in a word, deviant). In this way each of the accounts in this study is framed by a pervasive denial of pornography in a commercial environment that is by definition completely so. For sex in public, it would seem, is still the banal though disguised point of many narratives from politics to shopping. These, in turn, variously connive in another point entirely—what Susan Stewart terms the "invention of the social." [11] Off to one side of the criminal action or "antisocial," you will find that each monster embodies and embroiders an eroticized tale, as each body is slowly stripped, deliciously moralized in public: the revelations of one, the exhibitions of another, the forced display of a third are moralized for the profit of the sentimental viewer. The obscene is offered as civic tableaux for the public good. As we shall see, however, that same high-minded gaze can also mask sadistic investment, in which a viewer profits less from moral uplift than he or she enjoys emotional pain.

Despite their unspeakable acts, or maybe because of them, the monsters in this study are astonishingly familiar. For example, in a recent poll, 100 percent correctly identified Jeffrey Dahmer, while only 63 percent could identify Jimmy Carter and 34 percent Gerald Ford.[12] Scapegoats we drive away, burdened with sin, real or imagined.[13] Monsters, however, are to be relished, if not exactly loved. The monster must be analyzed, fretted about, interpreted. Indeed, the vast machinery of interpretation invoked, for example, to stabilize Clinton's civil meaning makes him most truly a monster in the classical sense, since he was considered ominous, full of potential threat to the civic order.[14] The hyperventilated public rhetoric about the undressing of Bill Clinton is precisely why he is in a book dedicated to the complexities of monstrous, and thus (by implication) unspeakable, discourse.[15] Indeed, reading these recitatives of perversity, one asks: If what monsters do and are is so beyond moral reference as to escape speech itself, why then is so much spoken about them? What are the unspeakable pleasures of public perversity and why does no one talk about *these?* For the monster pleasures as well as polices, although we rarely talk about the pleasure. The monster-face is a mask placed on someone whose offense is obliquely desirable to us, however much we disguise that knowing from ourselves or call it something else—for instance, news, or interest in the moral tone of the community, or whatever. Monsters have, or seem to have, freedoms we lack. They transgress, cross over, do not stay put where—for the convenience of our categories of sex, race, class or creed—we would like them to stay. Sometimes it is their painful beauty, or untrammeled individuality; other times it is simply the liberties they take (and *that* they take them in the first place) that so astonish us. They get away with murder and that fascinates us. Monsters are supposed to do just what they desire, and that frightens us.

Monsters are created, and fear exploited, not only by cinema and other industries of commercial mayhem, but equally in the more mundane places where fear occurs as a byproduct of social intimacy. This study looks at the ad hoc creation of monsters as agents of moralized fear in political speech, in the pathologizing homogeneity of the evening news, in the double-edged altruism of church prayer and managerial state polemic— anywhere, that is, where rhetorical as well as social cruelty is normalized in the name of "the civil." Why, for instance, make monsters of failed mothers, homosexual killers, oversexed presidents? Why the violence done them? And thus, why the violence done ourselves? There are, I think, three pragmatic reasons for the success of these narratives, and these can be distantly traced in the etymological burden carried by the word "monster": Monsters warn; they provide public shows of differing kinds; they redefine boundaries that have become frayed. In sum, monsters help a community reinterpret itself. Sometimes, any given narrative cycle may demonstrate all these at once, as indeed did the moral venting about Bill Clinton's prodigious appetites.

I. The Book of Monsters: *Modus Legendi*

From antiquity the monster had a well-defined role as an ad hoc public servant. The ancients interpreted the strange birth as *portenta,* "A showing forth of the divine will." [16] Even as late as 1512 authorities agreed that the collapse of Ravenna had been foretold by the birth, a month previously, of a badly deformed child in the town. Reading the monster's exceptional body was never a simple task, however, since the message was, like the body itself, often doubled, or partial. In pre-Christian times the monster or anomalous birth took its place among one of many forms of divination, the "voice of birds . . . [or] any other way of seer-lore" [17] In Roman civil religion, for instance, solicitation of the gods and divining their inscrutable will through augury and propitiation was accorded public ceremonial importance.[18] These *Fanatici*—"inspired soothsayers" or *augurers*—held civic authority for interpreting omens.[19] Today such augury is maintained by a different priesthood, an authority shared by state and church, itemized in tabloids high or low, in casual speech and determined polemic. All exploit the monster—a cash cow, as the expression goes, but a fear cow, as well, a rich source of emotional and economic exploitation.

In his Introduction to *Monster Theory: Reading Culture,* Jeffrey Jerome Cohen lists seven theses about the monster that remain as valid now as they might have been in ancient Rome. Cohen can be condensed here: the monster's body is a "cultural body"; the monster is a harbinger of "category crisis," escaping categories of knowledge as well as form; monstrous fear displaces, relocates, and sometimes exploits desires that are equally monstrous. In sum, the monster watches and wards at the gates of the human, policing "the borders of the Possible." Finally, in an apt theological allusion, Cohen says that the monster is "difference made flesh, come to dwell among us."[20] Cohen gives us a framework with which to begin. By asking who, or what, is the monster, I also seek to answer who or what is the human. The monster has no one history, and its many tellings will always be incomplete; elusive fragments of its narrative will usually miss the main cultural argument. On the other hand, each time the monster appears is, in some ways, the last, since the monster is, by definition, unique, one of a kind (despite the cartoonish formulas used to speak of it). Further, each monster embodies a different cultural trauma. Clinton, Smith, Cunanan: different dramas, indeed, yet all three added up to sex, violence, and sentiment. This is an intoxicating cocktail; it will be repeated again somewhere else. Each of their narratives, as we shall read them, is a stuttering into the speech of gesture of issues sometimes far distant from the trauma itself. Some of these we will consider—in particular, gender, beset and undone; the sanctities, often spurious, of the home; the collapse of the erotic and private (at least as traditionally understood). In each scene formal Gothic modes intersect with a theatric mode of melodrama and political need to shape public notions of the good and the civil. By locating monsters *off* the social map, we locate the human—and, thus, we hope, ourselves—*on* it. Shall we, ourselves, pass the "Monster Test"?[21] From day to day, the answer to *that* question is never clear, never certain. This, ultimately, is what is at stake.

The center of my argument will be a consideration of public fantasy in entertainment as well as politics, its covert presence in nationalist scripts—

especially in the stealth pornographies of polemic and propaganda. Lauren Berlant defines fantasy as the means by which "national culture becomes local—through the images, narratives, monuments and sites that circulate through personal/collective consciousness."[22] This study examines more narrowly the production of a Gothic narrative nationalism, whose imperatives blend fear and desire. Monsters are agents, often unwitting, of ideology. They are a "fantasy screen" upon which the literal nonmeaning of the monster can be projected as a public scene.[23] The monster, in short, is a pedagogue; he, she teaches fear.

Some distinctions are first necessary. A vast gulf exists between Aristotle's description, in *De Generationes,* of the *teras*—the unusual birth—and the special-effects monster of contemporary pulp cinema. An even wider gulf separates movie monsters from those that end up on the cover of *Time* magazine, or get talked about on Geraldo, Rikki Lake, or the dozens of other interactive shows. The word itself is monstrous—multiple, complex, promiscuous, capable of endless nuance. In the secularization of a once-theological civil order, monstrosity lost its association with the divine and accrued other meanings instead. Visible deformity coincided, it was thought, with moral infirmity. Where external form failed, by extension moral or spiritual form was found to be deficient as well. In time, those who were markedly different helped define national identities, securing the geography of the normal by showing how and where it failed. That way, the maps said, lived the monstrous races, those unlike us in every way.[24] In *Natural History* (A.D. 77) the Roman naturalist Pliny propped up Roman centrality by arranging around it those races of people, mostly imagined, whose strangeness and threat were defused into exoticism by their distance from Rome. Even today the fantasy places of Ultima Thule and the Antipodes convey a sense not so much of otherworldiness as this-worldly exclusion.

The word "monster" slipped its biological moorings very early, becoming a categorizing term for the unusual, abnormal, the exotic and alien. In its disparate manifestations—as wonder, freak, oddity—the monster represented deviations from a presumptive natural order. As often as not, this unnaturality was invested with negative weight, read as perversion, deviance, and transgression.[25] An unexpected consequence followed: monstrosity gave human failure a legitimate place, at least marginally, on human maps. Monstrosity became a flexible tool of civil repudiation—sometimes literal, sometimes metaphorical.[26] From the Age of Exploration forward, local differences of nearby peoples were politicized. Competing definitions of the human were battled out over the exceptional body. During the Enlightenment "human nature"—at least as defined according to Western thought—became fixed, implicitly hierarchized within a system of interlocking evaluations of reason, race, and gender. Partly as a response to these social classifications, monsters likewise became more and more obvious—visibly more ugly, occasionally more beautiful. Strange and weird, in the widest sense of that word, they moved from halls of interpretation to fairs and carnivals, and to the wonder-closets of the wealthy. Ultimately the monster received new life by means of the simple, neo-Gothic plots of the creature feature, although this new life was tawdry in comparison to its ancient complexity. Thanks to the wide screen, the monster shed his vexed humanity altogether and became a simple code for the alien and the inhuman. What had once been an omen of awe became a trigger of fear—a civic fright monitor that was, in addition, profitable as well. Mystery gave way to movies. Omen became economy while metaphor flattened into allegory.[27]

History suggests that monsters are made as often as born; in physical and symbolic ways they carry the stigmata of civic discredit.[28] The malformed or misformed body is invariably read as civic allegory. That is, the abnormal and the different show by inversion what the normal is—or, minimally, what it ought to be. Each society has its own maps, the boundaries it feels are nonnegotiable. This means that the possibilities for civic reprisal mounted in the name of the monstrous are as varied as the fantasies of normality they support. For example, Smith, Cunanan, and Clinton are three monsters of notoriety, but think of others and the faults for which they achieved celebrity: Jeffrey Dahmer, fantasy cannibal; JonBenet Ramsey, the *enfant érotique* in a consumer society which eroticizes the young and then denies its interest; Fr. James R. Porter, cleric, a man who never understood his erotic interest, but still, who never disguised it either.[29] And then there are Willie Horton and Gregory Louganis, black killer and beautiful homosexual AIDS carrier. Each had his own drearily formulaic notoriety—augmented in the first case by politcs and in the second by a phobic response I argue to a rhetoric of diversity that locks upon the scandal (and allure) of visible difference while rarely moving beyond it.[30] Matthew Shepard was truly *monstrum:* sacred from one perspective, horrific from another, a reminder or warning from either vantage point. Another candidate for the title would include the amorphous, shadowy group known as the Trench Coat Mafia and the gun-packing youthful hordes they are thought to typify. It is easy to sentimentalize youth, of course; it is even easier to demonize them as monstrous, blaming them for our ills (and for the consequences of our guns).[31] The point, however, is not how many monsters can be named—there are many more. To be remarked is how similar, in reception and in narrative shape, each monster is to the next—despite the uniqueness suggested by the charge of monstrosity.

II. Rubrics and Tactics

Thus far I have employed a metaphor derived from the Gothic cinema, riffed with no apparent recognition from Aristotelian biology. In *Metaphors We Live By,* George Lakoff and Mark Johnson argue that metaphors are "tactics," and that their use "constitute[s] a license . . . for action."[32] "Monster" is such a tactic, a figure of speech used to demonize and to alienate. The discourse which it anchors consists of a chant-like litany used to shut sense down, even as the words themselves continue in a torrent. Gothic genres, modes, and technologies of fear are found everywhere in popular culture, and these are not my direct subject. I am interested, however, in how these forms and consumer habits are exploited in commercial and moral economies.[33] Since at least the fifties the formula of the monster story has been so familiar that its terms—and the violence that accompanies them—can be transferred from movie to political forum without acknowledgment. Still, maybe the mixed delights of this violence are chiefly responsible for this lack of recognition.

In its late-modern phase, the cinematic monster narrative is elegantly simple. A monster cannot be allowed to live; as historical precedent insists, the monster must be put to death. In the movies this requires that the monster be staked, burned, dismembered, or otherwise dispatched in the final reel. Thus simplified, however, the narrative tells only half the story. That is, before the monster can be staked it must be found. Whether on the screen or in the civic arena, the monster needs to be visible, a show that warns. *Creating* and locating the monster is at least as important to society as the creature's exorcism—repeated ad infinitum in horror film and pulp text. Such a ritual (creating or staking) is not, however, limited to films. Consider the logic, for instance, that in July 1997 saw S.W.A.T. teams, helicopters, dogs, and elite troops massing a street in Miami to "take [Andrew Cunanan] out." Against the power of the fantasized urban threat (not to mention the armament), the unusually inept Mr. Cunanan never stood a chance. This is the general point of this book. Fear on the streets might borrow the words and the rubric of the movie house, although on the streets fear moves to a qualitatively different closure. The difference? Real people die. This book argues that making monsters is a perennially useful social tool, part of an arsenal of weapons of fearful pedagogy by which societies define themselves in a complicated dance of *fort, da:* be driven away, stay close. This study argues a variation of *Civilization and Its Discontents,* in which Freud notes that aggression is provoked by a "narcissism of minor difference."[34] In short, monsters are too much like us, in too many ways. There is so much energy invested in staking the monster because "the monster is man turned upside-down, negated."[35]

A dense forgetting of history is necessary before the term "monster" can be shoehorned into the Gothic grade-B movie box. More forgetting is necessary before the figure can be wedged into grade-B politics, where "monster" is used to disavow people we don't like or do not understand. The power of any discursive system, including narrative, lies in its unquestioned veracity and the invisibility of its terms. Pliny's anxious fear about difference—his need to cast it far away—is still a customary habit of individuals, groups and states, enacted so regularly in public places and speech that it causes no comment. The rhetoric of monstrosity is a particularly virulent form, since the brutality produced by the discourse is rarely attended to. Monster-talk fuels polite as well as impolite discourse, news as well as talk show, sermons as well as presidential speech. It sells tabloids and *Time* magazine; it fills churches and ballot boxes.

This book culled examples of this projectile metaphor from many different sources to show how pulp prejudice shapes the attitudes of everyday social intercourse, often with very little comment about the questionable exchange. It is astonishing to realize that formulas of fright originally found in drugstore racks or on late-night fright TV now come and go in the halls of governance, providing, at least superficially, a language of moral evaluation.[36] Sometimes monsters are made in time of war, as when President Bush excoriated "that devil Saddam." Sometimes the monster is made in the heat of local politics: "Save my child from the sexual monster."[37] Sometimes, however, monsters are made with deliberation and forethought, by darkening faces on magazine covers, as *Time* did with O. J. Simpson's photograph in 1994 (27 June). Monster-talk might be cheap, but it is easy to use and takes its toll in human lives. To pay no attention to the dynamics is to accord this figure of speech an ancient authority, which it banks on, surely, but which it does not deserve.

Time's fabrication of the Simpson photograph was easily revealed as rabble-rousing. At other times, however, monsters are less obvious, constructed in the patient reasonability of Supreme Court decisions, the benign commonsense rationality of ecclesiastical injunction or timely medical warning. Thus, mantled within the unquestioned authority of (choose one) theological argument, legal code, or stump electioneering, monsters make their way into our homes, unnoticed (their presence usually attached, sentimentally, to the safety of children).[38] As a rule these monsters do not display their artificiality in obvious ways. Sometimes it takes wisdom and a keen eye to discover the seams and cracks in the logic. James Whale knew the formula for monstrosity seventy years ago. While the clamps and bolts of the creature in *Frankenstein* (1932) might have been obvious to audiences, Whale's choice of victim (a young blonde girl) passed without comment, as did his choice of villain (a blocky, uncouth loner). Susan Smith likewise knew the formula when she claimed that a smelly (black) man took her children at gunpoint. *Newsweek* called her story "a lurid fabrication seemingly drawn from tabloid crime reporting."[39] This book asks, where did the tabloids get it? The answer is, they didn't have to go very far. Generations of received racial viciousness underwrote Smith. Indeed, Smith's choice of monsters was astute. Because it was such a cliché, Smith's plea was, at least initially, accepted without question. Monstrosity depends upon instant recognition; insuring the conditions of that familiarity is a prerequisite for making monsters, whether in James Whale's film studio; Union, South Carolina; *Time*'s editorial room; or in the White House's press room.

One might remark, with Humpty Dumpty, that all this is a lot of work for such a little word like "monster" to do. Indeed, it's the little words that often make the big trouble. I am most interested in the way a discourse of cheap fear can pass so easily for ethical discussion. Who profits when the language of Gothic horror becomes legitimated—to borrow a phrase from Eve Kosofsky Sedgwick—as a "never quite explicit ethical schema"?[40] What kind of news do these monsters bring? On the other hand, it *is* easy to see what profits can be made from this kind of talk. Monster-talk is an integral feature of the arsenal of fear which underlies the practice of those modern, liberal states who nonetheless come to self-definition by making "perfect enemies." Indeed, the cultivation of hate is practically synonymous with civility, as thinkers as diverse as Walter Benjamin and René Girard have observed. Peter Gay locates the production of hate within the civilizing bourgeois project itself.[41] The dispersal of fear, in other words, is a civic duty. It might represent, in Freud's phrase, "the psychological poverty of groups," but this poverty is apparently common to many societies.[42]

Are there consequences of permitting monstrous rhetoric to pass unchallenged, either in tabloid or worse, in the courtroom? (This happened in the trials of Susan Smith, Fr. James R. Porter, and Jeffrey Dahmer.) What are the consequences for such speech in the feverish sound bites about Andrew Cunanan, the boys from Littleton, or countless others? The repudiative punch of this talk "makes [an individual] a huge, terrifying monster. And because they are no longer human, we can act towards them in any way we like."[43] Yet can we say nothing positive about such language? Doesn't this form of speech endure because it has a specific civic function? What urban stability and political consensus does monster-sticking insure? One woman, discussing her husband's abuse of their child, said, "he's a monster for want of a better word."[44] It is "for want of a better word" that I write this book. Because something happens to Jane *and* to her husband when, in a stumbling attempt at ethical evaluation, she resorts to the language of horror film—a language that derives, many times removed, from an ancient civil hermeneutic in which the ill-born child turns attention heavenward. Already we see the ironies proliferate. Making monsters is one activity in which the vaunted separation of church and state does not apply, since one language often covers both.

III. The Monster Speaks with the Master's Voice

If they speak at all. Indeed, in most horror films the monster's inarticulateness customarily denotes its alienation.[45] In a radical departure from Shelley's text, in his *Frankenstein* James Whale purposefully deprives the creature of speech, abandoning it voiceless, pursued by a mob, to a crushing death in a burning, cross-shaped mill.[46] Similarly, Cunanan's media coverage was so satisfying because he never lived to spoil it by telling his side of the story. Although he may have put a gun in his mouth in South Beach, his voice had been silenced long before. The effect of narratives *about* him, however, was to maintain Cunanan in a kind of faux-life, vampire-like, long after his death.[47] As one columnist noted, "Cunanan's death keeps us in his grip a little longer."[48] And makes us money, too, while distracting us from the things about our commodity-driven culture that are *really* threatening, such as the social conventions and formulas that govern our daily economic and social lives; these pass, largely, unsaid, and intentionally so, for to speak them would be to diminish their hold upon us.

In the same way, the boys in Littleton conveniently removed themselves from the debate; by killing themselves they left the papers free to make myth of them—in fact, they planned on it—"they wanted to be famous," concluded one FBI investigator, after reviewing the boys' journals and the five secret video tapes they left behind.[49] Almost by cultural necessity the myth took its usual shape in such matters. Linking gender-deviancy to viciousness remains a most useful cliché, and so the *National Enquirer, People,* and other sources began suggesting (hoping?) that the kids were gay, or at least sexually disturbed. A fellow student remarked about the two killers that "they're a bunch of homos."[50] Monster metaphors are projectile fictions of the most capacious kind. One size generally fits all, and for almost half a century criminality (real or imagined) has brought along with it suspicions of homosexuality.[51]

An age-old moral allegory governs the vampire myth; it dictates that evil does not compel us against our will. The same might be said of the monster. It is practically a cliché of trash film that no monster enters without invitation or some form of human connivance. Someone must say "come in," someone must leave the door or window unlatched, someone must leave the (always innocent) "victim" and, against all reason, go off for a walk. The monster narrative is deeply moral, an allegorical rendering of desires deeply conflicted. This is the submerged point of the monster-figure. Evil cannot possess without permission. So no matter how heinous we think the monster to be, we have, after all, entrusted him or her with very serious social questions about what shall be normal and acceptable, and who shall—or shall not—be human. How, then, did we instruct these monstrous persons (Clinton, Smith, Cunanan, et al.) to tell us in deep, dark, often painful detail about *ourselves*—without of course letting us know it?[52] Why do we make monsters; of whom, really, are we afraid?

Lastly, how is it that monsters, unspeakable themselves, became such a popular excuse for talk—harangued at length about in church, Congress, and tabloid? This book tells, at least partially, the story that the monster is not permitted to speak. Putting aside those monsters we stable in the cinema, on a pay-per-view basis, I focus, instead, on those sites (Miami Beach, Colorado, Union, Georgia, Washington D.C., Laramie, San Diego, Los Angeles) where daily news and speech announce the discovery of the latest monster—some new child killer, homosexual, serial murderer, killing doctor, Aryan terrorist. Monsters, the papers cry, walk our streets, occupy our libraries, and invade the sanctuaries of our homes, militaries, churches. But should we be surprised if, as *USA Today* intones, this "society produces monsters"?[53] Or that in the end they are all routinely alike?

IV. Chapter Overviews

Chapter one, "Gothic Returns," surveys commercial Gothic production of the fifties and sixties. During these years nostalgia and horror collude in the scripting of an American nationalism fueled by fright, which then becomes an economy in its own right—partly rhetorical, partly moral, and invariably commercial. The instability of the normal—or rather, the *fantasy* of a stable and serene normality—fixes the Gothic impulse as part of everyday life. Civility is supported by fear, retailed in newspaper, boutique, and civic polemic for our delicious comfort.

In chapter two, "Drive-by Shouting," I explore the dangers to language as one primary consequence of making monsters. Rhetorics of monstrosity propose a hierarchy of fear, yet the project of evaluation is undercut by the linguistic resources available. Monsters must be individualized, singled out, made much over, but the language employed to do so is common, formulaic, banal. Because of such incoherencies, the monster's individuality is lost to semantic collapse. What happens to language when it reaches the end of its ability to signify? How does Gothic effect of unspeakability present itself, not in the collapse of language, but *as* the collapse itself?

Chapters three, four, and five offer specific examinations of the rite of monster-staking, showing how each appearance of the monster has a political scene and social purpose whose outlines can be teased out from the formula presentation. Chapter three, "Redressing Andrew: Cunanan's Killing Queerness," argues that the Gothic methodologies of fear described in chapters one and two hijack a variety of nationalist discourses to justify and permit open displays of sex and violence in public. Andrew Cunanan's brief killing career transfixed media for three months; his criminality was largely circumstantial and his actions framed as unintelligible (i.e., "motiveless"). His "private" life, to the contrary, was pronounced scandalous and thus properly viewable in public. The absence of criminal record wrenched Cunanan's narrative into the blend of fantasy sex and homosexual perversion into which he was read. With ancient warrant Cunanan's ambiguous body, always visible, sustained an erotic public spectacle of fear.[54]

In chapter four, "Susan Smith: When Angels Fall," I track how trauma erupts, not in public and across the nation, but in the private place of children and home. In a truly Gothic moment, the creation of sexual danger from without is countered by the failure of domesticity from within, as evidenced in the narrative of Susan Smith, killing mother. That is, the horror "fantasy" of the dangerous intruder in public space has its double: a national fantasy of private security coded as Family Values. The crisis provoked by Smith's nonmotherly and therefore nationally subversive action was to be managed in terms of formulas—horror and domesticity. In the end, however, the formulas reversed themselves and the horrible monster became, instead, the victim of economic as well as representational systems.

Chapter five, "Reading the Starr: Scandal and Auguries," examines the interactive dynamics of scandal into which Bill Clinton was figured as a celebrity deviant and civil omen. The public theatrics mounted around Clinton's liaison with an intern helps focus the question, What social profit is there to be gained from speaking unspeakables in public, whether for moral pay or just plain cash? In this chapter I contest the conventional understanding of pornography as something we do shamefully in private; to the contrary, I argue that it is a ubiquitous mode of representation, commercially and politically central to conservative definitions *of* "the public"—and, as such, something we do shamefully in public.

Chapter six, "Death by Narrative," examines the process of storytelling through which prejudice masks itself as fear—a simulation (and stimulation) of public feelings similar to the pornographic mode examined previously. The monster story justifies violent commonality, even while it relieves individuals from responsibility for these emotions. The merchandizing of hate permits a rhetoric of the monster to seep into court, into news, into prison, and finally into oblivion, as its effects go unnoticed.

Chapter seven, "Sacred Monster," builds on the religious discourse from which the monster derives its ancient hermeneutical authority. The chapter opens at the scene of Matthew Shepard's funeral, in October 1988, in which homosexuals dressed as angels stood down evangelical Christians waving hate signs. The chapter examines how religious fundamentalism fosters a political fundamentalism that passes itself off as national civil religion. This chapter, finally, directly touches the complex sign of the monster we shall track throughout: in its awfulness the monster brings awe; the scandal of its presentation is unavoidably linked to the revelation it intends.

Conclusion

The monster must be identified and staked: this is the compulsive (and often comic) energy of horror films. Yet the urgency of the task is undercut by an unavoidable ambiguity, reflected in the fact that monster movies are so often screened at night, set in the dark, even *watched* at night. How are we to read this ambient darkness? Does it implicate the viewer who, sitting in the dark, cannot detect the monster? Or does the darkness hide the monster from view, and thus keep *us* in danger? Or is the darkness the occasion for which the monster is, at least symbolically, a warning? Nonetheless, from any direction, the monster is a luminous presence, a source of light, however dim. It is their vocation to be watched, to elicit warning and to signal judgment. However, after one leaves the safety of the theater monsters are not always as visible as we would like. Thus the work of staking the monster is done, as the movies too often remind us, in another sort of darkness as well—the dark places of social evasions, the blank and forgotten margins of things we cannot or will not acknowledge to ourselves. Among these unspeakables are the numerous ways that citizenship requires of us to collude in public fantasy, either about the lives we desire or those we disown and deny. It is no small irony, then, that the newspaper headlines that made Jeffrey Dahmer a monster missed the point entirely. If Jeffrey Dahmer *is* a monster, he has an illustrious past. And like all monsters, he is ominous, full of civic intention, with meanings crucial to communal health. We owe Jeffrey Dahmer at least this much: to do as ethically by his memory as we try to do by the men he killed—who, equally, get lost in the representational flotsam and jetsam. In order to do so we need to get beyond the surreal Gothics of his (and their) public lives.

This ancient augury in the dark is achieved only slowly and partially, as we seek the meanings of socially distressed, and distressing, bodies. Unlike the movies, or the three-week fright cycle of a scandal, a project like this book does not have a guaranteed formula ending. I may not detail the social trauma provoked by a monster—or, more accurately, the one for which it is blamed. Even if I were to succeed and free up one monster from the cage of language, there will always be others to anticipate. It seems we need monsters for our peace of mind—or, at least, to help make up our minds. No narrative is value-free, even, and especially, this one. My study is, after all, "academic"—and one hears the social dismissal carried by that word. Indeed, as an academic, I may be the worst of American monsters, at least from the perspective of rough-riding American anti-intellectualism from Roosevelt to Gingrich and Pat Buchanan.[55] For this reason, then, I must make one last point. My study isn't, for me, merely academic. By this I mean that my fear focuses me and gives me excuse, if not permission, to speak. The grammar of monster rhetoric acts like a spell of sorts, and this book is a work of counter-enchantment, a dis/spelling of chants, hexes, and fantasies of a very potent, political kind.

What do I mean? The monsters I have chosen here partly reflect the obsessions that have shaped me since my earliest days as both Christian and monster. That is, as a homosexual child, long before I knew the word "gay," much of my imaginative and spiritual life was born in the cauldron of resistance, refusing precisely the intentions of monstrosity that even "well-meaning" people intended toward me and others of my distaff kind. In writing this book, so often I have positioned myself behind the monster. Wide-eyed, I wondered, what must the monster think, as the crowd draws near, stake and flame in hand, cross raised high? This book is my answer: "This is my life you are talking about; these are the words you refuse me to speak in my own behalf."

More monstrous than any individual experience, including mine, is the social burden of this slant speech, and its appalling consequences — the leaden identification of religion and civility with brutality and violence. This book ends with a discussion of the primary monster of the Christian tradition: the bloodied body of Jesus — God, yet human as well — spirit, outrageously enough, in flesh. Philosophically, of course, the Inhumation is a monstrous concept, "logically odd" as theologian Schubert Ogden puts it.[56] In sentimental Christianity, however, the broken body of the crucified Jesus is monstrous in other ways, as well — particularly in the pious moralism it authorizes and in the death so easily dispensed in its name. Mandated by metaphysical authority, the image of the bloody Jesus dying for our sins is used to justify the rituals of fundamentalist — religious *or* political — staking by which individuals and groups are sacrificed to doctrinal purity. The monster, of manifold types, must die — in God's name and so it cannot be our fault.

The millennial threshold we cross is still ordered by that first death, perversely, "for the good of the people." Two thousand years later it is still the case that Christianity has not sorted out its own ambiguous devotion to this scandalous image of Jesus, pained and displayed on the criminal's cross.[57] This book considers some of those investments — scandal, offense, monstrosity — in the hopes they can be renegotiated. As Augustine reminds us in *The City of God:* A monstrous man is nevertheless a man.[58] We who connive in twisting humans into monsters, for whatever reason of thrill, shortcut moralizing or pay, thereby create our own peril. Ghost-like our language returns to haunt us. As we use this language to create a world of safety, we thereby make of ourselves monsters as well.

Does not our own epoch help us to understand the beginnings of European modernity? . . . We have reentered the "country of fear" and, following a classic process of "projection," we never weary of evoking it in both words and images. Mixing the present and a hypothetical future, science and fiction, sadism and eroticism, our fears for tomorrow and our experience of daily dangers, voyages into outer space . . .we propagate violent, barbaric, dehumanized and flashy stories with graphic imagery.

Jean Delumeau, *Sin and Fear: The Emergence of a Western Guilt Culture, 13th–18th Centuries*, 96–97

"Real Life isn't a Fu Manchu novel."
Luther shrugged. "I'm not so sure. You been watching the news lately?"

Dean Koontz, *The Door to December*, 148

. . . the monster has become a portrait of ourselves

Rudolf Arnheim, "A Note on Monsters," in *Toward a Psychology of Art*, 257

CHAPTER ONE

GOTHIC RETURNS:
HAUNTS AND PROFITS

Introduction

Generally speaking, movie monsters are clumsy things—often an excuse for gore, cool special effects, and maybe some illicit sex on the side. Such interpretive thinness has not always been the case, however. From Plato to Aristotle, Homer to Augustine, Chaucer to Burke, Locke to Shelley, Marx to Freud, Zola to D. H. Lawrence—and from Stephen King to Jesse Helms to Lionel Dahmer—a distinguished array of authors and thinkers have used the word "monster" to sometimes startling effect. The history of the word signals abnormality and deviancy, but, in addition, it conveys a sense of wonder. The word itself is monstrous—noun, verb, sometimes adjective. It transgresses linguistic and social boundaries, collapsing categories of biology, sociology, ethics and aesthetics, theology and philosophy.[1] Its exclusionary force has been applied to individuals, races, genders, even culture and society. Truman used it to describe a conspiracy of communism while Marx used it to bash capitalism.[2] Freud suggests that the "border-creature, the Ego" is monstrous, since its constituent parts do not always cohere.[3] Currently the word is applied to rock concerts, killers, radio hits, trucks, job markets, ball games, old people's homes, excessive revelry, the Y2K bug, bad coaches, bad metaphors, D.C.'s metro system—even excessive language itself.[4]

As this brief catalogue suggests, a short history of the word would be a long narrative of civilization and its discontents. Even in its contemporary American use, where the word is shrink-wrapped to fit commodity horror, "monster" still reflects traces of its ancient meaning—the unnatu-

ral birth that announces social crisis, epistemological trauma, and civic disarray. This book asks, How did Aristotle's misborn child become popular
culture allegory, on the cheap?[5] The creatures drifting through the half-
light of the cinema, crawling out of black lagoons, dropping in from beyond the stars, or digging up from the earth's core are, like cinema, of fairly
recent origin. Nonetheless, there has always been a social "beyond" and
that way monsters invariably lie. On screen as well as on the streets, monsters, and talk of monsters, have served as ideological police since ancient
times. They secure the normal; the exclusions they exercise and the violence encoded in language about them are supported by the triumvirate of
religion, state, civility. This fact alone is one reason why Hobbes, Locke,
Burke, and other theorists of the modern state would disagree with Freud's
claim that aggression represents "psychological poverty."[6] To the contrary,
each would argue that some sort of fear and aggression is a necessary social
cohesive.[7] Making monsters is one way aggression becomes an unremarked
trauma of everyday life.[8]

I. Ceremonies

An intimate and reciprocal exchange exists between private anxiety and
the public systems through which fear—and by extension, violence—is
awarded social approbation. In what I am calling "ceremonies of fear,"
private emotions—monstrous because they are, precisely, perceived as *private*—must be negotiated into public shape, massaged into socially appropriate forms.[9] Nina Auerbach writes that "no fear is only personal: it must
steep itself in its political and ideological ambience, without which our
solitary terrors have no contagious resonance."[10] Civil disorder and its
public display thus has pragmatic social purpose, especially when the disorder links fear *to* desire, as is typical in the rite of scandal. The social grammars of monstrosity capitalize upon such links, making spectacles out of
punishment and rituals out of shame—all of which are state sponsored, as
the saying goes, for "your" own good.[11] Socializing agencies and discourses—media, government, church, markets and manufacturers, consumers, readers and viewers—all contribute to this "odious landscape of
punishment" in which transgression is awarded civic sponsorship.[12] In the
final analysis, decency rests upon the cultivation of public incivility.[13]

Numerous commentators have explored how fear, originally religious
in nature, found a home within secular governance, systemized for state as
well as for religious purposes.[14] Foucault takes note, in particular, of the
ritual aspects of this theatrics of fear, by which a state's "designs" are in-

scribed upon the docile emotional bodies of the citizenry by means of spectacular public scenes.[15] Such occasions are rituals; as Clifford Geertz explains, ritual provides "models not only of what a people believe, but models for the believing of it."[16] The theater of fear, then, is pedagogical, teaching by preemptive example. It is also participatory and interactive, intended to be habit-forming. In painfully literal ways civic occasions, like the highly media-ized pursuit of Andrew Cunanan, have designs upon us. Nonetheless, these systems of spiritual or bodily governance do not exist in isolation, nor do they appear in such simplistic forms as this quick overview suggests. Rather, ceremonies of fear, like other social theatrics, adopt for their own ends conventions, motifs, and images pilfered from many sources. For example, from Diocletian to Bentham even the most determinedly secular models of punishment have been justified by the language of corporate moral uplift and religious discipline.[17] The discourse of monster-talk, similarly, draws its expulsive speech from many sources, from both high and low on the social register. In addition, the discourse acts like a rubric, making possible actions that embody beliefs—no matter how sketchy or implausible such beliefs might be.

This chapter examines the accidental, as well as deeply ironic, convergence of Aristotle's monster—the socially uncanny body—with the neo-Gothic image of the cinema "monster." At issue is a period in American culture drenched in Gothic sensibility. Why so many monsters, why now? Is the energy behind alienation, reprisal, enemy-making, and monster-staking millennial? That is, does the need to find monsters everywhere reflect "eschatological anguish," as Frank Kermode or Norman Cohn might argue?[18] Or is the need chronic and systemic in nature? Does the energy derive from external pressure and economic alienation, as Marx suggests, or from psychological predisposition, as Freud believed? What about the hybrid, ancient/new language itself? That is, while its use today is largely secular, the term "monster" draws upon a submerged but nonetheless *metaphysical* argument, with just a hint of conventional religious discipline added as spice. From Aristotle onward, the monster's showy body implied a (discordant) relation between deity and human, a dark cloud between transcendence and mortality. In every age it has been the monster's imperative to signify; its imperfection requires human augury and action.[19]

In classical epistemology as well as in Gothic narrative, the trope of monstrosity turns upon anxieties of generation and reproduction, drawing attention to the potentially unnatural consequences of these natural actions. As Marx observed, capitalism makes possible a monstrous reproduction entirely different from Aristotle's, yet one that is similar in effect. Aristotle's uncanny "monster" predates eighteenth-century Gothic; however, figured within an economy of political horror partially derived from that genre, the word's hex-like power to condemn, alienate, and dehumanize is heightened by its elaborate reinforcement within a "cult of horror."[20] Contemporary American culture is undeniably Gothic, from the movies on its screens to the rhetoric on presidential lips, to the elections of presidents themselves.[21] Fear is produced as genre requirement through the literary motifs of werewolf, vampire and ghoul, but the civic unrest historically coded in—and contained by—these figural expressions is also dramatized by the mythicizing of slashers, terrorists, lurking child abusers, and unnatural mothers. All these are now clichés derived from slasher films, media-presented horror, and good old-fashioned Gothic shock. In turn, clichés of dysfunction and social terror are disseminated through the cinema, to churches, government, markets and vernacular address, where they constitute the visible shadow of social life that Fredric Jameson terms the political unconscious.[22] Through the interlocking structure of language, institutional allegiance, and commercial economy, the political unconscious establishes and enforces a formal epistemology of normality based upon likeness and difference.[23] In this way, through the covert policies of managerial terror common to market and city hall alike, private nightmares become public. The "psychopathology of everyday life" is, partially at least, their consequence.[24]

II. Producing Monsters, Making Citizens

Is it possible to historicize the social work of fear and its metaphor of alienation? In its American context, for instance, how does an aesthetic/religious tradition of awe and ominous dread collide with the camp theatrics of consumer fright? Through what means of commercial product placement and psychological inversion do rhetorical and economic structures of fear become, instead, machineries of a rather peculiar joy?[25] In its modern phase, and as reflected in the economics of fear, the Gothic is almost evangelical, a rite as monstrously regenerative and interactive as shopping. Indeed, being frightened to death and shopping to death might be termed emotional equivalencies, since each jointly connives in making subjects who are proper citizens. As an aid to this process, fear is materially produced as well as imaginatively endured; indeed, both of these aspects are keyed to, and reinforce, another system of political fantasy, desire.[26] Gothic ideological effect, then, is economic effect as well as narrative plot, and both come together in the neo-Gothic hybridities of cinema and vernacular speech. Consumers are nickeled and dimed into propriety by desire-organized shopping; however, the same might be said of the way fear directs the contours of civil life, both the public performances we call "consumer" as well as those aspects given traditional political sanction as "citizen." Fright narrative and its ceremonies may be said, then, to produce the ideal genre viewer or reader. Appropriate civility of this sort is also produced by means of the representations and artifacts of fear cluttering the social landscape. One alleviates desire by shopping, it is true; and sometimes buying fear (material object and emotion) is the only way to *reduce* a different kind of anxiety, as well.

Fear, like *Trix,* then, is not *only* for kids, although it starts there readily enough. Pocket Monsters (abbreviated *Pokemon*) are collectable, of course, because they are shoppable. Even at a young age we are trained in lack, as desire is seduced even as it is created.[27] In not very subtle ways, then, citizenship is supported by the emotional commerce through which often spurious individualities are packaged, bought and sold courtesy of the narratives, artifacts, rubrics of scandal and spectacular shame that define public representational space. These might include the overt moralism of *Nightmare on Elm Street,* the generically gendered Barbie and her friend Ken, kid's "toys" such as Freddie Krueger's knife-fingered glove, the poems of Charles Manson found in pop songs, or the moral posturing around Susan Smith or Bill Clinton.[28] No place is safe from triggers of fear and explosive rhetoric—not toy shelf, Supreme Court decision, not even state law, as witness Oregon's 1992 Measure 9.[29] In each exchange the iteration of fear whitewashes anxiety into some other, less directly tangible emotion. Terror is silently elided, remaining only as unspoken trace, all the more comfortable for what it has forgotten.

Even as an unspoken trace, however, terror's parentage is complex. Awe and fear are not the same, although terror contains elements of both. To take one example: The power of the vampire myth draws its energy from numerous places (distantly, for instance, from early church preachment about the resurrected body of Jesus). One of the general aims of this book will be to show how a banal mechanics of social fear derives at one remove from a discourse of transcendence and sublimity. The use of fear as a "weapon for mass pedagogy" is of ancient origin, as Delumeau argues in *Sin and Fear.*[30] Its use presumed, at least initially, spiritual discipline, in that *pietas*—fearful awe—was the proper response to encounters with the Divine.[31] Such an experience overran reason and representation both; it could not be put into words, only gestured at. At this point of unspeakability devotional awe permits another movement entirely, the plunge into unspeakable fear.[32] Both responses are built in the narrative method of Gothic, which also exploits a desire for the sublime it nonetheless cannot satisfy.[33]

The close alliance between theology and civil governance remains more honored than breached in many public contexts, since theology provides an emotional habit of public address even in the most obdurately secular institutions. In *Powers of Horror,* Julia Kristeva notes that the sacred "has left us without leaving us alone," and that, almost as a consequence, the power that horror has is a "sacred power."[34] George Bush's condemnation of a world leader by means of a dusty religious bromide is merely one example of the promiscuity—and emptiness—of the language. A firewall is thought to exist between highbrow politics and the tawdriness of popular culture, though to hear one president bash Saddam or his predecessor denounce "that evil empire," one is not so sure of how effective the separation is. Popular cultures, whether Chaucerian, Shakespearean, Bakhtinian, or contemporary, *might* seem to be without politics or to be above ideological concerns. Yet literary texts are formally meaningful sites in all cultures. Genres—no less than other regulatory devices, like gender or racial codes—constitute readerships to different purposes, and therein lies their politics.[35] Gabriele Schwab argues that "literary texts are conceptually granted the capacity to work against or even undo certain forms of cultural repression and to provide a mode of communication that allows for a meaningful engagement of unconscious experience."[36] The Gothic genre and its campy derivatives exhibit this effect in particularly condensed forms, since this literary mode—so redolent of metaphors of slashing and cutting—is resolutely dismissed as culturally worthless, as "marginal." Nonetheless, one wonders how such a genre could *not* be significant in a social world where a similar form of dismembering routinely describes economic intercourse in terms of consumer and consumption?

In her study of murder narratives, Karen Halttunen argues the development of an indigenous American Gothic mode that took root and thrived in political self-address, markets, and in other sites of popular exchange. This new mode of talking about citizens and selfhood obscured the real issue—an ongoing anxiety of nationhood and a sense of cultural insecurity.[37] At issue, Halttunen suggests, was the transformation of the precolonial spiritual Pilgrim into the young republic's secular citizen. Crèvecoeur's "new man" was more concerned with successful passing in this world—not to say survival—than with passing to a world hereafter.[38] As only one of many such nationalist unrests of the time, the American

Revolution coincided with what might be called a global managerial crisis. An epistemology of the sacred gave way to a different hermeneutic entirely, as Calvinist forms of Christian apocalypticism were presented, in post-Enlightenment terms, as transcendent hope, and continual progress.[39] Sentimentality and the required happy ending banked, then, upon older religious habits of termination.

Halttunen charts similar effects in the development of American civic narrative. Puritan moralized expositions of sin and crime emphasized its mystery, horror, and guilt—all embodied in the "exemplary sinner" narrative.[40] This gave way to a different sort of horror and a newer sense of mystery in which guilt was spectacular and voyeuristic ("humanistic") rather than narcissistic and inward ("spiritual"). Horror became a matter of watching, rather than undergoing. Ultimately, recounting horrid crimes was intended to shock, rather than to convert. Readers, says Halttunen, "were instructed to shrink, with a sense of *horror* that confirmed their own 'normalcy' in the face of the morally alien."[41] Gothic narrative investments, then, in sites as distant as the penny papers, courts of law, psychology, and theological polemic together gave shape to a new criminal. A purposeful economy of fear—part theological discourse, part aesthetics, part politics—helped reshape the understood terms of civility. In *The Thrill of Fear,* Walter Kendrick underscores the consequences: " . . . there's nothing eternal about the paraphernalia of scary fiction. . . . We have learned to be frightened by these things; they have a history."[42] The prejudice sedimented in the language is part of the history often covered over by the flamboyant metaphoricity of the language itself.[43]

In many post-Reformation countries, and in the United States in particular, religion and civility explicitly overlapped. The use of fear—once aimed at refurbishing souls and now entwined within a discourse of Gothic horrorography—became transferred into the public discourses of state- and citizen-making. In a transitional moment between these two eras, for example, John Winthrop gave the following advice to the wayward Anne Hutchinson: "Your conscience you must keep else it must be kept for you."[44] In *Democracy in America,* Tocqueville came to the following conclusion about the periodic campaigns of fear he observed: "When there is no authority in religion or in politics, men are soon frightened by the limitless independence with which they are faced. They are worried and worn out by the constant restlessness of everything."[45] Even Freud explicitly aligned what might be termed the American political unconscious with patterns of its nation-building. He writes that American society "would give us a good opportunity for studying the damage to civilization which is thus to be feared."[46] David M. Kennedy concurs: "American culture is an especially fertile breeding ground for the particular psychopathology [Freud] conjures."[47]

Why should this be? What about the American experience lends itself to aggression and making "perfect enemies"? Born out of the revolutionary impulse that swept Europe, American culture early had to counter charges of being something of a monster itself (and borrowing a rhetoric used by Marx in *Das Kapital*)—hybridic, multicultural, centerless and plural, bits and parts which could only be reconciled in the rhetorical purging of the melting-pot.[48] This insecurity would forever color national self-reference; it would never be far from needs to explain, excuse, and deny the country's (or its population's) sometimes *outré* behaviors. Identity panic would manifest itself in recurrent bouts of nation-clutching fear, obsessing about how other people—Indians, Negroes, old and husbandless women, Irish, Chinese, Japs and other "Orientals," gays, Cubans, et al.— were "naturally" different and so liable for eviction, exile, even death. The recent fulminations of an Atlanta Braves pitcher against "foreigners," "queers with AIDS," and "dudes" from prison are typical of this slant speech, in which violence, disowned into words, becomes a tactical although unacknowledged bludgeon.[49] The stake, sometimes actual, as often verbal, was a handy weapon directed against the many who "need not apply."[50]

Rhetorics of monstrosity and the repudiations they intend are resilient enough to accommodate a variety of forms and cultural imperatives. This is the beauty of formula's almost infinite elasticity. It says nothing, or everything at once, all at a high pitch. In one era the discourse of civic unrest can be styled as jeremiad, in another era as McCarthyist paranoia, in another as moral panics around perverse adults and sometimes monstrous children (and the adult weapons they carry). The shuttered thinking of conspiracy can be mounted on the right, sometimes left, sometimes center. When it is a question of identity politics (spiritual or national, ethnic, sexual, religious), this culture is remarkably adept at making monsters. I include here of course the melting-pot selves of its citizenry, those monstrous collations of narrative, populist fantasy, and ever-ready credit card by which "identity" is formed. In this respect monsters among us are an allegory, not so much of a specific difference, but more generally of the logic of "otherness" itself. Carriers of social anxiety, they reflect a constant fretting at the difference by which America was constituted—theologically as well as civilly—as a Utopia. In so many respects a land begotten in fantasy, in some respects its citizens must still depend upon fantasy to make their daily way.[51] The difference that is built-in as rhetorical ideal must, in practice, be firmly defended against.

In this brief exploration of the uses of the word "monster" I have touched upon biology, sociology, theology, history, aesthetics. Each of these discourses has political consequences, as Joyce Carol Oates observes: "Where the 'human' crosses over into the 'monstrous' is . . . a matter of law, theology, or aesthetic taste."[52] The language we use as insult and reprisal collapses an astonishingly varied history. Monsters, and monstrous bodies, were portents of great significance, wherever and through whatever means different societies created, and sustained, their monsters—whether these were defined as the visibly different or the invisibly alien.[53] In current practice the term "monster" still registers an uneasy alliance between the abnormal as spectacle and the abnormal marked out as moral failure; its show is always a special kind of warning: "Societies have always tried to unburden their disasters on the strange and the stranger, oscillating between blaming divine wrath, rumor, and conspiracy."[54]

Gothic formulas of difference exploit cultural dissonance, places where daily rhetoric of civility and action necessary for life divide, where social systems of comfort and fear undercut each other. Mark Edmundson can thus argue that "the major media's Gothic rendering of the [O. J. Simpson] case served to *deepen* race hatred in America."[55] The language of monsters works in similar fashion; it sweeps together bits and emotion, leftovers from previous cycles of fear—which, while they may have run their course, may still be tapped into. When such formulas of Gothic reprisal leave movie theaters—calling Jeffrey Dahmer a "vampire," for instance— they mimic material tensions inscribed in everyday social intercourse. Nonetheless these effects of dislocation, anxiety, social destabilization recede from view at the same time that they are reproduced in movie, tabloid, toy, and fright scandal. This ongoing self-erasure is the point of the rhetorics of monstrosity. Both its content as well as its delivery system go willfully unnoticed, and this might be said to constitute the ideological burden carried by the genre: the unspeakable is often literally unheard. Nonetheless, despite being dismissed as a marginal genre, as pulp, or pop, and being consigned to video back rooms, the Gothic has important work to do. Making monsters is a necessary social hygiene, helping to keep citizens straight (in that word's widest as well as narrowest senses, as we shall see). Monsters are merely the vehicle—the occasion or excuse—for the presentation of social ill or "ideological tensions."[56] Thus, to be called a monster is not something one should take personally, although consequences of such naming will always be felt personally. Freud, again, is helpful: "It is always possible to bind together a considerable number of people in love, so long as there are other people left over to receive the manifestations of their aggressiveness."[57] Monsters are those "other people."

In such a dense political/moral atmosphere, the claim of monstrosity—such as the one made against Clinton in the august chambers of the House of Representatives—is a multifaceted civic moment, worthy of the awe and dread the charge provoked. Monsters, Michael Uebel writes, are "charged with the insoluble task of resolving real social contradictions"; they are given the "function of inventing symbolic solutions to imaginary contradictions."[58] Monsters announce, work through, and negotiate social trauma in the very formulaic terms of which they are thought to be unique. As a monster Clinton is freak and alien, yet somehow he is also divine agency, bearing dreadful news as well. In Clinton's case, for example, the location of sex *in* the halls of power suggests a great deal about the historical meaning of both power and sex in this culture. Nonetheless, the rhetoric used to contain the monster cannot do so, despite its best intentions. Rhetorics of monstrosity bear a certain resemblance to magic, whose incantatory rhythms they emulate. They are spells, words that describe an action; their cadences intend powerful results. Yet by virtue of their formal emptiness, as Homi Bhabha argues in a different connection, the stereotypes of the monster are themselves doubled. They pass as ethical speech yet are not; they undercut the seeming stability of conventions and yet are themselves conventions.[59] Stereotypes also reconfirm—or seem to at any rate—a category that seems natural and preexisting. This linguistic indecisiveness accounts, at least in part, for the compulsive reiteration of the formulas in question and the resulting Gothic quality of the discourse; the need always to say more means that words, overused, always mean less and less.

In *The Coherence of Gothic Conventions,* Eve Kosofsky Sedgwick remarks that the Gothic's "most obvious structural significance" is "the difficulty the story has in getting itself told."[60] The public inadmissibility of whatever scandal is being publicized is generally coded into speech by sighs, expostulations, and linguistic excess. Indeed, the greater the moral transgression, the more deeply strictured becomes the speech announcing it. This makes for some interesting questions about the direction taken by contemporary media. How does speechlessness—a customary Gothic equivalence to public policies of "don't ask, don't tell"—make for the wordless gesturing of melodrama? How does the interpretive mechanics of the monster permit Gothic scenes of personal disability, staged around bad mothers and worse presidents? These scenes, announced by disabled speech and silence, connive with a media-driven compulsion to gaze and leer. At this point moral consumerism and social inadmissibility terminate in a different public silence altogether—the "sharp edge of conventional" speech and genre formula.[61] One is led to ask, Can the moral paralysis signified by speechlessness, caught within a torrent of representation, ever shut up?

Practically speaking, making monsters—willfully by state policy or media agency, or accidentally by slapdash language—is bound to fail, however sophisticated the rubric. Why? Monsters invariably suggest multiplicity of meaning; nonetheless, read against the constraints of formula expression and the emptiness of the metaphor, the speech undoes itself, disrupts the sense it presumes to make. Such narrative instability almost by necessity creates a captive, entrapped reader, which is how Gothic narrative technique achieves its goal: the story that doesn't tell, finally, leaves its reader grasping for formula. This failure in turn explains why the production of monsters out of a ragtag supply of marginal and unwanted persons seems endless. Neither political fantasy nor Gothic completely encompass its subject; neither discourse ever completely permits what needs to be said. The parents of Steven Hicks—the man reported to be Jeffrey Dahmer's first victim—underscore why Dahmer was spliced into the Gothic role: "We have spent a great deal of time trying to understand the motivation for such a heinous crime and concluded that some acts are so evil they simply cannot be explained."[62] Dahmer became genre-fodder, processed to exploit the power of "the unexplainable." William Veeder argues that "societies inflict terrible wounds upon themselves and *at the same time* develop mechanisms that can help heal these wounds." The Gothic mode, he remarks, is "one such mechanism."[63] As we observe in the Hicks' conclusion, unexplainability, then, is social effect as well as dramatic answer.

Why then so many monsters in this particular historical, political climate of fearful haunts and fear-driven profits? In Fitzgerald's *The Great Gatsby*, Nick Carraway reflects that "personality is an unbroken series of successful gestures."[64] Bourgeois civility is similarly repetitive; it presumes a coherent narrative of the humane and civilized, yet in reality such coherency of "self" is never possessed. To the contrary it is only incrementally, and provisionally, achieved. The civil life is as much a mode of restraint as it is a habit of doing. Fear, not unlike Aristotle's definition of virtue, is habit-forming, successful most when its presence is unnoticed. We are educated into civility *and* fear narratively.[65] Civility is the cluster of actions that are deemed appropriate to us as we accommodate ourselves more or less successfully to the plot of life emerging scene by scene around us at home, job, school, mall, cinema. Still, civility is not as successfully achieved as we might like, and this is where the judicious application of fear makes itself necessary. Narratives of civility don't always say it all, do not always account for discrepancies. They do not, in a word, always have room for the single, separate person—especially one not well subjected into the nuances of moral citizenship. Civility includes, of course, the possibility of incivility, as the word suggests; and if the monster escapes categories, the same can be said for our frail selves. Day by day the scripts we repeat are meant to rescue us from monstrosity (we think), even as we are narrated into a different form of monstrous hybridity in our desire to become proper citizens and consumers.[66]

Teresa A. Goddu argues that the Gothic fantasy "exposes the cultural contradictions of national myth."[67] Arguably, in democratic society "the public" *is* the legitimate expression of fantasy politics. The Gothic "has always been fascinated at the prospect of *undoing the human*."[68] The presence of monsters—camped up in cinema-drag, beclawed, furred, and otherwise de-manned, the better to fit tabloid cliché—reflects the instability of those disciplinary norms that, on the one hand, define our political systems as well as, on the other hand, the fantasies that control the movements of our hearts and pocketbooks. Those who are chosen as monsters direct our attention, further, toward a deeper anxiety; they ask us to consider the problematic status of the body in a culture of consumption—economized as product on one hand and morally devalued on the other. This anxiety indirectly evidences it in the way popular culture projects its desires into dramas of the erotic body and its fears into the paranoid fantasy of the criminalized, sexed public body. Transfixed in the steely repetition of the scandalous gaze, these are the two bodies which commodity economics reproduces, monstrously, again and again.[69] We see shadows of them over the years in the outcries made around Willie Horton, Jeffrey Dahmer, and more recently O. J. Simpson, Timothy McVeigh, Susan Smith, and Matthew Shepard. Their narratives are knots of dreams and fears, tangles we fret at, though fear to untangle lest we, ourselves, come undone.

III. They Came from Space and Met Donna Reed

Many reasons can be enumerated for the Gothic tilt of American culture. I suggested earlier that its monster rhetorics import language, unacknowledged, from many sources, including theological.[70] This is not a remark-able conclusion, given the intense religiousness common to the culture and genre alike. From John Winthrop's "A Model of Christian Charity" (1630) to Ronald Reagan, one finds an intellectual habit of discounting the visible for what might lie behind it, or above it. Such double vision argu-ably shapes American attitudes to worlds that can be seen as well as those that can't be seen.[71] This sense of "otherness" is evidenced in metaphysics, in politics, as well as in the creation of perfect enemies—of which no more perfect one exists than the monster, ready to die for our sins.[72] Religious energy, however, takes numerous forms. American civil cultures of the past fifty years have exhibited extravagant shows of deflected spiritual energy.[73] The fifties and sixties, in particular, were marked by what might be called wholesale spiritual eruption. During these years and through the seventies a social order tamped down following the Second World War began un-raveling. Daniel Snowman and Malcolm Bradbury write that "anti-war protests, urban riots, black militancy and a revolt of youth against their elders were soon to create insurrectionary situations . . . [which] persuaded many that a major change in the political and social order of the West was impending."[74] Empty closets became as familiar as Donna Reed's well-secured kitchen had been a few years before.[75]

With the ending of the war, national attention turned to enemies within. The House Committee on Un-American Activities (HUAC) and other policing agencies were intended to return the United States to a pre-war normalcy—as much a fantasy as Donna Reed's kitchen lock-up. A spurious commonality gave birth to public nightmares of the uncommon, the alien and deviant; the organizational man of the fifties was not so much invisible as transparent, since anything *not* made public was viewed with suspicion. Vance Packard's *The Hidden Persuaders* (1957) found the enemy in the group-think of American consumer society, while from another ideological place entirely, J. Edgar Hoover found the *Masters of Deceit* (1958) in a communist conspiracy that likewise lurked within.[76] This pre-occupation with hiddenness was paralleled in the fiction and cinema of the time, as a Plinean fascination with the strange and exotic was reflected in movies of invasion and the eruption of inner monsters. Subversive pos-sibilities in cells and closets were duplicated in the anxious despoilment of hideous monsters, all dimly pornographic, all traumatically visible. But there was another side to this fear, as well—the desire sometimes hidden by the fear. Closets were in—at least so long as they were partly open. Voyeur TV had its start in Cold War paranoia.

Through the fifties the slightly tatty horrors of a generation of comic books clawed their way into film via the equally déclassé American International Productions, the gimmicky thrillers of William Castle, and England's Hammer Studios (beginning with its 1957 classic *The Curse of Frankenstein* and in 1958 *The Horror of Dracula*). Frights more imaginary than real were commonplace, although the frights related in distinct ways to actual life. Gregory Waller notes that Hammer productions of fright "reaffirm what are assumed to be the 'normal' values of heterosexual romance, clearly defined sexual roles, and the middle-class family."[77] Clichés may not say much, but they say it often, and the rhetoric of the monster underwent a slow evaporation. No longer Aristotle's divinely uncanny birth, the monster had become a cinematic convention—teaching adolescents, not too subtly, how to behave, while giving their parents something with which to reinvent their own youth.[78] And indeed, the monster took readily to a culture famed for its immigration panics on the one hand and its melting-pot rhetoric on the other. By 1953, writes David Skal, "More Americans were reading horror comics than were reading *Reader's Digest* or the *Saturday Evening Post*."[79]

In March of 1950 Faulkner noted that all questions of the spirit had been exhausted. Only one remained, he said—"When will I be blown up?" Through the ensuing decade, the troubling implications of human agency posed by Faulkner's Nobel Address had been displaced by another question, one which shifted agency elsewhere and blame onto someone else: When will we be invaded, and who will the monster be?[80] So whether "post" refers to World War I, II, to Korea or Viet Nam, or to the -modern, -post-modern, or -human, interesting parallels develop in the fantasies that were (1) encouraged during these years in the name of politics, and (2) discouraged in the name of escapist horror. In both directions monsters lay hidden. The American citizen-consumer was the primary fiction of the time, the civil face steadfastly locked in place. Such a hothouse of horror produced a generation accustomed to easily identifiable monsters, and they applied the same principle to their national enemies as well. Quite simply, perfect enemies were "different." Cristoph Grunenberg writes that the "internal characteristics that unite the contemporary Gothic have been defined as a preoccupation with 'paranoia,'" something the generation of the fifties had in excess.[81] Inevitably, however, the logic went in the other direction as well. That is, to an ideologically Anglo audience, if monsters were Other, those who were different from us were necessarily monsters—mole people, beast men, slime people, or something from a swarm or a lagoon.[82] In the cultural fermentation of the time, and in the accompanying political fragmentation, the socially different were recast in formulas of the inhuman and the unhuman, borrowing for the purpose a shorthand of repudiation lifted without pause from cinema horrorography.

Neither the language nor the impulse of the monster was new, however. Blacks, feminists, gays were engulfed by metaphors of monstrosity as banal as they were ancient; this denunciatory rhetoric, taken directly from the film halls, was itself derived from the public spectacles of earlier centuries—markets, fairs and freak shows, even lynchings and other public stagings. There were differences, of course. Nonetheless, a popular interest in the erotic commerce of bodies confirmed an older practice in which the monstrous body and its parts (enormous or small; whole or partial) were displayed for economic profit and moral remonstrance. Created out of civic necessity, social warrant, and simple greed, monstrous lives were policed and displayed in equal measure. Politics became variants on the cinematic, while monsters, once exceptional, became the rule. The ideal viewer, meanwhile, feminized by the spectatorial role allotted her in horror cinema, and undone in the gore and trauma she watched on screen, likewise found herself redone according to similar expectations and formulas.[83]

Self-narratives rarely tell all, or even much, of the truth. National rhetorics and ideals, whether political or literary, are no different, leaving unspoken as much as they think they say. In *American Violence: A Documentary History,* Richard Hofstadter notes, with some understatement, that "[American] civil violence is quite out of keeping with our image of ourselves as one of the world's most advanced political cultures."[84] A paradox, then, emerges in American popular and political cultures of the period. The more visibly national mythologies of the civil and domestic lay in tatters, the more visibly they were restitched in nostalgic wholeness. Janice Radway observes of popular literature that it "assiduously avoids disappointing its readers' expectations. . . . It strives to reaffirm the validity of the strategies and conventions that they, as readers, have for making meaning of the world."[85] Radway's comment underscores the ideological content of reading—that its methods, the skills required for it, as well as its intentions pass unremarked. Whether flickering on the screen or in the lurid prose of the newspaper, Gothic fantasies of invasion and terror so characteristic of the fifties generated their opposite, sentimental fantasies of romance and domesticity.[86] As a result, ideological operations of public fantasy produced what might be called the normalized citizen, but it also made possible the monstrous, secret alien. The two were flip sides of one impulse to find a Platonic world elsewhere better than this. Indeed, romance and Gothic are a generic Siamese twin, doubled even in American literary ideology.[87] The problem, however, was that even here Gothic trope was at work. Identity and its possibilities were doubled, or fragmented, and the horrifying other was seen, inevitably, to be an intimate other. When one considers the genres separately, however, domesticity and horror are not always recognized as being related, even though treacle and terror share common borders on cultural maps of the last two centuries.[88] If domestic policies, fictional as well as political, produced angels in the house, they also made possible the necessary trigger of fear—the monster who lurks on city streets, near schools, or near our homes.[89] Angels, finally, cannot be separated from the monstrous threats that they become when disowned.

IV. Acting It *Outré:* Gothic on the Sly

Americans forget the nightmare in the resurgence of warmth and comfort.

Arthur Schlesinger, *The Vital Center: The Politics of Freedom,* 2

The collapsing national certainties in the sixties produced a revisionist civic moralism whose horrors led directly to the minatory. Lessons in political correction were not, of course, the main intent of creature features, nor, later, of the slasher films of the seventies. Nonetheless, a pedagogic moment or two got the films past watchdogs and moral censors.[90] The great bulk of the genre fictions of this time were as censorious as they were formulaic. "Entertainment has replaced religion and ideology as the primary source of moral guidance and for representations of evil."[91] King, for instance, cites William Peter Blatty's *The Exorcist* as an example of the "Humorless, Thudding Tract School of Horror."[92] Partly for its pseudo-religious content, Blatty's novel of a young Georgetown girl possessed by an ancient demon from a faraway foreign land is an important ideological mirror of the time; it registers ethnic anxieties, fears of invasion, parental concerns and domesticity, even governmental collapse. In sum the book ably demonstrates that the center does not—is not—holding. Further, *The Exorcist* is remarkable for what followed it, and what in fact it may have made possible. Noel Carroll suggests that the horror revival of the period derives from the success of Friedkin's film of the novel, which channeled a crypto-religious energy into a form so hackneyed it was an immediate success.[93] In *Recreational Terror,* Isabel Pinedo writes that a "dense thicket of Catholic imagery prepared me for . . . televised horror."[94] She later acknowledges, with almost convert-like zeal, the "salutary role that horror played in my life."[95] Fictional horror is "tolerable but pleasurable," as Pinedo writes, not only because it "simulates danger" and "produces a bounded experience of fear."[96] In addition, I surmise that part of the pleasure is the deeply ingrained spiritual memory that accompanies the re-enactment of the fear. Somewhat indirectly, then, via the comfort economies of fear and shopping, during these years monsters regained a sense of their ancient dignity. A production of interiority had begun, taking the form of moral entrepreneurship organized through fear. During the late years of the century a pornography of the soul emerged intending to scare the hell out of its viewers, all the while shaking them free of their money. It was an intoxicating combination. The body was to be shopped and stared at; equally, however, the soul became merely another sort of place to fuss over and furnish.

The comforts derived from anxiety, exploited through commercial fear, brought with them their own attendant familiar spirits and minions, shadows not always dealt with directly. What I am calling "commodity Gothic"—the formula comforts of King's middle period, market tie-ins to slasher films, terror toys from the films for the kids—was not, finally, where the moment of real social disconnect would appear. Stephen King writes that beginning in the forties monsters adapted the Hollywood comic mode of "The Three Stooges" by becoming "stooges" themselves.[97] The trend of parody would be confirmed and redoubled in subsequent decades, as horror and market, fear and comfort, became less and less separable. Terror, accordingly, vacated from cinematic production (or at least reworked as an odd sort of comfort) made its way into markets and onto toy shelves. Alan Smith and Victor Sage write that "contemporary use of the Gothic register strikes a darker and more disturbing note. It is the horror now that is real, and the resolution that is fanciful."[98] The horror aesthetic of a pulp film genre was at least partially responsible, then, for the Horror Politic that covertly supported the ideological lock-up of the time. Fear is a multipurpose social adhesive, as political masters from Plato to Machiavelli and beyond have noted.[99] The Gothic technologies of fear that swept the United States in the early seventies included fantasies of invasive horror as well as a kitschy-Christian sentimentality. The results were a peculiar mix of pornography and apocalypse, part moralism and theological treatise. The genre was, in sum, a pragmatic, cool-eyed licensing of social perversity. As John O'Connor puts it, the diffusion of horror from comic books to the front pages of newspapers had its effects. "Horror is not limited to comic books. . . . Primal nightmares are rooted in reality, and the overlapping of images can be disorienting."[100]

Public panics, construed as invasive terrors of a various kinds, are relatively easy to spot. Public terror is also seemingly easy to manipulate, as Orson Welles demonstrated in 1938 with his broadcast of H. G. Wells's *War of the Worlds*. However, reviewing media coverage of Andrew Cunanan in 1997, one is less confident that such manipulation is always recognized. Nonetheless, public nightmares, whether spoof or serious news, are useful because they can distract us from equivalents that are less obviously "fantasy." I refer here to those cherished fancies that are afforded the dignity of political dress—political ideals, libertarian commitments, American "values." Peter Gay terms these "alibis for aggression." That is, in his opinion, these "rhetorical platitudes . . . legitimated verbal or physical militancy." [101] Flip through the Cunanan reports, for instance, and one finds Gay's comments accurate, since so much of the Cunanan reportage was framed as a threat to the national—or to a national self-image—with little relation to Cunanan himself. It may be that the very act of making public discourse out of the various rhetorics of normalcy needs a counterbalancing rhetoric of fear to hold them in place—one reason why horror is usually bundled with another sentiment, that of romance. In the practice of the rhetoric of family values, for instance, sometimes the horror *is* the romance, or what the romance subtly implies. The sentimentalities of horror are not materially different from the sentimentalities of love. [102]

Whether viewed as horror or as domestic sentiment, then, the Gothic never fully disentangles itself from the worldly pressures of silence and deflection. It speaks against a constant pressure to shut up. The seeming literary focus of the genre, then, reflects the way the genre keeps its politics in the closet, politically speaking, even while closets and enclosures characterize its metaphorical structures. Such deflections and displacements become necessary wherever categories and formulas of knowledge no longer "tell." In such cases the Gothic mode parallels the social-epistemological fissure visually announced by the monster, whose ugliness (often) is an objective correlative of the chaos it evidences. Staking the monster—the ritual closure of cinematic Gothic—is an epistemological necessity as well as formula ending: Who, where, *what* is the monster? Thus, the Gothic is a way of doing fear-based politics in other, less obvious words. The genre, William Patrick Day argues, "illuminates the unbroken connections between our imaginative life and our economic, social and political life." [103] Eugenia DeLamotte, similarly, writes that what "the Gothic had always known" was "the way the perils of the soul in its darkest night reflect, in magnified and revealing forms, the quotidian realities of life in the daylight world of money, work, and social rank." [104] Less politely,

Stephen King puts it this way: the horror tale "scream[s] at the top of its lungs: 'Aren't you afraid that your normality is in itself a lie? That there is no such thing as normality?'" [105] Such a question seems all the more imperative as normality becomes increasingly problematic—another way of recognizing that normality is, like other products, produced under certain conditions and for certain ends. For this reason, the literary genre called Gothic is deeply implicated within contemporary American political and economic systems. Evidence for the American horror aesthetic that I will be tracking will be found, then, not by examination of trope and content, not by cataloging a genre's faux-Gothic furniture, castles, opaque mirrors. Instead, the evidence will be found listening to, reading, and hearing the textual melodramas of silence and negation in public discourse. Evidence will include the bleeding bodies cut and pasted across newspapers and TV. These become visible in the scandalous public rites and the public rites of scandal—both of which are so crucial to a society in which "don't ask, don't tell" is an economic as well as political boon.

The rhetoric of monstrosity is part of a political system of fantasy that is intended to *discipline,* in the word's conjoined meanings of teach and punish. It is awe-ful, full of *pietas.* The pleasures of the Gothic have always involved fears of things coming undone; the torn body in evident pain at the center of so many Gothic narratives asks us to consider a similar pained body, the social order in which these dramas enact cultural crisis.[106] Where social things fall apart, a dissembling is likewise apparent in language, as aesthetics always mirrors, however distantly, political practice. The textual leaps, deflections, fissures, silences, and absences characteristic of Gothic discourse are also typical of the interpretive melodramas of monstrosity that circulate through popular representation. Acting in unison they reflect how what is socially unrepresentable or inadmissible can pressure a language to extremity, pushing it over the edge, perhaps, or better, over the top. Such a language might already find itself *in extremis,* pushed beyond the limits of sense in the service of systemic banality, euphemistic evasion, and outright dissembling: *"It depends upon what the meaning of the word 'is' is."* [107] Adapted as a political mode (as Bill Clinton did, in public policy as well as in his personal defense, as we see he does here), the Gothic evacuation of language we shall be examining is a peculiar mode of address. Almost by requirement it is designed for moments whose representation is made to ride upon paradox: an excess of words will be undone by an abscess of meaning.

The epistemological breakdown evident in Gothic discourse is at once an attempt to register, while containing, cultural distress.[108] Gothic modes and monstrous metaphors will not mimic culture so much as echo the discrepancies of its forms back to itself. A rhetoric of sentimental humanity, then, gives rise to the troubled public fantasies centering on sites, scenes or persons conventionally held sacred (or taboo) in sentimental discourse: the church, the school, the military; mothers, priests, children. In dramas about the killing of kids (soul or body) and kids who kill, one finds the Gothic troubling—evidenced as much in the drama of the story trying to tell itself as in any particular feature of the storyline. Consider the disjunction, for example, in *Time*'s cover story about the two boys who shot up Columbine High School ("The Monsters Next Door"). Nowhere in this report do the authors refer to, explain, or even apologize for the use of the word "monster" in that context. Even if ironic, and it may well be, the Gothic reference is legally inappropriate and politically inflammatory. In other words, the reference is doing the sleight-of-hand for which such language is designed. That is, Gothic monsters are all talk, obsessive attempts to cover gaps in the sensefulness of everyday speech. They are, in short, a form of linguistic last resort, called into play when language and civic resources otherwise fail to signify. Monsters are "for want of a better word"—they demonstrate the failure of linguistic commerce, serving as mute witness to the collapse of language as an economy of social exchange.

A density of wishful thinking and voyeuristic fabrication occurs whenever sex and intimacy occurs in public—whatever the legal or social forms these take. The same can be said about the eroticized media exemplars of these acts, which invariably take the form of invasive death or killing in public. Often panic narratives collapse both, as for example in the plots of killers such as Jeffrey Dahmer and Andrew Cunanan. Similar collapse occurred in the presentations of Susan Smith, who killed her children for "unrequited" love (the motive was registered as crucial) or Fr. James Porter, who molested children (but who was framed as homicidal nonetheless, figured as a "soul killer").[109] Who needs Gothic novels, when much of American life goes on so horrifically, to paraphrase William Dean Howells? Rather than the fake gore and special effects of the movies, we have the scary uplift of the evening news. Move over Moreau, Dracula, wolfman, and perhaps Freddy Krueger and Michael Myers, even Hannibal Lecter. *We* have children who kill in schoolyards; babies dumped in garbage cans by promgoers, cooked up as revenge dinners, or driven into lakes to drown. We have Andrew Cunanan who, we are told, changed his shape constantly, and we have Jeffrey Dahmer, cannibal, killer, wannabe star of *The Exorcist*.[110] We have parents who kill for love as well as those who kill because they are afraid of what love might mean. Who need fear erotic death at the hands of the vampire, or the shape-shifting werewolf? We have erotic death aplenty, Cunanan, McVeigh, Dr. Kevorkian—all competitors in the American way of the flashy ending, and all dismissed as the doing of that "monster," Hollywood. Well, maybe. "Watch my lips" the put-down goes. Maybe Mr. Bush père isn't the only one whose lips need to be watched. Still, the point must be made that the cannibalistic and dismembering fantasies of the award-winning *Silence of the Lambs* can be said to have made the public story of Jeffrey Dahmer possible. Entertainment does give us ordinary politics in distilled form, although it is not wholly to blame. Other people's bodies are, indeed, our business as well as our pleasure, displaced aggressively into fantasy—whether the pornography is the consumption of emotional, talk-show bodies or the detailing of their erotic potential.

Conclusion

Gooble, gobble . . . we accept her, we accept her.
The wedding toast to Cleopatra in Todd Browning's *Freaks* (1932)

The processes of exclusion, denial, and difference that drive the dynamics of monstrosity are bound up in American political fancies, rooted in deeply ingrained theological habits. These fancies and habits are in turn reproduced in and through various exercises of public display, scandal, rhetorical and polemic pronouncements, economies of desire and languages of fear. My discussion of monstrous bodies argues that politics, entertainment, ideological concord, and theological habit combine in civil rites of panic in which the dread-ful body is displayed for erotic or terroristic gain. Monstrosity, however, is always double-edged. In many ways the individuals who populate the pages of this study are distinguished, in the first place, by a social ineptness that, indeed, borders upon the criminal—to borrow a cliché to confirm a cliché. In the case of Clinton and Smith, this is literally the truth, when one considers the banal stupidity—either of their actions or the "cartoon" narrative concocted to explain and adjudicate them. While the hermeneutic of monstrosity seems to underscore the depravity of horrible intimacies, the reverse is the case. That is, repeat killers, killing mothers, child molesters, criminal sexual beings—no matter how inept they might personally be—become the unspeakable *occasions* by which a continuous intimacy is maintained with a naively unpoliticized traditional genre. This rhetoric frames very real political problems and provides a vocabulary, however deficient, of speaking them. For example, a country that has never fought a foreign enemy on its own land instead construes invasions and terrorism in terms of intimacies and intimate places from *within* homes: homosexuals, domestic terrorists.

In its earliest plots Gothic was all about sudden unaccounted visibilities, returning ghosts, dispossessions and the shock of repossession. Gothic still registers a fear that something hidden this way comes, or that what we see is about to become something else, entirely, or has already done so. Especially congenial to the Gothic systems of mis-speaking—its narrative codes of monsters and expostulations of the unspeakable—are those disruptions in the visual choreographies of normalcy, whether race, gender, class, or even the newer formulas of public deviancy by which we are educated.[111] Fantasies of the closet, of the hidden and the threateningly visible, have high social impact, no matter how trivial the knowledge presumed. Secrets become significant in an order where public and private are spliced into a continuous loop of exposure, resulting in a culturally mandated civil pornography. These are, then, Gothic times, and no greater proof than closets and closeting increasingly describe an array of citizens, all considered exotic in that they are thought to be hiding something—and all carefully positioned as sacrificial spectacles for the voyeuristic good of the whole.

I will argue that a contemporary equivalence of the closet must include that structure of excess called the scandal, in which someone's privates make for a visibly productive social scene. The policing of interior dispositions guarantees the ideological placement of bodies thus pressed. In the spate of new "voyeur TV" shows—spectacles, really—privacies are traded in as public coin, exploiting the always already pornographic appeal of lives for exhibition and sale at supermarket checkout—on Oprah or Geraldo, or, now, post-Clinton, in the Congressional Record and on the Internet. The "don't ask, don't tell, just stare" social order is precisely Gothic in that it is organized by what is not seen—either the (ob)scene or the merely unacknowledged. Such an order is thereby monstrous in a most primary sense, in that it produces a show that is a warning, a looking that is moralized gaze.

Political narratives occasioned by such Gothic structures of emotion—fear-based and distrustful, voyeuristic and shame-inducing—are familiar to us from news broadcasts and a media blanket saturated with the threat (hope, possibility?) of some terrifying anticipatory revelation. Su preme Court judges, presidential candidates, religious leaders: the list is extensive of those who punctuate their meanings with fear—or rather, who hide the fear in what they pretend otherwise to say. These nightmare narratives are particularly suited for social policies that are similarly intended to compel an entranced citizenry—titillated by pay-per-view sex but also deeply mired in a scripted shame because of their complicity in the show. In this way a rhetoric for making monsters finds its political utility well laid out: the rubric inscribes abnormality, deviancy, *oddness* in the individual, while keeping attention away from the systems, public "spheres," and bureaucracies of public management that so often constitute the monstrousness of society. Hannah Arendt's observation in *Eichmann in Jerusalem* is to the point: "[The judges] knew, of course, that it would have been very comforting indeed to believe that Eichmann was a monster. . . . [Yet the] trouble with Eichmann was precisely that so many were like him, and that the many were neither perverted nor sadistic, that they were, and still are, terribly and terrifyingly normal."[112] It is the normal from which the monstrous emerges: that, itself, is the terrifying conclusion.

Such deflections also hide the vehicle itself—language. In subsequent chapters I will explore a variety of social monsters, those moments of cultural epiphany staged around anomaly and collapse—collapse of authority, class, motherhood, appropriate gender. In each of these cases visible failure becomes transposed into a different medium, the instability of metaphor. Trauma becomes symbolized as invasion, collapse, monsters among us. The narrow, close-ended feeling of the Gothic—its encastled entrapment—is, finally, emblematic of the compulsive teleology of prejudice, its rush to preempt thought with feeling. Prejudice trains us to read beforehand, as it were, the text in front of us that waits to be read. Thus prejudice binds us to formula and its comforts.[113] "An explanatory gap haunts the case," writes Matthew Ruben about Susan Smith.[114] Rhetorics of the monster paper over that gap, but in addition they paper over Susan Smith, as well. The monster rarely speaks, though she or he always signifies. In each narrative eruption the monster is the epistemological suture between what is seen and what must be meant. The telling of the monster, caught up in ideology, can only be spoken in formulas that preexist it, despite the promise of uniqueness the monster brings, which, finally, undoes the monster more than any stake or exorcistic rite. Formulas of horror, sentimentality, and spectacle must be called upon to complete the story so monstrous that language itself leaves it untold.

~❧~

. . . this nameless mode of naming the unnameable.

Mary Shelley to Leigh Hunt, 9 September 1823

In the language of the man on the street, he was a monster. He would always be a monster.

Ann Rule (pseudonym Andy Stack), *Lust Killer,* 166

If Clinton is guilty of everything alleged, he is still a far better person than Starr, who is using tactics as if *Clinton* were a *monster* like Timothy McVeigh.

Tom Gaumer, letter to the editor, *Denver Rocky Mountain News,* 7 March 1998 (italics in original)

I am not the monster I have been made out to be.

Adolf Eichmann, at his sentencing, from "In His Own Words"

CHAPTER TWO

DRIVE-BY SHOUTING

Introduction

In this chapter I consider how a mode of address common to sacred as well as profane space—found in churches, government halls, tabloids as well as in spitfire epithet—functions to monitor, and police, civility. How does the "monster"—an antique, even archaic title with significant metaphysical echoes—become a vernacular put-down in the "language of the man on the street"?[1] In other words, how do metaphors derived from pulp horror, folklore, and supernatural narrative stabilize the representational world of fear in daily news and social interchange? Finally, how do these expressions of projectile contempt pass unreflected into the realm of ethical speech?[2]

To be successful, pogrom and hate crime must go unnoticed. In other words they need a long incubation in a language designed to hide the violence they enact. Monster-talk is that sort of speech; its metaphors of extreme violence are hurled like verbal grenades. It is also and always a form of indirect address, talk *about,* or aimed *at.* Rarely is it speech initiated by the subject in question. Monster-talk, then, is narrative and meta-narrative, all at once; it tells a story, explains that story, and draws moral conclusions, simultaneously. The discourse *explains* while it pretends only to describe, and moralizes while it thinks to organize. Such fantasy speech develops a taxonomy of the horrible similar to the arguments once used to prove the existence of God. In the ontological argument, some *imagined* thing or person is deemed categorically superior than an actual thing or person, precisely because of its imagined quality. Similarly, in the grammar of monstrosity, the person or action thus nominated is categorically *different* from any actual person by virtue of failing even the category *of* person. In *Partings Welded Together,* David Musselwhite argues that the monster "is monstrous, because it escapes classification, because it scrambles codes, confounds rules, causes administrative chaos."[3] Speaking from the viewpoint of social peacekeepers, then, that chaos alone is enough to consign monstrous persons to the edge of the civilized map. There they function as guards, strangers marking the gates. At that always dangerous place of potential crossing and transgression, the monster brings spurious closure to that which, obsessively and obviously, cannot be closed.[4]

The rhetoric's fundamental strength is its power to command interpretive authority while disguising the ineptness of that authority. That is, the language of monstrosity, like the word itself, is categorically promiscuous. It acts metonymically rather than metaphorically, proposing association rather than direct comparison. Nonetheless, such rhetoric functions with the paradox of metaphor, in that it links unlikeness across divisions and systems (biological, social, moral, aesthetic) while suppressing evidence of the seam. A typical construction begins, "He, she is *like*"—and from that point forward the attempt to describe, to portray, to encapsulate, leaps into another register entirely. "Like" is such a little word to be so burdened with the linguistic processes heaped upon it, "condensation, displacement, verbal and visual overdetermination, slippages, puns, and the like."[5] Upon the slippage, unacknowledged, from simile to metaphor, rests a formidable structure of exclusion and alienation. The simile—"like"—announces itself; the metaphor, on the other hand, suppresses visible announcement, with potentially deadly consequences.

The power of the monstrous lies, then, in the cognitive dissonance it first signals and then hides. The use of such rhetoric, as Moretti points out, "starts from presuppositions . . . which it supposes to be present and at work in its audience."[6] The naming of the monster constantly undoes itself; the words used, themselves supplements, need supplementation. That is, the instability of its claims to rank and to distinguish undercuts the rhetoric's apparent authority, since the use of monster-talk defines nothing except its own commitment to foreclose speech and to shut down discussion. Think of the casual way in which *ad hominem* vilification lumps together as monster Hitler, Stalin, Eichmann, Pol Pot, Milosevic, Pinochet, Kim, the president of North Korea, placing them in the same category with Susan Smith, Andrew Cunanan, animal killers, and, surprisingly, the founder of the Boy Scouts.[7] The crimes attributed to these persons range in importance from the global to the national and individual, and include even offenses against sentimentality. Variously they are charged with violence against single persons, multiple persons, nations, and nonhuman creatures. Yet named as monster, distinctions and gradations among these individuals are lost. The one word capaciously covers all, and thereby is adequate to none.

Invariably, the term "monster" is always "for want of a better word," since neither language nor social permission extends where that word wants to take us. That is, monster-talk incites an intimacy that the narrative told about the monster prejudicially forecloses; similarly, the discourse exploits an intense desire to know against a fierce need to repudiate that intimacy. The effect of such contradiction is discursive failure, speech that misses one point, while making another. However, while monster-talk does not in the end explain very much, on the other hand it permits a great deal. Specifically, it is an approved mechanism for the disguise, and discharge, of social violence (all honorably) in the pursuit of civility, and in the name of humanity.

I. Saying the Unsayable

The words *horrible, monstrous, villainous, infamous,* and the like never cease
to spice up [Sade's] sentences. The transvaluation of all values does not
find a new language; rather, it reinforces the sharp edge of conventional
terms.

Roger Shattuck, *Forbidden Knowledge,* 277

The management of fear is a customary aspect of social life, serving the varied economies of moral sensationalism, civic pedagogy, and erotic show. Yet to be successful the diffusion of fear must be unrelenting, routine, and repetitious. In other words it must be ordinary and unrecognizable. Thus, even modern fears have a sense of antiquity about them, an incantatory diction that would seem quaint were it not dismissed as "formulaic" when (rarely) it is noticed. Karen Halttunen argues that in the transition from a spiritual to a secular epistemology of crime, the construction of murder (to take one example) as "narratives of incomprehension" (46) adopted Gothic codes for its narrative coherence. As Halttunen suggests, that coherence was really wishful thinking; the discourse was designed to "try *and fail.*"[8]

Questions of motivation in these accounts gave way to more practical ones of "who done it?" This shift was partly a result of demographics; in small villages one would likely know a serious malefactor and so identity rather than spiritual uplift would be important. From another point of view, however, this shift occurred because of the "peculiar kind of coherence" generated by the legal models of criminality and its uncertain causation. Judicial humility about the nature of evil superseded theological conceptions in which evil was expected, even accepted as part of human nature, after the Fall. Thus, one way to understand references to the supernatural in narratives of serial killers (among others) is to see them as details left over from a cosmology in which evil and murder had originally functioned as indicators, however perversely, of grace. Epithets such as "fiend" and "monster" found their way into early Gothic formulas of evil from bestiary and pulpit. They were as popular in the late eighteenth century as now—the one a remnant of vanishing theological coherence, the other indicating the alienization characteristic of the newer mode of thinking about crime.[9]

The tension between the newer content and an older form of expression is evident each time Dahmer, for example, is named a vampire, or whenever Ted Bundy is referred to as a shape-shifting werewolf. The instabilities of address give rise to questions concerning the form itself. Monstrous scenes exploit, as a matter of course, the monster's uniqueness. Generally they detail his or her specific failing, underscoring the danger and civil carnage that results from the monster's presence. Nonetheless the explanatory metaphors and plots cannot convey *all* the emotions they would like—principally because, in relation to the monster, no one emotional response is ever intended. As noted earlier, in *Wonders and the Order of Nature,* for instance, Daston and Park argue that "three separate complexes of interpretations and associated emotions—horror, pleasure, and repugnance" are traditionally associated with the monstrous birth.[10] The language of contemporary monstrosity is likewise overloaded with contradictory emotion. Uniqueness is diffused through the codes and leaden metaphors of impulsive scattershot speech. Such a collusion of genre-need and metaphorical incoherency evacuates the monster of the exceptionality the word claims. The emptiness of the narrative shell results in a diffuse sense of echo, evidenced in mythopoetic representations of killers and other agents of public trauma whose descriptions recede into a linguistic past while we, reading, never notice. This is arguably one reason why narratives of exemplary criminality (where evil is displayed as a "teaching moment") seem engaged in competitive adverbial shouting. The incredulity and moral indeterminacy they signal are underscored by emotions ratcheted beyond pitch. The language follows suit, eventually reaching a cadence of speech characterized, oddly, as "unspeakable." The experience is "overwhelming" and so the language must likewise be overwhelmed. The event is most horrible, "not to be believed," and as a consequence, neither can the language be believed. Taxonomy collapses in a language freighted with excess. A terrible desire to outdo, undoes.

Reading through reports of Dahmer or Bundy or other celebrity killers, it is apparent that belief in werewolves and vampires is hardly the point, and there are many other uses for the ballistic speech in which they come to visibility. One in particular will concern me here. Describing dastardly events and villainous persons as beyond human speech implicitly places them beyond moral evaluation, even while the language is intended, ostensibly, to reach ethical conclusion. Indeed, such a technique constitutes the normal means by which ethical conversation about criminality is currently posed. News accounts implicitly position readers in places of moralized judgment in which high moral tone is signaled by the evacuation of speech. "Unspeakable is how some were describing the state of network news," writes Richard Zoglin in *Time*.[11] In an example typical of the genre, a 1991 issue of *People* magazine calls Jeffrey Dahmer's apartment an "unimaginable horror" and then, notwithstanding, goes on in the accustomed Gothic mode to describe the "unspeakable discovery" in delicious detail.[12] A scholarly study intending to dismantle the gendering of serial killers nonetheless employs the usual Gothic formulas to do so; it notes that unlike female serial killers the crimes of their male counterparts "are indescribable in their brutality"—after having spent the previous page engaged in just such description.[13]

Prompted by the arrest of Jeffrey Dahmer in 1991, a *Time* essay observes that "there is a moment of black epiphany at the revelation of a particularly heinous crime—a moment that is both oracular and inexpressible."[14] A few years later, Keith Giese, the assistant prosecutor in the Susan Smith case, summed up the dislocations at work when he addressed the jury in this curiously disjointed manner: "Look at it in the eye, face to face, and see it for the unspeakable horror that it is."[15] Despite the intimacy surreptitiously solicited between reader and subject, there is none. The language resolutely forecloses it. Yet as we shall see, the one-size-fits-all language eventually returns to haunt the speaker. The social rebuke aimed at someone else and at some social trauma elsewhere reflects, instead, an anxiety in the reverse direction. The rhetoric of monstrosity suggests an anxiety that monsters can neither be kept at bay, nor with any certainty confined within the certainties of grammar. The pretence at ethical pronouncement of such statements as found in *Time*, or at Smith's trial, is less about the villainous persons under discussion than about the anxieties in us they provoke. Further, the shifting rhetorical registers are an indication of the problem that the law has when such language comes into court, as I shall explore subsequently. In popular culture representation, speechlessness and visuality collude, and in this collision we observe the power and paradox of media: the unspeakable becomes endlessly exploitable, an industry of showy non-utterance, a situation summed up by Mary Shelley's reaction when she saw her novel *Frankenstein* produced on stage, and her creature played by an anonymous actor. Mary later wrote a friend that "the play bill amused me extremely, for in the list of dramatis personae came, ——— by Mr. T. Cooke: this nameless mode of naming the unnameable is rather good."

The Gothic's "singular moral function," argues Angela Carter, is that of "provoking unease," a dis-ease apparent, even if unaddressed, in the linguistic collapse we are following.[16] Nonetheless, the double bind of the language—to speak and yet to say nothing—is also a double injunction to show and yet not show. If the formula-drift of the language terminates in ethical silence, the visual component of any media representation likewise counters itself, since it must distance itself from the legal and social taboos in place against what can't be shown. In other words, the showy, exemplary moment of displaying evil must negotiate (by means of legal or other social process) the complex network of social proscription of the "obscene." This semiotic gridlock needs some sorting out, since the verbal congestion— the disorder between visuality and speech—says as much about the powers and limitations of discourse as it does about the subjects. Paradoxically, the subjects are only permitted into discourse to the extent that they suffer interdiction. However, as will become clear, the apparent contradiction between visuality and unspeakablity is only a seeming one. Contradiction, even duplicity, is a civil-pedagogical method common to the rubric of scandal, in which everything is spoken aslant, but in which nothing is actually *meant*.

Even if it is not made adverbially clear in the discursive logjam of their formal presentation in news or journal, it is nonetheless evident that all monsters are *not* equal. The difference, say, between a Dahmer and some other less notorious killer is arguably less a matter of depravity than of language and representation. In an analysis of the Jeffrey Dahmer media, Richard Tithecott argues that the dark romance of serial killers, rather than the killers themselves, establishes—indeed guarantees and confirms—the public scene of intimate violence into which Dahmer was fitted.[17] Tithecott also argues a subsidiary point, similar to one I am making: that the cutting and snipping of lives in these tableaux of civic horror enacts a violence different only in degree from the more literal violence engaged in—or presumed to be—by the subjects in question.[18] In *Using Murder,* Philip Jenkins likewise argues that some accounts of public killing are exemplary in the fullest sense of that word. They achieve public recognition, and are narratively framed as fear triggers ("serial killer"), not because they are "intrinsically more dangerous or threatening, but because they are more 'useful' than others."[19]

How can murder be said to be useful? Among other benefits, the utility of these melodramas of interpersonal mayhem lies in their pliancy and elasticity. Murders qualify as "useful" when they focus "symbolic campaigns." For instance, despite the largely vacuous pronouncements made about Jeffrey Dahmer's relationship to the state of American morals, the case brought local and national attention to a long-festering local problem—the adequacy (and racial selectivity) of police care in Dahmer's city. In a similar manner, the killing of Matthew Shepard was exploited in numerous incompatible political directions, framed by conservative, liberal, as well as sentimental constituencies. Murders can also anchor scenes of "moral panic" about institutions held in public esteem; such was the case with Susan Smith and the explicitly political defense of marriage into which her actions were scripted. Andrew Cunanan's reported series of killings also became civic allegory, although *narrative* panic, rather than moral, best characterizes the inflated attention he received. As these examples indicate, the ritual of the moral melodrama is especially useful when framed around some especially valued ideal, since the starkly metaphysical terms of the demonizing confrontation make possible "an ultimate, fundamental, and eternal moral cleansing."[20]

Ceremonies of civic fear *teach* trauma. They keep its effects somberly on exhibit—the nearer home the better, to borrow from Hitchcock's formulation of fear. But public scenes also can redirect the force of trauma's discontent. Emotions elicited in public can be distracted and quieted as well, organized into rhetorical campaigns, shopped, polemicized—and in different ways exploited for their unstable content.[21] The monster's usefulness, therefore, depends upon a variety of factors, some related to narrative and genre, others more directly a factor of marketing and commerce.[22] Still others are political in nature, as the extensive work of Philip Jenkins on moral panics demonstrates. Considered from any of these directions, the monster's appearance masks important questions regarding its material production and ideological need. For instance, in what sort of society does any particular monster become possible, even necessary?[23] (Differing societies *do* have different requirements for their monsters.) I am arguing that the discourse individually crafted around any particular monster—be it Susan Smith or Bill Clinton—permits such questions of origin, purpose, and political function to be acknowledged, while its vacuous formula and syntactic indirection voids them of significant answer. This disavowal is the ideological commitment of monster-talk's movement into sense.

Why, for example, was Susan Smith elevated to media monster while some other child-killing parent was not? Child killing, unfortunately, is all too common; at least one other case was making news when the Smith story broke.[24] A Florida state attorney involved with that case said it most directly: "We're burying too many kids who died at the hands of their parents."[25] Most cases of infanticide never garner the media sponsorship accorded Smith's. Or consider the panic scenes aroused by killing in public. Both Dahmer and Cunanan were determinedly wedged into the "serial killer" crisis formula—in Dahmer's case, at the expense of the facts, and in Cunanan's, at the expense of FBI guidelines.[26] Yet why either of these was awarded "star" status is not self-evident. Evaluated according to "the phenomenon of the body count," they do not compare to other cases of multiple murder.[27] Consider Joel Rifkin, for example, who was arrested in August 1993—almost exactly two years after Dahmer. Rifkin has none of Dahmer's fame; he was neither interviewed nor remembered for his crimes, although he killed more persons than Dahmer (eighteen women, mostly prostitutes).[28] Arthur Shawcross, convicted of fewer murders, also had wider fame.[29] Dahmer, convicted of seventeen deaths of mostly Asian and black homosexuals, was interviewed multiple times—by *Inside Edition* (with father and stepmother, Shari), ABC's *Day One, Dateline NBC* (with his father, Lionel, who also appeared on *Oprah*). There were numerous other invitations, but the warden finally banned further interviews.[30] Was the interest in Dahmer a product of the serendipitous appearance of *The Silence of the Lambs* a few months later? Was it the leering glimpse into a forbidden homosexual life? Dahmer's reported (although unproved) cannibalism?

People magazine thought Dahmer one of the "25 Most-Intriguing People of 1991." Apparently others thought so, too, since *Dateline*'s Dahmer show received its highest ratings ever. Likewise, a few years later when the dust settled on Andrew Cunanan's ignominious suicide, one had the sense of coming off a media-drunk: now what was *that* all about? A commentator in the *American Spectator* acerbically harrumphed that "*Newsweek* . . . could not get enough of [Cunanan]."[31] Nor was *Newsweek* alone. One is tempted to conclude that the erotic subtext of homosexuality—always so delicious in a climate where sex is policed as well as shopped—is responsible for

Dahmer's and Cunanan's fame. To the contrary, an absence of a note-worthy erotic component accounts for Rifkin's obscurity.[32] In other words, there was little political leverage to be made out of Rifkin's killings of so-cially déclassé prostitutes. Indeed, a *straight* man killing a woman already grievously breaches public gender expectations; while this is common enough, its very commonness *must* be managed—by silence, if possible.

In other words, a clear hierarchy exists in public taste as to the types and ranges of its preferred criminality. A canon of deviance can be dis-cerned, shaped around sentimentalized notions of children and sexuality. It forms what I call a heuristic of the monstrous—a taxonomy, a classifi-catory system of civility. How is that hermeneutic constituted, and in what ways does the logically odd language of monstrosity signify?

II. Talking Trash

Candidates for the role of monster are as varied as the rhetoric about them is trite and the money made off them extensive. "What a guy—indeed, what a monster!" exclaim the authors of *Overkill,* a book about Ted Bundy, the one cliché as banal as the next.[33] Robert McNamara, former secretary of defense is one.[34] Martha Stewart is jokingly called a monster; Robert Frost, not so jokingly, by an outraged biographer. Bill Clinton is nomi-nated by none other than Newt Gingrich, Christopher Hitchens, and—in what is surely a preemptive strike—even by his quondam friend Dick Morris.[35] David Berkowitz, "Son of Sam," nominated himself as "Mr. Monster."[36] Colin Ferguson, who opened fire on the Long Island railroad, is "an animal, a monster."[37] Timothy McVeigh and Terry Nichols are "this country's most vicious monsters."[38] The comment was made in response to a *USA Today* editorial a few days previously which asked, possibly with irony, "who would regret the death penalty for a monster's apprentice?"[39] O. J. Simpson is paired with McVeigh in, one hopes, the ironic title "White America's Monster and Patriot."[40] Andrew Cunanan is a "homo-sexual golem."[41] Charles Manson is, variously, "our very own Gothic monster" or a "real monster" or a "celebrity monster."[42] Nor is this speech merely the emotional flailing of the wounded or the illiterate. A law pro-fessor at Oklahoma City University remarked that Terry Nichols was "not the zombie monster McVeigh was."[43] In 1977, Geraldo Rivera, then a re-porter for ABC News, announces the arrest of the "beast and monster" David Berkowitz.[44] Roman Polanski, with some irony, describes himself as a monster.[45] As observed earlier, *Time* magazine's cover about the murders in Columbine High School reads "The Monsters Next Door."[46]

In each of these cases something odd is happening; this oddness, while indicated by the cartoon-talk rhetoric, nonetheless is not supported by it. The casual metaphors signal a violence different from the acts reportedly committed by these persons, but it is a violence nonetheless. Individuals nominated as monsters become textually undone, victim of metonymy and metaphor, prey to sloppy habits of public thinking, linguistic failure, and a narrative rush to closure that is tantamount to an act of direct prejudice.[47] In these clamorous texts about child killers and home invaders, part- or full-time civic terrorists, predatory homosexuals, child-killing mothers, and loose presidents, an extraordinary energy is invested in referring the heinous person outside him- or herself to the fictional, cinematic, folkloric, or comic-book creature they are thought to embody, represent, or evoke. Examples are readily available. A woman screams across the courtroom at Joel Rifkin, "I want to spit on the face of the monster who took my daughter's life."[48] The father of a woman allegedly killed by a man called the "Cross-Country Killer" remarked, "We're going to have a glass of champagne and toast this jury that had enough sense to know that this monster had no right to live."[49] The sister of Jeffrey Trail (one of the men reportedly killed by Cunanan) announced with confidence, "What I've realized, having met Andrew Cunanan, is that there really are monsters out there."[50] What she makes less clear is that she had met him months earlier, for "only minutes." Nonetheless she can be serene in her judgment. Richard Davis, convicted killer of Polly Klaas, is called "monster" and "vampire" by the girl's father.[51] Timothy McVeigh, found guilty of blowing up the Alfred P. Murrah Federal Building in Oklahoma City on April 19, 1995, killing 168 persons, is given pointed ears and Dracula fangs; the celebrity-shock biography waiting in the wings even titles him an "all-American Monster."[52]

The case of Jeffrey Dahmer proved altogether unmanageable, either morally or linguistically. Attempts to put him into words signally failed. A vast stable of creatures, an array of machines, a compendium of legends, and references both occult and cosmological were called into service. Dahmer is a "specimen to be studied by experts."[53] He walks "with the near-drop pace of a zombie";[54] he reportedly emits "wolflike howling" and "demonic screams" when arrested;[55] he is a "human time bomb";[56] and, says Geraldo, a "monster."[57] With Faulknerian zeal one account lays into Dahmer. He is "The Ghoul," a "human flesh-eating vampire of the night."[58] Even homely sports metaphors saw play. Don Davis writes that Dahmer sent his "awful scoreboard" into "double-digits."[59] In each case the formularies intend to *convict* the killer of responsibility and to emphasize the personal depravity of "these beasts in human form." [60] Nonetheless, such asides to the supernatural, references to bestiaries and the occult, the mysterious and demonic, subvert those intentions entirely. Like the holes in Jason's hockey mask, the rhetoric allows the monster to see us. That is, it makes the speaker's needs for narrative coherency visible. In reverse, however, the reader or viewer loses sight of what, ostensibly, is sought: moral comprehension, ethical discussion, human insight. Dennis Nilsen, arrested in London for multiple killings, makes a similar point: "No one wants to believe ever that I am just an ordinary man come to an extraordinary and overwhelming conclusion." [61] Part of that "extraordinary . . . conclusion" was the discourse in which he himself was retrofitted for public company. Built into the public narration of serial killing is a prejudice of alienation—one that is, already, a conclusion. Nilsen is narratively served up as a perfectly intimate public enemy.

Two questions might be asked. Why should the grotesquery of Gothic lore and commercial horror be used, often without apology, to locate criminality within a paradigm of the "authentic," the "true," and the "real"? Second, how can such language be welcomed in the "news" without even so much as a wink in the direction of the camera? That is, so many of these scenes of civic crisis are plagued by an anxiety of adequate telling—no wonder, given the blenderized speech through which they are presented. Ever conscious of the air of fantasy hovering about them, and eager to confirm their own veracity, reports about crime that make up the stock in trade of such weeklies as *Newsweek, Time,* and other middlebrow periodicals establish their "truth" by sideways appeals to other genres: textual and televisual forms; fiction, drama, and metaphors of the literary; the supernatural and the monstrous. This alone is evidence enough of textual discomfort; it, rather than specific content analysis, direct us to the effects of the Gothic, as these are evidenced within the text and as they work themselves upon the reader. As Maggie Kilgour observes, "At times the Gothic seems hardly a unified narrative at all, but a series of framed conventions, static moments of extreme emotions—displayed by characters or in the landscape, and reproduced in the reader." [62]

Although pushed to the limit of grammatical resources and what is civilly permitted, discourse nonetheless negotiates these constraints, speaking *indirectly* in fragmented and sidelong ways what custom, genre, and civic convention forbid. In the curious crab-like movement of monstrous metaphors, sideways and backwards, language is understood to be supplemental, yet necessary. It is supplemental in that no language can be trusted to encompass the subject; nonetheless, language is necessary for what speech implies—a capacity for social intercourse sentimentally attributed "only" to human beings. The failure or absence of speech is, in fact, a conventional way to signal the inhuman, as for example James Whale does by eliminating Boris Karloff's speaking lines in *Frankenstein*. The discourse passes beyond speech into realms of emotions, ideas, attitudes that cannot be contained within "ordinary" speech. Monster-making thus conjures a language that moves beyond the moral limits of speech in order to accomplish its task.[63] Violence is, as a result, not far away.

Let me address for a moment what Hayden White might call the ideological "content of the form" of such language acts.[64] The *vérité* genres (true crime and the like)—whether passing as documentary or tossed off as tabloid "fact"—disclose in concentrated form an anxiety regarding the competency of language to "tell" what the genre form insists is its métier—*ipsa acta,* the facts and only the facts. For that reason the genre will serve as the center of my discussion, since its techniques exemplify methods found elsewhere in daily news and casual speech.[65] The very name of the genre reflects both its promise as well as its failure. On the one hand it offers to identify stigmatized behavior (crime), while, on the other, claiming to represent such behavior as "true." Yet the genre can neither alleviate this anxiety nor substantiate its claims for veracity. That is, the "truth" promised—usually "shocking," "chilling," "haunting"—exactly states what these texts cannot deliver. Nor, I think, do they intend to. "Truth" in this sense is merely another sort of metaphor, perhaps analogy, serving as a justificatory cover text. Its presence authorizes the consumption of material otherwise forbidden or denied. One thinks of the ubiquitous "eight pages of shocking photographs," whose grainy non sequiturs (odd shots of doors, house fronts, unrecognizable persons in the distance) need sometimes lengthy annotations for us to "see" how shocking they are. Shock, here, has to be produced textually. An anxiety of deficiency is represented in the demand for *more* representation.[66] (A similar anxiety—and result—will evidence itself in the crisis of representation provoked by Bill Clinton.)

Why should anxiety demand more, rather than less, representation? In true crime and reality TV documentary mode, a presumption of fact exists, at least from the point of the viewer (producers, to the contrary, rarely presume this). The text or show is thought to be transparent, above ideology, guilelessly in pursuit of some hidden truth which it uncovers and then dispassionately delivers to an ever-sober reader. Narrative is read as essay, in a manner of speaking, although the essay is a peculiar one, since its effect is neither to speak clearly nor to specify directly. Just as the monster exists within a verbal fog, in a similar manner "truth" is likewise lost to generic mismatch, as it is jostled and bumped in these texts at every turn by the untrue and the improbable.

One would think that a text eager to exploit claims for "truth" would avoid any reference that might lead a reader to suspect otherwise about the text in question. Yet precisely the opposite is the case in many of these tabloids, shows, and documentaries. Sideways glances are consistently made to texts and genres supposedly different in kind. Dramatic, fictional, or televisual examples are called upon to confirm the text's protestations of transparent honesty. Consider one of the original highbrow crossovers of this pulp genre, *The Boston Strangler* (1966). In the first few lines of the his prefatory note, Gerold Frank writes that he will consider a crime "under circumstances as baffling as any in fiction." [67] In those publications that are accorded "newsworthy" status, one still experiences the slightly wobbly sensation of being afloat a sea of unstable reference. *Time* magazine, for example, is particularly fond of funhouse speech. For example, an initial report about Andrew Cunanan compares the events to a "chilling campfire tale" and a "real-life horror movie." [68] Three months later, following Cunanan's death, the argumentation has not materially improved. In August the case is described as "Pulp Fiction" and "coup de théâtre." [69] These references intend to confirm the "real" but in fact the contrary happens; the real evaporates, leaving only representation and readerly expectation. In turn, what the reader expects is only remembrance of *earlier* representations that differ in *kind* even when they do not vary a bit in method. The reader indulges not so much a desire for truth but for the genre conventions whose closure makes narrative coherence seem true because it *is* coherent.

The obvious discomfort with the truth-capacity of words, and the need to supplement them, extends beyond the ideological residue of narrative form, or the effects of generic structure, to include matters of content itself. This is Wendy Lesser's point in *Pictures at an Execution,* when she writes that "real murders . . . feed our wish for narrative." [70] In *Using Murder,* Jenkins likewise notes the symbiotic relation:

> There exists a complex feedback relationship between fact-based and fictitious accounts of the serial murder phenomenon. Fictional accounts often derive heavily from real-life cases, though with significant alterations; while in turn, the fiction has done at least as much to shape popular stereotypes of the serial killer as any avowedly factual book or news program. [71]

Jenkins's point can be extended from fictions into legal processes and formation of governmental policies.[72] As we have seen in *Time* and *Newsweek* reports about Cunanan or Dahmer, for instance, actual persons and situations slip and slop across literarily degradable boundaries. The interactive nature of the genre—its dependence upon a readership priorly educated in genre and media—suggests the uneasy conclusion that language must fail in order that formal genre constraints might succeed. Mark Seltzer observes that the most "visible" aspect of the "proliferating, "[sic] official literature on serial killing" is its "relentless banality."[73] Bundy's "death-row interviews are endless strings of mass media and pop-academic clichés."[74] A *New Yorker* essay a month after Bundy's execution-day interview dismissed Bundy's efforts on the basis of the format, rather than the words: "After one glance at the setup, you understood its premises and pre-arrangements; you could have turned off the set at any point and not missed much . . . that silent grinding is the medium's mammoth forget-tery."[75] By this conclusion we should never watch anything, or, at least we should never conclude anything from what we watch. Since this is impossible, the least we can ask for is better familiarity with genre.

Similarly, the extremity of the crime or the depravity of the criminal is tightly locked into genre-expectation. Terror is underwritten by appeal to occult, supernatural, diabolical, or other meta-human force, even as the human agency of it recedes. Nilsen remarked that he gave interviewers "a psychiatrist's cliché."[76] In an attempt to speak definitively about the nature of the act in question, language collapses. Sometimes the reach is quite low; a priest accused of sexual misconduct is "a useless piece of human excrement."[77] Susan Smith is "slime; just slime"; Cunanan is "garbage"; Richard Davis is "a terror . . . a real lowlife."[78] Bundy, in prison, further imprisons himself, referring to himself as a "hunchback," an "entity" (Michaud and Aynesworth, 6, 13). Mythological allusion, fairy tales, and literary characters spike the narrative; "murderous mutants" (226) are blamed.[79] Cinema favorites Jason and Freddy (and of course Norman Bates) are called in as support, condemning the killer or other miscreant to death by proxy.[80] The evildoer in these texts undergoes a transubstantiation not unlike the bread and wine in Catholic Eucharistic services; material reality becomes metaphysically reconfigured, symbolically charged. Indeed, supernatural reference is almost obligatory in the genre. Bundy is said to have a "preter-natural power to manipulate, a capacity whose effect was akin to magic."[81] Dahmer "was a sorcerer, making magic."[82] What is served, one wonders, by according such powers to these persons? Must we increase their threat in order to feel better about killing them off?

Such free-range semiotic grazing extends from the campy to the banal and inept. *Time* magazine, always handy with the already known, titles an essay on serial killers "Dances with Werewolves."[83] This combines two effects in one—horror formulaic and cinema allusion. Mixed metaphors of this sort abound. Indeed, mix-matched speech seems *required* in exorcising monsters, whose discordant civic parts make them mixed metaphors, as well. Commenting on the cross-country chase of Andrew Cunanan, former FBI specialist Robert Ressler unhelpfully observes that "the victim pool is widening. . . . Now he's like a mad dog running through the countryside."[84] But as Mary Noel remarks in *Villains Galore,* being original is not really the intention, since "lack of originality is not only the essence of popular culture, but its definition."[85] The point of monster rhetoric is to show that the monster, while suddenly upon us, is not, after all, *new,* nor really much of a surprise. The old language still functions to contain its newer progeny—a radically conservative gesture, as one might imagine, and so it is worth considering who might find it worthwhile to employ such a tactic.

As for mixed metaphors, one could argue that the monster is such a metaphor—a jumble of ends, effects and emotions, whose objective correlative is the fractured bits of language sutured together in his behalf. Gerald Boyle, Jeffrey Dahmer's defense attorney, was sturdily inventive in this regard, a savvy weaver of mixed metaphors and the mixed messages they intend. His descriptions of Dahmer are memorable: "Halley's Comet," a "steamrolling killing machine," "a runaway train on a track of madness, picking up steam all the time. . . ."[86] Boyle did not actually need to *call* Dahmer a monster; the fractured language he employed demonstrated quite clearly what a conceptual mess a monster *is,* and thus, made the point for him. Indeed, his hypertrophic speech intended just the evacuation of responsibility I am arguing. In other words, it could be argued that Boyle was doing his job; he defended Dahmer as best he could from bad language by heaping that bad language upon him in return, knowing that nothing succeeds more in this respect than excess. Evacuated of his humanity Dahmer becomes anything *but* a human agent who might be accountable for his actions. From another view, Boyle's slapdash inventiveness demonstrates how Gothic is less a genre where sloppy thinking goes than a mode in which language collides with the limits of its civic and linguistic resources. What can be expressed and what may be uttered are not always the same thing. Even in America one cannot say everything one wants, or even anything. Sentimentalized notions of the Bill of Rights and commodity-driven notions of freedom aside, the grammar, sense of language, and formal discourse simply cannot sustain such conceptual chaos.

The bullet-like evocations of monstrosity we are examining share a common trait. They are contentless expressions of an ill-considered, if not actually thoughtless, violence. Self-confirmatory, they are caught in a loop of the already-represented. A September 12, 1991, episode on *Geraldo* is titled "Jeffrey Dahmer: Diary of a Monster." In a similar manner Ressler titles an interview with John Wayne Gacy "Interview with a Monster."[87] In each of these cases, "monster" begs definition, being a formula of reprisal and prejudice rather than description. Ressler and Geraldo further undercut the already limited authority of the metaphor by appealing to linguistic capacities and literary categories—diary and interview—from which monsters, usually speechless, are excluded.[88] As if these methods do not in themselves suffice, and in case his readers don't see the shadow cast by Anne Rice's *Interview with a Vampire,* Ressler reruns the already-said with Dahmer: "Interview with a Cannibal."[89] Here again artifice first identifies the monstrous by aligning it with a prehistory of representation; this is *the* necessary prerequisite for the genre to work effectively. It then underwrites and confirms the already-said with literary allusion, which—like the text clarifying the "eight pages of shocking photographs" (always eight, never six, never ten)—steadily directs the consumer's (a description intended in literal ways, here) "reading" to specified conclusions. It is thus interesting to observe that Ressler's codifying of Dahmer *as* a monster is not unlike Boyle's attempt to defend him from that charge. The one accuses, the other defends, and the same fissured language serves both. Ressler says it was his task to "evaluate Dahmer for Boyle within the larger context of serial killers and the patterns to which they most frequently adhere."[90] Those "patterns," it should be clear, have very little to do with killing and a great deal to do with "feed[ing] our wish for narrative."[91]

III. "Yes, he's a monster."[92]

It would be entirely reasonable at this point if, bewildered by the drunken speech evidenced in the popular press, one tossed one's hands in the air and retired to read the OED. Whoever these individuals and whatever their crimes might be, one marvels at the energies taken to render them as generic and inhuman as possible. Given any of Boyle's descriptions of Dahmer, for example, no one is likely to mistake him for a human being. The happy result of this, of course, is that it makes dealing with Dahmer as if he *isn't* one so much easier. Similar conclusions can be drawn about the transformation of other criminals into public theater. There is a mad energy to make these disturbers of the civil peace into something—literally—other than what they are. This, I think, is Charles Manson's point, bitterly made, "I am what you have made of me and the mad dog devil killer fiend leper is a reflection of your society."[93] One turns with anticipation and relief, then, to a different realm of report—studies, academic presentations, professional assessments of criminal etiologies and sociological conclusions. Here, one thinks, will be found a sober use of language commensurate with high moral purpose.

Even here, however, genre overcomes purpose. A prominent literary critic, for example, writing in *Salmagundi,* comments upon the "public response to real monsters like Charles Manson. . . ."[94] John Douglas and Mark Olshaker solemnly assure their readers that a serial killer will not always be "easily recognized as a monster."[95] Let me take another example. In *I Have Lived in the Monster: Report from the Abyss,* criminologist Robert Ressler combines his experience in law and detection to mount a loosely sociological analysis of serial killing.[96] Ressler is initially at pains to distinguish the humanity of serial killers and separate it off from mythology and horrorography. Ressler argues that in "old times" the "incomprehensibility" of DeSalvo's "Boston Strangler" killings would have elicited "supernatural causes" to explain "excessively savage murders, blood-draining, and other monstrous acts."[97] He intends here to confirm Albert DeSalvo's humanity. Ressler's motivation for doing so is unexceptional, considering his profession. That is, human beings are subject to the law in ways monsters are not. Ressler wishes to underscore that killers are moral agents and thus punishable. Yet even mantled in the combined dignity of sociological rhetoric and the "priesthood" of FBI authority, Ressler loses whatever focus he might have intended. Listing "known killers" from the nineteenth century onward, he concludes with "such latter-day vampires as Richard Trenton Chase, Edmund Kemper."[98] And, if direct attribution as vampire is not enough, Ressler adds confirmatory detail of a suitably Gothic sort. He notes that one of his "latter-day vampires," John Haigh, "had dreams of drinking blood."[99]

Ressler's catalogue—and he is certainly not alone in plundering Gothic warehouses for descriptive aid—thus subsumes individuals under criminal stigma back into the horror mythology he initially sets out to discredit. The "supernatural"—which in previous times provided "the only logical explanations"[100]—is evidently still useful. Ressler, however, is not particularly to be blamed, since such linguistic flatulence is characteristic of most speech in the discourse, regardless of the level of audience or diction. Philip Jenkins has made a career soberly deflating moral panics by analyzing their representational incoherencies. Yet even Jenkins argues that killers permit "society to project its worst nightmares and fantasies, images that in other years . . . might well be fastened onto supernatural or imaginary folk-devils—vampires, werewolves, witches, evil sorcerers, conspiratorial Jews." [101]

A glance at any "news" weekly or supermarket true-crime text will show that projectile fantasizing of this sort occurs regularly now, not in "other years." The punch-drunk metaphors; the fissures and gaps these partially cover; the silences and deflections of language: all these aspects betray a debt to Gothic narrative technique, where a multiplicity of narrators and a shifting point of view—in addition to escalating violence of language—signal, in Eve Kosofsky Sedgwick's expression, the "difficulty the tale has in getting itself told." [102] Sedgwick's point is well taken. In any telling of the monster, something remains unspoken despite all the energy to speak it, while something else continues to speak, despite all efforts to shut it up. Geraldo, for instance, makes no claim for higher sociological analysis when he calls Dahmer a monster on his public broadcast. Even so, one wonders how a contemporary discourse of civil fear, prosaically criminalized and talk-showed as it is, is served by a revision into a language of "shopworn . . . occult"? [103]

To repeat the obvious, the occult is not the problem. It was not the problem for the men killed by Dahmer, nor, indeed, was it the problem faced by Dahmer at the end of his life. As John Gacy wryly observed to Ressler, "The dead won't bother you. It's the living you got to worry about." [104] Jeffrey Dahmer might agree, if he could, as indeed, so might *his* victims if they could. This is one irony of the discourse. Rather than confirming the depravity of serial killers, the empty syllables of monstrosity do the reverse. Narrowly circumscribing the humanity in which depravity is grounded, it substitutes—well, what *does* it substitute? Narrative pleasure? Social approval for retributive violence? Closure? Ask Christopher J. Scarver, who found in the monster narrative a mandate from God to bludgeon Dahmer to death. Gacy rightly notes that occasions of interpersonal violence are the responsibility of living persons—the Haighs, Kempers, Chases, Bundys, Lucases, Dahmers, Cunanans. The methods used by these murderers may range from the mundane to the criminally inventive, but assuredly they are not spooks or haunts, nor do they kill by haunting means. Nonetheless their transmutation into ritual Gothic metaphor is useful *because* so doing permits the continuance of a ceremony of the horrible, and this repetition is the teaching required by civic stability.

Robert Keppel says it best: "the warnings on the eleven o'clock news, the ominous headlines on page one of the local papers" had "almost become a ritual." [105] Thus, Albert Fish, a killer who achieved notoriety in New York in the early years of the century, was given the sobriquet "Brooklyn Vampire." [106] One could argue with Feuerbach, and later with Marx and Engels, that not only is religion an opiate, but other discourses are, as well; they place us in proper abject dependency to agencies and forces who profit most from our subjection.

IV. Uncivil Tales: Horror Politic

The various examples I have detailed might seem to suggest otherwise. Nonetheless, horror fictions, like other modes of genre-writing (such as sentimental domestic novel or the western) are acutely sensitive to the social register in which they are written. The formula-bound heaviness of horror *confirms* its generally conservative ideological base, rather than contradicting it. That the formulas of fiction can slip without recognition into news and academic treatment is ample evidence of this. Let me return for a moment to a previous example. Partly as a result of political pressures during the preceding two decades, and partly due to the steady, gravitational pull of genre, Ressler's ostensibly humanist, reasoned and compassionate study of criminal detection shades into a genre of an entirely different sort, as he presents a litany of killers who are *not* just themselves. The word *litany* is appropriate, because in this borderline genre of politically reconstituted academia, the speech acts in question have reverted from sociology to a different metaphysical plane entirely. Notwithstanding the differences in the narratives themselves, these compressed stories (of vampire, beast, werewolf, monster, ghoul) economically distill distinct processes of civic alienation, repudiation, and purposeful unnaming. Each of these processes is a requirement, as well as an effect, of making monsters.

A civic order distances itself in various ways from those whom it perceives to be carriers of its destruction. The distance, however, extends in two directions. Monstrous rhetorics simultaneously establish *who* the monster is, while insuring that its depredations are, nonetheless, out of reach of any human (i.e. governmental) energy. In these tightly coiled metaphors of prejudice, a double sleight of hand occurs. Systems and political structures are relieved of responsibility by means of a blame collectively applied to the inhuman and the monstrous. In turn, however, this collectivity is exported back onto individuals whose lives are transformed into necessary Gothic fantasies, whether of invasion, terrorism, murder, domestic trauma, or other fright-trigger. In this way, the "black headlines that would label Ted a monster" cage Bundy more securely than the prisons from which he escaped so readily.[107] This may be the point, however. Narrative is far more secure, and stable, than political systems, prisons, and ideological demand.

The rubric of the monstrous depends for its success upon two simultaneous movements, a political forgetting on the one hand, and an ideological remembering on the other. As we have seen, the forgetting erases the idiosyncratic humanity of the individuals who are caught up in formula as well as done in by it. (The interpolation of Dahmer into a fantasy of cannibalism, for instance, was imposed by the need to retrofit him *into* an already-familiar plot.) The genre makeover necessitates an erasure—a forgetting guaranteed by genre as part of its comforting spell. We see that process in one reporter's curious ambivalence to the "real" Jeffrey Dahmer. Before Dahmer's arrival in court, Anne E. Schwartz speaks of her "strange sense of anticipation" as she waited to see "what a serial killer looked like. I was shocked to see that he looked just like an ordinary fellow." Yet a few sentences later, that ordinariness becomes dense with significance: "The times I saw him up close, I saw nothing there. . . . There was just nothing to him." [108] Ordinary, normal: "nothing there." A photo caption in her shockumentary *The Man Who Could Not Kill Enough* describes Dahmer as the "average-looking man." [109] Schwartz gazes at Dahmer through the lens of pre-representation and admits to being disappointed when she realizes that what she has been observing all along is the lens, not Dahmer—who in fact is nothing without the lens.

In the television documentary *Murder: No Apparent Motive,* Detective Salerno observes that killers like Wayne Williams (Atlanta) and Kenneth Bianchi (the Hillside Strangler) are more like us than not. The "frightening truth is that serial killers like Ted Bundy and Jeffrey Dahmer are incredibly credible and, therefore, so very dangerous." [110] They are also very intimate, or at least made out to be. Gacy was "everyone's nextdoor neighbor." [111] Similarly, " 'Ted was one of us' ";[112] he was a "perfect son, the perfect student, the Boy Scout." [113] And so he was. The past-tense verb describing Bundy is well chosen for the work it must do. Erasing the closeness (and the terror?) of that intimacy, and eliminating that first-name basis, is where the real work of making monsters begins, and the essential movement behind the narratives. Brian Masters indirectly makes this point: "It is Nilsen's inhuman detachment . . . that makes him finally unrecognizable." [114]

The logical dysfunction of the discourse, then, presents itself as a confusing tracery of troubled speaking, a splatter text of eclectic genres and modes, and a methodological incoherency that goes unchallenged. What remains as evidence of this categorical collapse points toward a much wider semantic breakdown. In *Deformed Discourse,* David Williams notes that "language of the monstrous is parasitic, depending on the existence of conventional languages; it feeds . . . at their margins, . . . and, true to its etymology . . . , it points to utterances that lie beyond logic."[115] Except that to argue that monsters lie *beyond* logic is again to deny the reality by which *in* language they have such lethal effect. Placing them beyond logic exculpates the discursive grammars by which stigmatized persons are lost to metaphor—whether monstrous or academic—when they become, for example, "condensed symptoms of the social," "microcosmic histories," "maladies of sociality or pathologies of the soul."[116] Not only is the monster a blank category, the evaluative discourse through which monstrosity becomes visible is equally a blank. Into its formal emptiness hyperventilated public speech rushes, exploiting some topic not otherwise addressed. Stephen King makes this point in *Carrie,* through the character of Sue Snell: "They've forgotten [Carrie]. . . . They've made her into some kind of a symbol and forgotten that she was a human being."[117] In place of these "monsters" will be an endless loop of speech stuttering into [non]sense, repeatedly stopping just short of having anything to say. Individuals get caught in these loops—whether in the first- or secondary-degree fictions of King's *Carrie,* or those of Susan Smith, Andrew Cunanan, Timothy McVeigh, Pat Buchanan's Hitler, or the high school boys in Littleton. All of these persons will fade away, trapped in a repudiative cycle characterized, in Gary Indiana's phrase, by "phobia-laden mendacity."[118]

Making monsters is bloody business as well as hard work. Time, commitment, forethought, and perseverance are necessary. Perhaps, then, this is why Dahmer, among so many others, occasioned such a frenzy of misaddress. "Dress [Dahmer] in a suit and he looks like ten other men," remarked a court psychiatrist.[119] This reasonable looking, quiet white male in the buttoned-down Oxford shirt was, like Bundy, evidently "one of us." We accept Dahmer's monstrosity without question because of the coherency of the formula. It will be his humanity—painfully, excruciatingly evident—that is problematic. Therefore it will be that humanity that troubles the reports about him and the numerous interviews with him and that disturbs the fictions about his life. Similarly, it is the humanity of this or that killer or raper or baby-killer that we need to visit, and revisit, again and again.[120] Such unfinished business is twofold; it assures the reader of the monstrosity we expect to find while building a firewall between ourselves and any memory of humanity that might move us to compassion.

This accounts for the palpable sense of release in so many of the accounts of Dahmer's death. He ceased to trouble us with the potentialities we share with him, alive.

Nonetheless, despite the rigorous metamorphosis they undergo, these miscreants are never inhuman *enough*—reason enough why the work of transforming them continues so desperately. Don Davis's hastily written *The Milwaukee Murders* poignantly demonstrates this anxiety.[121] Opposite the now fairly standard picture of a mute Jeffrey Dahmer in court, the caption reads, "The face of a monster: accused serial killer Jeffrey Dahmer."[122] It is important to note that Dahmer is merely *accused* at this point. The text rightly notes that he had not yet been convicted of any crime, nor even charged with one. But these sobering facts aside, the work of making monsters must go on, for *our* sake, not *their* good. And so, legally innocent, Dahmer nonetheless assumes his role in a melodrama scripted out long before, losing his humanity so that readers might confirm theirs.[123] In another recent case, Luke Woodham was arraigned in court for bludgeoning his mother to death. Although he had not yet been tried, the *USA Today* report can nonetheless hold him up as an exemplar, noting that "a killer didn't necessarily have the face of a monster."[124] Clearly, these persons can't win for losing.

The presence of monster-talk at the arraignments of Dahmer and Woodham deserves comment, since legal precision and Gothic abandon are increasingly powerful allies in juridical processes. Listen, for instance, to Judge Cowart's sentencing of Ted Bundy: "This court finds that the killings were indeed heinous, atrocious, and cruel in that they were extremely wicked, shockingly evil, vile, and the product of a design to inflict a high degree of pain and with utter indifference to human life."[125] What purposes can possibly be served by the archaic diction, with its suggestions of a manic, Gothic vengefulness? None related to the exercise of law, perhaps, although the cadences do serve as a civic rubric. Nor is Bundy's case an isolated instance. For a more direct hex, we turn to New York Supreme Court Justice Edwin Torres, who in 1994 sentenced John Rosado to 50 to 100 years in prison. Calling his prisoner "the devil incarnate," Torres declaimed: "A collective pox on the parole board that ever sees fit to unleash this demon on society again. . . . And if necessary, I will arise from my mouldy grave to visit it on them myself."[126]

Whether encoded as legal or as Gothic, social modes of address mirror each other's possibilities while underscoring the different anxieties driving each discourse. If Torres's prisoner is "the devil incarnate," or if Susan Smith is a monster according to her prosecuting attorney, they claim a transcendence that places them beyond any court. This recalls the ascription of magic to Bundy, or the preternaturally canny Dahmer. Inevitably, such codes "eliminate society's responsibility for such violence, so that murderers are regarded as deviants, sex beasts and monsters rather than the inevitable products of our own society." [127] The schizophrenia is doubled, however, since the making as well as unmaking of monsters are simultaneous actions. On the one hand law itself is a formula that codifies speech acts; in so doing it inscribes their history *into* law, however silently. Law thus *normalizes,* conventionalizes, a gesture that is otherwise human. That is, it takes an action that is erratic, idiotic (of or related to an individual) and makes it tellable, shareable, repeatable. It also limits the event, obviously, to the terms in which it can be told. In the same way Gothic narratology exploits and codifies the silences that are necessarily part of any speech act, and which themselves articulate silences in the civic text.

Finally, it ought to be noted that the ritual denunciations of Judges Cowart and Torres confirm Daniel A. Cohen's observation in *Pillars of Salt* that increasingly through the nineteenth century "lawyers and judges replaced ministers as the primary spokesmen of public authority." [128] Although they are agents of human law, Cowart and Torres speak as well in support of a higher law. The law in question is not necessarily a religious one, although these sober judges might admonish me for putting the matter in these terms, using language of religion, higher laws, etc. For surely their culture of violence, its lure to magic and metaphysics, speaks through them. Judge Cowart and Judge Torres are casting spells: a *hex* by *lex*. Invoking the horrific sublime conjures up that other awfulness, the holy somewhere hidden, still, in our rhetorics of the hellish—the holy we have thrown out, mistakenly, as trash.

Albert DeSalvo, known as the Boston Strangler, was accused of killing thirteen women. There is some debate whether DeSalvo actually was the killer in question, and even his own reminiscence of the affair is ambiguous. [129] He confessed to some perplexity, confusing, he said, "the things that [he] did do, that I have read in books about [with the things] that other people do, that I didn't think or realize that I would ever do these things." [130] If we have a hard time following the grammar of DeSalvo's intentions, so, apparently, did he have difficulties fitting into the script assigned him—even if it was, quite possibly, just a role he was playing. Dennis Nilsen and Jeffrey Dahmer likewise admitted to being confused by what they were reported to have done. The confusion of these men is no doubt partly willful, as when the Son of Sam attributed his killings to the prompting of a neighbor's dog. Nonetheless, more than personal agency is at work in the confusion. To the contrary, while all three killers were writing texts that they could not understand, so, too, the society in which they lived was intent upon scripting them into the hermeneutic of the monstrous. The appropriate question to be asked, then, is less concerned with the actor than the ritual itself: Did it work?

Conclusion

As in any ritual, the *sense* of the matter isn't the matter, *doesn't* matter. Verisimilitude is not the point. The term "monster" had originally signified a human being—even if, as Augustine noted, the signification was troubling in terms of its biological, not theological, import. Such attitudes naively inform cultural scripts of deviancy still, as Anne E. Schwartz demonstrates in her account of Dahmer: "So many of us wanted to believe that something had traumatized little Jeffrey Dahmer, otherwise we must believe that some people simply give birth to monsters."[131] There is nothing simple about such social births, however. The policies and politics of monstrosity anchor an array of cultural narratives that are said to be distinctly different but which are often indistinguishable from each other. Among the crossovers can be included true crime procedural, the moralized tales of rue and gore called the evening news, the Gothic fantasies of the documentary form, and the moral panic. In these latter, one can find bits and scraps of monster-speech in the most socially rarefied air, employed by presidents, presidential candidates, law courts Supreme and other. As a result monsters find themselves made welcome in drawing room and in all the places from which once they would have been immediately banished.

It is hard to escape the conclusion that the almost gleeful traffic in finding private monsters only makes profit of fear in more useful social formats. What are the pleasures of public violence? How do these differ from the pleasures of perversity? The Gothic celebration of fear that was the Andrew Cunanan reportage, for example, enacted a ritual not different in kind from the sexy, emotional overripeness of the Super Bowl.[132] How, and in what ways, do social orders license deviancy, and stigmatize its deviants, and for what pragmatic ends? What sort of contract with a reader does Joel Norris make, whose jacket copy for *Serial Killers* reads: "What you are about to read in this extraordinary book will shock, terrify, and sometimes repel and enrage you."[133] Why, then, would anyone *want* to read it? How can readers "enjoy the display of crime, detection, retribution" without at the same time being "drawn into a . . . contemplation of themselves as audience"?[134]

Monsters by definition are to be seen, watched, made much over. They are spectacles of reprisal; the sinuous, unacknowledged pleasure of administering this pain, and watching it, needs to be considered. Making monsters licenses, organizes that hate in a socially approved manner, while stopping short of according it legal sanction. As an interpretive category, the metaphor of monstrosity resembles the psychoanalytic processes of scapegoating and demonization, although the monster hints at an allure and desire for which scapegoating does not completely account.[135] In *Fanaticism: A Historical and Psychoanalytic Study,* scapegoating is defined as the process of affixing "an exclusive fixation of hatred or fear on[to] an object serving as a safety valve and scapegoat."[136] For this reason the monster differs from the scapegoat, because in some fashion or other it must remain emotionally nearby. Unlike the scapegoat, the monster displays as well as despoils. Its visibility is a complex balance of the beautiful and the terrible, by which it recalls the ancient Greek sense of the fabulous creature, carried over into Judeo-Christian iconography as the messenger of the Gods. If the scapegoat carries blame away, the monster wears it as ward. The monster, then, is rather less a scapegoat and more an angel; it anticipates and warns.[137]

Finally, monstrosity is at once a meaning and a failure of meaning, a tale never completely told, one whose meanings are multiple and multiplying. In each appearance, the monster needs to be interpreted uneclipsed—or universalized—by genre.[138] Joseph Grixti explores this process of "genre-fication." In an essay entitled "Consuming Cannibals," he argues that "designating serial killers as monsters can be read as little more than the first step towards making them less threatening by locating them within a multi-layered entertainment industry." This process of symbiotic identification, says Grixti, allows serial killers "to be habitually perceived in the same unthreatening terms as is the case with domesticated mythic monsters like the werewolf or the vampire."[139] To the contrary, it is likely that the extravagant array of meta-human comparisons fixes the deviant or transgressor within a preexisting discourse of social anxiety designed for civic stability. Such a genre-determined loop is socially distabilizing, permitting, even orchestrating, necessary violence in daily social intercourse. Its ritual cadences say: Be afraid, be very afraid. Your life—and our lives together—depend upon it.

David Scruton writes that fear "is a social act which occurs within a cultural matrix. 'To fear' and 'to be afraid' are social events which have social consequences."[140] Fear is a public emotion to be expended in the service of "the norm." It is never to be wasted. Thus, in the naive realism of the daily news, the appeal to monstrosity is not an argument about what has, or has not, been done. The "facts," however they are certified, are not really the point. Rather, those who confect these monsters—Ressler, Norris, Davis, Schwartz, et al.—do so in order to insure that public distress is both continuous and properly interpreted. A rubric provides instructions, not in reading, necessarily, but in staging. Monstrosity is civic triage, panic first-aid, responding however ineffectually to the crisis provoked by the failure of a system of human categories. Monstrosity makes sense of everyday and ordinary social failure by reading it through the exemplary lens of one noteworthy failure. The discourse is, then, homeopathic. Persons nominated as monster embody, in sometimes startling ways, the conflicts they are said to represent—whether the trauma of racial collapse, religious fanaticism, or sexual or other social ambiguity. Dahmer, who was just like us in so many ways, lived out perhaps too intensely, we fear, our identity as Consumer. The showy, hermaphroditic grammar of the monster offers up a body for social sacrifice. This indirection, this switching of the allegorical for the real body, "serves to protect the entire community from its own violence" by forbidding violence on the one hand yet, on the other, by justifying it under conditions that approach the formality of a ritual event.[141]

The doubleness of monstrous rubrics is the point, after all, of ritualizing fear in a moral panic. Many different social emotions may be elicited in the cadences of panic, although by that same token responsibility need be taken for none. The effort to locate and to fix, and to insure the appropriately human, is a more important conflict than wars for land or political gain. Fear is a personal moment as well as guarantor of a wider social cohesion, understanding, of what a society accepts as true, normal, right. However unwilling an agent, the monster exists to "reaffirm the virtues of the norm"[142]—one reason why the link between the entertainment mode and the policing mode, as in the Cunanan case, goes unquestioned. Expressed as narrative, the prejudice coded into these displays of fear "breeds fear and anger, shuts down the power to make humane distinctions, eclipses thought."[143]

In *Pictures at an Execution,* Wendy Lesser writes, "Part of the point of these [biographies and studies] about real-life killers like Bundy or Gary Gilmore is that their reputation precedes them."[144] I would put the matter slightly differently. *Genre and its requirements* shape the reputation that precedes the killers in question. This is why the accused Jeffrey Dahmer is *already* a monster, long before he appears in court; why, too, Rule's Jerry Brudos will, in the vernacular of the street, *always* be a monster.[145] Ted

Bundy understood the complex role he was called to play in the civic repertoire and he exploited it to the fullest. He was both criminal and attorney, monster and defense, cagily playing all parts and doing all voices. He parodied his own monstrosity while profiting from the terror and covert desires he provoked.[146] Bundy knew that by virtue of his complicity in a social drama that extended beyond him, whatever he might want or need as a human being were "considerations which foaming-at-the-mouth, blood-thirsty, escape-prone monsters don't receive."[147] On ABC's *Day One,* Dahmer confessed that he "made [his] fantasy life more powerful than [his] real one."[148] Mike Wallace closes the program "America's Serial Killer Epidemic" by what we can understand as the usual token closure in these affairs—the expected solicitation of yet more fear: "Serial crime experts admit that what is so disturbing is that the very nature of our society— open, free, mobile—makes it almost inevitable that we will forever be reading about yet another serial killer on the loose in our midst." Maybe Dahmer is not alone in pursuing the desires of his fantasy life. Maybe we are, too, attending so carefully to the monstrous bodies of those whom we think get away with murder.

It had almost become a ritual by now, the warnings on the eleven o'clock news, the ominous headlines on page one of the local papers: "Madman Still at Loose."

Robert D. Keppel, with William J. Birnes, *Signature Killers*, xix

What follows is a case study about odd, disturbing, and violent sexual fantasies, but just whose fantasies were they?

Laura Kipnis, *Bound and Gagged: Pornography and the Politics of Fantasy in America*, 4

Cunanan's life has been a psychodrama played for maximum applause—or horror.

Evan Thomas, "Facing Death," *Newsweek* (28 July 1997): 25

Like an unkillable film freak in a grade-B horror flick, Andrew Cunanan's back and ready for another close up.

David Blake, "Dead Man Walking," *Advocate* (13 April 1999): 77

CHAPTER THREE

REDRESSING ANDREW:
CUNANAN'S KILLING QUEERNESS

Introduction

In *Killers Among Us,* Colin and Damon Wilson write that since the fifties "the 'crazy gunman' syndrome [has] become almost as familiar as the closely related problems of the political terrorist and the serial killer."[1] Their pairing is especially revealing considering the current Gothic paradigm of fear in which the reporting around Andrew Cunanan, for instance, becomes not only possible, but *believable* as well.[2] Cunanan, a 27-year-old San Diego man, is alleged to have killed five persons, including, it is thought, Gianni Versace, the fashion designer. For a period of three months he remained at large, the object of massive media hysteria. On July 24, 1997, trapped by police in a houseboat not far from where Versace was killed, Cunanan took his own life by putting a gun in his mouth and pulling the trigger. Formulas of deviancy *as* criminal violence, long circulating in the social preconscious, were subsequently used to confirm the elliptic reportage of Cunanan as "unquestionably" true despite the factual thinness of the narrative—which, in the words of one observer, had little more than a "fanciful relationship to reality."[3]

The media coverage of Andrew Cunanan reprises many motifs of fear adrift in American popular culture for at least half a century, specifically fears of gender failure, invasion, and at-large terrorism. In addition, however, the Cunanan coverage was intended to be something much more mundane—an erotic display of sex in public which usefully instructed viewers in their civic roles. In short, it fulfilled the rubric of scandal. Furthermore, the combination of threat, warning, and spectacle framed Cunanan as a monster, making violent reprisal inevitable. Thus, tracking Andrew Cunanan's tangled passage through contemporary media entails scrutinizing the politics through which he was awarded celebrity. That is, from the inception in the early to mid-eighties of the serial killer "crisis," a lexicon of cultural monstrosity—characterized by "inauthenticity, dissimulation, and disguise"—was already in place by which to frame any threat to the discourse of intimacy.[4] A cult of domesticity equated national security and personal purity with domestic orderliness and sexual virtue; its hermeneutic of the anti-erotic marked as deviant, first and foremost the homosexual, and then by extrapolation, those who were perceived as threats to domestic intimacy. In the codes of the times, "domesticity" was metaphorically applied to a range of scenes, public as well as private, and usually yoked to some issue or other of security or policed boundaries.

The crisis triggered by the serial killer, then, can be seen as less about killing than about the perceived disarray of cultural intimacies themselves. Certainly the narratives of famous killers from Bundy to Dahmer have rich subtexts. In the same way, the overheated paranoia provoked by Andrew Cunanan originates not in the streets of San Diego, but in the homes of middle America, which admits itself to be as much threatened by the fragmentation of gender codes as by killers. The threat, however, is not new. The category of a "male in gender distress," as Carol J. Clover terms it,[5] has had a long and venerable history of representation in premillennial America. Indeed, since the 1950s, gender violation or failure has been an implied component of national security discourses, civic polemic, as well as a common feature of commercial horror film.[6] Indeed, the success of one film in particular—Hitchcock's *Psycho* (1960; along with William Castle's derivative, transvestite-themed *Homicidal,* 1961)—so firmly cemented the popular link between homicide and gender-deviancy that forty years and thousands of cinematic knockoffs later, gender dysfunction can be naively read as a prognostic sign of the serial killer (violent offenders more generally are also interpreted in this manner).[7] There was no shortage of these links in the reporting about Andrew Cunanan, in which odd references to sex or gender were made often without apparent justification: Cunanan was dressed like a woman; he was seen in a peach dress, shopping for cereal; he shaved his body hair like a woman; he was found with the gun by his groin; he shopped and spent extravagantly and was loose sexually. The cumulative effect of these details was to underscore that this killer was not, conventionally speaking, a "man." Given the representational codes of the last thirty years, this was an unexceptional conclusion, even if it was never remarked as such in any report about Cunanan. Standard-issue

American Gothic and criminal narrative since the fifties has equated a failed performance of gender—more accurately, the failure of manhood—with criminality, while further defining effeminacy as lack and deficiency. NBC news anchor Tom Brokaw thus collapses years of representational viciousness when he calls Andrew Cunanan a "homicidal homosexual."[8]

I. Manliness and Civic Virtue

The notion of a killer propelled by psychosexual fury, more particularly
a male in gender distress, has proved a durable one, and the progeny of
Norman Bates stalk the genre up to the present day.

Carol J. Clover, *Men, Women, and Chain Saws*

Numerous critics note the centrality of gender, in subtle as well as obvious ways, to American notions of public and private, national and domestic. In the social regrouping following World War II, the consumer fantasy of the American Dream compensated for the awareness that internationally, the U.S. was no longer insulated from its enemies nor safe from them.[9] Domesticity became the all-important symbol of American health and unity. Indeed, in the years following the demobilization after the war, discourses of the domestic and the national blended, with the result that any visible failure of expected gender was thought to reflect other failures, as well. Such failures were more "social" in nature and less "private" in consequence.[10] For instance, a telling example of the conflation is the case of an LBJ aide arrested for homosexual solicitation; his police record listed the charge as "disorderly conduct (pervert)."[11] Stephen Cohan argues that a "normative masculinity functioned . . . to mask the social differences that stratified U.S. society during the Fifties."[12] As William Strauss and Neil Howe write in *Generations,* "Valuing outer life over inner, G.I.'s came of age preferring crisp sex-role definitions. . . . G.I.'s matured into a father-worshiping and heavily male-fixated generation. As rising adults, they came to disdain womanish influences on public life."[13] And as Robert J. Corber notes in *Homosexuality in Cold War America,* "Homosexuality was understood as a form of psychopathology that undermined the nation's defenses against Communist infiltration." At issue, he says, was the fact that "gay men were virtually indistinguishable from straight men."[14] The ability of homosexuals to pass "produce[d] an extraordinary degree of interpretive anxiety for heterosexuals—and especially for heterosexual men."[15]

Such fears could be exported from political to social use, and vice-versa, as civic need arose. Political paranoia, transposed, gave birth to the

Homintern; like the Comintern or hidden communist, the "passing," hidden homosexual subverted American politics and its morals from within.[16] Accordingly, in 1950 *Coronet* magazine could describe homosexuality as "that new menace."[17] In the "gender-rigid landscape of the fifties," the masculine served as the presumed baseline in private as well as in public.[18] This masculinity functioned as a principal metaphor of political consensus, which later found humorous expression as a kind of rough-hewn, man-about-the-frontier John Wayne-ism. As the unexceptional ground of social comparison, then, masculinity was invisible and unmarked except where its violation or potential failure drew attention. Simon Watkins sums up the political effects. In such an atmosphere homosexuality could only be "an intrusion, . . . an infernal and bestial domain which is virtually non-human."[19]

The homosexual's private failure of gender was never really private, however, since the publication and broadcast of that failure had demonstrable public benefits. That is, pragmatic moral effect as well as erotic economic use could be made of it. Like murder—increasingly its analogue in the public press—queerness was seen, invariably, to out itself. Press of the period were shy about—even in some cases legally restrained from—making overt references to homosexuality. As a consequence any suggestion of it had to be made indirectly. This was often done by portraying it as a grotesque hybrid of customary gender roles: the feminine male. Edward Alwood, for instance, cites a 1953 *Miami Herald* article in which the police chief complains about a strip of beach where men congregate "who try hard to look and act like women."[20] Such presentations of homosexuality were the norm in the strident gender cheerleading after World War II, when national energies were marshaled in the service of regularizing social scenes and national economies. Getting men back into public jobs was a major reason why women had to be gotten back into the homes, and extolling traditional gender roles was thought to be the way to accomplish this. These roles had been thrown into disarray by the war, of course, but they had also been significantly disrupted by the Kinsey reports on male and female sexuality (men, 1948; women, 1953). Peter Michelson writes that what Kinsey's reports announced were received like "an unanticipated bombshell."[21] In the 1948 study, for example, Kinsey's researchers concluded that the practice of masculinity was merely that—a practice, habit. Masculinity differed in differing situations across regions, class, and race. Particularly vexing to many was the implied critique of "masculine" power contained in the report.[22] Kinsey's reading of personal gender failure quickly became civic allegory. One commentator, writing in the journal

Marriage and Family Living, argued—apropos of Kinsey's conclusions of widespread homosexual activity among American men—that homosexuality was an "index of the burdens of masculinity" and in fact a "flight from masculinity." [23]

Before the dismantling of the stereotypic image in the early 1970s, being homosexual was thus indistinguishable from a model of public criminality, particularly evidenced in promiscuity and violence. Child psychologist Fredric Wertham, speaking before a 1954 Senate subcommittee on juvenile delinquency, makes a telling comparison: "Nobody would believe that you teach a boy homosexuality without introducing him to it. The same thing with crime." [24] Fourteen years later, the same association is still thought appropriate. In *Growing Up Straight: What Every Thoughtful Parent Should Know about Homosexuality,* Barbara and Peter Wyden directly align the two as they admonish parents: "No parent sets out deliberately to produce a delinquent—or a homosexual. Yet it is recognized today that delinquency and homosexuality are both rooted in the home." [25] As the Wydens indicate, the connection between the failure of masculinity (in particular) and criminal behavior was an accepted refrain in the jeremiad of national deficiency. [26] Criminality and gender violation—especially in the perverse femininity of masculine failure—was a pervasive, not to say persuasive anxiety of American life in the latter half of the century. [27]

Despite the liberalizing of some social attitudes, homosexuality in the United States still functions as an "index of the burdens of masculinity." As Jesse Green writes, homosexuality is "America's favorite goblin. . . . [T]he subject has become so much a part of popular discourse that it is available to anyone, however cynical or unscrupulous, to define and use as he wishes." [28] As a consequence, the interpolation of the serial killer into this "flight from masculinity" is politically astute. Like the homosexual, and often in the same terms and for many of the same political reasons, the killer is construed as a larger-than-life force, one who threatens not only private domesticity, but the entire fabric of national civility as well. Public manhood is put at risk by men who do not know how to be men.

This failure and risk was remarked upon early and often. In 1973, Harvard Medical School expert and psychiatrist Shervert Frazier argued in *Time* magazine that in sixty-five murderers analyzed by him a "common" trait was they did not "know how to be men." [29] If the normal practice of masculinity is violence, sometimes manifested sexually, then "violent" homosexuals are paradoxically very manly. Still, while homosexuals "know" how to be men in some fashion (i.e. the violence associated with its "condition"), in other ways they do not. [30] The division—and disconnect—between erotic attraction and violent action is, by now, an expected feature of the slasher cycle of horror films and a commonplace statement made whenever a killer is brought to light.[31] Consider a handful of disparate cases. In *Milwaukee Murders,* Don Davis remarks that Jeffrey Dahmer "never had a decent relationship with a woman."[32] Similarly, Brian Masters cites Dahmer's homosexuality as "compensation for the impossibility of having a relationship with a woman."[33] In *Whoever Fights Monsters,* Robert Ressler writes that David Berkowitz, "Son of Sam," "admitted that his real reason for shooting women was out of resentment toward his own mother, and because of his inability to establish good relationships with women."[34] Ressler clarifies Berkowitz a few pages later to mean that "his envy of normal people involved in normal heterosexual relationships" prompted his killings.[35] Timothy McVeigh, most recently, was described as an "evil bomber," but one who was so socially incompetent that "in his mid-20s, [he] did not even know how to kiss a girl."[36] These are more than journalistically unearned remarks about a killer's "personal" life. The comments are hardly asides. To the contrary, they are directly related to the current politicized discourse of nightmare in which the serial killer is an ideological agent who usefully helps sharpen what such terms as "personal," and indeed, even "intimacy," are construed to mean. By exhibiting a *demonstrable* social failure, these persons are understood to oppose the public manhood of heteronormativity. Their criminality follows, silently, from this premise, and the inept sociality of Cunanan, Dahmer, or McVeigh, among many others, is exploited to confirm that meaning. As a marker of social deviancy, then, gender distress has proven itself a remarkably effective rhetorical tool, capable of expansion and modification whenever political need arises or entertainment permits.[37]

II. Killers and Queens

Now that gayness is public domain, the delicate fairy has largely been eclipsed by the predatory queer.

Jesse Green, "Gays and Monsters," *New York Times Magazine*
(13 June 1999): 14

Since the early eighties the visibility of failed gender into which homosexuals are figured has been reattached to new threats: the aggressive sexuality, showy deficiency, and social perversity of the fifties "queen" lurking in the shadows would be split—reproduced on the one hand in the sexual aggression of the pedophile, and on the other, in the darkly perverse desires of ministers and priests. At about the same time both threats to normal sexuality were grafted onto the "boilerplate" mythology of serial murder—an extension, we note, of Hitchcock's initial lead. A famous example of this is the film *The Silence of the Lambs,* in which homosexuality, gender inadequacy, and repeat killings are inextricably linked. One might argue that these scripts of criminality are "only fantasies"; nonetheless, interlocking images of failed men, criminal intention, and psychological weakness cast their confirmatory spells in news accounts, police gazette, cinema, and the like. Writing some years before Cunanan was making headlines, Philip Jenkins observes that "even when it is not directly stated that the offenders are actively homosexual, the implication is still that homosexuality is part of a spectrum of deviant behaviors that culminate in violence and multiple murder."[38] Jesse Green likewise concurs that as late as 1998 a "jury of ordinary Americans would still see homosexuality as vile, and see violence as normal in a homosexual act."[39]

In the ongoing devolution of entertainment into policing, and vice-versa, killers (whether guilty or merely accused) assumed roles in a drama that is part Gothic fantasy and part pragmatic politics. In either case the drama would be cast in a traditional rhetoric of erotic fear, through which the omnipresent anxiety of gender defection, troped as invasion and threat, saw service.[40] No surprise, then, in the chilly political climate of the Reagan years and beyond, as Jenkins writes, the "gay-killer connection is so frequent . . . as to be overwhelming."[41] Diana Fuss writes that the serendipitous linkage of Jeffrey Dahmer's trial and Jonathan Demme's 1991 film *The Silence of the Lambs,* noted above, reflects "how the advent of a new public fear of cannibal murder and the intensification of an old and especially virulent form of homosexual panic can converge in a potent, explosive, and dangerous way to brand homosexuality itself as 'serial killing.'"[42]

Serial killers are now commonplaces in a Gothicized production of fear. Industries have developed around them in cinema, pulp fiction, TV exploitation documentary, and from popular culture sources like games, lyrics, and comic books.[43] The marks of stitching that join the factual to the representational and the suppositional are less and less evident. Further, the collapse of formulas of queens and killers, and the elision of distressed gender and criminality, go unnoticed, so common are they. A cover subtitle to a headline in *Vanity Fair* about Andrew Cunanan, for example— "On the Trail of the Gay Serial Killer"—suggests a seemingly self-evident category, but one which is in fact neither self-evident nor very old.[44] Indeed, the self-evidence of such a category has been carefully nurtured to answer questions indigenous to the political practicalities and civic folk-wisdom of this culture. *Vanity Fair*'s cover, then, is remarkable for the history of (non)representation it *presumes*. In other words, there is no contrasting category precisely *as* category. One hardly ever hears reference to the "straight serial killer" (although numerically these far exceed the other).[45] More to the point, even killers who are "straight" (that is, heterosexual) are nonetheless characterized in terms generally accorded homosexuals. In the impoverished banalities of formulaic crime as well as formulaic gender, straight killers (and these, often, are married) are marked as failed men—as effeminate, perverse in private, scandalous when public.[46] The refiguring of straight erotic killers (killers thought to be motivated by lust, as in the older usage, lust-murderers) as effeminate is a point that makes the evolution of the serial killer panic a provocative study of American political culture. It indicates that previously unquestioned scripts of civic normalcy—domesticity, for one, and its buttress, masculinity, for another—become sources of anxiety as these are prised farther and farther apart in political practice. That is, the ideologically sanctioned "natural" links between heterosexual desire, marriage, and a domestic violence-free zone are evidently not so natural any longer.[47]

Many texts could be cited to demonstrate the overlap between gender anxiety and criminality during the period under discussion. Gerold Frank's *The Boston Strangler* (1966) and Truman Capote's *In Cold Blood* (1965), however, particularly deserve attention.[48] Frank's text is noteworthy because its stated documentary purpose masks other forces at work, notably the collapse of genre, news, and formula entertainment that will dominate the media in the eighties. Frank and Capote are writing at the moment when paranoia about the socially queer man or woman was most widespread.[49] Given the ethos of the time, the hint of gender deficiency circulating around the killers in Capote's *In Cold Blood* can be dismissed as the conventional wisdom of the time—not an unimportant consideration itself.[50] What is important to note about *The Boston Strangler,* however, is the author's assumption, in the absence of a definite suspect, that the killer skulking around the streets of Boston is a homosexual. As in Capote, although without his suspects, Frank's unknown killer is aligned with a public representation of the homosexual. Both are invisible, secret; indeed, the criminality of each is offered as explanation—perhaps justification—of their secretiveness. One of the killings, Frank explains, shows "earmarks of a classical homosexual stabbing" (208). Furthermore, Frank's vocabulary is directly prejudicial, at least according to current standards. The homosexual is a "pervert" (108) and a "sexual deviate" (172, 207).

Yet, however hidden they seem to be, homosexuals are, to the contrary, quite evident. Frank notes that Mellon "had an almost unerring eye in picking out homosexuals" (207). However, this should not be too difficult, since, as Mellon observes and as social iconographies of the time demanded, the homosexual was thought to be perfectly obvious, limp-wristed and ladylike, pomaded and adorned. They are "obviously homosexuals by their manner" (207). That manner is aligned with the performance of femininity and spelled out a few lines earlier: "this powdered, elaborate man" (207), in his "inch-and-a-half crepe rubber soles . . . ," the hair "carefully pomaded, the face shaved to the quick, the clothes a little too sharp." Here, as Inspector Mellon identifies him, is "the King of the Fags" (207)—a parody of the feminine available as street display.

Similar formulas control the narrative of Andrew Cunanan, to which I now turn. Without changing more than a phrase or two, Frank's fantasy homosexual killer could be Andrew Cunanan. Without too much change, many of the terms, images, and anxieties circulating around the unknown Boston killer marked Cunanan, whose criminal sexuality, salaciously reported, often eclipsed the murders he was thought to commit. Cunanan's short public life dramatizes what Andrew Ross terms "the political nature of the *popularity* of *sexually explicit representations*." [51] However, ideological necessity and erotic show did not always cohere in the Cunanan coverage and it is interesting to consider where the two discourses parted, and to evaluate the crisis of representation that resulted from the divergence of the twain. [52]

III. The Horror Narrative of Andrew Cunanan

> Now the panic has eased. Cunanan is a name that echoes only in night-mares, like Bundy, like Dahmer, another lesson in how a monster can put on a pretty face.
>
> Howard Chua-Eoan, "Dead Men Tell No Tales,"
> *Time* (4 August 1997): 32

From the earliest reports Cunanan was described as "a mystery," and a threatening one: "He could be anywhere," was a constant refrain. [53] His death, as discussed on National Public Radio, "leaves questions unanswered." [54] "We had to start from scratch to figure out who Cunanan was," said Bill Sorukas, deputy U.S. marshal. [55] Part of that "figuring" out was, in fact, a figuring *in*—piecing the monster together in the manner of Victor Frankenstein, scouring "charnel houses" of old gossip and secondhand tales of customary civic bogeymen. In terms of media interest, however,

Andrew Cunanan was much more interesting as a *homosexual* than as a killer, serial or otherwise, since his killings left too many questions of fact and motivation unanswered. For one thing, as even FBI commentary noted, he escaped categories—spree, mass, serial—as easily as he escaped detection. Second, at least initially, Cunanan contradicted the accepted and gendered formula of public killing; this occurred when it was made clear that Cunanan was a threat not only to "other" homosexuals with whom he might have been intimate, but to straight men as well. The former could be written off as blameworthy, at least by extension, while straight men—like masculinity itself, always at risk—seemed somehow even more victimized by the whole affair.

These factors explain the rapidity with which Cunanan underwent a media makeover. Figured as a monster of sexual depravity rather than as a killer, all matters of his motivation and intention had already been answered long ago—decades, even, before Cunanan was born.[56] Indeed, as we have seen, the contestation of gender since the onset of the Cold War had worked to insure that the answer to people like Cunanan was precisely predetermined, stable, and socially available as a cultural norm. That is, homosexuality signified a range of unacceptable secrecies and criminality; these were private lives *not* "Growing Up Straight"—lives in public that were out of disciplinary control. What remained to be done was the public work of confirming this answer, obsessively repeating it, serially enacting it in media, political speech, and other compulsory civic platforms. For this reason Cunanan was transformed from a bumbling, unemployed, socially inept young man without a penny of his own into an icon of fast, libidinous living—his public celebrity made possible by the complex visual demands of scandal. In Diane Sawyer's words on ABC's *PrimeTime,* the threatening killer became a "family star." He was to be civil admonishment and public lesson in fear, and this meant he was to be erotic show, as well.[57]

Cunanan lacked even the rudiments of a criminal past. He had no previous convictions and thus had never been fingerprinted.[58] Nonetheless, a past was quickly cobbled together of the representational flotsam of decades of American gender anxiety. Cunanan embodied the crazed and thoroughly undomestic homosexual whose fatal body usefully buttresses American notions of the public, and intimate, self—even as the passing of time dramatizes the inadequacy of these formulas to any actual life, male or female. Cunanan, it was reported, hid in cheap hotels, pawned coins in order to live; he surfaced only to kill, or to buy sexually suggestive materials, after which he disappeared again. In this way his accounts dramatized the contradictory demands made upon the homosexual body: that it be rootless, mobile, and dangerous; that it be promiscuous, diseased, and everywhere at the edge of visibility. Finally, and paradoxically, that homosexual body had to be revealed as weak, effeminate, unmanned.

The display of Cunanan's sexual "mystery" (read "perversity") thus enabled media to give only perfunctory coverage to the murders he was alleged to have committed; indeed, to this day only circumstantial evidence connects Cunanan to the murders of five men. The fact of his suicide further insured that Cunanan's guilt or innocence would never be adjudicated in a court of law. But no matter, since the real engine driving the exhausting and contradictory coverage was not Cunanan's guilt—not homicidal guilt, anyway. Murder merely announced the deeper crisis that was teased out of the rather more exciting sexual life Cunanan was seen to live. Cunanan orchestrated a drama of sexual outlawry in which he was the lone sex criminal crossing class boundaries with eros and abandon. This was the sexualized fantasy offered the common reader, a tale established by careful cultural solicitation over the years, one which could be collapsed into scenes of murder in order to give them "motive." For the narrative of homicide to be awarded its full benefit, that is, a homosexual was needed to star as instigator of public mayhem, if one was to be had or could be invented (as did Frank's *Boston Strangler*). The role, however, is a costly one; Cunanan's fate in representation was not far removed from his fate as a homosexual in the political order itself. In *Sexual Dissidence,* Jonathan Dollimore writes that "we should never forget the cost: death, mutilation, and incarceration have been, and remain, the fate of those who are deemed to have perverted nature." [59]

To read the coverage generated by Cunanan's passage from San Diego to South Beach is to see how readily incidental the actual man became to these twin social burdens of criminality and eroticism—the modern equivalent, one is led to suggest, of state-offered bread and circuses. Cunanan's presumed criminality very quickly became scandalized denunciation, an operatic mode of civil address in which transgression is offered as moralized display. In accordance with this mode, the straightforward demand for "news" of Andrew Cunanan's exciting sexual life was glossed over, obscured, by a breathless rhetoric of moral reprisal. That is, Cunanan's public body had to be sexually exciting, but symbolically affrighting and politically useful as well. Finally, from the point of view of the reader or viewer, the means by which these ends were secured had to be indirect. As a result the sex, while in the front of the narrative, functioned rather as backdrop. In what Michelson calls the "econo-erotic code" [60] of the national imaginary, sex could be acknowledged in public so long as good, moral reason existed for doing so. Thus, so long as it was occasioned by bullets, accompanied by erotic terror and deploring expressions of shock and surprise, Cunanan's sex life was thought to provide moral example to readers.

Over the three-month period of Cunanan's public career, three broadly distinguishable themes could be detected, although in practice these often overlapped: the killer; the homicidal homosexual; the chameleon gigolo who changed faces and identities at will; in *Time*'s hyperventilating rhetoric, the "fugitive of a thousand faces—seen everywhere and nowhere." [61] An early headline, for example, is typical of the initial reports. It reads simply "Murder Charges Filed in Minnesota Killings" [62] This statement, approximately ten days after Jeffrey Trail was found beaten to death (on April 29), is reasonably circumspect. Within three days, however, a second theme will appear, and provoking a rhetoric of a different kind: "Fugitive 'Gay' Killer Strikes in New Jersey." [63] A *Newsday* headline another three days later reads "Dangerous Hunt: Wide-Ranging Serial-Killer Suspect Sought" [64] (5/11/97, A19). This early, and inaccurate, use of the term "serial killer" will remain unchallenged throughout. The New Jersey killing referred to coincided with new information about Cunanan's San Diego existence, and thereafter it becomes evident that neither facts nor circumspection are being sought. Through the rubric of scandal, detection gives way to exposé, and the criminal body becomes, rather, a pornographic body, one watched and moralized for public delectation. A headline late in the narrative cycle (in fact, days after Cunanan's death) reprises all three elements of scandal, detection, and exposé, while showing the jocular, splatter-text narration so characteristic of the case: "Tagged for Murder: The Strange Life and Gaudy Times of Andrew Cunanan and How He Came to Be the Most Wanted Man in America." [65]

"With Cunanan dead, police turned to filling in the many gaps in his story." [66] It might be more accurate to say that the man's life was retrieved in death, recreated, however, in terms of the fantasy desires long projected onto the homosexual body. While the Cunanan story failed as criminal narrative, it succeeded as Gothic. Critics regularly draw attention to the generic requirement of Gothic—that, as Punter remarks, it "has to do with terror," and that its "central dialectic is a continuous oscillation between reassurance and threat." [67] In the Cunanan coverage, two separate motives, threat and desire, merged with two methods—spectacle and exposé. The resulting narrative, in which Cunanan was construed as Public Threat, distracted from the unanswerability of some questions by posing spurious other ones. Elizabeth Napier argues that Gothic semiotics intend a "standardized, absolutely formulaic system . . . in which a reader's sensibility toward fear and horror is exercised in predictable ways."[68] The "predictable" quality in the Cunanan reports was that speculative horror replaced fact unannounced. The constant appeal to "facts"—even when these directly contradicted each other—signaled the instability of the factual, or at least, pointed to its provisional nature. Gary Indiana notes that interviews with Cunanan's acquaintances and friends were "stunningly impoverished, imprecise, almost amnesiac in [their] generality." He concludes that "the most sensational of these tabloidal revelations were freely invented."[69] In terms of their place in a Gothic scene, of course, facts were never the point; to the contrary, the elicitation of a monster, his repudiation and exorcism—all public moments—were.

Judith Halberstam observes that if "the Gothic novel produces an easy answer to the question of what threatens national security and prosperity . . . , the Gothic monster represents many answers to the question of who must be removed from the community at large."[70] True to the Gothic formulas called in to undergird a superficially newsy realism, Cunanan is fleshed out in Gothic drag; the lack of concrete evidence placing him in any locale for long led, inevitably it seemed, back to the Gothic. A phrase occurs early in the cycle that will occur frequently. Cunanan has a "thousand faces."[71] Another journal refers to "the other scary hit of the summer [1997] . . . The Many Faces of Andrew Cunanan."[72] He "tried on identities as easily as other people change hairstyles."[73] He is a "chameleon who invents his history by absorbing facts from the lives of people he's met."[74] "Nobody really knows the truth" about him, Cunanan was reported to have said.[75] Surely, the media reports were no help. Reading through the coverage, it is not so much Cunanan who invented lives as the various lives that were invented for him, sometimes literally over his dead body. *Time* magazine traffics in the hype as much as it creates it, reporting that "with his death the portraits of Cunanan only seem to multiply."[76] Despite all the hyperbole, however, in fact there were only variations of one portrait, numbingly repeated: the erotic homosexual terrorist—a favorite bogeyman since Gerold Frank first hypothesized that the unknown killer ravaging Boston streets was "evidently" homosexual.

For an example of the endless-loop quality of even the early reporting, on May 9 the *Atlanta Journal-Constitution* briefly references Cunanan as "a known quantity in San Diego's gay community, a 'party boy' who tapped a seemingly endless cash flow that he spent on lavish meals and extravagant gifts."[77] Already, hardly a week into the "crisis," phrases are in use whose cadences will thereafter merely be repeated. A few days later, for example, another newspaper in a different city states that Cunanan had "an unending supply of cash that he used to pick up tabs for dinner parties several times a week."[78] The seeming density of these pseudo-facts disguises an overall resolute indifference to facts, while signaling the dissonant combination of interest and repudiation intended by the narrative line. A week later, a *Los Angeles Times* headline repeats an earlier description verbatim. Cunanan is "a man known in San Diego's gay community as a charming 'party boy.'" "Party boy" is already in quotes, because already borrowed, as indeed the entire headline should be in quotations.[79] The "known quantity" is what plays, and the text of the story, likewise, freely avails itself of the already known. In a similar manner Cunanan's own very real body was tacitly given over to public prurience, whose examination of its oddities and desires proceeded apace with a steadfast disavowal of interest in such topics. Indiana comments that "with little or no regard for accuracy, Cunanan's life was transformed from the somewhat poignant and depressing but fairly ordinary thing it was into a narrative overripe with tabloid evil: ugly sex, drug dealing, prostitution."[80]

Even as genre formula, however, the narrative is clumsily and ineptly stitched together, generated from homogenizing news sources like Reuters, AP, and UPI. Tales of sex, riches and lascivious living, for example, are jumbled together; these often contradict each other and as often are at odds with Cunanan's actual hand-to-mouth existence as recounted by those who lived and worked with him in San Diego. As stated, Cunanan's criminality is rarely perceived to be as interesting as Cunanan's sexual deviancy. Even after Cunanan's alleged killing of Gianni Versace increased the fury of the criminal manhunt, the *Atlanta Journal-Constitution,* among others, is still more interested in Cunanan's "other life." The journal describes him "jetting off to other cities"; he is "often seen in the arms of older men."[81] Indeed, Versace's killing greatly expanded the readerly leer into homosexual decadence, since now there were two "known" homosexuals available for tongue-clucking speculation.

IV. Cunanan as Civic Pedagogy

Mark Edmundson argues that Cunanan's appeal was "partly" because he was gay. To the contrary, despite the seeming liberality of American society, the very *thought* of gay sex occurring precisely *in* public produces high anxiety, even, in a phrase, heterosexual panic. To borrow Eve Kosofsky Sedgwick's phrase from another context, "the surplus charge . . . of . . . heightened sexiness around this topic comes from its unspecified proximity to an exciting and furiously stigmatized sexual field."[82] To put it perhaps not charitably, just as scenes of "lesbian" sex are a required performance in much "straight" porn (and thus at least commercially necessary to the pornographic fantasies of many heterosexual men), so gay sex is a welcome fantasy/nightmare in heteronormative America.[83] One can watch the lesbian in the porn film, or read about Cunanan in the newspaper; either way the performance of deviancy confirms the privilege of the nondeviant, who can be involved without fear of consequent shame or arrest.

It was this Gothic rent in the civic fabric that the display and consumption of Cunanan's moralized body helped to create as well as suture together again. Andrew Cunanan's deviancy was literally "made up" so that the Body Politic might likewise reinforce its mind about the important issues being contested by that ambiguously racialized, dramatically sexualized body to which so many persons lay claim. The moralized deviancy of Andrew Cunanan was used to clarify issues of gender, intimacy and domesticity, but also, jealousies over race, class privilege, access to sex, finances and drugs as well. Despite this, however, the Cunanan narrative was thought to originate as a purely (and safely) private matter. Nonetheless, narrative pressure and media economic sponsorship quickly transformed that "gay lovers' quarrel" into a national threat.[84] A May 13 USA Today story (one of the earliest major spreads on the case) leads with: "A Spree Killer Is on the Loose in the USA" (3A); even at that early date Cunanan's potential as national crisis has been underscored.[85] Cunanan's actions were dramatized as a threat to domestic space, as he went from home to home leaving death in his wake. Nonetheless, for reasons suggested earlier, the domestic was subsumed into the national. The burden of much of the news coverage of Andrew Cunanan is invasive criminality, writ large as threat to the national scene. The announcement of his death was pointedly directed at an audience whose point of association was common nationality: "Tonight, all across the nation, our citizens can stand down and breathe a sigh of relief. The reign of terror brought upon us by Andrew Cunanan is over"—this from Richard Barreto, chief of the Miami Beach police.[86] Yet was "the reign of terror" "over"? And was it "brought upon us" by Cunanan, as Barreto ponderously intoned? The endlessly running, looped rubric of scandal suggests otherwise (as does the made-for-TV movie announced by Cunanan's father shortly after the son's death).[87] The normal politics of dread weren't over, nor could they be. Cunanan's death merely insured that the drama of finding perfect enemies would continue by any means possible, fueled by empty speculation, and the suggestion of sex—a combination which need be not so much true as titillating.

The *USA Today* account of May 13—"Murder Suspect Eluding Manhunt"—is worth considering at some length because of Gannett's determinedly "general" audience for its publications and its overt ideological nationalism. This report is one of the earliest to present the outlines of the full formulaic narrative of the homosexual, emphasizing the overt threat of perverse sex as well as demonstrating its covert appeal. The tone of the report is breathlessly voyeuristic, pawing over Cunanan's life while quickly establishing boundaries between him and the reader; the implicit premise of the report is that Cunanan is a threat because the boundaries are unstable, provisional, always verging on collapse. In order to distinguish the monster from "us," the front-page story references "gay" and/or coded terms signifying queer perversity. References to lavish spending, former lovers, suggestions of erotic torture overload the opening short paragraphs. Where "gay" itself is not used, Cunanan is marked as deviant in other ways. Andrew is a "flamboyant character," he "liked to club-hop." Sexual extremity is aligned with class privilege. Cunanan "usually picked up the tab, tipped generously and gave expensive gifts"; he "was secretive but hinted that his family was wealthy." Finally, the tugs of desire throughout these paragraphs merge into, and finally terminate in, salacious fear: Friends are "running scared"; "One former lover, a wealthy businessman who provided him money and a home . . . , departed for New York."[88]

The fear of what Cunanan represents thus never quite separates from a desire for the monster that remains textually unspeakable, except as it can be deflected into a remark about "friends"—who, the reader is to understand, is like "them" in wishing to keep a distance between themselves and Cunanan. Desire, however, is only one aspect of the Cunanan narrative that is occluded. Aspects of Cunanan's life that resist formula narrative likewise assume the character of duplicity and hiddenness. Lack of information about wealth, perhaps, or how Cunanan lived, that "puzzled" friends or that didn't "add up"[89] become "secrets" that don't "add up" for the reader's designs upon Andrew, as well. Questions remaining unanswered become, somehow, evidence of Cunanan's devious intelligence at work, thwarting the reader's unquestioned "right to know."[90] This involves the reader in a pattern of what Noel Carrol calls "the drama of iterated disclosure"[91] that helps increase the drama's intensity. In other words, regular and persistent inquiry, even prying, into material never legitimately anyone's "business" disguises the banality of the information sought. From the point of view of the reader, this is potentially the most troubling aspect of the Cunanan case—the subtle alignment of the public with "the normal" and the private with the suspect and criminal. The reader is directly targeted in a work of ideology. Musing about terror and crimes safe in his or her home, the reader faces subtle but direct consequences. *Any* private life is potentially criminal, alive with the prospect of scandal.[92]

Whether Cunanan's life was considered as a private affair or a public threat, secrets were the public coin of the Cunanan reportage. Paid out in the erotic economies of spectacle and speculation, this insured a covering and uncovering of sexualized bodies, with the attendant economic and moral payoff usual in such matters. The *USA Today* account offers, and exploits as secrets, three relatively banal aspects of the Cunanan story—his relation to the military, his presumed HIV status, and the rich life he supposedly led. The first two of these were, at least initially, side narratives. In time, however, they will centrally underpin the overall civic meaning of the Cunanan narrative. Cunanan's relationship to the military was, from various viewpoints (his own, the military's itself, and readership), largely one of fantasy. This network of fantasy included, by symbolic extension, two others—the relationship of homosexuals to the military as well as the reader's largely fanciful relations with both groups, homosexuals *and* military. Initial accounts in the saga do not reference the military angle, although two weeks into the coverage the *USA Today* report (May 13), refers to the military experience of Cunanan's first murder victim, referring to Trail as a "former Navy lieutenant." This incidental point of connection quickly becomes a central preoccupation. *Newsday,* the next day, amplifies, calling Jeffrey Trail a "gay graduate of the US Naval Academy," featuring the reference prominently in the early portion of the essay.[93] Once the military connection is raised it rapidly becomes a central component of the story: Cunanan, son of a military man, consorting with military (perhaps, later reports imply, even *kept* by them); and, apparently by his hand, a military officer is dead.

One might argue that Cunanan's coverage becomes most transparently ideological at this point. While references to the military are made casually, there is obvious energy around the issue, reflecting investments in consolidating a readership who can agree with certain politically sensitive, contested issues. In the first place, the fantasized discipline and gender purity of the military is posed against the promiscuity and gender diffuseness of the failed man, the homosexual. From a different perspective, however, the association of homosexuality and the military suggests the odd perceptions about the military held by a "commonsense" public (aside from the unrecognized masculinization of both categories) that in some ways homosexuals and soldiers *are* alike. They resemble each other by virtue of what they are not—that is, their lives differ markedly from middle-class suburban domestic virtue. One marker of that social difference—transience and mobility, for example—no matter how it might be justified or tolerated, still prompts a need to negate its public effects. Further, gays and military alike are positioned as being mysterious, adventurous, exotic, exciting, and powerful. The *Los Angeles Times* distinguishes itself in this respect with its gossipy asides to a *Dynasty*-like military shadow life: "Cunanan and Trail had met in San Diego when the latter was stationed at the amphibious-warfare base in Coronado. Cunanan, the son of a retired Navy officer, liked to frequent gay bars where military officers congregate, and he sometimes introduced himself as Cmdr. Andy Cummings."[94] Earlier, that same report picks up details referenced in a previous *USA Today* version and elaborates upon them, focusing especially upon titles and awards. Jeffrey Trail, first identified as a "Naval Academy graduate," is now further distinguished as a "Persian Gulf War veteran."[95] The notion of well-decorated military queers certainly gives a new twist to an old gay stereotype. A manhood once reserved to straight men—uniformed, butch, and heroic—is now doubly used, first to describe the queer and then to indict him as well.

To be fair, however, the whiff of erotic energy circulating around Cunanan and the military had, often, less to do with him and more to do with the salacious pleasure presumably attendant on his status as a "kept boy" for closet military. Thus, it is quite conceivable that Bill Clinton and his "homosexual agenda" politics are broadly entangled with Cunanan. That is, indirectly at least Cunanan (and the military persons he dated) served to exemplify the public depravity decried by conservative elements about gays in the military. This energy draws on some peculiar metonymy between Clinton, the military, and sex—a gendered public discourse that accompanied much of Clinton's political career as president. The combination reaches soap-operatic proportions in *Time* magazine's report of August 4, shortly after Cunanan's death.[96] The account in question retreads material from an earlier *Los Angeles Times* report in which Cunanan is seen dancing "bare-chested at hard-rock bars preferred by young professionals and off-duty military personnel."[97] In similar fashion *Time* makes steamy, raised-eyebrow references to "closeted military men at San Diego's naval base." The essay singles out for attention an author "who writes books about the gay subculture in the military." In the first place this statement is remarkable for the presumption it makes about an extant gay life in the military—especially in light of "don't ask, don't tell" policies around the subject. *Time* paraphrases the author's complaint that "he and Cunanan, the son of a Navy man, were rivals for the attention of Marines and sailors in San Diego." These latter, *Time* helpfully clarifies, include "Jeffrey Trail, the former naval officer who would become the first of Cunanan's five victims." [98] The author's pique raises an interesting point; in context, does it (and the essay more generally) want to suggest that Trail chose the wrong man (Cunanan), when he could have had one who knew, as the formula goes, "how to treat him right"? That readers find themselves privy to dating tips and extended descriptions of gay military culture underscores my earlier point that Cunanan was much more interesting as an uppity homosexual than as a killer. Desire, however covert, destabilizes the more direct movement toward horror. Further, and gendered romance formulas aside, what, one wonders, is this military fantasy about? Apparently straight readers love undressing men in uniform as much as the stereotypic homosexual—equally a production of fantasy. *Time*'s odd reference to a queer-tainted military—doing "alpha male" behavior by "displaying their genitals" [99]—is almost as resonant an image as the other that came to predominate in the Cunanan reports. Entwined and sometimes crossing the military narrative was another—the vengeful homosexual whose life of public havoc begins (naturally) with the failure of personal intimacies.

The closeted gay soldier is as provoking an image as that of the AIDS-sick homosexual, whose casual street partying is thought to be a kind of sexual serial revenge. Nevertheless, while there was reason to associate Cunanan with military men, it must be said that no evidence existed at any time to justify the linking of Cunanan with HIV+. (In fact this claim was repudiated within a few days of Cunanan's death.) But AIDS is a formula of reprisal, not medical fact, as Douglas Crimp reminds us; as such it has no existence outside of its phobic representations. [100] That fact, however, did not interfere with the spectacle of speculation that proceeded on the assumption that Cunanan had "AIDS." A July 17 headline in the *New York Post,* happily disconnected from fact, screams "AIDS Fuels His Frenzy." *Maclean's,* likewise confident in its ignorance, baldly puts it this way: "Inevitably, given his sexual orientation, some suggested that Cunanan might have discovered he had contracted AIDS." [101] The combination of the conditional past perfect and the indefinite subject indicates the thinness of the factual ice here, although that is of little import. Few readers will attend

closely enough to remember the convoluted disavowal of authorial responsibility. Given Cunanan's stigmatization as a public homosexual, as well as
the narrative requirements dictating the dispersal of fear, it is undoubtedly
more accurate to say that the *New York Post,* and its English-language
equivalents internationally, would make such a link very early.

On May 13, 1997, *USA Today*—the early page-three spread mentioned above—laid out what would be the final form of the Cunanan
narrative, and it includes already the AIDS justification. That is, the homicidal homosexual narrative spun out around the invisible threat of Andrew
Cunanan receives its justification as "public news" precisely because of this
potential medical threat. This, again, reflects an established genre of medical crisis that developed around "AIDS" and into which he was uncom-
fortably wedged. On May 14 *Newsday* cites the chief of the Minneapolis
police homicide unit: "The strongest theory is that he's HIV positive, or
thinks he is, and is out to settle a score with past lovers." The officer then
adds, "But that's just a theory." [102] Two of the four men killed to that
point—Miglin in Chicago and the cemetery caretaker in Pennsylvania—
were neither gay nor, for that reason one guesses (in the assumption of
heterosexual America, at least), HIV+. If this is the strongest theory police
can come up with, perhaps they should stop theorizing. But the police here
are not so much theorizing as fictionalizing, and the formulas they weave
together include the newer model of medical threat, but supporting this is
a different, and older formula—a fiction as old as the "mingling of sex and
violence" that a murder researcher in the mid-seventies found to be "characteristic" of killers. [103]

The AIDS narrative prompted the most visibly Gothic effects of the
Cunanan cycle. It combined the hint of sexual secret, contagion, revenge
and aggression—a combination of elements borrowed it seemed straight
from Randy Shilts's *And the Band Played On.* [104] Shilts establishes a fantasy
of origins by which "Patient Zero"—Gaetan Dugas, the airline steward
who is blamed as the source of the virus—sleeps his way across the nation,
infecting his partners with death. Cunanan's perceived medical threat is
thus used to underscore and confirm the other threats he was thought to
pose. Again, "friends" were called in to help guide the reader in her or his
response. The observation was made repeatedly that acquaintances of
Cunanan's were "running scared." [105] Tony Perry's May 16 report for the
Los Angeles Times parodies the language of hurricane reporting: "Gay communities in New York and San Francisco are afraid that Cunanan is headed
their way"; a former roommate "has gone into hiding," and prominent

men "are said to be worried." [106] The implication here is that Cunanan is seeking revenge upon someone who had infected him with HIV. Behind this implication lies still another one—the assumed fact of homosexual promiscuity. This makes for a certain instability in the way "friend" operates in the narrative. On the one hand the "friend" is a stand-in for the reader, but in another way such "acquaintances" are definitely *not* the reader. That is, in the context of the AIDS narrative, "acquaintance" or "friend" means sex partner. Anxieties of contagion, and the presumption that intimacy equals revenge, gained currency in the Cunanan coverage—even rapidly begin to drive the narrative, despite the evident facts.[107] One source, typical of this form of heterosexual panic, claimed that Cunanan was "aiming his vengeance at the gay community."[108] The *Daily Telegraph* puts the prejudicial spin on it as baldly as *Maclean's,* and adds further manic punch: Cunanan "was killing fellow homosexuals in a black rage and murdering others so that he could swap cars." [109]

In summary, from about May 15—a mere three weeks into the Cunanan drama—the public fantasy of his homosexual deviancy is in place. Until the Versace murder, this narrative all but occludes the murders he is thought to commit. *Newsweek's* first major story on May 19 sells the news this way, couching it as shock and scandal—necessary, in fact, since the main crime drama is yet to come: "An openly gay teenager, [Cunanan] would whistle at the boys on the water-polo team, and he once came to a school dance in a tight red jumpsuit with an older man as his date." [110] Subsequent reports will rarely add anything new, merely elaborating upon already printed versions. Conventional elements of the cherished homosexual narrative are so useful because its shocking sexuality contrasts the domestic virtue of middle-class America. The Virtuous Public finds readerly coherence in these reports by a conviction of apocalyptic degeneracy that might have come out of a Patrick Buchanan stump speech, frightening mothers and causing dogs to bark: the unmarried and the unable-to-be-married are seen, in quite public ways, partaking in erotic pleasures once reserved only to the married (and, in theory, still so reserved).

A report from the *Los Angeles Times* near the end of the Cunanan cycle dutifully records the deviancy that its wide-eyed readership has come to expect. Note is taken of Cunanan's stay at a South Beach hotel. This account is the only one to note, with barely concealed leer, that it is a hotel that "caters to a gay clientele and where clothing is optional." His room in the hotel is searched, notes the essay, and is found "still brimming with fashion magazines (some with ads for Versace clothing) and sexually explicit material."[111] Gratuitous sexualized nudges—like the aside to "optional" clothing—are frequent. In addition, Cunanan's perverse threat is ratcheted upward by a tie-in to the Dahmer story (pointedly to the fantasy of cannibalism associated with that case).[112] The report explains—apparently unaware of how silly it sounds—that a "search" is being made for dental charts in Cunanan's apartment. And though no dental plates turn up (we keep them at home?), the report breathlessly details finding "something more ominous": "two videos . . . showing homosexual bondage and sadomasochism." And then, of course, one is given the equivalent of the text accompanying the "eight pages" of grainy photos in True Crime pulp; reading instructions are given on how to understand these arcane practices: "'It looked like a training film for the Miglin incident,' said one law enforcement official [referring to the third man whose death was attributed to Cunanan]."[113] In sum, fueled by eroticized lack and conventional class envy, the narrative lurches from Gothic motif to motif: frightened gays in San Diego, sadomasochism, and, forebodingly, fashion magazines in Cunanan's room "with some ads for Versace clothing"; even early on the alignment of class and deviancy were in place, establishing parallel systems of reprisal.

Conclusion

> Andrew, come out, the whole world is watching!
>> "Bullhorns at Cunanan's last stand"; reported in Chua-Eoan,
>>> "Dead Men Tell No Tales, *Time*

The Cunanan drama indulged, developed, and circulated a variety of fears, some material in nature, others less tangible but nonetheless powerful. Countless daily papers, journals, and magazines might be cited to support these points. The *USA Today, Los Angeles Times* and *Time* magazine reportage examined here are merely indicative of the whole. Their formulaic content owes its consistency to the Reuters, AP or UPI news services, each separate links in the ideological chain. Nor can it be said that gay-identified reportage—the *Advocate,* for example—always avoided representational pitfalls. Often they did not, to some extent participating in the abuse implicitly aimed at them. But Cunanan had been lost to his own coverage before this. Another way of thinking about these issues is that Cunanan, slipped loose from his life and fixed within the ideological gravity of public *narrative,* could only function as a serial killer in the codes already established in the national imaginary—that is, as the contradictory amalgam of the fast-living, killing homosexual that had been narrative boilerplate through the years.[114]

On occasion, however, a headline or report would daringly contradict the narrative flow, and suggest, as the *Los Angeles Times* did, that that "Cunanan Doesn't Fit Serial Killer Mold."[115] Those who were interested in the details of the case understood that Cunanan "defied the easy categorizations"—by which is meant legal definitions—used by criminal investigators to "describe multiple-murder suspects as either serial or spree."[116] Nonetheless, Cunanan evidently did not escape the other too-easy categorizations of commodity sex culture. He does not, in other words, escape the speculative traffic in body parts that is the conventional—and customarily pornographic—homosexual narrative. Homi Bhabha notes that stereotype "is a form of knowledge and identification that vacillates between what is always 'in place,' already known, and something that must be anxiously repeated."[117] Formula narratives of the "news," similarly, work because they are *not* news; we have already heard them before. In the precise sense of the metaphor, they bank upon our presumed assent. These are stories "we" know. They are, in short, prejudice, as indeed scandal is a rubric organized to insure the smooth flow of prejudicial narrative. Formula emotions depend upon formula conventions, and thus a Gothic methodology of monstrosity, already in civic play, becomes useful.

Benedict Anderson argues that "print capitalism"—the novel and newspaper—make possible the anonymity that is the foundation of "the modern community."[118] In the Cunanan coverage what was being "invented" was the noncriminal—the sentimentally egalitarian, middle-class body against which Cunanan's civic excesses were demonstrated, a prurient gaze made possible by subterranean currents of envy as well as bitter disappointment. Throughout, fashion and sexual deviancy, consistently paralleled, establish a baseline of sexual normalcy, one linked directly to class, and sometimes to gender. The reports broadly remark Cunanan's fashion-aping as signifying his membership in a class of persons whose *wealth* marks them, like Cunanan, as *also* sexually troubling to civic mores. The difference of these two groups—sexual deviants and the ostentatiously wealthy—from *the general public* is marked in many of these accounts by the ability they share to shock the common reader with sexual and economic license. Versace's death, sadly but serendipitously, *confirmed* the association, raising the Cunanan reports to a morality play of sorts, criminality exposed, even venerated, for its teaching moment.

A petty dig at Cunanan in *Newsweek,* written before the announcement of his death but dated the week following, compresses the fantasy
link between Versace and Cunanan into a bond that must, certainly, include the reader as well: "Cunanan . . . liked to wear Versace label under-
wear, was a wanna-be in a wondrous kingdom of make-believe."[119] The
threat of a killer on the loose, then, is confirmed by a different threat entirely, that of a profligate and well-traveled member of the upper-class,
whose mobility, like the killer's, is also the stuff of myth. Both of these
deviancies are read onto the body of the homosexual, to facilitate, in
Edelman's words, "internalization of the repressive supervisory mechanisms of the State."[120] Readers can be interested in deviancy thus authorized precisely because they can be so moral about refusing to acknowledge that interest. Sex and money—however alluring might be tales of
their use and dispersal—are still to be repudiated by those whose access to
either is limited by law and economic ability.

One also senses an additional urgency in these texts. Behind the ex-
postulating and stuttering, metaphor-drunk exclamatory sentences, with
their desperate reliance upon cliché and banality, lies a deeper issue, and a
deeper fear. Indeed, this fear might be the source of the energy behind
detailing scandals like Cunanan in the first place. That is, the anxiety about
locating Cunanan was, equally, about marking the line where the profligacy
of the homosexual and the profligacy of the texts announcing his visibility
explicitly merge in a culture where sex is defined increasingly as a public,
textual and possibly criminal, act. This, of course, will drive the Clinton
sequel to Cunanan, where sex is clearly employed as commodity, pushing
the *vérité* drive to documentation to its limit in a "found" pornography.
Reading the Cunanan accounts one finally begins to understand the paranoia that fuels the arguments behind censorship and the moral lock-up
they espouse.

The fear, I think, concerns the potential criminality of the private,
undisciplined life, especially in the representational methods commonly
used to set such a life *loose* in public, there to work its titillating, although
always destabilizing havoc. In this manner, however, *any* public text is
liable to be (indeed, is intended to be?) pornographic, unable to keep
its privates—intentions as well as meanings—to itself.[121] In this respect,
conservative definitions of pornography are not nearly broad enough
to cover their subject—nor, however, are they intended to. Quite to
the contrary. "Homicidal texts"[122] are like homosexuals, everywhere.
Both are potentially lethal since no text (or homosexual, apparently) is to

be trusted to keep its seductive influence to itself. This anxiety is reflected in the reports considered here, which appear of two minds—whether to incarcerate Cunanan or star him in an X-rated video (numerous references were made to the possibility). These texts, in other words, are visibly anxious about their own complicity in what they denounce as immoral acts—making the homosexual visible, and speaking the unspeakable for pay.[123] The pornographic motivation driving the economy of popular culture, then, must always be shielded from its direct involvement with that *other* pornography which conservative, liberals, and feminists alike agree to bash.

The narrative inconsistency and factual incoherence of the various reports only slightly disguises the virulent aggression circulating throughout them—a virulence accounted for by the anxiety just discussed. One report suggests that the police will "take him out";[124] another waits for Cunanan to be "run to ground."[125] Such aggression has its fictional consequences. Cunanan was personally, socially, and economically inept in so many ways; this much, at least, many reports obliquely acknowledge. Yet he is morphed by the constraints of formula necessity and readerly expectation (and thus economic need) into a Gay Hulk in order to support the testosterone-pumped gendered narrative that required a suitable enemy—however contradictory (nay, monstrous) that enemy might be. For example, one publication writes in unwieldy prose that "FBI agents carrying machine-guns, helicopters, boats, dogs and a Swat team in black armour [sic] bearing shields surrounded the boat."[126] In order to make Cunanan *equal* to the armament massed against him, the formula effeminacy of the homosexual must be reworked. Gone is the fey Andrew at his high school dance in red jump suit, forgotten are his always obscure dalliances with older men. He becomes, instead, another creature entirely, the Gothic monster besieging not individuals so much as the city and the country.[127]

The need to make Cunanan a terrifying force was justified, simply, by the need for the story's ending—civic reprisal. However, this was accompanied by an additional need to humiliate and demean him. In particular, toward the end of the cycle, hysteria of this sort explodes textual coherency. Numerous accounts make note of the possibility that Cunanan's gender-deficiency may include "masquerading as a woman" to escape detection. However, only *Time* quotes the puzzling remark of a spokesman for the Miami police, "He may have shaved all of his body hair to enhance this appearance."[128] The low-lying erotic edge of *this* image is unmistakable, and suggests a complicity at some level in the very dark sexual practices horrifyingly indulged by Cunanan. The inevitability of the formula conclusion to the portrait might be underscored by turning again to Carol J. Clover, who observes that in the genre of the slasher film the "killer's phallic purpose . . . is unmistakable," although "his masculinity is severely qualified: he ranges from the virginal or sexually inert to the transvestite or transsexual."[129] Horror films follow civic practice. Often enough,they replay in cinema scenes of everyday life, partly to address, partly to confirm. Cunanan's life, as dramatized in public, was a continuation of the gender parody enforced by forty years of political contestation. In the formulaic contest, the gender-failed man demanded an answering parody, and so, poised against Cunanan we find massed the war-porn imagery of a "Men in Black" fantasy (swat teams, FBI helicopters, gas, dogs; martial imagery of shooting and chasing that circulated at the scene of Cunanan's siege). Less directly we find the genocidal terror and its compensatory obsession with location and control. The narrative is obsessively gendered, clearly to the edge of panic, and clearly intended nationally.

Finally, one last remark about the duplicity of the current pornography debate in this country, mentioned briefly above. The argument as it is cast is willfully deceptive. While certain classically defined pornographies ("displays of genital action") might be limited, a glance at any conventional talk show, or reading the Cunanan reports, demonstrates that pornographies of all sorts are welcome everywhere money is to be made. For arguably, by fixating upon self-evidently "commercial porn," the anti-porn lobby has deflected attention away from a pervasive cultural commercialization of the flesh whose sexual explicitness is, without question, one reason for that culture's continued success. For this reason, the narrative aggression throughout these texts can also be explained as the text taking aim at itself for the possibilities it generates. Because even those who deploy scandal for social purposes realize that scandal's pedagogical effect is partly derived by its traffic in the taboo. The effects stirred by scandal, while including titillation and excitement, also include guilt and shame, always useful for making subjects by reminding them of their abjected, subjected place: "Abject terror . . . is gendered feminine, and the more concerned a given film [is] with that condition—and it is the essence of modern horror—the more likely the femaleness of the victim."[130] And this is the point of Cunanan narratives: scandal's other face is fear; any one of us might be next: "he might even be stalking you"—sums up the thrust of the story for one reviewer.[131] Yes, any one of us might be *next* from a different per-spective, as well: each of us might be a Cunanan-in-training, each of us regendered in abjection, by narrative and civic duty alike. And so the stri-dent tones of revenge against the monster warn us away from testing boundaries we might otherwise think to try.

Should Nature change, and Mothers Monsters prove . . .

Isaac Watts, *Hymns and Spiritual Songs* (1809)

But we confronted . . . an even harder lesson about how much evil can lurk in even a mother's heart.

Jerry Adler, "Innocents Lost,"
Newsweek (14 November 1994): 28

It's the saddest story I've seen in my 60 years. God bless those sweet, sweet souls.

Kathy Lee Gifford[1]

Dave is a monster. . . . It's very simple.
You touch a child, you should die.

"Readers Reply to Child Molester,"
St. Louis Dispatch, 31 October 1995

CHAPTER FOUR

SUSAN SMITH:
WHEN ANGELS FALL

Introduction

The attorney prosecuting Susan Smith had devised a jury-simple strategy. Smith, who killed her two children, was a monster, a small-town Medea who could not be allowed to live. Tommy Pope was wise to shape the narrative in this fashion. Thus framed, the story was old news of a sort, with a conclusion already predetermined.[2] The ending to which the narrative moved, if left unchecked, would take a considered toll on the defendant—even if that toll was not legally sanctioned.[3] This serves to remind us that "the monster" is never just an isolated individual, although certainly the rhetoric suggests, and intends, such an effect. To the contrary, the person singled out as monstrous is, already, a collusion, a prejudice, a ritual and community effort. Monsters are nominated by popular, not singular, acclaim. They only play to crowds.

Like so many contemporary scenes of the American monstrous, Smith's is a morality tale of horrific intimacy, the banal romance of top 40 love turned inside out. Her tale, however, was not just one of horror, since alongside the Smith narrative ran another plot-line that accentuated and made sense out of Smith's civic affronts. That is, in order to make visible the monster who would terrorize the domestic space, the private Utopia of home and hearth needed first to be established as under potential threat. Smith's monstrosity, reprised and repudiated for months, is thus deeply inscribed in a narrative of tender familial devotion it seems to oppose. Further, Smith's tale is not a new one, nor particularly American, since the opposition of sentimentality and horror is far older than Smith. Infanticide itself has a long history. The abandonment or killing of children, while now shocking, has not always been so. Even language itself—for example, the word "foundling"—draws attention to this fact.[4] Smith's crime, does, however, have an indigenous American context, with specific American antecedents and consequences. Puritan preaching, for example, singled out infanticide as an inerrant sign of communal failure.

Smith's action—killing her two children—was likewise held up as demonstrating some larger civic failure. As Matthew Ruben observes, much of the commentary produced around Susan Smith was devoted to "explain[ing] Smith's insane or inexplicable deviation from the 'universal' maternal role."[5] Why was this "deviation" so profoundly unsettling? Kenneth Anderson (writing in 1997) observes that during the previous two decades "childhood has been raised . . . to transcendental status, especially in the United States."[6] In the popular idioms of American self-address, the cultic presentation of motherhood at times impresses itself into another discourse entirely, that of the national.[7] Yet for this transition to have its full effect, the horror fantasy of threat must be countered by an answering fantasy of the natural and good. These rhetorics intersect with, rather than oppose, each other. Just before his execution in Florida, Ted Bundy spoke to James Dobson, of the conservative *Focus on the Family,* slyly making the point from a reverse direction: "Those of us who have been so much influenced by violence in the media—in particular pornographic violence— aren't some kind of inherent monsters. We are your sons, and we are your husbands. We grew up in regular families."[8]

Bundy's point, if I may theorize it for him, is that the monstrous invariably lurks on and around the edges of the domestic. The monster is said (implicitly, sometimes explicitly) to impinge upon, to taint and touch the innocent and pure. Such Gothic patterns thrive in the sentimentality of late twentieth-century American politics. In a discussion of Gothic motifs in art, Christoph Grunenberg addresses anxieties that since the fifties have been American obsessions: "Over the last decades, the last refuge of the middle class [the home] has become the preferred site for encounters with strangers, serial killers, and the supernatural."[9] For all the shock it produces, then, the monstrous will always retain traces of the "familiar" from which, extrapolated, will emerge the political "equivalencies" of "family and normal, pervert and criminal, sexual deviance and disease."[10]

The Smith narrative compactly articulated multiple narrative lines that coalesce in a particular genre often called domestic Gothic. Anne Williams suggests that the peculiar tension of family Gothic is that it is a narrative "built over a cultural fault line—the point of conjunction between the discourses of alliance and sexuality."[11] That is, sex, at home in the family, is considered a private matter, unimportant beyond the confines *of* the family. However, when sex becomes visible *within* the familial discourse, its figurations are almost always problematic, taking the form of child abuse, incest, domestic violence, or the eroticized child. Three recent cases—Susan Smith, O. J. Simpson, and JonBenet Ramsey, for instance— exploit the political possibilities of this hydra-headed Gothic frame. It can be argued that the Smith narrative in particular was so successful *as* a media event because displaced private intimacies took all these proscribed public forms. The stodgy *New York Times* seemed painfully undone as it disclosed the "backdrops" to the instance of child-murder—aspects of life that rarely make it to its august pages: "molestation, incest, jealousy, class distinction, sex and more sex."[12] Nina Auerbach observes that "women are culturally constructed as vehicles of intimacy . . . and thus . . . are freer than men to act out embarrassments like desire or death."[13] Smith's textual body was the narrative line upon which a multiplicity of civic intentions and meanings were displayed; desire as well as death drove the public reading.[14]

I. Home Alone

In July 1995, 23-year-old Susan Smith was convicted by a South Carolina jury of murdering her two children, Michael, aged 3, and Alex, 14 months. Nine months earlier, at the beginning of the drama, Smith had told police that a black man forced her at gunpoint to relinquish her red Mazda and then drove away with the two children in the back of the car. Smith maintained her story for nine days, even appearing on local and national TV networks pleading for the return of the boys. Finally, on November 3, mere hours after a string of three network talk shows, Smith confessed that she strapped the boys into the car, and then rolled it into a lake near the edge of town. "Unspeakable" was a common adjective used to describe the scene, although there was no shortage of attempts to speak at length about Smith and what her action implied about mothers and national mores in general.[15] From the start, however, it was never exactly clear just what *was* unspeakable since many aspects could have been cited. The "unspeakable savagery" of the killings caused outcry, although part of the public outrage was doubtless guilty anger at being duped by Smith.[16] Smith's initial claim about a black abductor was taken with great seriousness. The *New York Times* called Smith's ploy "the great lie," although Smith's fabrication was in fact common enough in the history of American racial contest.[17] Doubtless Smith used the story in her defense for the same reason that Pope used the monster-narrative in her prosecution. She knew that the horror of the black invading beast would have the immediate ring of truth, precisely because it *was* so obviously a horror formula.

Most public response, however, reflected anguish and shock about the fate of the children. In particular many reacted to the pointedly cruel method of the killing itself. Smith engineered the boys' deaths by strapping them into baby seats, rolling up the windows (thereby insuring a prolonged death), and then permitting the car to roll into a lake. One of the divers who found the car testified that he "saw a little hand pressed against the glass.[18]" The detail is poignant and powerful, and given the social context of the reportage, itself not without premeditation.[19] The representational focus on the child alone is twofold; in the first place it demonstrates the vulnerability of the child, whose safety "home" is sentimentally said to guarantee. Additionally, and deriving from this point, focus upon the child intensified the political gaze upon the scene, showing how the place of safety—home, and thus nation—is under threat. Further, the pictorial isolation of the child likewise isolates the mother within a pre-established narrative of reprisal. Historically, removed from the security of home, the undomesticated woman (without husband and worse, without child) is accorded few representational options. She can only be a witch, a troubler of the scripts of civic normalcy, or "loose"—like her counterpart the homosexual—someone who disrespects civic norms, especially those coded in sexual conduct.[20]

Walter Kendrick observes that popular culture narratives are "designed to make their audiences feel certain clearly defined emotions."[21] Commercial as well as political purpose lost no opportunity to seize upon the stark image of Smith's cast-off children, in order to exploit "clearly defined emotions" for various purposes. The little boy's hand "pressed against the glass" took on added significance, given its closeness to conventional renderings, in a sentimental mode, of the death of children. Children are the *sine qua non* of moral panics, and the dying moments of children are sources of great writerly interest, although rarely do the lachrymose scenes address the underlying causes behind the event. So successful was the dying of Little Nell in Charles Dickens's serialization of *The Old Curiosity Shop* that he extended the process of her dissolution through another issue.[22] Children stand in as symbols for a dense set of social emotions and cultural desiderata. They signify the primary reason for the existence of culture and family. The customary representation, then, of civil danger—a rhetoric often as contradictory as it is inflammatory—requires a child for its dramatic effect. J. Edgar Hoover's paranoia about strangers lurking near schoolyards or Fredric Wertham's insistence about the evil of comic books, or Anita Bryant's "Save Our Children, Inc." campaign (1977) dramatize how such rhetoric works; in broad outline it remains the same even as local detail changes. If women's bodies ground the Gothic, then, children's bodies stabilize the sentimental.[23] Finally, bodies of mothers and children jointly support the favorite American self-narrative, being a haven for domestic virtue.

It was from this submerged conflation of the national and the domestic that a number of commentators tried to parallel O. J. Simpson's trial for murder and the Susan Smith child-murder case. The attempts were unsuccessful, in my opinion; in the first place the reason given for such connections—family and domesticity—merely underscored how different the cases were, and indeed, emphasized how that difference turned upon conventions of gender that function to guarantee domesticity. For example, Murray Kempton's discussion of the Smith case has for its title "A Mother's Shame." To my knowledge a parallel expression ("A Father's Shame") does not exist in the Simpson case.[24] That is, however much Simpson is read *through* Gothic codes of doubleness and dissimulation (hiding "a private face" behind a "public face"), he is never referenced directly as "bad dad," "accused father" or "accused husband"—however much the charges laid against him may have implied all these things.[25] Simpson's role or function as father is never called into question, nor is he referred to as "monster" (except once, and then with ironic intent).[26]

Susan Smith is similarly doubled, although in a different manner than Simpson. Unlike him Smith has no extant public body which can be disassociated under the pressure, unless it is her role as Mother—an already unstable representation, as we shall see. As a result Smith was made to bear the burden of Gothic splitting herself. *Newsweek* says she "has never been what she seemed"; a *New York Times* title focuses on the division between "Susan Smith's Lies and a Smile."[27] If Simpson, then, is separable from his role as "father," Smith on the contrary is submerged into her role of mother. From there she is unequivocally elided into a corrupter of domesticity more generally. Expressions—epithets, really—like "child-killer" and "bad mom" abound.[28] Transcripts of NPR's "All Things Considered," the day before she confessed to the killings, identify Susan Smith as "Accused Mother" (2 November 1994). A book about the Smith killings— published a mere two months following her confession, and even before her trial had been set—is entitled "Sins of the Mother."[29]

It is the violated role, rather than the violator herself, then, that organizes the terms of the panic and gives us a clue to its Gothic, national focus.

The panic is not, after all, about Susan Smith, but rather about an ideal reader who is a composite of civic virtue and who comes to definition by reacting to Susan Smith. Numerous reports vented upon the question "Why does a mother kill her child"?[30] "A shocked S.C. town asks: Why?" intoned the *USA Today*.[31] A woman interviewed on NPR says, "I just can't imagine any mother doing that."[32] In some disheartening way, as the narrative cycle concluded in the July, 1995 trial, it seemed clear that the story line was ideologically directed to make such public statements possible. These preachments were intended less at Smith and more at "Parents Everywhere."[33] One headline asked, or rather declared, "Mothers Wonder: How?"[34] Another report notes that Smith (and Pauline Zile) will suffer "great pain"—not primarily for the deaths of their children, but, in addition, for charges even more daunting than these. The two women are guilty of "betraying motherhood," indeed, but also of betraying the "rest of the country," *and,* finally, for "all the frightened little children who will be lost or kidnapped from now on."[35]

The obvious conclusion to be reached from considering the Smith and Simpson trials separately must be that mommies and daddies serve different narrative functions. Considering them jointly suggests that representations of marriage are meant to stabilize a different allegorical scene altogether. This is a first clue into the gendering differences of the narrative developing around Susan Smith, and it permits a view of the larger crisis of domesticity that is unfolding. Let me consider for a moment that fantasy of national domesticity and the political economics it supports.[36] In the bourgeois view of marriage—i.e. "for love"—threats against domesticity are typically understood to come from outside the union. Thus, any example of violence from *within* is ideologically volatile, since it casts into high relief the seeming inviolability of marriage as a sanctuary of "natural affections."[37] Likewise, if economic systems make the domestic possible, a narrative economy is needed by which to portray and justify that "domesticity."[38] It is within this narrative economy that certain types of violence, operatically displayed, become both permitted and *visible*—no matter how unintelligible they might be within with the sentimental codes of marriage. Thus, while spousal murder (by men, at least) can be accommodated as, in Philip Jenkins's phrase, "routine homicide," child murder (at least by women), although equally common, must nonetheless be shifted into a different register entirely. It invariably provokes a Gothic display of moral declamation, textual sputterings, and exclamatory sighs—all of which, in typical misdirection, pass as implicit ethical statement.

Again, the starkly contrasting responses to Simpson and Smith reflect some of these issues. For example, Judge Lance Ito, who presided over the Simpson trial, remarked, "Loving the children is one thing. Killing the mom is something else." In an editorial whose headline addresses this point ("Why Are We Shocked When Mothers Kill Their Children?"), Wendy Kaminer lays out the implications of Ito's remark: "We expect some men to kill their wives; we're shocked when a mother kills her children. Smith's act was an affront to the natural order; Simpson's alleged crime merely confirmed it." [39] In support of her contention Kaminer cites a woman at a Boston subway stop who reacts with thoughts of violence to Smith ("I'd like to strangle her"), while, on the other hand, noting with sympathy that Simpson "just lost control." One can only conclude that while Judge Ito may be overstating the case, Kaminer isn't. Murder is by definition excluded from the *representational* role of motherhood in a way that it is not from what ought to be a parallel representation of fatherhood.

II. Parents at Risk

The discussion so far has ranged across literary as well as political economies of marriage and family life. It is perhaps not completely possible ever to separate these discourses. Halberstam comments that the "power of literary horror . . . lies in its ability to transform political struggles into psychological conditions and then to blur the distinction between the two." [40] Her remark is apt here. Pope's attempt to isolate Smith as the monster in the case (plenty of other candidates emerged, as we shall see) was socially astute. Pope's action was, additionally, intended to support legal maneuvers, although legal discourse and prosecutorial narrative diverged. Pope's narrative distracts from having to consider the political and economic elements of the dysfunctional social/political fantasy of domestic tranquility touched upon earlier. These include, although are not limited to, the financial and economic inequities built into marriage; the de facto authority of the man to tyrannize at will, often without legal or social reprisal; and finally, the woman who must suffer the constraints not only of economic penury but those of narrative as well. Indeed, the elliptical but speedy condensation made possible by Gothic shorthand—a shorthand intended by Pope—has similar prejudicial equivalents. Notably, it moves legal discourse in a direction it might not go otherwise. Jenkins observes how representational pressure affects legal discourse:

> Partly in response to pressures emanating from the media and the culture
> at large, far more resources are devoted to tracking, identifying, and stop-

ping the tiny number of serial killers than to preventing the great majority of routine homicide cases, in which victim and offender are related by marriage, kinship, or close acquaintance.[41]

Prosecutor Pope offered the jury a short-course in domestic horror by framing Smith as a monster of unnatural affections. Nonetheless, it wasn't easy to stabilize the formulas of horror around Susan Smith. Simply put, as the cycle of reportage moved toward its culmination in the trial, too many monsters appeared bearing too much meaning. The case rapidly threatened to founder upon the shoals of politics as well as Gothics. The gazes of sympathy and horror split apart. In the first place, as previously noted, gender became the politicized focus here as race had been in the Simpson trial; in each instance the metaphor provided the lens through which the cases were primarily viewed. Months before the trial opened, for example, Pope was criticized for actions that underscored how typical the Smith case was of a tradition of legal practice—that is in which mothers were held morally accountable for infanticide while fathers were not, at least not in the same way or to the same degree.[42] Pope had announced that he would seek the death penalty for Smith. Subsequently it emerged that Pope had previously permitted a father who smothered his child to plea-bargain (the man eventually received eight years for manslaughter).[43] Laws aside, a random check anecdotally confirms that fathers who kill their children *are* treated representationally different than mothers. For example, the *Washington Post* places on the last page of its news section a very brief article accompanying the headline "Father Confesses to Killing Baby Son as Revenge on Wife."[44] In exasperation at the alleged differences in the legal treatment (and perhaps representation) of "fathers" and "mothers," one letter to an Atlanta paper writes: "I want all felons hung out to dry, not just mothers. Bring equality to the media coverage of all criminals."[45] The letter's grammatical imbalance—its collapse of the categories of felons and mothers—unwittingly underscores the moral weight attached to the role even in the best of circumstances.

According to sentimental convention the mother is the "angel in the home," as vulnerable as her ward, the innocent and defenseless child. In the Smith narrative motherhood itself seems particularly beleaguered, as the angel, fallen, turns demonic. The potential threat of "failed maternity" of course, does not stop as children grow up. Faulty maternity commonly anchors, sometimes excuses, a variety of criminal behaviors engaged in by children, sometimes long after they are no longer children. Indeed, the "turning" of a child later in life, whether criminally or sexually, is often traced back to the mother.[46] Ann Rule sentimentally asks of her "lust monster"—a married man who kidnaps, tortures, and kills women—"What happens to change a chubby-cheeked, freckled five-year-old into a monster?"[47] All too often, it is the failed mother who *happens*. This is not an exceptional conclusion, given the reigning certainties of gender politics. In sum, whether a child is turned to some nameless evil, fails in the performance of gender, or else is killed in infancy or childhood, such danger increases the representational pressure upon the mother.

Nonetheless, considering its narrative requirements, one is led to ask an obvious question. Even if, as Blanch McCrary Boyd remarks, the "pop situation" of the Smith case required the choice between a monster or a victim, why then was Smith chosen to be the monster when so many other cases presented themselves? As Boyd herself ruefully notes, "Mothers who hurt or kill their children are, unfortunately, not that uncommon."[48] Indeed, in October of 1994, when the Smith case first received nationwide attention, several media cases competed for space. Three days before Smith reported her two boys kidnapped, Pauline Zile told police that her 7-year-old daughter Christina had disappeared while they had been shopping. On October 27—two days *after* Smith went public with her story—Zile and her husband led police to the child's grave. Zile's case merited only a short sidebar in *Newsweek,* an accompaniment to the Smith narrative which assumed larger and more dramatic proportions.

Cases of child-murder make the news frequently, each with its particular element of the lurid or the shocking—recall, for example, the image noted earlier of the small hand pressing against the car window. *Time*'s cover story "Parents Who Kill," two weeks after Smith confessed her carjacking hoax, detailed some nasty examples of parental care.[49] These include the case of Paula Sims, who, in 1986, like Zile, initially claimed her daughters' disappearance and later confessed to their murders.[50] Or consider Claudette Kibble, who confessed to suffocating her baby and drowning two other children years before. Additionally, subsequent to Susan Smith's trial other incidents of child-killing have briefly made the news— again, charged mostly against mothers. None of them, however, made a lasting impression upon the media, nor are any of the culprits now recognized as household names (a possible exception is the JonBenet Ramsey affair). For example, in 1997, Darlie Routier, 27, was found guilty of killing her young sons Damon and Devon. She was sentenced to death by lethal injection.[51] Carla Lockwood was arrested in September 1996, for killing her 4-year-old daughter. Authorities said the child had been confined to a covered crib for a year, and had starved to death.[52]

It is hard to keep the names separate. *Time*'s report summarily notes that children had been smothered, fed pills, even cooked and offered as a revenge meal.[53] A set of Los Angeles parents are charged with "burning, biting and breaking"—and finally killing—their two-year-old daughter.[54] The statistics derived from cases like these are grim enough: "kidnapped children are a hundred times more likely to be taken by friends, loved ones, parents, than by strangers," unequivocally claims *Time*.[55] Children's rights activists claim that "three children in the United States are killed, on an average day, by a parent or guardian."[56] *Time* cites FBI figures for 1992 which state that "662 children under the age of five were murdered." To the point of this discussion, the president of the National Center for Missing and Exploited Children "estimates that about two-thirds of those victims were killed by one or both of their parents."[57] Listing all these incidents in some detail may seem excessive, but doing so throws into relief a number of unasked questions, while demonstrating how purposefully phrases like "baby killer" are used to obscure, even erase, complex economic and social factors behind the incidents themselves. The phrase contains the hard density of a narrative punch that answers, or seems to answer, such questions by attributing unspeakable depravity to the offending individual. What does the formula hide in this instance? What discussion about systems and structural inequities does it foreclose? Why Smith and why not Zile or Routier? The answer, to some extent, lies in the compression to which the Smith case is open. Like all effective civic performance it tells in a ritualized manner a story already familiar, one in which Gothic and sentimental formulas twine together. Susan Smith's narrative permitted the defense of domestic virtue by braiding sentimental elements of compassion and pity together with Gothic elements of appalled horror. It succeeded as a public story because it has those aspects that, as Mary Noel observed, are "unchanging elements of popular culture"—"sweetness and violence."[58]

The Smith narrative also had politics. It is often the case that elections, and those who win them, profit from rhetorically advancing values not economically supported. The association of motherhood and America is almost compulsory in American political mythologies, even if domestic justice and economic parity are not likewise compulsory subjects of discussion. Smith quickly became a late-October drama, a social sing-along and choral presentation accompanying the 1994 off-year American election. Smith's failure as mother was orchestrated at a national pitch, the crime mourned around the country. Her confession "stunned the US"; it "shook the town and the nation"; "the "Murders Still Stun the Nation."[59]

Another report emphasizes the "shock waves that rippled across the US when Susan Smith . . . confessed."[60] Clearly, however, there is more at stake in these expostulations of shock than a mom's private failure, or even the terrible dying of two children, or even the always-anxious concern for socializing adequate parents. There was a feeling not only of personal affront but, more largely, a sense of communal betrayal as well—as one columnist put it, anger arising from "Mrs. Smith's betrayal of the community."[61] *Newsweek* speaks indignantly of Smith's "duping the nation"[62] The scene was directly nationalized, from high to low: "What person watching—and parents from the President on down couldn't turn their eyes away—had not felt the sleep-depriving, soul-splitting pressures of parenting and worried about their own capacity for violence."[63] Indeed, Newt Gingrich profited from astutely reading the situation and choreographing Smith into the political drama and the victory he had hoped to achieve.

III. "Very Mayberry": National Fantasy

Gingrich's civic apocalyptic used Smith as a pedagogical device to decry democratic leadership—a pernicious force responsible, in his opinion, for the weakening of American moral fiber.[64] In Gingrich's view, Susan Smith was monstrous in a most classical sense: she interpreted a failed community for itself. She "vividly reminds every American how sick the society is getting and how much we need to change things." The political agenda intended by Gingrich was readily transparent. Since the Democrats were, in Gingrich's words, "the enemy of normal Americans," change necessitated "vot[ing] Republican."[65] Gingrich's revisionism was hardly exceptional. Nor were the formulas of back-to-the-land moral nostalgia he employed unusual. They were, and remain, the *lingua politica* of a folkish nationalism as old as Crèvecoeur's *Letters from an American Farmer* and as arguably American as Jeffersonian (itself derived from the book of Genesis). "The End of INNOCENCE"—reads the *Atlanta Journal-Constitution* the week Smith went on trial. The report summed up the situation in the town as "Very Mayberry," reaching for representation to fill in the rough edges of truth: "The town of 10,000 is the kind of place where folks get their picture in the newspaper when elected Rotary Club president or after catching a prize catfish—not for killing their kids.[66] As before, to be noted is the resolute gendering of the social scene. While this ordering is out of sight, nonetheless it significantly weights the argument. Men are elected Rotary Club president and catch prize-winning catfish. Women, on the other hand, are accorded publicity for killing their kids. Clearly, the town and implicitly some aspect, real or imagined, of a culture is on trial as well.[67]

The cartoonish terms of the melodrama were highlighted by the serendipitous universality of Smith's name—and that of the town, as well. Union, Smith: the names were ready-made for an American Rousseauian fantasy of the democratic and the egalitarian. And that played well in the urban economies for which such fantasies are produced. The *New York Times* writes patronizingly that the prosecutor, in summing up the case, "relied on the small-town conscience and common sense of the people . . . to see through the defense lawyers' claims."[68] The "good people of Union" become the proxy for the larger national body, the "general public."[69] "Common sense," as used here, cuts two ways. In the first place it suggests regularity, ordinariness—experience so banal as to be completely shareable by all. Conversely, it signals a language so sophisticated (and yet so transparent) that it covers all experiences equally and is adequate to each in particular. In Gingrich's estimation, such "common sense" would also necessitate a one-size-fits-all politics, both banal and extraordinary, in which Susan Smith was the one-size-fits-all monster, a stand-in for an evil government which must be staked at all costs.

Nonetheless, the facts of the case, as they emerged, turned against Gingrich's political design. The GOP's "Contract with America" rapidly seemed to become a "contract *on* the family" as first one gossipy bit of "news" after the next emerged from Union City. Jammed with TV and news cameras, the town hosted a number of national talk shows that week. Many of the "revelations" undercut Gingrich's critique of Democratic morals. The particular irony, not available when Gingrich appropriated the Smith case to his electioneering, was that one of the persons negatively involved in Smith's troubles was her stepfather, Beverly Russell—a Pat Robertson operative and member of the executive committee of the state GOP. Frank Rich writes that Russell had sex with Susan Smith "after he'd returned from plastering the town with 'Pat Robertson for President' posters.'" These trysts continued, Rich writes, "as Mr. Russell became country chairman of the Christian Coalition and country coordinator of the South Carolina Citizens for Life."[70] These facts, like others that emerged, were irrelevant to the legal charges against Smith. Nonetheless, they were distracting to Gingrich's call for a return of Republican morality. As more and more information of this exculpatory sort became public, reasonable people cautiously began suggesting that Smith's crime, while certainly terrible, was well-matched by the mendacity and abuse exercised *upon* Smith by trusted persons near her. Defense and prosecution alike found themselves having to do spin-management. Prosecution tried to keep the criminalized narratives separate and distinct—Smith, the heartless monster on one side, the damage done her by others elsewhere. Defense collapsed the narratives, in traditional liberal fashion reading damage done to Smith as *causing* her to damage others. In the defense's formulation of the issues, both a sentimentalized concern for children, as well as horror at the monster-mother, coalesced in a third—a standard of Harlequin Romance, narrative of the victimized woman.

However it was viewed, the power of the Smith narrative was its ability to permit a lens of moralizing scandal to expand or contract the field of sight. From any direction Smith becomes the center of narrative crisis, while the children, lost in death, are lost again to the demands of representation. One can view Smith as murderer and sole agent ("Baby killer!" as one person screamed at Smith; another person weighed in with "Baby-killing bitch").[71] One can also consider the case more generally as about motherhood failed or betrayed, whether through tragic ineptness or mental incapacity; to do so, however, is to become a readerly victim of the ideology intended by the narrative. Or, alternatively, one can choose to view Smith as victim—first of abandoning fathers, then of seducing men, and finally, ideologically, of a system in which abandonment by men seems written into law. In any of these directions, the system that demands virtue of mothers without giving them the necessary economic means remains hidden out of sight.[72] Carol E. Tracy, executive director of the Philadelphia Mayor's Commission for Women, makes the point that "we live in a society that romanticizes motherhood but provides virtually no structural supports for mothers."[73] Whichever possibility is chosen, Smith's bondage in the representational stocks of scandal permits an open display of the issues that are concealed within, but nonetheless denied by, the formula Gothic emptiness: (1) that American economic reality puts young children at emotional and sometimes physical risk, especially with inadequate resources allotted for single parents; (2) that motherhood, as scripted in the male-centric national imaginary, is an impossible fantasy, and that its practice also diverges wildly from a different fantasy, the wife; (3) that all these options are equally true.

Further, the Smith story garnered media space because its telling relies upon a narrative mythology that preceded it and whose rubrics govern how it can be read. From the earliest examples of the genre, the Gothic finds itself the center of political energy—indeed, often producing it, despite the routine denial that astute policy intervention is possible by clever use of genre. Pope of course attempted something like this when he instructed the jury that one should appropriately "read" Smith's actions as monstrous, inhuman, and beyond moral evaluation. The paradox here is that, as we see, even construed as monstrous, implicitly beyond moral evaluation, Smith's actions are not at the same time considered beyond legal reprisal. Similar rubrics for reading accompanied various media reports, as details of the story were trimmed, edited into appropriate genre form. As the time approached for the opening of the Smith trial, numerous reports worked overtime to properly align readerly investment, inserting the cues "required," as Boyd remarks, by the "pop situation." In some cases readerly management was very direct. One newspaper managed the scene this way: "This was something straight out of Tennessee Williams, very Southern Gothic."[74] *Newsweek* employs the "Southern Gothic" reference a week later, giving it prominence as a headline: "Southern Gothic on Trial." The inflammatory tenor of the title is merely confirmed by an added punch; "Will the Child-Killer be Put to Death?" reads the subtitle.[75] Both phrases guide readers in the choices ideologically pertinent to them and to the case.

As we have seen before, the sideways glance to genre fiction is meant to deny the story's status as representation while at the same time exploiting the familiar but complicated mix of horror, voyeurism, and spectacle customarily associated with the representational needs of the genre. In sum, Gothic references (asides to Faulkner and Tennessee Williams) instruct readers how to "read" the Smith case, while implicitly controlling any "damage" the story might have in terms of the national scene. Aligned with the "Gothic," the public trauma of Susan Smith is effectively emptied of significance, contained within clear ideological parameters by which Gothic fantasy is explicitly cast to the margins of literary or cultural value. Further, the point of view organizing the dismissive gaze is urban and sophisticated—Mayberry need not apply, here; it need only offer itself up for evaluative critique. That is, headlines like "Southern Secrets" reinforce a century of locating "regional" and discredited genre texts in a "remote Southern town." Smith becomes a "symbol of small-town decadence," and Union becomes "Sin City."[76] These directives might not add up to "leading the witness," although clearly the reader is positioned, in advance, to concur with the formula's inevitable denouement. *Time*'s account, written when the Smith case first broke, anticipates the conclusion that the cycle's end will move to confirm: "The town reared up in horror" at Smith's actions, "and everywhere parents suffered."[77]

IV. Reading Writing

Why are such cues for readers necessary? Sentimental narrative demands that a reader vicariously share imagined pain; it invites—compels, often—the reader into a presumptive intimacy with the suffering person on the other side of the text. This mix of distance and closeness is part of the allure of the sensation mode. Sensation genres derive at one remove from the post-Enlightenment shift in representations in which the suffering body was considered to be a pedagogical object—to be viewed, appreciated, sympathized with or appalled by. In short, suffering (someone else's, at least), was to be an occasion for the exercise of, and hopefully increase in, "moral sentiments" on the part of the spectator or reader. Through the eighteenth century the senses were seen to be directly implicated in the production of moral responses; thus readers were thought to read *for* sensation—that is, in order to be thrilled, moved (either to horror or pity), and in other ways to have visible evidence of an internal moral change. The man or woman "of feeling" was one whose "sensibilities" presumed an innate capacity to feel, and in whom the activation of proper "sentiments" would result from the exercise of sensibility.[78] Traditionally, "sensation" genres—varieties of romance, including Gothic, and their sentimental forebears—were critically discounted, since the manner in which they elicited sentiments was thought to be excessive. That is, the obvious array of mechanisms in place for production of emotion precluded such texts from being "artful."

Horror narrative works in a similar fashion, and with similar critical contempt for the obvious way it seeks to elicit "sensations" from readers. However, Gothic variants of horror differ from sentimental romance in that its narrative structure positions the reader less as witness to suffering than as voyeur, keeping her or him at a distance safely away from untoward emotional distress. "Untoward," here, as read through a Newt Gingrich squint, means socially "unusable." That is, it signifies emotional distress that unsettles the civic scene—as sometimes happens in these major public events.[79] Marianne Noble explains that "detachment of the reader from a scene of anguish [is] a diagnostic feature of sentimentality, . . . terror for the Gothic reader, tears for the sentimental reader."[80] Sentimental and Gothic idioms invite readers, in differing ways, to collude in experiences of pain that are, if truth be told, one of the signal pleasures of the excitation common to sensation genres. This fact, however, has consequences that might not at first be expected. Any text can move, ultimately, to the point of the pornographic, offering to indulge emotions that are neither owned by readers nor earned by them. Such emotional colonization is not of course limited to texts, but in fact could be considered one of the primary economies in a commodity culture. Emotional and physical trauma take their place as scenes of representation as well as evidence of "real life." In this manner Gothic and sentimental variations of explicit pain, displayed, can be said to be useful in a political world, as an association is directly made between terror and intimacy. According to Laura Hinton, "A mimetic bondage exists . . . between the sadomasochist and the sentimentalist." [81] Such a bondage exists between the text of suffering and the reader who suffers the text, as well.

Many accounts of Smith show the instability outlined above in process. A leer of voyeurism alternates with sentimentality in the *People* account.[82] Finally, however, the distancing methods of horror win out over compassion. Smith becomes an object of the appalled, rather than the sympathetic, gaze. Throughout the narrative, however, the reader likewise assumes both positions, directly responding to the shifting placement of Smith herself. In this respect *People* merely follows the example of other presses. *Newsweek,* for instance, offers Smith first as the pained heroine, wept over and identified with, and then as the Gothic monster who must be quickly repudiated: "crowds that once agonized for Smith jeered her." [83] But this transformation is not easily managed. For the formulas of reprisal to work, Smith must be undone representationally, and made over as the unnatural mother whose actions reveal her "true," horrific self. During this process, Smith gains a Gothic shadow, and, additionally, Gothic depth. Some days after her confession, the *New York Times* announced that Smith "seemed to be a perfect mother and so hard-working and devout." [84] The *Newsweek* account, however, states the contrary with conviction: Smith "had never been what she seemed. Party to enough infidelities and suicides to make Faulkner . . . proud, she's a Southern Gothic come to life." [85]

Smith's change from the Mother of Sorrows to the Unnatural Mother intends, as noted, a response in the reader, who transfers compassion into the safety of horror. The emotion-tugging tale of violated motherhood quickly collapses, as the fantasy of bad mothering is almost completely effaced by the extensive corruption of the domestic scene itself. This fantasy nightmare, in its turn, is used to support the wider positioning of the South as a *Gothic* place—that is, graveyard site to which are consigned personal haunts, civic unmentionables, and social grotesquery. In many of the reports linguistic collapse enunciates the problem, but whether the language serves as antidote or response is not clear. For example, one newspaper report collapses superlative, negation, and Gothic rubric to dramatize the author's conviction that "the saddest day of all will be when a mother's misdeeds no longer produce shock."[86] In another response only the violence endemic to swearing will suffice. The case of Smith presents, a resident of Union says, "one hell of a problem."[87] And when language fails, a reach for the pre-represented, or the violent, is not far away. A former South Carolina prosecutor observes that "[the case is] going to be a hell of a soap opera."[88] Just what kind of soap opera *Newsweek* is suggesting had been laid out a few days earlier by an Atlanta press: the "testimony is expected to center on molestation, attempted suicide, adultery, and unrequited love in [Smith's] past."[89] Throughout all the narratives, gone, completely, is any sense of legal responsibility to the memory of two children.

But if the memories of Michael and Alex are lost, so, too, is Susan Smith. When *Newsweek* first covered this story on November 14, Smith's "past" was dismissed in one sentence. The "one exceptional incident" that was found worthy of note was the suicide of her father. At cycle's end, however, Smith's past life has magnified in event and drama—"attempted suicide, adultery, and unrequited love"—the vast production of which seems oddly disassociated from the legal case being built around Smith. Through it all, Smith plays the role of monster very well; that is, she enables the "soap-operatic" melodrama to be staged by being its excuse. As she becomes the body sacrificed to the political and representational economies of scandal, she is lost to its rhythms and so nowhere in sight.[90] Her Gothic depth is gained at the expense of her representational individuality. Notably, Smith loses her right to tell the story at all. The *People* essay mentioned earlier demonstrates this. A telling detail is the magazine's decision to make Susan Smith's confession visually center to the layout of the article about her, without ever addressing this text *as* a human statement that might warrant comment. In the early Gothic, villains and evildoers are voluble, generally loquacious about their suffering and the reasons for their depravity. Nonetheless, civic monsters in the neo-Gothic exemplary mode are rarely given power of speech, since voice shatters the effect of distance and alienation the monster is charged with provoking. *People*'s unaddressed photograph of Smith's confession exploits this visual/verbal disconnect. Smith's confession, however, deserves attention, since looking at it changes the narrative focus again, moving away from the condemnatory direction *People* wished to go—reason enough why *People* chose to downplay it: "I didn't want to live anymore! . . . I felt I couldn't be a good mom anymore but I didn't want my children to grow up without a mom. . . . I felt I had to end our lives to protect us all from any grief or harm."[91] However, it must be said that the confession itself suffers from representational overload; Smith did not end "our" lives, only theirs.

Smith is characterized as *evil,* first, because she is a *failed* mother, and failure of our individual social selves is, perhaps, the great fear circulating through commodity culture—the sometimes unseemly haste with which we subject ourselves to commercial prosthesis, shopping to fulfill imagined or real lacks, indicates its extent. The crosshatched and contradictory narratives of representational motherhood, when set beside the financial imperatives and the political consequences that trouble actual mothering, make it almost inevitable that *individual* mothers will—indeed, must— fail. No individual life is equal to the burden of the civic narrative, although each life is asked to carry such responsibility. Smith's mother remarked, "Some people don't want to think Susan is a good person who loved her children. . . . So they have to make her a mean, terrible somebody. If not, they think, 'Whatever happened to her could happen to me.' And that scares them."[92] This is the point of socialized fear. It keeps us ever vigilant to the potential of our own duplicity, alert to the way our slip(s) show(s), and to whom. None of us passes all the time, every day.

Moving away from politics and representations, then, what else might Smith represent? At issue in Union, and extrapolated into election national Gothic, is no less than a society's sense of itself. In framing Smith as a monster, the social order anticipates, even as it repudiates, such an unthinkable (but always thinkable) thought. In this instance, the unspeakable possibility is the killing of a child, but more generally, the fear is the failure of social codes of identity more widely understood. Consequently the allegorical dimensions of Smith's crime required major social-stigma management, and interested parties from Gingrich to *People* magazine to countless members of the press busily apportioned blame elsewhere. Susan Smith made possible the horror fantasy of the Bad Mother which, in truth, *any* reader—particularly female ones—might have been (and who might yet be at any time). This was a major reason for the narrative cycle, since pious meditation upon her example helps insure that no reader *will* be. Further, when Smith meets some extralegal end in prison, much and loud will be the remarks about making prisons safer, etc. etc. Heads will be shaken in sympathy, but yes, there will be general agreement. We know the story of Susan Smith the monster, the version circulated in court by prosecutor Pope, or the "baby-killing bitch" that went the rounds of the press.[93] These mutually supporting narratives tell us all we need to know. Monsters are exemplars; as meditative aids, their actual lives are forfeit. If

Smith is "slime, just slime,"[94] then her death (if not her first, in print, then her second, in prison) will not be our fault.

Monsters show how far the liberal state extends beyond the skin of representation. The monster is by definition the private self—the logical consequence of a very unliberal need for boundaries and social closure. Monsters "call into question the extent of our power and status, the contours of our sexuality, the nature of our 'humanity.' They are, in this sense, us, which means that it is we who are different."[95] Indeed, once could argue that the case of Susan Smith functions in this homeopathic fashion; one fantasy confirms another, while a visible monster is vanquished in order to ward against monstrosity hidden, and potentially available, in ourselves. In the public fantasy called domesticity, and electioneered as Family Values, Smith must be alienated—her name erased from civil consciousness, crossed sticks (rather than yellow ribbons) planted over her memory. This must be done not because she is so unusual, but to the contrary because she is so typical. And in her typicality is her danger: the unimaginable act she performed, is, after all, horrific in its very ordinariness. Murray Kempton remarks that "her deed remains beyond earthly absolution; but . . . her feelings are not as unfamiliar as they ought to be."[96] What parent or guardian has not at some time or another, under duress and stress, imagined a way out of the bone-grinding burden of giving care?

Monsters serve as exemplars of a social inadequacy rarely served by speech, as discussed above. Speechless and unspeakable, they can only provoke dramatic and spectacular commentary *about*—never dialogue *with,* or, God forbid, speech *by.* Endlessly spoken about, they lose their voice for the good of those who might have to listen to them explain. The Smith case poignantly demonstrated this process of silencing in a number of ways. We have seen how, in turning Smith into Representation, for example, *People* turned her confession into visual aid. Yet a further violent silencing occurred in a different venue entirely. At the funeral of Alex and Michael Smith, on November 6, 1994, four pastors officiated. The mother, under suicide watch, was not permitted to attend, nor, as one observer in attendance noted, were any prayers offered for her. Was the silence shame, or complicity? To keep her safe, or to keep us?

A successful text produces the reader best qualified to read it. James W. Carey, writing about "good" journalism, marks as a "necessary" condition "a profound collaboration between the writer and his audience."[97] David Punter argues that any "text . . . enacts the construction of a 'we'; produces a readership which is at all points coterminous with US norms."[98] Similar points can be made about the narrative processes driving the Smith and

Cunanan cycles, although I am less convinced than Punter that such narratives are "at all points" a reflection of norms. Many points sometimes are, but just as often resistance to norms is a major source of energy sustaining the Gothic cadences of monstrosity we are following. Particularly interesting is the way such civic recitatives split the Gothic into its component parts, fear and sentiment, monsters and angels, via the privileged fantasy of enclosed, and safe, domesticity. Susan Smith, for example, is an angel in an angelizing society who refused her wings. The woman who wouldn't—or who because of personal as well as social constriction, couldn't—play the sentimental role demanded of her, was cast as its opposite.

Conclusion

Nonetheless, reading these broadsides, newspapers, journals and opinions, the questions begin to change. In particular, it becomes evident that at least one motive supporting the inflammatory writing lies in circulating private fear in public—in order, ironically, to guide a discussion of the conduct of the private. One might say that at issue in Susan Smith's public tale (and that of Cunanan and Clinton, as well) is a short-course in the definition and conduct of the erotic. For all its renowned stodginess the *New York Times* shows how this works. One *Times* analysis notes that the "case has not just given outsiders a peek into the closets of Union, it has lifted the roofs off its bedrooms and reopened old, hidden crimes." [99] How is it that the death of a child should make possible such an erotic leer? Indeed, it can be argued that in all the representational cycles under consideration, the killing mother, the serial killer who comes from nowhere, or other civic haunt has not so much *violated* the domestic as he or she has been the narrative trigger by which one fantasy can erupt into another. [100]

In *The Feminization of American Culture,* Ann Douglas argues that in American vernacular address the iconic mother and child assume a tremendous importance; they formalize a tableaux of the nationalized domestic space in which every day is "Mother's Day." [101] Maggie Kilgour remarks that "the Gothic uses the woman's whole body as pawn: she is moved, threatened, discarded, and lost." [102] But if her body grounds the Gothic, helplessness (as noted, epitomized in the child's body), grounds the sentimental. Joined in a representational Möbius strip, failed mother and murdered child dramatize the collapse *from within* of the domestic safe place, which even in its earliest figurations in bourgeois civility carried a heavily gendered burden. The establishment of the private space of the home, an enclave securely away from the workaday world is, as Maggie Kilgour

notes, an effect of two movements, one a reformation and the other a revolution, Protestant and industrial. It is a "separation of public and private
that is bourgeois, and Protestant, in origins." [103] At the same time, the
imagining of this space was, equally, the creation of a class and ideological
space—middle, "private"—which had not previously existed, at least in
quite that fashion. By the eighteenth century the energy around *creating*
this new space was manifested by the amount of defensive public speech
accorded its potential demise.

The cascading, disproportionate outrage at Susan Smith marks a similar entwining of opposing movements—demise and construction—
played out as a crisis in national fantasy. In these tableaux of traumatic
undoing, Smith and other always-failing parents take their places as apocalyptic agents of a particular Americanized Eden, a geography as useful now
as it was to Crèvecoeur and Jefferson. Additionally, failed parents are joined
by other domestic and erotic terrorists who could be named as accessories
to the crimes that are so necessary to establish, and ground, the political
fancy of democratic normality. Discussing his favorite topic of the serial
killer, Robert Ressler nicely shows how Gothic and sentimental images
jumble together in a representational heap: "The monsters among us do
live on. The American scene has become apple pie and Mom and serial
murder." [104] But we need not look to Ressler for this link. The paranoid
linkage of invasion and sentimentality can be found embodied in legal policy and structure, most directly in such agencies and programs as the Child
Abduction and Serial Killer Unit of the FBI, or the U.S. Department of
Justice's sponsorship of the "National Missing/Abducted Children and Serial Murder Tracking and Prevention Program." [105] Gingrich's investment
in Susan Smith perhaps sheds some light onto why these two investigative
agencies should be linked, either in the popular or political mind. One can
argue, however, that the conjunction in law confirms the public gravity of
the fantasies we are tracking. The S.W.A.T. team fantasies mobilized
around the body of Andrew Cunanan and the doleful cries around Susan
Smith (who also rated S.W.A.T. teams, for her "protection") are not disconnected. Andrew Cunanan, the boy next door (and some mother's son)
is a queer and a killer, but so is "the mother next door." [106] Whether father
is absent or, more frighteningly, mother is home alone: the private constraint of gender is undone, and that publicly marks the crisis. The defense
of marriage was, finally, about the defense of gender. This was the reason
Smith was of interest to Gingrich.

Smith, inadequate parents, and the dying child (or, with JonBenet, the
eroticized child): the failure of the domestic narrative is complete. The

crisis of the child, indirectly addressed through the Smith narrative, and the crisis of the killer in public places are flip sides of a common anxiety. The increase of social legislation around children since the early seventies is less about children than about the site that sentimentally exists "for" them—i.e. the home. Douglas W. Pryor, in *Unspeakable Acts: Why Men Sexually Abuse Children,* notes that the "last fifteen years have been largely an era of 'protectionism,' as parents have become preoccupied with the safekeeping of their children from various perceived threats."[107] The energy is high, but misleading as to the nature of the threats.[108] "Home Repairs," as Ann Hulbert terms it in the *New Republic,* has prompted a national ideological crisis since at least the fifties, when the retooling of domesticity accompanied a shifting away from international focus to the private implications of the national.[109] In differing ways, the focus on children and those who slay them (physically or spiritually, as sexual abuse is said to do), confirms the fantasy of home as a place like no other.[110] Home sweet home, indeed. What more persistent political preoccupation is there in contemporary fantasy America than this one, even as the social and economic conditions increasingly call homes into question?

As only one moment in the ongoing ritual theater of the monstrous, the media presentation of the Smith case seems initially very different from the cases of Andrew Cunanan, or Jeffrey Dahmer, or Timothy McVeigh. In the screaming headlines of paper and news, serial killers and civil terrorists are, after all, "public threats" in the way Susan Smith is not.[111] And this has little to do with biological gender, and lots to do with representational gender. However dispersed such incidents are in terms of scene or location, they are nonetheless connected by rigid behavioral formulas which inhere in what Josephine McDonagh calls the "aesthetics of murder."[112] Thus, while Smith is accorded the public nomination of "monster," she is one of a severely limited kind. The warning announced by the monster's presence need not be couched in terror, directly; it might be figured as communal guilt rather than in individual fear. Smith's action, nationalized through Gingrich's political squint (among others), for example, is of this sort. In the attempted prosecutorial frame-up, legal remonstrance draws upon Gothic support. If a monster, Smith is a troubling aberration, a monstrosity of failed coherence and formulaic collapse (formulas of motherhood, and perhaps less obviously, though as significantly, of the "feminine" as well). Smith is not, however, construed as a monster whose direct action is "publicly threatening." The failed mother might be dangerous to the weak and vulnerable child, so the argument goes, but nonetheless, like femininity, such actions—indeed, such persons—are essentially private matters.[113]

She is no Andrew Cunanan, killing adult men, even though her crimes, like his, are made to carry a public burden.

Of course, to view the cases in this way is to see how thoroughly gendered is the notion of "threat" in the first place. Economically, women are ennobled by rhetoric and devalued in practice; in similar ways they are representationally disarmed as well. In sentimental discourse women are rarely represented as public dangers of the gun-toting kind. Any threat they might mount is detailed as moral, rather than physical. Nowhere is this more evident than in popular, even academic "studies" of serial killers, for instance, where women, if they appear, do so with some apology. Their killing is circumscribed, its incitement if not its effect explained away as "compassion killing." Indeed, it is almost with apology that women are said to kill in hospitals, homes, or other sites of the feminine. Or else they are seen to kill only family members, practicing their dire trade within domesticity itself, while the male killer cruising highways and navigating across continents traffics in mayhem with panache and "mobility." [114] In sum, when women are portrayed as monstrous, it is because they threaten, usually, the sanctity of the domestic scene, and children. The assumption seems to be that deaths in these places are somehow less violent than others. Finally, monstrosity in women is somehow always connected with *their* mobility—when, that is, they violate the sanctity of the home by leaving it and "going public"—a disgrace usually characterized in terms of a sexual lapse or offense. [115]

The crisis of gender can also be seen aslant in the counterformations mounted to stabilize it. These guerrilla movements off to one side of the peculiarly focused moments of public fright maintain socioeconomically approved formulas of intimacy. This is the gendered structure of public life that undergirds a public "national-political masculinity." [116] In the emotional shorthand of family values, monstrosity lurks, particularly, in those who repudiate gender or fail it—the homosexual or the bad mother. From another, equally revisionist perspective, one finds a regrouping of gender essentialism in the cults and movements established to restrict the play of gender and, at the same time, to extend its significance. Such restriction often consists of performance cues—some literary, as we see in the Smith reporting, but others physical, as well. These are injunctions to act or dress in specific ways. The movements in question derive from secular as well as religious principles, from "straight" groups to "straightening up" groups for "ex-gays." Among others, these include the various Men's Movements, and the Million Man marches, and the Promise Keepers, for example. In these Utopian, back-to-gendered-basics movements, masculinity is thought to be wounded, its trauma the result of numerous possible causes—the women's movement, the realignment of the civic imagination in the sixties, and finally lesbian and gay challenges to gender hegemony.[117] The economy of the masculine, bankrupt, in telling the tale had to make monsters of its women and women of its monsters.[118] Why? As Michelle Masse suggestively observes: "The Gothic is [a narrative of the infamous] and its infamous scandal is a suffering woman."[119] This is the only way the story works, its voyeurism dependent upon the body of the woman.[120]

In summation, Susan Smith, Darlie Routier, or any other killing mother could only emerge as a visible carrier of social unrest in a bodily-schizophrenic order, in which bodies and their intensities disappear from polite converse except as they can be shopped, shot (with gun or film), sexed and undressed. This asks us to consider the way the ideological oddities of gender are said to be confirmed in the uncanny scene of the home. I began this chapter with a remark by Ted Bundy, who announced that monsters are found at home. We could end by agreeing with Bundy, that, indeed, monsters *start* there, in the site once deemed the province of angels. The association of domestic felicity and monstrous affect is a commonplace much older than Bundy, of course. Freud's "uncanny" originates in the familial scene, as did E.T.A. Hoffman's, nearly a century earlier. But more to the point of this chapter is Mary Wollstonecraft Shelley's *Frankenstein*. In the preface to the first and anonymous 1818 edition, speaking for (as?) the unknown author (his wife), Percy Bysshe Shelley writes that the text's motive was "the exhibition of the amiableness of domestic affection."[121] So maybe the narrative of the monster is not merely a subversion of homes, angels, and family virtue. Maybe the monster declares, not a contempt for family values, but their illusory nature to begin with. This, finally, is how Harlequin and Gothic versions of the Smith tale were balanced. As each undercut the other, the narrative became as empty as the political formulas driving it. There are no angels in the house because the prior domestic fantasy cannot support the heavy additional weight of fantasy: angels have fallen, not into sin, but into the plain ordinary old gravity of economic reality and the psychosis it can generate.

Angels—no wonder our boutiques are crowded with them. They are necessary reminders to shoppers of their out-of-this-world duties as caregivers—not only to children, but more generally to national mythologies. Remarkably, such a culture defines as rhetorically valuable a political regime known as family values and yet on the other hand supports an economic order which makes families practically impossible to maintain. That this "order" already partakes of more than an element of fantasy should be clear. Thus one sees its utility for fantasy merchants like Disney, who trade on a different regime of nostalgia and sentiment. Henry Giroux writes that

> the white, nuclear, middle-class family becomes the ethical referent for linking consumerism, gender roles, motherhood, and class chivalry. It is around the family as the primary unity of stability, culture, ethics, and agency that Disney circulates in many of its films the articulating principles that link, say Morley and Robins, "individuals and their families at the centers of national life, offering the audience an image of itself and of the nation as a knowable community." [122]

It is toward the forming of that knowable community, and the schooling of it in the theatric presentation of scandal, that I turn next.

≋

Life was so much simpler before they found that dress, wasn't it?

David Schippers, counsel to the Judiciary Committee
Republicans, testifying before the committee[1]

Congress, when the time came, pushed titillating material immediately and unthinkingly into the public domain. This howling after sex stoked the fires of Republican moralists.

"The End?" *Economist* (13 February 1999): 17

They cannot be called pornographic. They can be bought at any
bookstall.

Testimony in a capital murder case, cited in Roger Shattuck,
Forbidden Knowledge, 258

If you are going to rely in this proceeding on a *Time Magazine*
essay . . . then I think the standards are not quite as lofty as I
thought they would be this evening.

Kenneth Starr[2]

CHAPTER FIVE

READING THE STARR:

SCANDAL AND AUGURIES

Introduction

In Bret Easton Ellis's much-villified *American Psycho* (1991), the narrator Patrick Bateman has two favorite compulsions, which he indulges serially—cutting up women and watching the Patty Winters talk show. Often he would do the one while watching the other. Somehow these activities are conjoined in his mind, and why should they not be? Dismembering, exhibition, and commentary define a public space taken for granted in his fictional world. It is also a favored theatric mode of media culture, in which the eroticized display of bodies (and their emotional equivalencies) support activities as seemingly diverse as shopping, beauty pageants for children, and the rites of political scandal.[3]

Mark Seltzer argues that American representation demonstrates a "wound culture": "It is around the wound—the torn and open body, the torn and open person, the opening and spilling and becoming-visible of interiors—that this culture gathers."[4] Referring to Patrick Bateman, Seltzer argues that his commodity fetishism "advertises, and trades on, the analogies or casual relations, between these two forms of compulsive repetition, consumerism and serial killing."[5] Bateman *is* fiction, of course. However, Seltzer could have made his point with reference to any daily news broadcast, whose pursuit of the "real" *collapses* killing and consumerism into one process called scandal. That is, shooting and cutting refer, appropriately enough, to the way media, as well as killers, process bodies. The coverage of Andrew Cunanan dramatically confirms Seltzer's point.

However, at a different social register, so does the mechanics of scandal initiated around Bill Clinton.

The chapter on Andrew Cunanan examined how fantasized criminality entwined erotic taboo and sexual display into a flexible narrative of public threat. This chapter considers a higher-toned collusion—where evangelical piety, served up as civic augury, likewise turns upon a moral detailing of bodies. If Cunanan's gun was proposed as a national threat, Bill Clinton's errant body, emotionally suppurating in public, was also presented as a civic trauma. In the Cunanan narrative, sexualized bodies and a Gothic apocalyptic mode staged a fantasy S-M tableaux in which moral disciplining alternated with demonstrable interest in the pleasures of pain.[6] The Clinton case, however, reached a closure as ambiguous as Cunanan's, though for different reasons. In what Gore Vidal terms the "Starr business," an evidentiary drive for accurate detailing of sex reaches an impasse: knowledge of bodies was endlessly sought, provoked, even incited, to use a word Foucault would like. Nonetheless, the knowledge thereby produced was constantly under threat of legal erasure as pornographic. As a result, whether treated as evidence or moral fact, knowledge could only be expressed within the formally empty cadence of Gothic. Too close an attention to the body resulted in a collapse of narrative possibility.

I. Moral Consumerism

One can make any claim, as long as it is shocking. . . . We do not want it to be all over with.

James R. Kincaid, *Child-loving*, 377, 341

In this chapter I wish to broaden Seltzer's point about "wound culture" to include the moral consumerism at work in the Clinton scandal.[7] But first to the drama of Mr. Clinton, by way of Ellis's fiction. Bateman's doubling of the Patty Winters show with his private violences draws a metonymic link between the consumption of bodies and their emotional interiors in shops and shows, and the consumption of bodies in more literal, if private, fashion. Indeed, Bateman's intimacies with those around him become grotesque literalizations of the violations of interiority he sees on the Winters talk show.[8] In this respect Bateman's fictional world has numerous analogues to our own. Indeed, Bateman's actions are unexceptional in light of the ways bodies are reproduced, displayed, and consumed in media culture. The difference, of course, is that the violence so much a part of therapy TV—whether Patty Winters, Oprah Winfrey, or even Rikki Lake—is justified as a therapeutic social encounter, and thus, as morally pedagogic and useful. Bateman's activity, while similar in symbolic kind, is to the contrary denounced as psychotic, pathological, unspeakable.[9]

One could argue therefore that the furor attending the publication of *American Psycho* was aimed not so much at Ellis or Bateman as at the not-so-gentle reader, who, Bateman-like, consumes the endlessly reproduced media bodies of Clinton, Smith, Cunanan while reading quietly at home.[10] The violence inherent in this activity is usually talked away as moral or ethical investment; as "news" and the "right to know"; or simply as "entertainment."[11] Bateman's psychosis—if one is to pathologize him and it that way—is his essential literalism. This habit, however, is not unlike media culture's production of pay-per-view bodies, its libidinal investment marking no difference between the morally exceptional, physically unusual, or the criminal.[12] Joshua Gamson questions the collapse of liberal categories of "diversity" into less benign categories of "deviancy." In the talk show, asks Gamson, "how . . . do poverty and lack of education, sex and gender nonconformity, and race come to be lumped together and condemned as monstrosities?"[13] Gamson here addresses the way a hermeneutics of civility—the discourses, gestures, and disciplinary techniques by which a society underwrites "normality"—is often a tangle of selling, reprisal, eroticizing and policing, each working at cross-purposes to the other. Grounding these procedures, as Jonathan Crane notes in *Terror and Everyday Life,* is a fantasy of the "perfectly broken body," the image of which is "the most interesting and most vital special effect in any contemporary horror film."[14] This body plays out the trauma *of* consumption, and the fantasy lack that consumption seeks to undo. Furthermore, this trauma is not contained within the horror genre, which only distills processes and effects diffused more widely through culture. Indeed, the perfectly broken body is—as Cunanan and Clinton understand—a characteristic requirement of contemporary moral evaluation. Public pleasure takes the form of public pain.[15]

It is in such a culture of consumption—unstably poised between the literal violences of Bateman and Cunanan (perhaps), and the symbolic modes indulged by the reader—that the sex scandal must be situated as a discursive form and disciplinary civic mode.[16] Scandal borrows techniques from what Michelson might call the "econo-code" of the obscene. Additionally, however, displaying abnormality for moral purpose has roots in the freak shows and, distantly, it derives from an ancient mode of preaching.[17] In this way both fictional example and real-time President collude. That is, the same voyeuristic drive for intimacy that organized Bateman's fetishes of cutting and watching—or Clinton's more complicated mix of exhibitionism and masochism, or Cunanan's binding and shooting—fold together in a moral theater. Discursive ethics gives way to the evaluation of scenes and performance. As the pursuit of the *ipsa acta* of Clinton's body demonstrated, when desires barred by law are brought before public scrutiny, bodies that shock and provoke can be said, perversely enough, to be moral bodies. That is, to the degree they are framed in a religious mode of exposition, scandalous bodies become objects of meditation, and, occasionally, of veneration as well. Secrets of inner lives are revealed and eroticized by the reader in a ritual of almost sacramental shame—one that leads, implicitly, to an epiphany or revelation. As a general method of civil management, then, scandal replaces earlier public ceremonies. It organizes the communally based activity of dismembering and displaying bodies, while insuring the proper interpretation of the opened body.

Clinton's exposition thus crossed the voyeuristic methods of the freak show with the classic designs made upon the extraordinary and ominous body: that it reveal in its ineptness and unnaturality dreadful news. Further troubling the public discourse around Clinton were the gotcha! exposé politics of a litigious society, which in turn was complicated by the moral economics of an evangelical culture. From the perspective of the Citizen-reader/viewer, in the interactive dynamic of scandal, what we watch as voyeurs we participate in as potential scandals ourselves. This is the point of civic melodrama, as Elaine Hadley reminds us in *Melodramatic Tactics*.[18] As a result, anxiety over Clinton's body was exploited as negative example and its shame internalized, even while the body was bought and sold in the markets of voyeurized pleasure. By means of this sleight of hand, energy that is directly erotic in nature is disguised, redistributed as moral stricture as well as commercial profit.

From the moment when the Lewinsky affair first became public, Clinton was positioned within a discourse of moral surveillance that was never very clear about its commitments. At different times commentary fore-grounded religious rhetoric (sin), the discourse of law (crime), and an obsession with the forensic (evidence). To return for a moment to Ellis's *American Psycho:* Patrick Bateman's scrupulous itemizing of clothing or accessories, while surely fiction, nonetheless compares to the documentary zeal that excused (as well as justified) the obsessive production of data/

evidence in Clinton's impeachment trial. That is, this scene of deviance—
and the moralizing narratives it encouraged—required bodies that were
readable; nonetheless the moral/legal inquisitions required by this exegetical mode *increased,* rather than lessened, the potential erotic value of
that body—hence, increasing its commercial appeal as well. These instabilities in the moral and economic pressures applied to the case had important consequences. In the first place, the pressure destabilized the nature
of the "fact" itself. Dates and times, positions of bodies in relation to each
other, although generated as factual, tilted either toward the illegal pornographic or to the inexpressible Grand Guignol Gothic.In either direction meaning escaped the judicial heuristic structure set up to generate it.[19]
Scenes of private intimacy, trumpeted as scandal and thereby permitted as
public example, lost their blushing civic demeanor and became, instead,
leering public show. Moral purpose was bleached out in the glare of erotic
display. The result was sheer verbal excess, as a multiplicity of words attempted to plug the epistemological gap.[20]

II. Scandal: Public Sacrament of Pain

Scandal can be studied from a variety of perspectives, as method or pro-
cedure, as discourse, as content, as public theater, finally as moralizing
gesture. Its rubrical processes borrow from theatrical exposition and moral
pedagogy, some ancient and religious, others modern, secular, and some
pornographic.[21] In it the freak show, spectacle, and forensic sensibility
merge, as the body is called on to exhibit, pose, underwrite, witness.[22]
Sometimes, however, tawdry commerce, freakery, and transcendent ideological mandate are indistinguishable. Indeed, in the Clinton investigations a moral imperative to chastise wrongdoing became, instead, political
machination, apocalyptic augury, and salacious narrative.[23] Despite world-
ending claims made for it, Clinton's case of the abuse of sex/power is not
unique. As Suzanne Garment observes, the rubric of scandal is "one of the
most pervasive elements of [American] history."[24] An adequate answer as
to why this should be demands an investigation beyond the scope of this
book. Nonetheless, America's complex pattern of public Christian discourse is one reason why the "search for the most disgusting, sinful, or
shocking possible facts . . . has deep roots in the American journalism of
the past two centuries."[25] Nor is Clinton's public "fall" likely to be the last
such scene, since a discursive habit of free-floating religious reference
makes for some irreligious politics, generally centered upon sex and its

voyeuristic potentials.[26] Garment suggests that the epistemological basis of the scandal has shifted away from a focus on financial or bureaucratic irregularity in the 1970s and '80s, and moved instead to a sexual economy.[27] It might be more appropriate to say that the rubric of scandal has returned to its origins within a sexual economy, since the allegorizing of the *sexual* Body Politic predates political and popular culture's commerce in wounded or eroticized bodies.[28]

The word "scandal" has two main roots: a Latin word meaning "cause of offense or stumbling" and a Greek word meaning "trap" or "snare."[29] In *Media Scandals,* editors James Lull and Stephen Hinerman define scandal as occurring "when private acts that disgrace or offend the idealized, dominant morality of a social community are made public and narrativized by the media, producing a range of effects." Disciplinary agencies (churches, secular governments, and media, among other forces) manipulate moral spectacles for a variety of purposes, as Lull and Hinerman note, "from ideological and cultural retrenchment to disruption and change."[30] Thus, however much a particular scandal might be thought as disruptive of an imagined normal life, the contrary is often the case. Scandal doesn't rupture social mores as much as it confirms the network of mores whose workings the scandal demonstrates. For this reason, perversity in public places—its elicitation, control, and management—requires institutional support, even while it seems the institution has most at stake to lose in the scandal. Indeed, it can be argued that the content of any scandal matters less than the interlocking media and civic rubric by which scandal continuously positions itself as new, late-breaking, as unexpected. Paul Soukup observes that scandal serves "three related functions: warning, for the scandal needs to generate shame and fear of transgression . . . ; justification, for the scandal needs to reinforce the community's right to define acceptable behavior; and entertainment, for a good scandal story must maintain group interest and be memorable to be effective."[31]

The sudden appearance of any scandal is thus belied by the sturdily consistent apparatus of reportage, announcement, and official commentary standing by, always ready to capitalize on the news (invariably "late-breaking") and the impending crisis such news portends.[32] As a socializing process, then, scandal is neither ancillary nor incidental to the civic norms it breaches. Scandals are engineered, not endured. John Thompson writes that scandals are "not just about actions which transgress certain values or norms: they are also about the cultivation or assertion of the values or norms themselves."[33] Scandals, then, insofar as they announce a moral position, are conservatively anchored to ideology as well as to economics, although the payoff is different for each. Ideology speaks its civilizing imperatives by means of a viewer/reader who becomes "the subject of as well as to the representation of meaning." Scandal organizes a narrative compulsion that "does not simply represent subjectivity to readers or viewers; more importantly, it also signifies their subjectivities for them."[34] The economic value of scandals, then, is the way quite simply that perversity in public generates income, as well as outcry, sometimes by the same persons.

Another consideration must be addressed. From suffering that ennobles, to suffering that appalls. Earlier, in my discussion of the construction of the Susan Smith narrative, I noted that there is, or can be, a metonymic exchange between exemplary pain and showy horror.[35] Given the almost explicit religious framing of the scandal, elements of *marturon* (witness) overlap with, and exploit, aspects of *monstrum* (show). Any scandal can be said to exploit a range of emotions simultaneously—moral zeal, certainly, even shame and pain, to some extent. Nonetheless excitement and erotic stimulation are part of the mix as well.[36] The rubric of scandal thus consolidates its powerful energy through an interlocking set of tactics from exhortation to exploitation, from teaching to commerce. These make possible moments of high address as well as vigilantly enforced silence. From another point of view, commercial commitments to pursue, uncover, and to know balance political and social investments in covering and hiding. Given the instabilities that govern the whole enterprise, it should be apparent that no scandal is either one-dimensional in effect or uniform in meaning. For instance, operatic invocations of scandalous criminality swirling around Clinton served as many purposes as there were readers libidinously, morally, or politically invested in him. At its most superficial aspect, the erotic framing of the narrative elicited interest while the intense moralistic reprisal helped articulate a readership who were bound, at least informally and momentarily, to an ideological consensus.

Finally, scandals maintain their power to effect, change, and stabilize civic meanings by remaining oblique about the power and pain they intend. That is, whether privileged as moral moment or decried as pornographic, what often passes without observation or comment is the viewer's submerged libidinal investment in these narrative scenes of stripping and evaluating. As Laura Mulvey remarked long ago in "Visual Pleasure and Narrative Cinema," "pleasure lies in ascertaining guilt . . . , asserting

132 · CHAPTER FIVE

control . . . through punishment or forgiveness." In short, "sadism demands a story."[37] Plato rightly understood that the storyteller affected the imagination as much or more than the intellect. It was the poet's capacity for destabilization that troubled him, and the scandal confirms Plato's insight. Narrative *is* powerfully persuasive. Nonetheless, the body's pain, produced in the time-honored manner of witness—or less benignly perhaps, "for [one's] own good"—and narratively produced, is ethically charged. Such representations deserve to be examined because they pleasure the reader in what must be considered a moral equivalent of the S-M exchange.[38] As Laura Hinton observes, the "gaze of sympathy" is also a "perverse" one, a manifest pleasure taken in the display of pain.[39]

These points can be considered in the staging of melodrama around Bill Clinton—whose public presence was a compound of very different machineries, including the dynamics of celebrity, monstrosity, the rubric of stardom, as well as the discourse of moral disclaimer. Each of these performances involved differing fantasies, although common to all methods was the way Clinton's body was placed under obligation to testify. As observed, however, testifying became horror, as the witnessing body was exploited to produce shock, titillation, and shame. All of this was accompanied by, or produced, commercial potential—thus edging the discourse into the gravitational pull of the pornographic.[40] Elaine Hadley argues that the melodramatic mode "operate[s] on the assumption that people are socially constituted and therefore recognizable to one another as long as they participate in sympathetic exchange." From "the perspective of those who deployed the melodramatic mode," Hadley suggests, the aim was "to uncover these hidden selves and reintegrate them into a society where public exchange remained possible."[41] The anxiety of the Clinton discourse—or at least the variant that anchored conservative moral readings—was that the meaning of civic public exchange was seriously compromised as a result of Clinton's actions. Nonetheless, Clinton's textual body paralleled his physical one; that is, the discourse was interpretively diffuse. Monstrous, it admitted of so many interpretations and significations. Why? Show-and-tell moralists from Augustine to Kenneth Starr have always had to face the uncomfortable realization that repudiating an action demands prior experience for the injunction to be completely effective. William Bennett, for example, can fulminate about popular culture, calling it a "rot" that threatens civilization. However, his remark typifies the conundrum faced by those who preach the jeremiad. At the very least, the documentation of civic woe as "proof" threatens to swamp the moral purpose for which it was designed—thus "perpetuat[ing]" the "cultural rot" it means to undo.[42]

III. "All Filthy Facts and Secret Acts"

All filthy facts and secret acts,
however closely done
and long concealed, are there revealed
before the mid-day sun.

Michael Wigglesworth, "The Day of Doom" (1662)[43]

The public undressing of Bill Clinton and Monica Lewinsky demonstrates how moral and pornographic discourses are hardly separable in the sinuous rubric of scandal.[44] In such an economy bodies are quite literally up for grabs. This is what exercised so many about Bill Clinton, who seemed clearly incapable of keeping his privates to himself. Nonetheless, the public distribution of these privates—moments as well as parts— became not solely Clinton's fault, nor, completely, the viewer's pleasure. Jonathan Alter noted that Clinton was partly helped in the Lewinsky debacle by a "wave of revulsion against the obliteration of private life in America." It is owing perhaps to the instability of the public/private binary that the Clinton affair assumed a monstrous power of regeneration, reproducing toxic versions of itself—thanks to news media, that, as Alter commented, "have lost control every bit as much as [Clinton] may have."[45] Yet an odd result could be observed. With the titillation came shame; imbricated in scandal's production, it could not be extricated from the pleasure. In the developing Clinton scandal, it became evident that any thought of pleasure in the proceedings was explicitly no one's right (in fact was to be denied *as* pleasure). On the other hand, shame—Clinton's as well as the reader's—was considered to be everyone's business. In actual fact the reverse of these two happened, and the unacknowledged pleasure outstripped the intended shame.

From the outset Clinton's body was considered monstrous in the word's most primary meaning, derived from Aristotle's ancient usage. It was deemed ominous, full of civic portent. Indeed, criticism of Bill Clinton's liaison with Lewinsky, a White House intern, explicitly linked him to the monstrous. Newt Gingrich—always ready with the formula *du jour*—named him a "monster"; others—friends, even the foreign press— followed suit.[46] Clinton's presumptive monstrosity was, additionally, used as comparison to evaluate the monstrosity of others. Gingrich's nomination of Clinton as "monster" in the House Manager's meeting was exactly to the point of this book, and it is more than likely that professorial Gingrich understood the word's significance better than people who heard him use it. Clinton's body—its markings, hungers, individuating peculiarities—were assumed to signify in metaphysical ways about the health of the state. Gingrich had made similar claims before, remember, when he read Susan Smith's life as morally central to a history of bad (i.e., Democratic) governance. So it was in this case, as well. Monster-like, Clinton's body was thought to compel moral advisories; examined, it would provide cautionary parables on the one hand and forensic evidence on the other. What was not always clear from the outset was that the examination of Clinton's body would become publicly mounted commercial pornography, as well.

Interpretation of the monstrous body was not a simple matter to the augurs entrusted the task in ancient Rome. Nor was it to be so in this case. The instability looming over these procedures of interrogating the Civil Body began with establishing that, indeed, Clinton's body was a text capable of civil exegesis. Bill Clinton's extended stay in the public stocks thus began with the Supreme Court's decision, May 27, 1997, that Citizen Clinton's body—and by extension organs on that body—*was* a public text, even if the *president*'s body was by definition inscrutable, unavailable for such readings.[47] The court ruled that Clinton's body could be read as evidence, and, in a manner of speaking, be inserted into the Paula Jones case. Nonetheless, the court took pains to separate Clinton's merely hyperactive penis from Clinton's morally oblique phallus, the in/visible sign of patriarchal authority. The court's efforts were in vain, however, and the situation was subsequently reversed with dramatic consequences. That is, the impeachment would place on trial the *presidential,* rather than the Clintonian, penis—even while those responsible denied that either effect was intended. "The case is not about sex or private conduct," read the brief against the president. "It is about multiple obstructions of justice, or perjury."[48] It was the misuse of *lips,* stupid, *not* the sex. Thus it happened that Clinton's body was deemed civilly monstrous, doubled as well as split, its often messy entrails necessitating interpretation at the highest level of government.[49]

Reports of Clinton's supposed sexual exploits had preceded him into the White House, and indeed, they almost swamped his campaign for the presidency in 1992. However, after the Lewinsky story broke, Clinton's errant dick assumed monstrous significance, deemed capable of almost uncanny powers of fascination and bilocation. It was, apparently, inescapable as well as implacable; one tabloid after the next discovered yet more distant sources of sexual malfeasance, many of which had very little if any further consequence. Like the scarlet letter on Hester Prynne's dress, Clinton's hapless organ began to organize and refract a complex spectrum of civic emotions. Red letter and physical organ became typological—rubrical in both senses of the word. At issue was the civic melodrama of communal identity, rather than individual failing, however. As Mark Seltzer observes,

> The spectacular public representation of violated bodies has come to function as a way of imagining and situating, albeit in violently pathologized form, the very idea of "the public" and, more exactly, the relations of bodies and persons to public spaces.[50]

Hawthorne was at pains to show in *The Scarlet Letter* that the letter on Hester Prynne's dress, while an emblem of individual sin, ultimately pointed beyond itself to other issues. Sometimes these issues energized the law, was Hawthorne's point; as often, however, they escaped its signifying power. Adulterer could be angel, sinner could be saint. And so it was in the Clinton proceedings. The law, like any text, demands but does not always achieve competent readership. Jesus' question to the Pharisees on the law's relation to public sin could have been addressed to the House Managers, as well: "Here is the law, how do you read it?" Clinton's errancy was read into civic, even cosmic portent. His actions, whatever they were (and despite the Starr Report, these were never conclusively itemized), were thought to signify something woeful about communal identity—although just exactly what that something was never became totally clear. Still, meaning aside, the scene was dramatized in a Christian rhetoric of shock, guilt, and apocalyptic revelation, all of which resulted in a narrative as rich in Gothic religiosity, protestations of metaphysical intensity, and religious guilt as earlier authors in the genre. Kenneth Starr's report, without much exaggeration, could be placed in the same civic apocalyptic mode as Michael Wigglesworth's "Day of Doom" (1662) or Cotton Mather's *Wonders of the Invisible World* (1692–93).

So knotted were the exchanges, charge and countercharge, by opponents and supporters alike of Mr. Clinton that resulting commentary produced a discourse never quite sure of its intentions; nor were observers ever sure of what they were observing. The reference to Mather, above, is an apt one, since the Clinton affair puts one in mind of an earlier case of civic wickedness, the legal proceedings against witchery in Salem. Mather's confusion in how to read the affair becomes a pronounced part of his narrative about the case. At one point in *Wonders of the Invisible World,* Mather confides to the reader, almost in an aside,"The whole business is become hereupon so Snarled, and the determination of the Question one way or another, so dismal, that . . . We know not what to do!"[51] The connection with Salem is not a casual one, either, since in terms of content, method, and even originating cause, Salem's 1692–93 civil unrest was brought to bear on Clinton. "Political Witch-Hunts, Then and Now," is the subtitle of an essay about the Clinton scene in the *New Republic.* John B. Judis took for his theme what I am arguing, that the conflicted discourse emerging around the president's body disguised the presence of a religious framework that Mather himself would have readily understood.[52] Indeed, the resemblance between the agents of state discourse—Cotton Mather and Kenneth Starr—is uncanny. Like Mather, Starr saw his role as civil, yet also transcending the civil good. As a civilian authority Starr defined his task as insuring that the information he garnered "met the statutory standard of substantial and credible information."[53] Mather, likewise, said he was in pursuit of "credible" evidence. At another level, however, both agents acted, it seemed, indifferent to statute and evidence alike. Mather, absent from the trials themselves, was left with a vast empirical emptiness as witness to the witches he thought to identify. In similar fashion, while he himself participated in "virtually none of the questioning of the scores of witnesses," tracking the exact facts of Clinton's body left Starr no sense of presence—only absences, stains, traces, and excruciating reconstructions of time lines.[54] This vacancy at the center was, in turn, largely responsible for the cumbersome length, detail, and overburdened quality of the Starr Report. In the absence of definitive fact, fine-combing was called for. Even grammar failed, as the parsing of the copulative possibilities between Bill and Monica included, finally, detailing those of the copulative verb: "It all depends on what the meaning of the word 'is' is."[55] Language, already overburdened by a press for evidentiary detail, evacuated itself in Gothic undersignification—a consequence which only increased as desire for narrative and legal process split further apart. Mather, reflecting upon "the dismal scene" of witches abroad in Salem, and, in the end, having very little evidence to sustain his case, wonders somewhat lamely that given all the commotion, surely *something* must have caused it. Starr, like Mather, arguably created the conspiracy he sought to unravel.

While moral rhetoric went high, ever topping off at a metaphysical or apocalyptic level, the drive for narrative pleasure went commensurately low. Even the most pristine news venues published disavowals of their complicity while rushing to print the latest "filthy fact" or "secret act." Writing a month after Clinton's grand jury deposition, and shortly after the Starr Report became public, an essay in *Time* leads with the title "High Crimes? Or Just a Sex Cover-Up?"[56] Despite this title, no one was fooled. The peculiar fact of the Starr Report was that it left very little to the imagination. At least in that respect, there was very little cover-up to be had. This is one reason many observers declared themselves so outraged by it. What Clinton had not the decency to keep to himself, neither did Starr. Writing for *Time,* Nancy Gibbs remarks: "The most shocking aspect of the report was the sheer quantity and raw quality of sexual detail." The material was, Gibbs wrote, "so gratuitously detailed and pornographic that it warranted warning stickers and a plain brown wrapper." Just prior to this Gibbs had put the matter slightly more delicately, referring to "the sad, smutty chronicle that Starr has provided."[57] The effects of this representational schizophrenia were in evidence before Starr's report became public, as he and his office constantly defended themselves against charges of voyeurism and intrusion. Afterward, however, Clinton's actions, whatever they might have been, receded into the background, while the acts of collation and representation epitomized the moral stakes. What may have been, in the truest sense of the word, obscene, now risked becoming another issue entirely—pornography. Indeed, Starr adverted to the commercial aspects of his report when he ruefully admitted to the president's lawyer that press spokesmen for the independent counsel's office, although sworn to secrecy and neutrality, had nonetheless been featured on as many as eleven talk shows.

So richly detailed was the report that by its very heft and bulk it became something like a Victorian novel in which the reader, once immersed, could be lost for days, maybe weeks. Gibbs comments that the Report—a "sad, smutty chronicle"—"was so novelistic that reading it had the effect of redrawing the characters we have watched now for so long."[58] The instability between detailing of evidence and narrative accounted for some confusion. One observer seemed to grasp the fact that it was *narrative* that he was critiquing, not legally admissible actions or evidentiary detail. Eric Pooley, accordingly, offered moral evaluation that edged into literary criticism: "As numbing and repetitive as any porn, the narrative is clinical and sad, a recitation of furtive gropings and panicky zipping-ups between two profoundly needy people." [59] Pooley's comment reflects the direction of much of the Clinton reporting in the popular press. Pornography becomes an inadvertent moral touchstone, an explicit baseline by which to judge ethical significance. The production of *public* discourse about ostensibly private intimacies is arguably a mode of pornographic retail, especially when the discourse is inserted into a variety of economies that are designed to profit from the display. Such a production does not materially differ from more traditional definitions—i.e. genital acts and personal intimacies displayed for pay. In this manner, the House Managers released the Starr Report as evidence, yet they fell afoul of its pornography, in content if not intention.

At least one famous flesh-trade retailer thought so. Larry Flynt saw his moment; if sex were to be the ground of moral evaluation, he reasoned, then he would be the "investigative pornographer" and more moral than the rest.[60] After the posting of the Starr Report on the Internet, a full-page ad appeared in the *Washington Post* offering $1,000,000 for proof of an "adulterous sexual encounter with a current member of the United States Congress or a high-ranking government official." [61] *Hustler* editor Allan MacDonell reports that the Monday morning following the ad's appearance, his office received over 2,000 calls—of which about 250 had actual evidence of such encounters. Larry Flynt, "overloard of porn," had become, in one critic's estimation, "avenging angel." [62] Flynt had previously written Kenneth Starr in mock praise of the Report: "I am impressed by the salacious and voyeuristic nature of your work," he is quoted as writing. Flynt further noted that the "quality and quantity of material you have assembled in the Starr report contains more pornographic references (50) than those provided by *Hustler Online Services* this month (44)." [63] Flynt's reported offer of employment to Starr heightened the bedroom comedy; at the same time Flynt made it subsequently impossible to deny what was, in fact, evident to all. Starr's evidentiary case was by that fact also a pornographic one in a very strict sense. That is, commercial profit was being realized from the buying and selling of graphic images of sex. Indeed, the parallels drawn between the two discourses were often this explicit. In a somber cover letter to a special insert of the Report, the *San Jose Mercury* political editor advises that "the prosecutor's case . . . is not suitable reading for young children." [64] Two letters to *Time* magazine cut through the high-toned wash of legalese and forensic defense. The first said, "I never thought it would come to this, my own government actively distributing pornography in the guise of the report from independent counsel Kenneth Starr." The second remarked, "What a rip-off! For all the money Starr has been billing the country, he could have included pictures."[65]

If one defines "porn" as representations of genital sex produced for erotic profit, the case *was* pornographic, even if Clinton's private actions (by definition) were *not* obscene. All Starr's report lacked, as the reader above quipped, were "pictures."[66] Howard Fineman and Mark Hosenball were among the more mild-mannered commentators who, nonetheless, registered how the issue had long ceased being Clinton's tawdry affair(s) and had become a matter of their tawdry management—in the report as well as in the House. Discounting Starr's content entirely, they focused instead on counting pages: "2,800 pages of raunchy 'supporting' documents."[67] In this respect the Report would have done even the obsessive Bateman proud, in its itemization of body parts and cataloging of soiled dresses and cigars. The case was likewise pornographic construed more broadly as a political text. Susan Stewart observes that "the work of pornographic discourse is the work of bureaucracy: the arrangement of bodies in and through social categories; the manipulation and reorganization of such categories themselves."[68] Indeed, Starr's implicit alternations between the modes of evaluation—bodily exegesis on the one hand, and metanarrative explanation on the other, including convoluted discussions about grammar and textual meaning—puts one in mind of the Marquis de Sade's systematic dismantling of social norms via a rigorously pornographic mode.[69]

One of the most interesting "ethnological aspects of pornography," suggests Susan Stewart, is "the invention of the social."[70] And it is in its ideological function of creating the adequate reader that Starr's report is most important. Ann Snitow observes that pornography acts more or less directly to establish the disciplining lines of society: "Pornography is a fantasy of an extreme state in which all social constaints [sic] are overwhelmed by a flood of sexual energy. . . . Class, age, custom—all are deliciously sacrificed, dissolved by sex."[71] Snitow's observation is pertinent to many of the accounts tracked in this study since arguably she defines the content—indeed, function—of media culture. Snitow makes another comment that is appropriate to the Starr Report: "Pornography is not only a reflector of social power imbalances, sexual pathologies, etc. but it is also all those imbalances run riot, run to excess, sometimes explored *ad absurdum,* exploded."[72] The Starr Report, then, was itself demonized as monstrous, an implacable agent of social ill. Nonetheless it must be asked whether the extreme discomfort with the report, and the hyperbolic speech it occasioned, made it possible for commentators to offer up *Starr* as the monster, thereby ignoring the way pornographic excess characterizes popular representational modes more generally.

IV. Hester Prynne, Bill Clinton, and Public Confession

In *Art of Darkness: A Poetics of Gothic,* Anne Williams writes that "charges of obscenity have haunted one strain of Gothic for its entire history."[73] Three things are important to recognize about the staging of civic theater around the Starr Report, and by implication, around Clinton himself. First, the charges of pornography signified offenses *taken* by the viewer (as well as by quondam producers) rather than offenses inherent within actions themselves. Nor in this case was it only readers who took note of the closet pornography; so did those responsible for it. Many of those who had a part in producing the text, on both sides (Starr, House Managers, White House lawyers and aides), constantly found it necessary to apologize for the affront they experienced at the (near)-pornographic quality of the narrative they produced. Representation, not action, was called into question. As observed earlier, one reviewer cited as "most shocking" not Clinton's actions so much as the "the sheer quantity and raw quality of sexual detail" with which the Independent Counsel's report presented Clinton. Obscenity, Justice Potter Stewart remarked, one knows when one sees it. That is, obscenity needs public presentation in order to qualify. Starr thus found himself in a situation comparable to the *felix culpa* argument of sin: moral appraisal demanded experiential content; thus legal adjudication called for a sexual calculus. Thus complicated, Starr's *legal* appraisal of the facts leading to impeachment became a moral one, at the same time implicating Starr in the moral fall it thought to chronicle. Additionally, from a viewer's perspective, it was also clear that moral exposition and closet pornography were only two of many possible interpretive modes made possible by the Starr Report. That is, while his legal purpose was to generate data and facts, by virtue of his moral pedagogy Starr intended the production of shame as well.[74] Nancy Gibbs commented that, indeed, rather than convicting the president of impeachable offenses, Starr's Report only proved his willingness "to humiliate the President" and "horrify the public."[75] In this manner covert aggression of different sorts drove the public demands for repudiation, confession, and moral uplift.

Legal penalty, religious indictment, and public discipline all came together in the traditional mode of Gothic reprisal. Almost in response, many commentators registered their affront in language as purple as the texts they criticized. This had the effect of further evacuating the already thin discourse and further bashing an already burdened language. Starr's report could stand as a monument to excess on any number of grounds, including linguistic. Even in terms of its simple heft, the sheer volume of the Report had the unprecedented effect of slowing down the Web when Congress narrowly authorized its publication. Web aside, however, one observer noted it collapsed other modalities and categories as well, "flooding the circuits of conscience and calculation and taste."[76] Such collapse, fittingly, deserved apocalyptic metaphors. These were plentiful, positioning the collapse of signification as terminal, even cosmic, employing language that derived, ultimately, from religion, even as the subject demeaned and parodied the reference: "And the real sexual Armageddon is yet to come." Though never very specific about what his comment means, Jonathan Alter ends with the suggestion that such a state might result from "paralyzing the country with porn."[77]

Alter's remarks show how the denunciation of pornography and civil malfeasance settle into the cadences of a familiar American discourse, sexual apocalypticism. The denunciation of Clinton's policies had reached high decibels long before Paula Jones or Monica Lewinsky appeared. Nonetheless, Clinton's purported or imagined liaisons with Flowers, Jones, Lewinsky, and possibly others rapidly transformed the ad hoc legal investigation of an individual into civic allegory in which sex became both vehicle as well as meaning. Anyone familiar with either American letters or American politics should have anticipated the collapse. Apocalypticism in general—and sexual apocalypticism in specific—is a mode of American self-address so customary that Hawthorne can assume it as a given for his narrative investigation of a similar case of exemplary sin, theological meaning, and civic governance—*The Scarlet Letter.* In the case of Mr. Clinton, a similar bifurcation can be evidenced. That is, any given act contains within itself often contradictory possibilities of interpretation. Public and private, symbolic and literal, phallus and penis engaged each other—perhaps provoked each other—into scenes of determined outrage in which the very heavens seem called upon as witness. Clinton's public display of his sexual life, however forced upon him it may have been, nonetheless provided the state occasion by which traditionally "private" (perhaps another word would be "silenced") topics erupted into speech in an exhaustive cycle of asking and telling, repudiation and denial. Rendered as scenes within this national theater, Mr. Clinton's intimate moments were retrieved from their privacy by being displayed in the most ideologically public "private space" of the nation, the White House.[78]

This contradictory volubility made for other cognitive dissonance as well. The publication of evidentiary detail provoked on the one hand angry, eroticized disavowal, and, on the other, incendiary repudiation. Following the logic of his excruciating parsing of grammar, Clinton may *not* have perjured himself; however he surely mimicked his "don't ask, don't tell" policies by becoming the chief example of the schizophrenia such policies mandate. Confession followed disclosure, as more and more persons—the subjects of inquisition and the inquisitors themselves—exploited the uncertainty of who knew what when, or who *didn't* know what when, and what they didn't do with what they didn't know. All of this verbal roughhousing was accompanied by denial, hedging, and an obfuscation that descended, finally, as we have seen, to grammatical parsing. So disrupted was the civic map that not even grammar, apparently, could police its own boundaries and meanings.

Throughout Clinton's presidency, his consistent alignment with the gays in the military issue insured, almost fatalistically, that his private affairs would likewise be enacted in a Gothic manner. And so they were; actors with multiple or mutating personalities and differing narrative voices alternated, visibilities of persons and evidence cast long shadows of presumed hidden secrets. In this way the complicated series of public erasures and revisions characteristic of the Clinton/Starr exchange reactivated the uneasy ghost of "don't ask, don't tell," which lurched into public consciousness again. This time, however, it was deployed as scandal, not politics, with the added aspect that bodies in question were measured out in economic erotic zones. Under the wonderfully suggestive heading "They Ask, He Told," Al Kamen's report in the *Washington Post* is worth quoting at length:

> There's little doubt some House trial managers are much put out over sex and the Clinton administration. "You look at what this president's policy has been from day one," Rep. Chris Cannon (R–Utah) told the *Salt Lake Tribune* recently. "The first thing he did was create a debate about homosexuality, by talking about homosexuals in the military." Another of his initial moves was "to hire Jocelyn Elders as his surgeon general. The whole point was to have an advocate for weird alternative lifestyles." [Kamen continues quoting Rep. Cannon] "This administration has had as a policy goal

the public discussion of weird sex," . . . "He didn't fire Jocelyn Elders until after she said some really weird things and said them many times. She talked about self-abuse. Sex when you're alone." Cannon concludes, "despite the administration's focus on 'weird alternative lifestyles' that includes [sic] 'homosexuality' and 'self-abuse' or masturbation, . . . There's no reason for us to talk about it." [79]

Oh, but there is; in American Anglo-Christian discourse, sex is very much a state issue—not so much for the sex itself, but what sex implies, suggests, means about the Social Body more generally. Alan M. Dershowitz mordantly comments that Monica Lewinsky "did want oral sex: she wanted to talk about it." [80] Sex is what a community does together in public, a point Michael Colacurcio makes in his discussion of Hester Prynne and Puritan governance.[81] Let me at this point return to *The Scarlet Letter,* and Colacurcio's discussion of that novel, to see what light that seemingly disconnected text might shed upon Mr. Clinton's public scenes in the stocks. As a vehicle for civic allegory there is indeed plenty of reason to talk about sex—even, as in Hester Prynne's or Bill Clinton's case, when there *isn't* any sex to talk about (both, after all, refused to acknowledge the encounter at issue, although Hester's child and the stained dress gave mute witness to "something"). For reasons too complicated to address here, sex assumes allegorical dimensions in Christian governance, oftentimes becoming state discourse as well as private act. This is especially true in post-Reformation Christianity, where sex becomes a public matter relative both to church and secular control. Sex, Alan Dershowitz bluntly puts it, is "politics and politics is sex, and never the twain shall be parted." [82] For this reason Arthur Miller derides commentators who want to blame a certain conservative view of Clinton's impeachment upon some spurious understanding of the Puritans or Puritanism. "The Puritan tradition, in brief," writes Miller, "is sex." [83]

Indeed, beginning with the colonies, the management of public sex—and intimacy more generally—has been, and continues to be, a much remarked feature in American moral discourse. During the precolonial era, sexual conduct of any (all) sorts was interpreted as a significantly public activity in theocratic settlements. The motions of bodies were not, as they so often seem to be, relegated to a realm of the private. The outward deportment of bodies signaled much about interior movements of the spirit, and so public discourse about public righteousness came to be demonstrated through "movements"—both those of the spirit as well as of the body.[84] John Winthrop, for example, the first governor of the Massachusetts Bay Colony, muses in his journal about the sexual liberties of the Antinomians and how their carnal excesses signified ominous consequences for the corporate body. Hawthorne's *The Scarlet Letter* derives at least in part from Hawthorne's reading of Winthrop and this history. Michael Colacurcio sums up the intertextual—as well as interhistorical—situation in a manner Bill Clinton might find appropriate: "Lust, Winthrop must have felt, he would always have with him. But an outbreak of hermeneutics he had hoped to avoid."[85]

But the hermeneutics are still what sex leaves us, uncontrolled and generative, long after bodies have cooled and stains have dried. It is ingenuous to say, when justifying the extensive, even obsessive pursuit of Clinton's private life, that "times have changed." In some fundamental ways they haven't.[86] Other presidents have hosted the ad hoc sexual advisory session with the occasional special friend, whether in side closets of the White House or elsewhere.[87] Clinton, indeed, learned more from John Kennedy than just charisma, as was made clear in a heated interchange with Donna Shalala. When she told the president that his personal life mattered as much as his policies, he snapped back, "If you were judging on personal behavior and not policies . . . then Richard Nixon should have been elected in 1960, not John Kennedy."[88]

Clinton's mistake, however, was acting like Hester Prynne. His failure was not the presumptive perjury and obstruction of justice for which he was tried; nor even for having sex in public where everyone could *see* it. Rather, he erred by trying to keep the action private, circumscribing its public epistemological function—in short, by obstructing public narrative. I observed earlier that Clinton's penis, although scandalously marked, was itself never precisely the scandal. It was merely the trigger, as it were, used to activate the mechanisms of moral exposition that always idle on the public sidelines. In the manner of point-and-tell theatrics of scandal, the interpretive promiscuity of the Clintonian sexual text signaled a mess of hermeneutics more broadly construed. This unstable civic condition was, in turn, announced as crisis by the verbal promiscuity that accompanied it. Typologically, Clinton's transgression pointed elsewhere to subjects and possibilities otherwise unspoken—subjects that could only be ritually enacted, never directly spoken (the equivalent of Prynne's scarlet A was analogically represented, in this instance, as a spot a little lower down). Chief among these subjects, of course, is the always-vexed status of the sexual body within an epistemology where bodies themselves are ultimately monstrous, sources of ambiguous revelation: marked as sacramental on the one hand and demonized on the other.[89]

John D'Emilio and Estelle B. Freedman observe that "because of its religious, Utopian nature, early New England society . . . [was] based on an ideal of extreme social cohesiveness and the practice of close surveillance of personal morality."[90] Indeed, D'Emilio and Freedman argue that in "Puritan theology, the entire community had responsibility for upholding morality."[91] Thus, in his meditation upon the body under the red letter of law, Hawthorne asks, What happens when Hester, avowed public sinner, wouldn't—indeed, didn't—confess? When Clinton, wouldn't—indeed, didn't—confess? What happens when, despite the asking, there is no telling? Finally, which presents more of a crisis—having unauthorized sex in private, or *not* having it in public?[92] Some falls are more *felix* that others, it appears, especially of the phallic kind. Talking dirty, especially in public, seems to be something of a Christian duty, then, directly useful for supporting civility. Further, duty aside, talking dirty clearly has its pleasures, political purposes, and other social consequences. Former secretary of education William Bennett thus assesses the doubled-sided task facing the moral pornographer: "Civilization depends upon keeping certain things under wraps. . . . There's clearly an underside to human beings. It's a little weird when you start celebrating the worst things in public."[93] But as we have seen, it was the moralists who "howl[ed] after sex" and "pushed titillating material immediately and unthinkingly into the public domain." So, indeed, it *was* the sex, stupid—as everyone said, trying to act appalled and trying not to be titillated. California Democrat Zoe Lofgren is quoted in *Time* as saying, "If you look at the supporting evidence, it's kind of shaky [on obstruction and tampering]. It's really about sex and lying about sex."[94]

Lofgren's point can be focused more sharply, since in fact it wasn't so much the sex—which many conceded was a given—as the lying about the sex. Bennett, after all, *is* right. Civilization does depend upon keeping some things under wraps, which is precisely *why* these things must be positioned in public—in order that they may be *put* under wraps. The agent and the force of the wrapping, here, is the issue, not any given action. That is, the important debate, often submerged in the flurry of dresses and DNA tests, was not about the *ipsa acta* of Clinton as much as it was about how those acts would mean, and to whom, and by whom the discourse of sex would be produced and managed. Who wraps it up, in word, legislation and meaning, and thus, who is given the delicious privilege and terribly stern duty of unwrapping it? Freud and Foucault would both agree, to this extent, with William Bennett, that some version of the repressive hypothesis not only defines the civilizing project but makes the discourse of Christian exemplary morality possible. Finally, one faces the remarkable conclusion that if Clinton had his Gothic side, so, too, did Kenneth Starr. One exhibition of hiding and secrets entailed, perhaps demanded, another. In a particularly Foucauldian moment, Eric Pooley underscores the Chinese-box wrapping, unwrapping, and rewrapping required to manufacture the sex upon which the prosecutorial case depended: "Starr's office had originally planned to confine the seamier material to a secret sex appendix."[95]

So maybe it *wasn't* the sex, stupid—or at least, not Clinton's stupid sex. In the fantasy life of political America, it is arguably the case that a chief political officer is, in twelve-step language, sex-addicted. Yet one could argue to the contrary that it is the public, or at least public discourse, that depends upon fantasies of publicized sex to give itself definition. The scandalizing body is the hagiographic body offered up as visual aid to meditation. Clinton's deviancy, performed in public, permits in a most obvious way a surplus of pornographies—sex for sale, sex for pay, sex on public view. The greeds of many different producers as well as consumers were all excused and exempted, to the degree they were framed as moralities, warnings, minatory social pedagogies. Sex, finally, as prayerful uplift was welcome, even while it was scorned as economic trade. The Clinton papers made possible a range of reading possibilities; in particular they offered verisimilitude physical description as well as emotional excitation—freely available for many whose squeamishness would not let them be seen enjoying pornography more directly, but whose interest in it, by virtue of their moral fixation, is nonetheless necessary. "Sex-police"—Diane Sawyer's perhaps aggressively ironic term for Kenneth Starr—have their hands full, it seems.[96]

Thus the grammatically squinting possibilities that could be detected in various reports actually did intend more, one thinks, than they set out to mean. For instance, as Lynette Clemetson and Pat Wingert write, "The fumbling liaisons chronicled in the independent counsel's report, many therapists say, read like a checklist for sexual compulsion."[97] Indeed they do, but whose compulsion are they evidence of? In *Scandal,* Garment makes something of the same point: "A scandal is created not only by the individual who scandalizes his community but, just as important, by the community that is scandalized when it learns what the miscreant has done."[98] The question remains, Whose addictions are we tracking here, and are they addictions to objects or to fantasies unknown, or fantasies pursued, learned, and perhaps invented? Are they moral, legal or erotic, Gothic? The answer, of course, is yes.

Conclusion

Social categories of the impolite and the unspeakable are all the more persuasive for their silence. When shame is the weapon, little need actually be said. Silence is a provocative power; reticence a powerful tool. Indeed, societies develop categories of the "obscene" not, as seems the case, to eliminate certain forms of representation, but rather to put the "off-stage" in use as a frame to consolidate the "on-stage" gaze. The maintenance of "prurience" as a category of social shame requires, then, the invention of the ob-scene. In her classic work on the subject, Lynn Hunt observes that early texts prosecuted for obscenity were politically motivated attacks against Charles II rather than directly sexual texts.[99] She further notes that through the early modern period obscenity was articulated as a category of *offense*—created by those who simultaneously were trying to repress it: "The police knew what they were looking for. Like the librarians, the police clearly had their own lists, lists which resembled, indeed shaped, those of the librarians."[100]

Similar conditions governed the transfixing of Bill Clinton in a discursive space cross-hatched with conflicting mechanisms of interrogation and repression. Often enough these were authorized within a conventional religious narrative of exemplary display. That is, political revelation, readerly satisfaction, and moral moment were all mutually served by some anticipated culmination—a body, in motion yet caught in stasis, available for various interpretive strategies, readerly investments, legal conclusions. Such a moment was unreachable, of course, and attempts to achieve it only dramatized its ephemeral quality. The readerly leer in January—when Bill Clinton publicly non-confessed, "I did not have sex with *that* woman"— became a cringe by October, when we knew more than we ever thought possible about either *that* woman or *that* man. The continuing display of the suffering body (scenes of Monica traveling internationally, selling her book and, still later, advertising for a weight loss clinic) created distance rather than intimacy. In either direction the Gothic was not far away, as a mode of containment for the distress to civic ideological security.[101]

Moral reading, like its sometimes twin, the pornographic, depends upon a set of common epistemological presumptions, and both share a common narrative impulse.[102] Clinton's intimacy could only be revealed *as* scandalous within an system of representation where the pursuit of "truth" presumes bodies that are appropriately docile to the surveilling gaze. These, in turn, are registered as "obscene" *to the extent* that they make moral evaluation possible. The legal epistemology, then, that removed the "stained dress" from a category of "laundry" and inserted it into testimony, moves incrementally but insistently toward a *fantasy* of "the real"—one however that approaches but never attains its goal. In the geometry of representations, the nearer one approached the certainty in question, the further certainty receded. The insistence on a putative magic moment in which symbol and symbolized confirm each other at every point—rather in the manner of theologians seeking the Real Presence—evidenced the illusoriness of representation rather than its stability. We have seen the result: legal grammars gave way to expositions of dismay, shock, disbelief, and panic speech.

Matching, sometimes competing vocabularies of the pornographic and moralistic circulated tighter and tighter around Clinton. Both reached for some culminating moment, either by which the stained dress would confess the body it represented, or that language would confess a moral moment of closure. In either apocalyptic scenario, narrative would run out. It would be the end of words. Neither happened, of course. As Garment ruefully observes, "by law, the independent counsel cannot shut up."[103] Neither of course can, or will, scandal, whose systems are always poised, ready to pre-announce the next scandal. Similar observations can be made about the ultimacies sought in the parallel worlds of the pornographic or the monstrous: There is never enough closure to anticipate. No definitive money shot will provide satisfactory evidence of real pleasure, just as no evidence will effectively convict of actual illegality.[104] Monstrous bodies enable interpretation, not legibility; no one reading will completely enunciate the monstrous body, not even Bill Clinton's. Patrick Bateman provides insight here, perhaps anticipating the gentle reader, musing over the scandal in private at home—Bateman, as he thinks ahead to his next brutal date, wondering about whether he should be using a different brand of skin cream. After the end of words, there are still more secrets to anticipate, more bodies to violate—and any particular one is merely transitional, "the segue from the previous narrative, extricat[ing] the public eye from the previous keyhole."[105]

In the desire for an end, for a revelation that would in fact be final, Starr's obsession with stains ("filthy facts and secret acts") connives with evangelical discourse and cultural habit of augury. What drives Starr, son of a preacher, is a fairly conventional form of crypto-religion dressed in the moral vestments of scandal. The political energy this makes possible finds its implicit justification in divine judgment, even as judgment shames us with the full knowledge of original sin.[106] Apocalypse, no longer merely narrative trope, becomes instead an accomplished fact. The Clinton saga was a morality play that got away from itself, becoming an exemplary por-nographic/Gothic recitative, fulminated against and decried, and, ironi-cally, as popular as a previous dry and dusty tome, the Meese Commission Report on Pornography.[107] Finally, it is worthwhile noting how Starr could be said, legitimately, to be aligned with a very real form of pornography. His insistence on tracking the ins and outs of Clinton's organ gave it a representational allure not unlike that other discourse's insistence in liter-alizing *its* body parts—except of course that pornography (even Meese's) so often makes shows of monstrosities, outsized bodies and parts, rather than, as in Starr's case, making shows of monsters.[108]

With age-old warrant, and even in contemporary practice, "extra-ordinary bodies" become, as Rosemary Thomson observes, visible markers of social grade: "the extraordinary body is fundamental to the narratives by which we make sense of ourselves and our world. . . . By its very pres-ence, the exceptional body seems to compel explanation, inspire represen-tation, and incite regulation."[109] This is the individual body allegorically etched over by social imperative and taboo, inscribed in a language of re-ligious intentionality. Pornography and sentimental moralism constitute reading populations as well as technologies. Yet something odd happens to these extraordinary bodies as they are rendered into civic learning. Whether physically or morally anomalous, they are rendered into equally extraordinary discourse, characterized by linguistic silence and melodra-matic display. Silence is "strategic form, not an absence, of representa-tion."[110] In that silence lie the mechanisms of the Gothic, which while augmenting the work of scandal, nonetheless *undercut* its epistemological zeal, in that it gives the last word to silence and to the showy, Gothic non-sense of the monster. To announce Clinton as a "monster"—Gingrich should have known—vitiates the need for any trial whatsoever.

There is a showy quality about the moral exercise of scandal; yet the show finally separates off from a production of speech that is formally guar-anteed to fail. The disjunction between the unspeakable and its clear visual appeal becomes apparent in the narrative codes of excess, and in the energy for sheer exposition and unveiling the conflict provokes, independent of political or social affiliation. *Time* magazine's collapse into metaphors of cinema and fiction in their reports about Cunanan, or their high-minded commentary criticizing Kenneth Starr—both reflect the limits to which representation can go. In this manner an eruption of the monstrous is signaled not by scandalous image but by the containment—or rather the curtailment—of speech: the verbal collapses in the glare of spectacle; words fail, the visual drowns out the sound of sense. This unavailability to language is significant for a complex set of reasons. First, of course, is the ironic fact of the densely *verbal* quality of the scandal, the seemingly endless production of words; this reflects the fear that in fact there are *not enough* words, or, implicitly, that words are *not enough.* The procedures of scandal, then, critiques the moral valuation of *language*—despite their overuse, establishing words as less credible than "seeing." What you see, in other words, is "what you get." In addition, the inaccessibility to language marks the event (or person) under question as existing somewhere off the moral map in other ways, as well. Medieval maps demarcated the alien by leaving it nameless, and thus, voiceless, appropriately consigned to edges and outer boundaries: "This way monsters lie" is one way of saying evaluative tools do not exist. Thus, as a final consequence, the refusal of speech reinforces the alignment with alienness—the enduring reason why we make monsters, in the first place.

The movements of "slick willy" Clinton's body were ambiguous to the end, and in the Senate resolution nothing was resolved, even though an end was civilly agreed upon—for the time being. Starr's office, however, would remain hard at work, since there were other venues for crimes to be vetted. Clinton's monstrosity had been evacuated in exhaustion. This, too, is what, or how, the monstrous body means. These are the questions held hostage in the declamations of scandal and shock. It is not that categories of civility—reality, pornography, morality—are clear and self-evident, but that they are never completely so. *The moral map does not, in fact, have a clear edge at which to locate the monster.* The monster of the day (Clinton, or . . . ?) is not so much found as gestured at.[111] It is because the monster cannot be fixed that attempts will be repeatedly made to fix it, to capture it in a narrative that never changes, and maybe never ends. This is why, to paraphrase P. T. Barnum, no one ever went broke underestimating the complex public uses of fear, nor the complex delights of retailing perversity in public places—a point to which I shall turn in the next chapter.[112]

The monster appears as the public display of all secret, and at times illegitimate, yearnings. There are no desires, shameful or innocent, that one's progeny does not publicly disclose.

Marie-Hélène Huet, *The Monstrous Imagination,* 17

Perfect enemies are a scarce commodity in today's world.

Economist (3 January 1998): 82

Something in the news production process was creating the crime wave. What was it?

Mark Fishman, *Manufacturing the News,* 5

CHAPTER SIX

DEATH BY NARRATIVE

Introduction

It is time to ask directly the question this study has implied throughout. Why does one make a monster? In order to watch it die, of course. The civic rubric of making monsters—like scandal, whose exemplary form it resembles—is a social mechanism regularly employed to deal with social crises whose real causes are, for one reason or another, not available to speech or to direct action. The success of such policies, however, is haphazard, like swinging a large bat at a fly on a window. More than just a "victim" suffers in the periodic moral cleansings, and in the pogroms and vigilante actions mounted "for the good of the people."[1] Indeed, those who are deemed monstrous, whether for reason of legal offense or social inadequacy, have as much to lose from these politics of repudiation as do the more obvious victims of crime and mayhem.

In *Natural History* (A.D. 77), Pliny catalogued the monstrous races— i.e., those exotic types like the dog-headed or the Ethiope, whose exceptional appearance marked them as foreign, alien, non-Roman. Even today a similar urgent need to separate out the abnormal (and thus, implicitly, the unnational) continues unabated. In its American variants, confirming the boundaries of the social map drives the denunciatory machinery by which the nonconforming person is staked as (name one) failed mother, baby killer, pedophile, fallen priest, black beast, religious fanatic, AIDS carrier. The mixed metaphors circulate like cogs in a finely oiled machine, sometimes working in resolute defiance of fact.[2] In each case the use of fear both simplifies and coerces, while the rhetoric distances the user from responsibility for what the language intends. As fear circulates within the narrative economy of prejudice, it distills problematic situations to already-known conclusions. Conversation and argument becomes, instead, chant and litany. As John Leo observes, the "media framing" behind such tactics can be so strong that it "can ward off even a sturdy set of actual facts."[3]

Further, the subjects of the monster hunt are as varied as communal or national need permits: communists, fifth columnists, and hominterns in the fifties; or later, Anita Bryant and the hidden threat of the homosexual (retroactively dramatized in the lives of Dahmer, Cunanan, and whomever else could be found). Recent candidates and causes include Susan Smith and the fraying of marriage (from inside as well as without); or Willie Horton, Tawana Brawley, and the Gothic fantasy of American racial purity; or O. J. Simpson—whose fantasized media representation collapses, for many, racial as well as domestic nightmare.[4] In each case, presumptive civic failure relies upon a fine sense of balance, as sentimental formulas are used to outline in stark contrast formulas of the horrific and appalling.[5] Susan Smith, as we have seen, was called a "baby-killing bitch";[6] she was also called a "suicidal zombie."[7] Even so, cast as a horror story, her life was also scripted, in an exquisite example of imaginative splitting, to defend a romance called Family Values. In the rite of monster-staking, formula answers formula. Banal answers the bane. From either direction, Gothic politics secures the ideological boundaries of "the American Creed."[8]

One needn't ask, then, where fantasy goes in a culture which dismisses it except as entertainment or political putdown (remember Anita Hill?). The answer is clear: Fantasy goes public, sentimentally, horribly, in the political last word called Democracy. The cartooning of national debate is the result, in which monster-talk ends up plundering the public till of the "already represented." Conservative and liberal alike reach into the cluttered cupboards of social denunciation, where they find ready to hand Gothic bromide. What results is a nationalist Realpolitik that is derived from prejudice, film, and genre formula. Whether about family safety, immigrants, civil rights, or gun control, "Manichean fantasies"[9] luridly announce a cluster of familiar, even threadbare anxieties. Where media meets movie, representation becomes little more than propaganda, although the collapse of these into each other is seldom addressed.[10]

Lionel Dahmer remarked that his son, Jeffrey, "was not born a monster. . . . He is not a monster."[11] To put the matter bluntly, the first part of Mr. Dahmer's statement is true, the second, false. The Jeffrey Dahmer who was arrested for a series of ritual murders in Milwaukee was not yet the "monster" bludgeoned to death in a prison bathroom (an aside: He is always *Jeffrey* Dahmer, never Mr. Dahmer—to succeed, the story needs this intimacy). Between Dahmer's arrest, his incarceration as Inmate 177252 and conviction on multiple counts of murder, and his death in the Columbia Correctional Institution, narrative intervened—a storyline useful precisely because it authorizes such "mandates" as Dahmer's death. Why? Although surely extralegal, Jeff's death did not lack its social uses. Dahmer was killed in prison, where he was serving a 999-year state-mandated prison sentence. Nonetheless, imprisonment was not enough; Dahmer still needed to die—his death clearly more for our comfort than his good.

Timothy McVeigh's mother echoed Lionel Dahmer. Weeping, she testified at her son's trial: "He is not the monster he has been portrayed as." [12] Nor was Mrs. McVeigh employing hyperbole. A biography would shortly be released awarding her son the title "All-American Monster." [13] In a third case, a boy caught up in an apparently consensual, intimate relationship with a teacher reported in court, "I have come to believe that she is a monster that has terrorized me and my family." [14] A fourth instance involves James R. Porter—an inactive priest accused of multiple counts of child molestation dating back thirty years. After sitting in a courtroom through hours of vituperation in which victims and their families called for his stoning, castration, and exile, Porter stood up and read from a previously written statement in which he gravely accepted another charge—this one a nonlegal but equally terminal judgment: "Every time I look in the mirror, my mind makes me see the monster I was." [15] The student's comment, as well as the priest's confession, show evidences of the extortion common to both. The tenth grader's convoluted verbs mark the constraint he is under to tell the tale in the manner his society will accept—whatever the truth of the incident may be. Like Porter, although from an opposing perspective, the boy becomes a token in the always-problematic interaction, in modern sentimental culture, between the child and the adult.

Why make a monster? Making monsters is a social process of persuasion, a confirmation of the normal contours of daily life for those who, from time to time, need persuading. Those assigned the role of monster—such as Timothy McVeigh, the tenth grade teacher, Bill Clinton, Susan Smith, or James Porter—teach us who we are and how we are to live. Their bodies, offered for ritual exorcism as it were, in the last reel, demonstrate the inventive, and casually approved, violences that follow upon a failure to abide by the civic norm. [16]

I. The Monster Story

—and this is a controversy built for the age of O. J., in which law, politics
and entertainment merge into one cable-ready obsession.

Howard Fineman, "The Counterattack,"
Newsweek (9 February 1998): 12–13

Reflecting upon the trial of Susan Smith, Blanche McCrary Boyd observed
that "we value narrative intelligence, we understand best through stories."[17] Garry Wills makes a similar point about a president: "Reagan's
achievement at home was largely rhetorical, his use of the bully Presidential pulpit." Noting that "Reagan's view of the past was largely shaped by
the movies he saw or made," Wills concludes that "Reagan was a great
communicator because he was a great storyteller."[18] Still, what needs to be
questioned is the ethics of the storytelling act—the consequences such
rhetoric has on individual lives, no matter where, pulpit or podium, it
originates. What effect, for example, did Reagan's storytelling have on
American foreign policy? Or less augustly, perhaps, and more currently,
what effects do metaphor have upon Timothy McVeigh or that tenth
grader's teacher? Or upon Willie Horton or Susan Smith? Or on Andrew
Cunanan, or even Bill Clinton? Or upon James Porter, delicately described
by one woman as "a sick, bad priest"?[19] In the case of the tenth-grade
teacher, someone familiar with the facts observed, speaking metaphorically, one assumes, that "it was like a Brecht play, only people died." In
Dahmer's case, there was no "like" or "as if" about it. Someone *did* die.
Nor can Dahmer be dismissed as the victim of a sloppily administered justice. To the extent that each of these persons functioned as a symbol of
reprisal and desire in a larger scene of national fantasy, each of them was
impressed into narrative in order to provide memorable sound bytes. Media urgency would have us believe that indeed the numbers of monsters are
legion, and everywhere gaining upon us. At the same time it is clear that
any individual monster—including those cited in this study—is made to
be forgotten; witness the canned discourse that obliterates them as quickly
as it makes them. Herein lies the contradiction; the transgression that is
so uniquely fascinating, monstrous, and worthy of press must also be (or
become) formula—banal, endlessly repeatable, and completely conventional—in order for it to be "read."[20]

How is such competent readership accomplished? The monster story
has, essentially, four points of emphasis: the monster must be exciting; the
monster must be frightening; the monster comes from nowhere and rav-

ages what culture most values (or, at least, *says* it values). Finally, the monster must die (and it cannot be my—or our—fault).[21] The compactness of the narrative is largely a reason for its continued success. Whether it poses as a documentary or as a glance into "real" life, monster-telling is a fiction with the grammar of a prejudice. Monsters or monstrous persons hardly ever need to be *proven,* in the same way that what they are accused of doing may or may not be true. For the narrative to work, the monster merely needs to be *identified,* pointed out, gossiped about. Put more pragmatically, every society needs a person (or group of persons) who live at the boundaries of social maps. Aliens on the social landscape, they can be pointed to as living beyond the social pact. As Joseph Grixti notes, "the process of ascribing [deviancy]" is neither "innocent [n]or ambiguous."[22] To the contrary, monsters are chosen with deliberation for quite specific social tasks. As Michael Levenson writes, "in learning how a community chooses its freaks and invents its deviants we construct a photographic negative of its social life."[23]

Persons on the margins of civil life, whose only safety is hiding in social crevices, are important largely because they demonstrate *the symbolic nature of the pact itself.* Sometimes such refugees are political aliens, made so by law. At other times they are alienized through a complex system of reprisal, social indifference, and narrative foreclosure. Often the failure with which they are charged will be underscored by means of their physical appearance, although abnormality, difference, exoticism of visual appearance are usually read into a different realm entirely. We can hear energy of distance and reprisal drummed up around human failure at all levels of society. For example, in *Shadow in the Land,* William Dannemeyer offers an exclusionary vision of a homosexual-free culture; but his praise of a Judeo-Christian tradition (with little of either) sounds as if it had been lifted straight from the audio portion of a cheaply made splatter film.[24] Or consider the professional baseball player whose comments about life in New York sound like H. P. Lovecraft's racial jeremiad about that city.[25] As these instances confirm, it is important to note that it takes at least two to Gothicize— one to use the discourse and the other to agree. That is, those who make monsters—Dannemeyer, Lovecraft, or the ballplayer—collude with those who *need* monsters. Both parties demonstrate the fundamental instability of the term "monster," but in addition they underscore the frailty of the other category, as well. Neither monster nor human is definitionally pure; each will fail all attempts to cage or categorize it. What passes as normal, always, is in the eye of the fearful beholder—whether that anxious eye is Pliny's, or Dannemeyer's, Lovecraft's, or the ballplayer's.

In *The Formation of a Persecuting Society,* R. I. Moore explores how violence came to be "deliberately sanctioned *through established governmental, judicial, and ecclesiastical institutions,* against groups of people defined by general characteristics such as race, religion, or way of life."[26] While accurate enough, as in many studies of this sort, Moore exculpates the usual delivery system of this violence. That is, he pays little attention to the discursive means by which language and metaphor create the ideological world in which brutality is accepted as good social manners—indeed, as action deemed appropriate to the state. Billy Jack Gaither, a gay man, was beaten and burned to death. His killer, however, was dismissed by someone who knew him as a "bully," someone who "was mostly talk."[27] The dismissal is important, since it is an explicit denial that language has any "real" effect whatsoever—despite the graphic evidence of the brutal death. To dismiss the agent ("all talk") is, likewise, to erase the action as well as any consequences accruing to it. The monster story works because of the totalizing energy it releases. Locating evil in one site makes its eventual elimination that much simpler. Such a strategy apparently supplied the ideological energy behind *Time*'s cover of Milosevic during the early stages of the 1999 Balkan crisis;[28] his picture, target cross-hairs drawn in, was (conveniently) accompanied by explanatory text: "The Face of Evil." One need look no further than this cover, or perhaps the one of the Littleton boys, a few months earlier ("The Monsters Next Door"), to see how fantasy becomes polemic, and how horror pulp become "news."[29] The political usefulness of the monster—demonstrated, in this case, by either of these two *Time* covers—is a result of the spell its narrative casts long after the telling is done. This is narrative's ideological residue—the emotional investment confirmed, if you will, even after the excitement has been forgotten. One might define prejudice, then, as the sense of conviction left by the formal presentation of story, irrespective of its content.

Genres, literary formulas as well as conventions of readerly response, come together seamlessly in these productions. Bird and Dardenne argue "that the totality of news as an enduring symbolic system 'teaches' audiences more than any of its component parts."[30] That is, narrative logic shapes "reality" by providing the script in which events cohere (or are patterned) into meaning. Thus, as *Time* and its countless knockoffs chew over the day's news, seeming to report the world, in fact they shape a world that they are under some economic duress to report.[31] Indeed, middle-range media of this sort, whether print, visual or audio, depends upon keeping their readership detached from too-close questioning. Their profitability insists upon keeping readers from observing the discourse at work.

A moment's reflection, then, will show that news is as much fiction as fact, and often a peculiar type of national fantasy. Like any narrative, news is constructed from a fund of literary motifs and shaped by the constraints of a point of view.[32] In this way it is perhaps inevitable that news narrative sometimes slips its accustomed moorings—at least that which grounds viewer investment—when the *reliability* of news (every night, six P.M.) is mistaken for its factuality. More cynically the news becomes, in David Sonenschein's formulation, a "branch of the entertainment world," or what Noam Chomsky dismisses as "necessary illusions" specifically tailored to the fantasy called democratic governance.[33]

Consider, for a moment, two very different sources of a rhetoric that is quite common. What is the political significance of—for example— Stephen King's use of horror motifs or narrative patterns and Patrick Buchanan's use of similar materials? Jeffrey Cohen argues that it "matters little" whether horror stories appear "in the *New York Times* news section or Stephen King's latest novel."[34] Buchanan's "moral politics" tilt toward one end of the political spectrum, while Stephen King's Maine liberality would seem to push him very far in another direction.[35] Nonetheless, the genre within which the latter works has a different gravity entirely, as King himself is aware. The horror genre, he writes, is as "conservative as an Illinois Republican in a three-piece suit"; and "within [its] framework . . . we find a moral code so strong it would make a Puritan smile."[36] For this reason one must have a fine eye to separate King from Buchanan. The "brimstone rhetoric" of Buchanan parallels in effect, and sometimes in political intention, same or similar materials used by King. For example, the categories that signify as traumatic in Buchanan's populist apocalypticism, examples of which clog his stump speeches—racial fear, gender collapse, national weakness, and foreign invasion—likewise motivate King's best work (e.g., *'Salem's Lot, The Shining,* or most apocalyptically, *The Stand*).[37]

King and Buchanan consider themselves to be guardians of the social body. King cheerfully admits to being a stealth policeman, an "agent of the norm." "The writer of horror fiction is," King observes, "an agent of the status quo."[38] Clearly, then, there is overlap between what King and Buchanan do. Because of the conservatism of the genre, authors who work in it might just as well be Buchanan operatives. Howard Fineman writes that Buchanan hoped to win the 1996 election by "preaching to fears no one else has the courage to name, sounding fire bells for the loss of the America in which he was reared. His views can be extreme, his language incendiary. But America is listening, and not entirely in horror." Buchanan, Fineman concludes, is "the GOP establishment's collective night-mare."[39] King might very well be a Buchanan agent, under fictional cover; nonetheless the reverse is also possible. Fineman's remarks about Buchanan could equally serve as a review for one of King's astonishingly successful novels. Alan Brinkley observes that Buchanan's starting point is "a heavy dose of homophobia, xenophobia, . . . ethnic and racial prejudice, anti-feminism and hints of antisemitism."[40] All of these "isms" might be dis-missed—and often are—as fatuous rantings. Arguably, however, they carry ancient authority as the *lingua Gothic* of American nationalist dis-course, whose political needs are not always distinguishable from its fan-tasies. One has only to recall the flap caused by the subliminal use of "RATS" in a Republican campaign advertisement for the 2000 presidential election to understand why Lovecraft's "Rats in the Walls" is so potent a story.[41] One can conclude that politicians and novelists often cover the same territory, and sometimes are doing the same work. For example, King's fiction, a nightly news broadcast, and Buchanan's presidential cam-paign employ similar techniques of persuasion, delighting in gory images of depredation, drawing from a common fund of monstrous rhetoric, trope, and image. The mutual antagonism among these three on the social register, however, perhaps keeps readers and viewers from attending too closely to the similarity of their materials.

Further, whether the source is news, fiction or speech, genre distinc-tions are often overlooked, or worse, dismissed. Good citizens-in-the-making, we assent to the reigning cultural lie that horror narrative and terror text are tawdry and beneath our attention (although sales records of horror video and terror tabloid do not support that conclusion). Probably motivated by a similar culture-wide denial, little attention is paid to the daily round of fear that organizes, perhaps orchestrates, our shared civic life, and which has done so as long as journalism has existed.[42] Thus, as a matter of custom we prefer our monsters "straight"—that is, as the Nightly News—rather than in the dubious form presented to us by the doyennes of gore and the masters of fright—Wesley Craven, King, and Buchanan. Nonetheless it passes without observation that indeed we do need these perfect enemies. In the evening news, after all, we have Rather's magisterial permission to traffic in monsters and so we treat the narrative he tells with respect. Yet for all his dignity and his cardigans, Dan Rather, like Buchanan, knows that the more lurid his presentation, the higher his ratings will be. Fear—whose use is discounted and whose effects upon us are dismissed—becomes our daily dread.

II. Sticks and Stones

Our politics, religion, news, athletics, education and commerce have been
transformed into congenial adjuncts of show business.
             Neil Postman, *Amusing Ourselves to Death,* 3–4

One might reasonably respond that "sticks and stones may break my
bones, but words will never hurt me"; that name-calling, however wicked,
is just words. This is of course not true, as anyone who has been verbally
brutalized will attest.[43] One might further argue that invective is *merely*
metaphorical and so not a speech act that requires answer, and that all intelligent readers know the difference between categories of the real and the
imaginary. Given the evidence, this is not wholly convincing. Invective is
not just intoned, not just a ritually empty sound. Like all discourse it carries powers of convincement that depend not only upon words, but upon
other factors as well. As Patricia O'Connor observes, whether prejudicial
narrative, propaganda or daily speech, "utterances . . . can be actions."
Indeed, language is sometimes "itself a violation."[44] Some of the consequences of this rhetoric are more obvious than others. As much as news or
a Gothic novel, "hate speech" depends for its credence upon the audience
commonality it intends and creates. Indeed, the discourse creates the conditions by which such commonality becomes possible.[45] Further, not only
does monster-talk create audience familiarity, its narrative impulse moves
to a particularly intimate, and violent, closure: "each [unchallenged accu-
sation] becomes a tacit validation, a passive approval of a lie."[46] In this way
monster-talk enacts sanctioned violence, although in such a patterned way
that it is not obvious. At the same time, such talk distances the speaking
agent from any of the more remote effects of speech. As Esther Madriz
argues, "A direct consequence of the dehumanized images" is that they
"restrict any type of public empathy toward those who break the law."[47]
Yet as we have seen, the restriction of empathy obtains, also, for many who
are innocent of lawbreaking—for those whose only fault is to have been
in the wrong place at the right time.

   A genre once confined to movies and cheap cinema passes into daily
intercourse, weaving into formula comfort daily anxieties of life, in public
settings as well as private. To take one example, the orgy of death visited
upon oversexed adolescents in *Halloween* meets its political equivalent in a
fantasy different in degree rather than in kind, when Russia is made over as
"that Evil Empire."[48] As we have seen, *Time* magazine racializes one cover

while, in another, locating Milosevic for the reader's comfort as evil, complete with trigger-lines conveniently drawn in.[49] It sometimes is hard to tell, then, whether the fantasy in play is cinematic or political in origin; in either case it exploits an expected commonality of response, often directly, or indirectly, violent. Monster-talk is a convenient break from thinking, a pause that refreshes. It admits no answer, as Jesse Helms knows with his ritual denunciation of homosexuals, or as George Bush knows with his remark about "that devil Saddam."[50] Defining someone as monstrous—homosexuals, Saddam, or the boys next door—provides a usual, conveniently extralegal, method of *social* repudiation. Reader and speaker alike use the language, hear the allusion; the banal metaphor circulates in daily speech and passes as newsworthy fact. Dahmer, we are told, is "a monster"; Willie Horton is "the bogeyman."[51] Reader and speaker alike *may* know that these phrases are "only" a manner of speech, but somehow this fact slips quickly out of awareness.

In this way figures more proper to Gothic cinema and cartoon (monsters, bogeymen, and the like) or churchy Gothic demonic (talk of devils and demons) do double duty as political ethics; they condense a stew of modern hate from a mixture of genres, modes of public presentation, religious and secular rites of identity and social cohesion. Meanwhile the instability of metaphor itself—and the complex histories of these words (monster, demon, etc.)—slip away behind the brute and ignorant force of their misuse in "fear mongering." Only when a Matt Shepard is tied to a fence, beaten senseless and left to die in freezing weather—only then do we consider how persons suffer the consequences of failed language. As the Latin reminds us, real people suffer (*sub-ferro,* to bear up under) the deathful consequences of bad language that becomes worse law. In Laramie, Wyoming, it was "just words"—specifically, his assailants fear of *a* word—that cost Matthew Shepard his life.

One place where Gothic metaphor is least expected—although incrementally present—is the arena of justice, courts, and the law. As any number of cases tried in the media reflect (including most of the ones cited in this study), monsters enter the most hallowed places quite easily. How? They do so unremarked, by virtue of their utter banality. That is, monsters achieve entry into even the most secure sites by means of the already-heard cadences of formula Gothic. For this weapon no security system exists. All narrative has a tremendous power of convincement. Words convey a sense of their own *reality,* even if not, necessarily, a sense of their own truth. This fact can pass for objectivity: *this* (what the words say) is how it *really* happened. However, some texts build in a further level of certitude, less by virtue of words used than by the authority of their context. Judicial transcripts and legal documents are of this sort. The "avowedly factual" matters that engage them seem, on the surface, to be so resistant to formula and so immune to the wiles of fantasy.[52] This, of course, is the rationale and selling point for *TV vérité*. Judge Judy is *really* Judge Judy and justice, it seems, is transparently *there,* on our TV screen, in fifteen-minute increments. A similar naive sense of presence governs an Arts and Entertainment network's documentary on Edmund Kemper, although the camera angles, scene cuts, and music employed in the production of the documentary demonstrably borrow from the Gothic. Despite that fact, the fabrication of the materials slips away in the power of their presentation; one thinks that here the anonymous actor playing Kemper (often it is the audience who occupies Kemper's viewpoint) is *really* Kemper and justice, likewise, is transparent. In the courtroom the forensic implications of the least detail are considered crucial to the juridical outcome. How is it, then, that the complicated act of weaving the tale *for* judicial review is rarely considered as important? When the monster enters the courtroom unannounced and passes as evidence, what has happened? Is it any less tainted than the glove that probably torpedoed a celebrity trial in Los Angeles?

Peter Brooks writes, "Conviction in the legal sense results from the conviction created in those who judge the story."[53] The problem here, as I have been arguing, is twofold. In the first place, as Liz McMillen writes, "Trial lawyers . . . try to tell the story that a jury is most likely to believe."[54] This is a delicate way of saying that a jurist is most likely to give credence to what he or she already *knows*.[55] And what she or he knows *already* is the sum of public presumption on the subject, narratively dispensed and so never recognized *as* the obvious prejudice it is. In the second place, as Boyd observes about the trial of Susan Smith, "The law, like other forms of storytelling, imposes structure on the chaos of experience, assigns meaning and responsibility."[56] The structure of law, however, moves to a different *form* of conclusion than does fiction. A legal trial is neither cumulative, nor *does* it conclude, in the narrative sense of the word. Rather, legal judgment admits ambiguity and lack of closure. Indeed, this is what *judgment* signifies—an intervention, codified by law, formally intervenes to conclude an otherwise ambiguous situation. Further, as I have tried to show, the storylines into which Susan Smith et al. are rendered have at best a symbolic function; they constitute an allegory or moral algebra into which are factored supposed correspondences. However, rarely are the terms precise, or even nearly equivalent.[57] Judgments have already been made, which anticipate as well as inform subsequent legal ones.

The difference between these systems of judgment can be seen in the sentencing of James Porter, cited earlier. Porter ritually submitted his person to the court, but in so doing, he submitted to narrative as well, when he acknowledged that he saw "the monster [he] was." His formal abjection before the crowd can be misunderstood as Porter's acceptance of legal guilt. However, Porter's remark did *not* affirm the court's legal verdict, nor was it intended to. Neither was the abasement an ethical coda to a legal structure. Indeed, Porter himself probably intended his statement as having other than legal significance. Instead, he offered narrative closure to a literary system (genre) that long before had hijacked the legal apparatus of his prosecution. For reasons known only to himself, Porter offered his person to the extralegal, Gothic denunciation that attended his sentencing. Why should he have done so? Whether he had ever thought about his situation in these terms, Porter was doubtlessly familiar with the way narratives of monsters *must* conclude. Porter's trial was no longer about *his* personal guilt, and surely he realized this fact. In a culture so overinvested in sexualized scenes of adults and children, something else was at stake, in that wonderfully pungent Gothic expression. For this reason Porter endured the heated energy of the crowd, listening stoically to their incantatory calls for castration, stoning, and exile. What else could he do, as the monster? A verdict of guilty or innocent would not have affected that judgment.

In sum, the examples of Porter, Smith, and Simpson, McVeigh and Dahmer demonstrate that it makes little sense to sequester jurors and snip their newspapers, when the tainted rhetoric from which jurors are protected slips into court via the official record. The rhetoric of monsters, a higher law, enters the courthouse unchallenged; no one notices—except, perhaps Porter, and others like him, who hear the death sentence intended in the rhetoric long before the court's verdict. Pressed into the one-size-fits-all role, these have most to lose in this diminution of language. The fundamental literalism of the discourse enabled the prosecuting attorney to present Smith's guilt in terms that the jury would understand. Susan Smith's trial proceeded as it did because the "pop situation required polarization: If Smith, who killed her children, was not a victim, she must be a monster."[58] Such a clearly defined choice between narrative modes works by means of a dense, although elegant simplicity. Depending upon the initial selection, the conclusion is already in sight. One commentator can thus knowingly observe that that the jury didn't give her the death penalty because they "concluded that she was a mom, not a monster."[59]

III. Cuts, Shots, the Live Feed: Dahmer or ABC?

The monster's eradication functions as an exorcism and, when retold and promulgated, as a catechism.

Cohen, "Monster Culture," 18

Genre familiarity underwrites the extensive newspaper coverage of the monster du jour. A representational history of treating women as over-sexed—or undersexed—made it possible to cast Susan Smith, failed mother, as a witch. In similar fashion, *Time's* cover of O. J. Simpson, in which a mug shot of Simpson was silently darkened, likewise profits from a tedious history of American fright-mongering. Indeed, such manipulation of genre makes such fright-fretting continuously plausible.[60] Like lynching, to which it can be compared, invective sanctions a readjustment of social roles, often in actions too violent for laws to support. Invective, however, depends upon resources other than language for its full effect. The surround-sound slippage of Jeffrey Dahmer into the fictional *Silence of the Lambs,* in particular, is a very good example of how fiction, a pervasive cultural discourse of fear, and the comforting fantasy of legal justice reinforce each other's claims.[61] After Dahmer's arrest, there was a sense that we *knew* this man with an intensity seldom accorded our friends. In truth, we *did* know Jeffrey Dahmer better than our friends. Dahmer became the fiction that had preceded him—the serial-killer bogey in the social imagination of the time, surely, but more specifically, Dahmer was scripted into the filmic version that had *preceded* Dahmer's arrest. *People* magazine immediately drew the connection, noting within days of Dahmer's arrest that Dahmer "eerily recalled" *The Silence of the Lambs.*[62] With stunning speed, categorical distinctions among cinema, legal process, and media representation collapsed.[63] Jonathan Demme's film of Thomas Harris's popular novel had been released a few months before Dahmer's arrest. A month *after* Dahmer's arrest, and following *People's* lead, Geraldo opens his show with "It's a Real-Life *Silence of the Lambs.*"[64] Thus, a predigested version of Dahmer's life immediately provided retrospective confirmation of a film that itself depended upon a further history of representation. From another direction, the film's sinuous "replay" (of events that happened *after* it), undoubtedly became a factor in the film's success at the Oscars. It was, after all, so "real life." This stroked the entertainment industry's sense of embattled cultural inadequacy; for once it could say was describing culture's violence, not anticipating (or creating) it.

Similar categorical collapse is evident elsewhere in the newspaper, magazine, and journal display of Dahmer—an examination of which would be a study in itself.[65] For instance, after Dahmer's arrest, an editorial in the *Atlanta Journal-Constitution* opens by asking—rhetorically one supposes—"How does a city cope with playing host to absolute evil?" The editorial muses that "cities wind up . . . at center stage in a real-life horror show"—referring to Milwaukee's unenvied position in the "macabre tale of Jeffrey Dahmer."[66] Here again one notices the epistemological anxiety that pervades the media representations. One must dismiss Gothic narrative as "macabre tale" and "horror show," while at the same time making the metaphors of that formula heuristically central to a civic "reading" of Dahmer. Dahmer's life is a horror show, readers are told, but nonetheless the show is "real." The conclusion which follows from this is the fact that Dahmer might be *any one of us.* For this reason what he does is of deeply conflicted interest to us.[67] Media coverage of Dahmer opted for horror and grotesquery rather than for the erotic titillation reflected in Andrew Cunanan's coverage. Nonetheless, both narrative cycles banked upon similar readerly investments in eliciting desire only to have it capped again by fear.

One can conclude, further, that the more emphatic the insistence upon "real life" the more probable the use of Gothic presentational effect. On April 18, 1993, *Day One* reenacted a montage of moments from Dahmer's "confession." Forrest Sawyer, speaking for ABC News, gravely assures viewers that "Dahmer's voice and those of the police officers" are spoken by actors, but the words are "exactly" what [Dahmer] wrote. Thus, supremely in the thrall of the fantasy of the word, viewers slip from hearing the "exact" words to judging these words to be "true." Throughout the show, meanwhile, Dahmer's "exact" words accumulate a residue of Gothic effect by camera work, scene and music manipulation. Dahmer's doubleness and moral duplicity is repeatedly emphasized both by verbal cues as well as by contextual ones. He is "seemingly normal" one day, while the next he is capable of "some of the most unspeakable crimes imaginable." He is said to change personalities in a "hideous, monstrous way." Throughout the documentary work-up a naive verisimilitude is supported by a cheaply approximate Gothic formula. More accurately, formula *becomes* as close an approximation of exact description as one gets. The "facts" of the case—largely imported on the basis of prior narrative expectations—provide the rationale for retelling Dahmer's story in terms of the film that had preceded it. The consequences of this have already been addressed. In a post-televisual mode of reality, fact appears less convincing than the fiction made of these facts. This, however, is a useful reminder that fictions *aim to convince*—reason enough for Plato to ban the poets and makers of fictions from his Republic; their presence was potentially disturbing to the civic order.[68]

Turning for a moment from the production of such fictions to the consumption of them, we see a similar misdirection at work. The Gothic reading process reproduces itself in a reader who rises to the occasion, as it were. Take, for example, the *Day One* program cited above. "One important note," solemnly intones the announcer, "this broadcast is not appropriate viewing for children."[69] Such a warning, however, is customary fare for those familiar with the Gothic's convoluted reading process, and thus it heightens, rather than decreases, viewerly interest.[70] One hardly considers it a sign of genuine readerly concern. However, tipped off with this cue, the audience can set in place the genre expectations appropriate to life in the Gothic Zone. Tracy Edwards, the first interviewee, further does important work. He sets the stage for the ensuing quasi-supernatural drama of captivity and escape by linking Dahmer—not to the psychosis of Demme's killer—but to something rather different this time. Edwards links Dahmer to the demonic—or at least to a cinematic, ultimately silly version of it: Dahmer acted "like he was wanting to be the character in [*The Exorcist*]." Of course, ABC judiciously edits this comment in because Edwards helps viewers place themselves in the appropriate subjectivity. Indeed, which character in the film is not specified, nor is it really important. The genre cue is the important consideration. This is similar, of course, to the way that a headline like "Southern Gothic on Trial"[71] functions; it doesn't so much *inform* our reading of Susan Smith as *direct* it.

The viewer, attending to this tale of Dahmer, may not be completely aware of the long foreground of knowing *about* Dahmer even if the name is new to her or him. That is, slight alterations must be made, perhaps, to fit Dahmer to the storyline that precedes him. We *have* heard Dahmer's narrative before—maybe not exactly in this form, but close enough. Or, more to the point, we must work to alter Dahmer to fit his life to the existing plot line, if the moralized narrative is to "ring" true. Indeed, this work is how ideology prepares the ideal viewer or reader, who can only "hear" stories with which they are familiar. For similar reasons *People* magazine must make an incoherent paragraph about Dahmer more nonsensical by stating very seriously that Dahmer "was fascinated by horror movies such as *Friday the 13th* and *A Nightmare on Elm Street*."[72] The points of ideological purchase here are many, and submerged. Listening to such a comment, one could challenge the house of cards upon which it is based by saying, So? According to sales statistics, *millions* of people enjoy these films. Nonetheless they do not feel compelled to reenact them. This is why, too, one account of Timothy McVeigh must make the observation that "he found inspiration in the 'Star Wars' movies and thought he was up against the 'evil empire.'"[73] The reader is constantly massaged into ideological submission by these, or equivalent, Gothic echoes. The narratives are designed to profit from our prior, often implied, assent to narrative habits and formulas we already know. Narratives arranged according to unfamiliar conventions recede from focus. Such "prehearing" prepares us to accept the pulp reading of Tracy Edwards. Viewers inwardly nod and thank Edwards for making the proper connection for us, as we thereby assent to his conclusion that Dahmer wanted "to be the character in the movie." Yes, that is how it is. Dahmer, flawed human being, drops out of discussion while another creature, beyond good and evil entirely, enters.

The ideologies sedimented in horror metaphors, like those of other genres, *produce* the legitimacy of the representations they portray while confirming the illegitimacy of those they repudiate. Thus, however horrible Dahmer's or McVeigh's actions might be, dealing with them as if they were creatures from late-night fright TV is neither ethically sound nor intellectually promising. Persons of sophistication can shake their heads in agreement when referring to Dahmer as a "monster," or when reading the "unauthorized" biography of McVeigh, or when Bush drapes Saddam in Gothic drag. This only underscores the extent to which made-for-movie emotions govern political processes that are ostensibly rational and ethical. Pressing Jeffrey Dahmer—or Timothy McVeigh, or Fr. Porter, or the leader of Iraq, or any others we might care to mention—into the role of horror-show "monster" is a rhetorical bait and switch. It speaks less about these individuals than about a society's need to protect itself from the fault lines opened up by monstrosity.

IV. The Master's Voice: Civics 101

How then do we talk about these things? What sorts of formal requirements should exist for the monitoring of a language that borders, in so many ways, upon the incoherence and silence of non-speech? Maybe that question would develop into other ones; for instance, what does a rage-inspired McVeigh *mean* given the vigilante ideology of American nationalism? Or how shall we interpret Kevorkian's slightly adolescent pose as the angel of comforting death? Or the cost of Smith's romantic *triste* to her children? In each of these scenes, a not-so-subtle Gothic exposition precedes, and makes possible, the coherent public face of the presenting melo-dramas, while effectively forestalling intelligent, ethical, or *moral* political conversation about the instigating occasions themselves. One wonders, further, does the mode of politics itself foreclose the possibility of ethical discourse? Persons chosen as representative monsters enable the accustomed cultural blink—the "don't ask, don't tell" squint at the open secret, plainly in sight but deprived of speech. For example, insert McVeigh, Kevorkian, and the questions of the preceding few paragraphs into the frame of an apparently different cultural fantasy entirely. Place this obsession with death—for it is that—into the mutually reinforcing network of idealized talk, polemic, and emotional attitudes defined as the "argument" of "pro-life."[74] To designate Susan Smith as the "baby-killer" situates her between the politics of choice on the one hand and its sentimental counterpart on the other. In both directions, however, the vocabulary is so unstable that at a moment's notice it can reverse, even undo itself. By the look-alike ethics thus established, formula constructions are wrenched from tabloids into equally leaden politics. However, the direction of slippage goes from politics to tabloids, as well: this looks like a little baby, and so it is; this doesn't look human, so it is a monster. The ease with which such textual incompetency empowers even the most privileged cultural observer should make us uneasy. "Jury found McVeigh didn't act like a human."[75] The submerged implication grounding a headline like that is, I think, inexcusable, because it is so clearly a lie with pernicious consequences. If McVeigh *weren't* human he wouldn't be in court in the first place. Although they may sell newspapers, monsters are not accountable in courts of law. Nor, as Fr. Porter demonstrates, do they have much security there, either.

Throughout this discussion, the danger is thinking that only persons of illiberal or meanly conservative persuasions use speech so laced with metaphorical non sequitur. However, the language of the monster is rhetorically available to all. It is a mode of address that is kin to the touted "common sense" that enables even high-minded speakers to say some very stupid things.[76] One journalist—"liberal" and clearly sympathetic to Matthew Shepard—writes, "It is precisely from such rhetoric [homophobic intolerance and hate speech] that monsters like the two 20-somethings accused of killing Matthew Shepard are born."[77] Here the stake is reversed, and the weapon skewers the person who wields it. That is, from anywhere within ideology, human bodies—those of homo-haters as well as the homos themselves—become monstrously etched. Sometimes this happens in literal ways; Adam Colton, a San Marin High School student, was beaten unconscious because he was gay. Unlike Matthew Shepard, however, Colton survived. When he regained consciousness, he found "Fag" carved into his forearm and abdomen.[78] Death was slow in coming for Matthew; terror will spend a lifetime with the other student.

Public ethics are only as resilient as the civic imagination that make them possible. In other words, appreciation of the true, the good, and the beautiful is constrained by the flexibility of the common language—or, conversely, by its enervation, a point made by George Steiner's eloquent *Language and Silence.* Neil Postman makes a similar observation when he says the "clearest way to see through a culture is to attend to its tools for conversation."[79] Plato of course argues that those who live in shadows have only shadowy knowledge of the real. Similarly, those who live only in metaphor suffer the tyranny of its misdirection.[80] In *Evil and the Demonic,* Paul Oppenheimer terms it an "ancient intuition, that an evil ambition must produce a linguistic straining, creaking, and collapse."[81] It was with this insight in mind that James Whale edited Boris Karloff's voice out of *Frankenstein* (1931).[82] Film directors can undercut human sympathy in other ways, too—for example, by controlling camera angle, as happens in *The Exorcist,* when the sympathetic girl-victim Regan is transformed into appalling spectacle by the clever use of a closed door and long hallway. Similar erasures are made possible by the requirements of civic speech. Silence, in the intricate and baroque forms in which it manifests itself, makes for powerful speech. Shepard was not a "monster," despite the Web pages and church groups that pronounced him such. Nor, however, were the men who savagely beat him to death. Timothy McVeigh is not a monster, either. Sadly enough, these individuals, with some changes, are only us—human, with all the disarray and formlessness implied by that word. Indeed, if monsters confirm anything, it is the terrible social burden of human individuality—what Karl Marx calls the work of wresting a moment of freedom from the jaws of grim necessity.

Why is it important to remember that "monster," or its equivalents, is an inappropriate term for those convicted of civil offense? For one thing, celluloid monsters are beyond the reach of law or any sophisticated morality. How many courts of law or judge's chambers does one find in horror films? I would bet few to none. Human beings, however, *are* remanded to courts and subjected to the closures of justice. These are often flawed and ambiguous, much less satisfying than narrative closure. If we wish to see actions like McVeigh's adjudicated in law, and justice done to the memory of those killed by his actions, then we cannot let him be dissolved into a monster. "We must do better than McVeigh," argues Kevin Acers (Oklahoma City Chapter, Amnesty International).[83] Why should we want to?

McVeigh's vigilante action against the Murrah Federal Building was made possible by *his* habit of making monsters—a habit of genre simplicity which enabled him to take matters of discontent into his own hands. He, too, fell for the spell which would later spell out his death. The monster story provides a narratively acceptable conclusion that avoids the mess of legal precision (and thus diffuseness). Indeed, monstrosity shares with prejudice a preemptive narrative lock in which powerful emotions receive telegraphic condensation. This is *why* specific individuals are named as monstrous—precisely to facilitate an extralegal closure that by all odds will be more satisfying than that permitted in law: The monster must die, yet it can never be the fault of those who want him or her dead. Rather than showing the richness of human discourse, the rhetorics, tactics, and formal grammars of monstrosity signal only its enervation.[84]

Conclusion

Horror fans know how determinedly simple-minded fright films can be. But films must be formulaic, since the cinematic monster's aim is comfort—albeit a peculiar one—rather than distress. The same can be said for the monsters in the daily news. The first rule of the comfortable is that it be familiar, intimate, even uncanny—with all the disturbing intimations of things, oddly enough, "too close" for comfort. The mechanism driving these films—and that which informs the rhetoric on the streets, as well—is, then, very simple. The monster must be found and staked. He must be *positioned,* finally, in order that he may be eliminated. In this way the community (the audience who pays for catharsis) must be released from the monster's complex power, its mix of fear, repudiation, and unacknowledged pleasure.

Yet the anxiety of monsters is more deeply linked to cultural obsessions than celluloid fantasies alone suggest. That is, despite all efforts to insure the monster's eccentricity and alienness by robbing it of voice and beauty, nonetheless, angel-like, the monster compels us to look homeward. There, in the common and the ordinary, on our streets and in our schools, celluloid fantasy wraps flesh around the fearful and the taboo of everyday life. As the one who (presumably) bears desires and energies deemed abnormal and unnatural, the monster defines the normal and the law-abiding.[85] By making a show of the conventionally awful the monsters of film imperceptibly nudge us into acceptable form(ula)s of the nice and normal: Elm Street, without the Nightmare. Whatever *else* they may be, then, the monsters among us are ciphers of anxiety. Not unlike the phantom limb, missing but still present, monsters signal lack as well as memory of that lack. They are representations of cultural trauma, but often as not they *are* the trauma themselves. What monsters intend is *who* we are to be—always anticipating guilt, yet somehow still innocent. In other words, the monster story is rarely about the monster, and usually not at all about his or her innocence.[86] Indeed, *who* the monster is of little interest; anyone can play the role, as an unnamed person played Shelley's creature onstage, and as Karloff was erased from *Frankenstein,* hidden beneath silence and mounds of special effects. A rather more interesting question is what sorts of social work does the identification, pursuit, and staking of the monster make possible?

Gothic speech is a rhetoric, but it is, as surely, also a rubric—a prompt to action that makes violence passable, even plausible. As such, monster-talk offers instructions for performance, justifying emotions, feelings, actions that otherwise remain under civil erasure. As a rubric, monster talk *incites* public displays of emotion, while, in the manner of a laser, narrowly directing them. Interviewing John Rocker, who was "shooting outrageously from the lip," the interviewer John Pearlman takes note of the ballplayer's "killing-spree scowl" and his "Manson-like feelings."[87] The transition from documentary interview to Gothic is casual and ordinary. However, it is also counterintuitive to the accustomed way in which violent language is studiously cordoned off from "real violence." By adapting Rocker's emotional energy to a vocabulary and cadence dismissed as antique, mythic, or "literary," the ritual of monster-staking *directs* his unacceptable excesses of violence and passion towards customary social ends. Out of sight, in this process, awaits the political conclusions to which these excesses move, and justify. For example, calling Dracula a vampire is an internally coherent speech act, so far as it goes. But to call *Dahmer* a vampire is *not* so coherent. In fact it signals a category collapse that, to borrow a pungent word from Margaret Atwood's *Handmaid's Tale,* permits a "particicution." We can all join in the execution of the monster.

Such linguistic promiscuity is surely responsible for the inevitability of Dahmer's death. On November 28, 1994, a fellow inmate attacked Dahmer in a prison bathroom, killing him and another prisoner. My earlier proposition—*the monster must be staked*—underscores the poignancy of Christopher J. Scarver's attack on the two men in the Columbia Correctional Institution in Portage, Wisconsin. Dahmer had been incarcerated in a maximum-security prison; care had been taken there to keep him safely under observation—presumably to prevent such vigilante action. This care was warranted; Dahmer had survived a similar attack a few months earlier. Despite these precautions, one guesses that the *ad hoc* justice of Dahmer's death (and that of fellow prisoner Jesse Anderson) was not underwritten by legal authority. Nonetheless, it probably wasn't much lamented, either.[88] The monster must die, so goes the narrative, but it cannot be my fault. If sentimental politics locates the burden of responsibility on individuals, Gothic politics, to the contrary, indirectly exculpates whole communities of blame, by justifying violence as necessary response to the monster's threat. *Newsday* writes, "Authorities said that because he is in custody, they are not rushing to bring charges against Scarver."[89] "So you do, so you get," the grandmother of one of Dahmer's victims said. Criminologist Jack Levin was quoted as saying that Dahmer "really wanted to die . . . in a sense, other inmates gave him the death penalty."[90]

From a variety of perspectives—Granny's homespun fatalism to the academic's odd and ultimately conservative bromide—Scarver's murderous act is exonerated. The act is given social sanction—legally, personally, and even linguistically.[91] A brutal bathroom killing becomes a matter of balancing scales, buried death wish, or indirect death penalty—administered, it would seem, by others who will one day suffer state-sponsored death themselves. Afterward, the Milwaukee District Attorney who prosecuted the case remarked: "I hope there will be no economic returns for the man that killed Jeffrey Dahmer."[92] McCann underscores my point that Dahmer's death, while itself illegal, was not necessarily lacking in social value. Care had been taken to isolate Dahmer and others in the prison house of language as monsters. As such, even in solitary confinement they were beyond any need for human courtesy or decency. Finally, in death Dahmer still suffered textual violence: "The Cannibal with a penchant for dark meat is dead."[93] The Gothic choreography of Dahmer's life prepares readers, narratively, to accept without murmur his death, and even to applaud it.

Anyone who thought about Dahmer's prospects knew what would befall him in prison. Indeed, one of the calculated points of monster rhetoric is to *prevent* such thinking from beginning. With similar considerations in mind Susan Smith is being held in isolation at the Women's Correctional Institution in Columbia, South Carolina, where she has "no contact with other inmates" and is under special twenty-four-hour guard.[94] One prison authority suggests why: "Baby killers are not popular in women's prisons."[95] Similar observations were made about McVeigh's safety when he received the death penalty. Capital punishment, said one writer, was clearly preferable to what awaited him in prison: "Do [McVeigh's parents] want their misguided son to suffer the fate of a Jeffrey Dahmer?"[96] Of course,

McVeigh *has* already suffered that fate; neither he nor Dahmer needed a court to find them guilty. Indeed, as the "All-American Monster," Mc-Veigh was evidently scripted as Dahmer's replacement.

Dahmer's death in prison was a sanctioned conclusion to a complex public drama. Like the litany of similar prison violences to notorious criminals, Dahmer's death was narratively determined, and its gruesome conclusion conceded, long before Dahmer's legal imprisonment. Why? Because the storyline dictates that the monster *must* die, and it *can never be* our fault. One headline after Dahmer's death read, "Jeffrey Dahmer is dead and we feel fine . . . Don't We?"[97] Dahmer meets his death in prison at the hands of another prisoner, armed with a broom and, he said, a mandate from God. Framing Dahmer as some creature from a bad pulp film—as, indeed, a "monster"—excuses us from complicity. We are unburdened but innocent. His demise enables *us* to rest in peace as well, since the monster *is* dead—but not at our hands, and besides, that's what monsters are for. Twitchell puts it pungently: "Monsters in popular culture must be violent enough to mandate still more violence against themselves."[98] A condensed example of the prejudicial punch at work can be found in the case of Richard Allen Davis, confessed killer of 12-year-old Polly Klaas. Says Marc Klaas, her father, "This guy is a monster. . . . If I had a gun, I would have put a bullet in the back of his head."[99] Monsters are both example and occasion. They confirm the rest of us in our normalcy, while the occasions of their deaths provide outlets, in various ways, for the times we likewise might be monstrous.

From ancient times the metaphor of the monster has existed as a shorthand narrative, a "confirmation of social prejudice through the stereotypes that are made to carry the necessary menace."[100] Thus, whether mounted against witches, heretics, backsliders, and recusants by Pope Innocent VIII in *Malleus Maleficarum* (1486); or against Jews and sodomites in Germany; or, against the Red menace in the late forties; or, less remote in time, against all things genderly-confused by Patrick Buchanan at the 1992 Republican National Convention, "the function of the monstrous," as Barbara Creed writes, "remains the same—to bring about an encounter between the symbolic order and that which threatens its stability."[101] Creed's statement is accurate enough, although it can be slightly emended. The *effect* of the monstrous is, in addition, to *permit,* even to orchestrate, a destabilizing encounter that confirms rather than subverts the symbolic order. So while the personalities change, the rituals of repudiation perdure. They remain constant and formulaic, insuring two very important social functions—first, the commonality of audience reception, and second, closely aligned with this, the economic profit derived from the titillating display of those who offend us.

Monsters are themselves exemplars as well as consequences. They demonstrate what we shall be if—or when—we fail to keep up our end of the performance of sociality. What performance? That by which we convince *ourselves,* day by day, moment by moment, that we are human—a "we," not "THEM." The concern, of course, is less the monster than ourselves. "We watch to be reassured that people who kill babies and who attack homosexuals are monsters, not at all like you and me. Included in this calculus, however, is the need to face the fear that in some basic ways they are *exactly* like you and me." [102] The more general narrative played out by the monster's life and death is that of civility—how to be good (mother, neighbor, citizen)—and what happens when one is not. Monsters show us what happens (to them, certainly, and possibly to us as well) when civility fails, when the line is crossed. The ancient words tell us true: they are *monere,* and *monstrare*—warnings and demonstrations—"signs and Portents." [103]

There is a final reason why monsters are welcome. They are socially purgative, mechanisms for stress release, judiciously available violence, upon need and upon request. Being good citizens is, after all, hard work. On occasion we need to drop our guard and indulge a little in the transgressions otherwise forbidden to us. After all, this is what monsters do that compels our fury; we, in turn, can go and do likewise. Monsters, by the violence they arouse, permit us an answering violence, one to which, in the prompting cause, we can give justificatory cover. The monster is dead, but not by our hands; long live the monster, who is so very like us, after all.

Ein jeder Engel ist schrecklich.

Rilke, First Duino Elegy [1]

. . . monsters proved themselves serviceable Christ-substitutes.

David Skal *The Monster Show,* 313

. . . lo! See, above the rest,
a monster to behold,
Proceding from a Christian brest,
to[o] monstrous to be tolde . . .

Cited in Dudley Wilson, *Signs and Portents,* 43

. . . the offense to Christian values . . . [2]

Candice Hughes, "Pope Denounces Gay Pride Parade,"
AP Online, 7 July 2000

CHAPTER SEVEN

SACRED MONSTER: MATTHEW SHEPARD

Introduction

In my initial meditation upon angels, I suggested that the decline of visible Christianity in secular cultures has not meant a diminishment in its power to persuade—rather to the contrary. The passing of creedal obligation has left in place a secular habit of consensus and a common civic vocabulary, often embodied nondiscursively in gestures, assimilated rites, and evocative religious images.[3] The effects of this persuasion are all the more powerful passing as they do unnoticed or forgotten. Taking one instance, the Gothic is a genre whose language and rubrics, as well as investment in fear, borrow extensively from religious aesthetics and hagiography's "grammar of sacred wounds."[4] Indeed, such religious echoes vibrate through secular space more generally. For example, there is a particular religious marker whose dire significance is insistent, provocative, but generally misunderstood— the Christian symbol of the cross. Representations of Jesus' brutal death, for believers, stands as sign of reproof against all who would challenge it— human, demonic, worldly, and otherworldly. However, as a religious memorial the cross has a profoundly ambiguous history, signifying first scandal and opprobrium, and later, power and victory. According to Roman law, death by cross was *mors supplicium,* the highest or "utmost" punishment, one reserved for outcasts and especially heinous crimes.[5] Nonetheless, despite its association with criminality, humiliation, and abasement, for many the cross signifies ultimate triumph over evil: in this sign, conquer—or so Constantine interpreted a dream on the eve of his battle against Maxentius in A.D. 312. On the strength of the dream, Constantine swept to victory, changing the course of Christian, as well as Roman, history.[6] Cinematic horror often parodies Constantine, perhaps unwittingly. That is, in many pulp films, crossed twigs (or its equivalent) thrust in the monster's face provide the *deus ex hex* by which the monster is vanquished and civility restored.

But we needn't go to the movies to see the hex in operation. A version of this scene also plays in American politics, as monsters, hexes, and the triumphant cross come together in a moment of political apocalypse. In the New Right's outraged war against all things anti-family, -nation and -civilization, the authority of Jesus, crucified and triumphant, is held out as potent augury against forces of evil. Drawing upon the eschatological energy of the millennium's end, evangelical Christians turned their attention to reformation—focusing not so much on themselves as upon the world in which they lived. For these groups, one "archenemy"[7] in particular exemplifies the forces of Satan and civil distress. The resulting scene of conflict could only be called *Gothic vérité:* The suffering, broken body of Jesus, whose blood is piously read as atonement, is poised in rebuke against the stigma-bearing body of the demonized homosexual, whose blood, Gothically read, signals private immorality, public domestic threat, and world-ending civic collapse.

This powerful clash of symbols could be seen at the funeral of a young man who was killed, most observers conclude, because his assailants thought he was gay.[8] On the evening of October 6, 1998, a diminutive freshman at the University of Wyoming was tied to a fence and struck eighteen times in the head with a .357 Magnum pistol. He was then abandoned, still tied and conscious, in freezing weather.[9] The assailants took Matthew Shepard's wallet and his shoes—the latter, one wrote, to insure that "he would have a hard time getting away."[10] There was little danger of that, however. Some twelve to eighteen hours later, Shepard's brutalized body was found strapped "scare-crow like" to a split-rail fence, suffering from severe head injuries, hypothermia, and possible cigarette burns on his arms.[11] After lingering five days in a coma, Matthew Shepard died in Poudre Valley Hospital, Fort Collins, Colorado.

Shepard's vicious beating, and his prolonged dying, could be discounted as merely one of many such incidents, common though regrettable, across the gun-pocked, violence-scarred landscape of American social life. At the very least it epitomizes an anxiety of identity common enough in vigilante America—reprisals directed at persons who differ in sometimes insignificant ways.[12] In Shepard's case the differences were slight; his killers were his age, also male, also white. However, Matthew and assailants alike were soon lost to the Wagnerian opera of guilt and sentimental fury that surged around them. Numerous groups hastened to claim Shepard's brutal death for their own purposes. Two, in particular, deserve note. Outside the church in which Shepard's funeral was being conducted, a group of mourners (many, although not all, homosexuals) clad in white robes and calling themselves "Angel Action," used large wings made of sheets to block a congregation of Baptists. These latter stood across the street, protesting Matthew's homosexuality—and his funeral—by chanted slogans and waved signs. Some of the signs read "FAG MATT in HELL";[13] "GOD HATES FAGS"; "FAGS DIE—GOD LAUGHS"; "No tears for queers."[14]

What looks like de more civic politics, although aggravated, was not what it seemed. Or rather, the confrontation staged over a gay man's funeral signified something else other than lack of taste. It is not enough to say that the contrast between angelic homosexuals and demonizing Christians merely reverses an accustomed shootout in which Christians are the good guys (angels) and homos are the bad (demons). To the contrary, in the engagement of demon and angel one sees a tense split within the heart of Christianity threatening, at whatever cost, to reconcile. At issue is the recognition, however dim, that the angel and the demon, the prayerful and depraved, mirror each other in ways more similar than different. It is historically the case that aesthetic as well as literary discourses of the sublime—the holy as well as the horrible—share a common fount of images and metaphors, and even prompt similar emotional responses.[15] Indeed, as Julia Kristeva declares, the power of horror is precisely its unacknowledged relation to the sacred.[16] Thus it is not surprising to find an incestuous link between the discourses, or to see that their agents can exchange faces, even roles, as happened at Laramie. Sometimes the images blend into each other; monsters—the fags—become angels, while the sentimentally angelic Christians bring news of a certainly dreadful kind.

Other transformations occurred, too, as Matthew lay dying. David Skal remarks that "monsters proved themselves serviceable Christ-substitutes."[17] So indeed, they did in Wyoming, where Matthew, the homosexual, was transfigured as Christ. This was a problematic makeover, however, as we shall see. The exchange asks us to understand, in Skal's expression, just how the monster is a Christ-substitute. In a context much wider than Shepard's death, how does the homosexual—historically bearer of stigma—provide legitimacy to and underwrite Christian doctrine? To understand these questions we need to revisit the very beginning of the Christian era. In the first place we have a religion born in stigma and offense, whose doctrinal basis (the Incarnation) proposes a hybrid blending of two persons—Divine and human—in Jesus. This doctrine has been regularly perceived (by theologians and philosophers alike) to be monstrous and, in its literal sense, logically incredible. An early formula enjoined belief in Christ precisely on such grounds: *Credo quare incredible est*. Throughout its history, Christian apologetics has struggled to accommodate not only the stigma associated with Jesus of Nazareth but, in addition, the incoherency *demanded* by its fundamental belief in the nature of the God-man. Such perceptions still exist, of course. Only recently, for instance, Garry Wills observed that the "idea of the Incarnation may be monstrous."[18] John Updike, an astute theologian in his own right, thus echoes an observation as old as St. Paul and as recent as Kierkegaard when he writes, "Orthodox doctrine bridges matter and spirit with a scandalous Incarnation, Jesus Christ."[19] More fundamentally, the scandal remains even when one turns from theological abstraction to the actual life of Jesus. According to the scriptures, Jesus' short life was marked continuously by scandal, beginning with his shame-filled birth out of wedlock in a stable and ending with the ignominious death of a criminal.[20]

Scandal, monstrous, offense: These words have deep Christian resonance.[21] Jesus' criminal death was a scandal to early believers. In *A Marginal Jew,* John Meier notes that "in Roman eyes, Jesus died the ghastly death of slaves and rebels; in Jewish eyes he fell under the stricture of Deut. 21:23: 'The one hanged [on a tree] is accursed by God. To both groups Jesus' trial and execution made him marginal in a terrifying and disgusting way.'"[22] The ironic offensiveness of Shepard's funeral, then, was due to the way it recalled the primary offense *of* Christianity—that is, Christ's problematic presence, even his often scandalizing body. Building upon this point, representations of Jesus—in life as well as in death, in pain as well as in resurrection—have explicit parallels to the homosexual body symbolically arrayed against it. Indeed, the visibility of both depends, to a large extent, upon the discourse of trauma and scandal which each typifies.

The stigma created by the interlocking legal and social taboo surrounding the homosexual body (symbolic as well as actual), extends an ironic tribute to the original scandal of Jesus—whose *sacred* body is likewise characterized by monstrosity, offense, and riddled with pain.[23] Both are bearers of social opprobrium. One is the bearer of a criminality generally overlooked; the other carries a criminality never forgotten. This was the potential reconciliation made possible, in a dreadfully literal manner, by Matthew Shepard's dead body. The holy and the horrible—in Christian discourse the authority of Christ's redemptive body and its abjected counterpart, the demonized homosexual—set out to scorn and repudiate the other. Instead, each brought the other to closure. Homosexuality marks a site of rupture in institutional Christian discourse, where its repressive energy is most pronounced. The return of this repressed energy was made visible in the uncompromising starkness of Matthew's death—especially as it was collapsed into a primal religious scene of abjection, the crucifixion. This confusion of sign and memory reawakens some longstanding moments of crisis in Christianity—anxieties that center on the nature of God, the meaning of Jesus' death, and ultimately the nature and scope of the sacred. Surveying the standoff at the funeral, one asks, Which is the monster and which is the hex—the angelic homosexual or the demonic Christian? Where does the scandal lie, in the homosexual, or in Christ? On the cross or in the violence done in the name of the cross? How, finally, is Matthew, homosexual (and thus, to many, monstrous), a bearer of sacred memory?

I. The Heretic and the Saint

"You need to be saved, that's what you need," one woman told a Gay man. "You're going straight to hell, all of you. . . . God's word is that you be put to death."

Washington Blade (26 March 1993): 8

While Shepard's death collapsed Gothic demonizing and religious discourse, an incident some years earlier had tried desperately to separate the two. In 1992, a noisy group marched outside the Arlington County Library to protest its decision to carry the *Washington Blade,* a gay and lesbian weekly. This fundamentalist Christian group carried signs and placards, one of which read, "Save my child from the sexual monster."[24] The provocative doubleness of this word should be obvious by now, although it was unrecognized at the time by the marchers. Indeed, the sign-carrying Christians would be scandalized—offended in the word's deepest sense—to discover that monsters are their born-again kin. For despite its cartoon dress, in its linguistic histories as well as in material practices, the monster functions as a *metaphysical* signifier. Carrying an authority from somewhere outside and beyond the normal maps of civil life, it is an omen or remonstrance that all is not well with the community. This is an obvious though forgotten reason why in formula horror, as noted, the cross—also such a signifier—is ultimate antidote to the monster's depredations. *In hoc signo vinces:* the odd homeopathy of horror in which awe-fullness vanquishes the awful. The repressed returns, simultaneously, as rupture as well as seal.

Nonetheless, observing the scene outside the library, one could also ask, How is it that street politics in a vigilantly detheologized culture could use such a word without anyone noticing its theological echoes?

For the marchers outside the library and the Christian protesters at Shepard's funeral, the alienating charge of monstrosity was intended not to *link* the homosexual to religion but in the name of Christ's authority to disavow it. Nonetheless, the attempt to cast it away only made evident how tightly the two are entwined. In a discussion of *Stoker's Dracula,* Francis Ford Coppola observes that Dracula's repudiation of Christianity proves that "the highest angel can turn into the most base devil by a simple act of renouncement." [25] In *Civilization and Its Discontents,* Freud puts a similar insight into slightly different words and context. Freud explored the psychic dynamics of repression, showing how projection gives rise to the "narcissism of minor difference." The aggression that results is, for a complicated mix of reasons, an enduring feature of the Christian worldview. A need to draw lines and separate out, to exclude and disassociate, is central to its rubrical, doctrinal, and institutional habits. Reviewing Elaine Pagel's *Satan,* for example, the millenarian scholar Norman Cohn writes that Pagel "has demonstrated . . . how ancient the demonizing tradition in Christianity is." [26] In *The Formation of a Persecuting Society,* R. I. Moore likewise observes that heretics and saints share the same bureaucratic and moral universes. Persecutor and persecuted are each complicit, sometimes willingly, in the other's designs.

To the extent that the marchers in Arlington County remained unaware of the history of the word "monster," the rebuke they intended for the homosexual missed its target. The same can be said for those who remade Matthew into Christ, exploiting religious imagery for a mix of private altruism and political gain. That is, what the marchers (as well as the liberal observers of the funeral) forgot is that the power of the word "monster" is not unlike the metonymic magic of the cross in Gothic lore; both in fact derive from a common source. That is, the monster's age-old function as an omen of transcendent judgment upon the community underscores the crucifixion's status, likewise, as *the monstra* of divine judgment. The hybrid God-man is thus monstrous in meaning as well as in category, both the ultimate monstrous body and monstrous demonstration. One can see how the logic of these metonymic identifications complicates any reading of Matthew Shepard as Christ; in other words, as Christ, Matthew becomes a different kind of *monstrum,* he is "something out of the ordinary; something that would cause one to point," [27] a remonstrance of a different order entirely. He becomes a bearer of grace as well as an agent of dread.

Representations of the cross, however simplified or attenuated, are never univocal in meaning. Whether the cross or crucifix appears as backdrop (for example, on an old grave in the opening scenes of *Frankenstein*), or hangs over the altar in a Christian church, or is taken to the streets in a protest march; in any of these instances the cross (and the power it represents) is no longer private preserve to believers. One can argue that since Constantine's Edict of Milan (A.D. 313), the hegemony intended by this Christian emblem can neither be contained within religious discourse nor held to a specific meaning. To the contrary, the cross is a transcultural image dense with conflict, pilloried as oppressive by as many who would applaud it. Sedimented in often contradictory forms of secular governance, it serves as many functions in Western culture as there are people to wear it, pray to it, institutionalize it, mock it, and, of course, sell it. Its meaning is as multiple and ambiguous today as it was to Paul and other apologists for the new faith.[28]

The iconography of the cross—for the most part, safely ignored today—retells an offense deeply scandalous to the Jewish nation of the first century A.D. Jewish religious law forbade capital punishment, and even St. Paul was aware of the degrading significance of the cross as *mors turpissima crucis*—the most abject of deaths.[29] In the first place, to a Jew, crucifixion represented a tainted death at the hands of a colonizing state. To preach Jesus' death in this way was, Paul knew, a stumbling block, a scandal.[30] Managing that task became, as Nigel Spivey explains, "the most formidable challenge undertaken by St. Paul and the first Christian evangelists. They had a cumulative conundrum at the heart of their message: contemptible lordliness and majestic folly perfectly demonstrated by a living corpse."[31] In order to accommodate this apparent stigma to the sensibilities of his Jewish readers, Paul rewrote the death, turning the scandal and "folly" of the cross into a demonstration, instead, of God's triumph.[32] Those who followed Jesus were not the wise, Paul wrote, but the foolish. In that reversal lies their ultimate triumph.[33]

Disputes over what Jesus meant, and *how*, occasioned controversy from the earliest days. Implications of deviancy and public shame thus circulate around the cross as in every age from first to last it reprises a haunted memory, a *memento mori* of shameful death. Observing the aphasia of Shepard's funeral (many other examples could be cited), one can nonetheless argue that contemporary Christians follow St. Paul's lead. For motives of class sensitivity, modern believers erase, forget, or else ignore the taint of Jesus' crucifixion that occludes its representation. Lenny Bruce quips that wearing the crucifix is akin to wearing an electric chair around one's neck; the nervous, shocked laughter of his audience makes the point well enough. For this audience to *think* about what the cross *means* is as much a taboo as *speaking* about it or representing it in public places.[34] Blinkered from history, then, contemporary believers rarely see the crucifix (or worse, its ideologically sanitized image, the cross) as the insufferable "sign of contradiction" that it is. Indeed, a respected Catholic churchman can say, with a breathtaking lack of historical consciousness, that "the cross coerces no one. It offends only those who are intolerant of the Catholic faith."[35] To the contrary, offense is central to its meaning.

Mourners arriving for a memorial service in honor of Matthew Shepard were greeted by a tableaux, whose "crude tree limbs roped together" recalled the scene of Matthew's death as well as the crucifixion of Jesus. The representation drew a "horrified gasp" from viewers at the Cathedral of Hope Metropolitan Community Church, who were thereby forced to remember Shepard's lashed and broken body hanging on a fence in subzero weather.[36] Elsewhere, at the funeral proper, the Rev. Anne Kitch made the horrifying allegory explicit. Wrote one observer, Rev. Kitch "evok[ed] the image of Jesus as another man whose body was broken, torn and abandoned on a wooden cross."[37] Shepard's death touched chords of outrage and sympathy. The narrative of his death—and the Christian allegory that seemed ready-made to encompass it—immediately became useful, if not completely without problems. Liberal persons, religious as well as secular, eager to mean well by the plight of homosexuals, quickly read Matthew as an image of Christ. Politically minded persons found in the starkly moralized dichotomy of the scene a chance to advance hate-crime legislation, then under interminable discussion in the Senate.[38] Other voices echoed and amplified. Writing in the *New Republic* little over a month afterward, theater critic Robert Brustein, reviewing Terrence McNally's new play "Corpus Christi," found occasion to recall Shepard's funeral. He wrote that Shepard's death bore "uncanny resemblance to a crucifixion."[39] Some, like *Vanity Fair,* saw in Shepard the potential for economic exploitation they had found earlier in Cunanan. Indeed, like Cunanan, Shepard warranted a cover story, redolently religious: "The Crucifixion of Matthew Shepard."[40]

Vanity Fair's religion of course was commodity window-dressing. Nonetheless, what even the most lucre-driven of these asides to Christ intended was broader than any specific religious meaning. Jesus' painful death was thought to sanctify Matthew's death by serving as its antitype or original. Some of the references, however, intended more narrowly a doctrinal reading; in true Christian redemptive abjection, Christ's death redeemed or atoned Shepard's appallingly useless death. Nonetheless, the equation of Matthew and Christ and the one-to-one correspondence of their deaths uncovered unacknowledged, or forgotten, implications of the original crucifixion. The comparison had the unsettling effect of turning a klieg light onto the various scandals associated with Jesus mentioned earlier—some of which were more basic than the torturous nature of his death. First there is the scandal of God's surely sadistic abandonment of "his son" to a criminal's death. This problem of familial relations circulates in Christian discourse—although it is rarely addressed as such in the sentimental construction of family values.[41] In the second place, the play of ironies about this scene necessarily recalls the use Jesus himself made of scandal. Scriptures attest that Jesus instigated offense purposely, employing what we might now call "act up" politics to move his auditors to conversion of heart.[42] In the third place, the scene unexpectedly reverses scandalized and scandalizer—a haunting memory of the stigmatization born by the early proto-Christians (Jews, actually). These "quintessential outsiders"[43] were ejected from the synagogue, hounded and martyred by religious and Roman authority alike, and now their children reenact that exclusion on still another group of outcasts.[44] The last and perhaps greatest scandal builds on these. In every age the crucifixion offers a scene drenched with violence, blood, and horror—actual as well as symbolic. Thus, in the context of Shepard's funeral, an image that is violent in origin monstrously reduplicates itself, first in the violence required *in* its name, and second, in the violence authorized *by* its model. Examples are numerous—take a recent attack on two gay men in California. "I'm guilty of obeying the laws of the creator," remarks a white supremacist when he admitted to killing a gay couple in their sleep.[45] In hoc signo—still a powerful intoxicant.

Other considerations were left unaddressed, particularly those relating to the theology of Christ's atoning death. If Matthew, made over as Christ, like Christ redeems and atones, who then benefits? Does Matthew bear the sin of all homosexuals and thus atone for them? If so, to whom? From the other direction, is Matthew's blood upon the killers as well as upon all the people? Hagiography can be defined as a "meditative enterprise" leading "to Christian perfection."[46] Such hermeneutics provide a customary method for reading the iconography of the saints, whose pained bodies and violent displays of death provide meditative uplift—a popular motif, as we have seen in the sentimental genre of the child death.[47] However, in the hagiography done up around Shepard, it is almost as if the practice of relics and saintly memory—repudiated during the iconoclastic Reformation—returns, although in a surely haunting embodiment. Finally, the intended effect of the Jesus/Matthew overlay was to read Matthew as martyr (the word derives from the Greek *marturon,* meaning witness) and to pig-gyback his appalling death onto the transfiguring death of Christ. Some-times the eye falters, however; meditative gaze becomes a stare, while compassion washes out in the glare of horror. Instead of Jesus' example sanctifying the viciousness of Matthew's death, the reverse happened. The juxtaposition of Jesus' cross and the fence onto which Matthew was tied instead draped Matthew with the scandal of the original. That is, the *offense* of Jesus' death, rather than its atoning action, is what the viewer remem-bers from the scene in Laramie. This has a twofold effect—undercutting those who would use Christ's authority to demonize Shepard's homosexu-ality, while rendering the homosexual Matthew as worthy of sympathy.

The hellish Christians waving signs and the bewinged homosexuals thereby cemented *in death* the identification of the holy and the horrible that Shepard's homosexual life (horrible at least in the eyes of evangelical Christians) had split apart. To thoughtful observers of this religious-Gothic drama, the only conclusion to be read was the (historically) accurate one that, indeed, Christ *was* the bearer of taint and that further, as David Skal observed, monsters *do* make good Christ-substitutes. Why should this be? Why was the scene outside the church so dread-ful, and thus—as the an-cient stories of angelic visitations remind us—so full of potential grace? Further, considering the omnipresence of scandal and offense to Jesus' life, preaching and death, perhaps the most significant question to adequately understanding the crucifixion is also central to understanding Shepard's funeral. In most cases the question is never asked, nor was it at Shepard's funeral. That is, are offense and scandal in some significant way preparatory moments for epiphany, grace, and the holy? Jesus' own blend of provoca-tion and offense as pedagogical method seems to affirm this. If so, what epiphany did the scandal of Mathew's death prepare us for?[48]

II. The Homosexual Monster

> People in homosexuality are incredibly evangelical. . . . It's pure sexu-ality. . . . It's such a rush. They are committed in almost a religious way.
>
> Dr. Paul Cameron[49]

The formulas of romance into which Shepard was read employed well-worn sentimental patterns and metaphors to achieve their effect. Eliciting sympathy and compassion, however, required certain changes in the facts of the case and in the life of Matthew himself. For the formulas to suc-ceed—that is, for them to pass unobtrusively *as* formula—the young man had to be regendered, portrayed as a naif, virginal, and innocent.[50] Accordingly, photographs of Matthew made much of his youthful, even sexless appearance. The owner of the bar in which Shepard met his assailants describes him as "nice and polite and quiet"; even his mother strikes the required note: "He has always been different . . . and that difference made him more thoughtful, sensitive, and empathetic."[51] At the same time, a contrasting hagiographic frame mantled Matthew with almost preternatural heroism and courage—traditional bulwarks to feminine purity and innocence. The implicit manliness of the hagiographic *heightened* Matthew's pictorial innocence, then, while nonetheless undercutting it. Further, claims made for Matthew centered upon his victimization as a gay man— an identity which is, in Erving Goffman's phrase, "spoiled identity."[52] The taint of that spoil had its consequences, as the representation of Matthew (the young man) became an example of monstrous hybridity. On the one hand Matthew's pained body was implicitly called as witness (martyr) to represent the incorporeal innocence of the angels. On the other hand, the heroizing text of hagiography drew attention to the sin-stained offensiveness of Matthew, the unmanly queer. Religious iconography, exploited against a Gothic mode of address, sharply underscored the mutual dependence of these discourses upon each other.

The conflicting pulls of discordant genre requirements (sentimentality/hagiography) only exacerbated the crisis of homosexuality crucial to the Christian right's politics, whose authority is grounded in an economic system of gender called "family." Within this system, homosexuality is doubly vexatious, unnatural as well as immoral. Spokespersons for various conservative groups marshal Biblical rhetoric and authority in the defense of their projects, among which the exclusion and repudiation of "non-family" perversions—particularly homosexuality—takes precedence.[53] Of course, tactics such as these are not limited to the Evangelical right. Indeed, relations of homosexuals to Protestant as well as to Catholic churches have rarely been peaceful in recent years. In Catholic practice, for instance, the initially sympathetic outreach to the homosexual set in motion by Vatican II met an abrupt end in 1986 with Cardinal Joseph Ratzinger's "Letter to the Bishops of the Catholic Church on the Pastoral Care of Homosexual Persons." In the fifteen years since, homosexual presence within the Roman Church has been seriously compromised; individuals have been silenced while advocacy groups have been evicted from church property. Theological positions underwriting this exclusion have hardened. For example, in a recent and much-publicized statement, the generally circumspect John Paul II responded to a millennial gathering of homosexuals in Rome by announcing from his balcony that he felt "bitterness for the insult" caused by the World Gay Pride march in Rome, and "for the offense to Christian values" caused by homosexuals.[54] The irony, of course, is the deeply pivotal significance of *offense* to Christianity itself.

Protestant doctrine, particularly in American contexts, has long viewed homosexuality with a mixture of contempt and disdain, while nonetheless treating individual homosexuals with pity and altruistic condescension. Yet recent decades have seen a change in this attitude. Evaluating the coverage of homosexuality in *Christianity Today,* Didi Herman writes that the journal's image of the homosexual was "once largely a benign portrait of unhappiness [in the fifties]." However, in recent decades a new "cultural genre" has emerged, "specifically dedicated to identifying the gay threat, and calling Christian believers to arms."[55] The martial rhetoric common to evangelists like Swaggart, Falwell, Robertson, Phelps, and others suggests that more is at risk than religion.[56] In his address to the GOP Convention in 1992, Buchanan thus distills two decades of ferment: "There is a religious war going on in this country for the soul of America. It is a cultural war . . . for the soul of America."[57]

Beginning about the mid-eighties, in radio and televangelism, in Christian TV talk show and evangelical publication, homosexuality assumed a more dire aspect, particularly related to medical issues of AIDS and other social crises of the times.[58] In part the increased wattage of the language was due to the success of post-Stonewall gay activism, through which homosexuality was accorded a degree of social tolerance, if not actual acceptance.[59] The New Right responded with alarm to this seeming liberalization by demonizing homosexuals as a group, judging them to fail in specifically domestic ways. That is, homosexuals were portrayed as sexually lawless—an affront not only to God's natural law but to the binary sexual orderliness of the family's gendered economy. As Robert Dreyfuss writes, "Abortion and homosexuality are the top preoccupations for much of the Christian right."[60] Considering Jesus' indifference to the latter topic and the total lack of Biblical insight on the former, these are surely odd topics for Christians to seize upon. Yet it is in these terms that one so often sees the confrontation between conservative evangelical forces and its "archenemy."[61]

Indeed, the language is directly gendered. The Christian culture of America is a "man-based culture," as Robert Knight terms it.[62] As characterized in Jerry Falwell's "Old-Time Gospel Hour," Jesus is a "he-man"[63]— the role model and exemplar for an explicitly masculinized culture of America. Rhona Berenstein argues that a central feature of classic monster horror films is the "bending" of gender expectations. Monsters are obvious in such films, Berenstein argues, in the way they twist and destroy appropriate gender: men fail to be men and are effeminized, while women—in theory sexless—become creatures of wanton lust. Patrick Buchanan's speech at the Republican National Convention—with its intimations of cross-dressing Democrats and calamitous national moral decline—derives from similar preoccupations about who bends gender, and who must straighten it back. Jesus (especially the pained Jesus triumphantly victim on his cross) takes it like a man. Jesus is the he-man whose potency wards off cultural flaccidity. His virility stiffs up the effeminate, whether pansies, fairies, queens, or other social ladies.

But as the narrative goes, monsters are made in order to die, and their death cannot be our fault. If for no other reason, then, monsters—"men ultra-swishy and ultraviolet, Frankenstein thug-women with bolts on their necks"[64]—are useful to have around if only to stake. Evidence of this preoccupation in the sponsorship of homosexuals is not hard to find. Jesus died for our sins, the billboard signs assure us. Another sign not far away stridently specifies what those sins are. AIDS is "divine retribution" against homosexuals, says Jerry Falwell, although Patrick Buchanan may have said it first: "The poor homosexuals, they have declared war against nature, and now nature is exacting an awful retribution."[65] Nonetheless, Buchanan's apoplectic speech some years later to Republican delegates was notable (aside from its content) in that anything had to be said *at all* about the subject of homosexuality—at least *in* public, and framed *as* a public statement. Buchanan's assumptions of rectitude and "straight living" had previously gone without saying—in the most literal of fashions. His disclaimers had been accepted as received wisdom and populist common sense. Indeed, as *Parade* magazine wistfully observed in 1987, perhaps with some attempt at humor, in the "good old days" homosexuals "stayed in the closet, not in the front pages."[66] Buchanan merely raised that sentiment to political sound bite, straightening up the culture for public exposition, as it were.[67] As he himself remarked in a campaign stop at Bob Jones University, homosexuality is "the love that will not shut up."[68]

During this period, the growing power and articulateness of homosexual presence helped sharply define a much older bogey, the "homosexual monster." Attributing legendary or monstrous sex is, in many Western cultures, a centuries-old code for mechanisms of scapegoating and repudiation.[69] The American version of this creature owes its current popularity to J. Edgar Hoover's fear campaigns of the thirties (although the formula preceded him and was ceaselessly revised after him). Its abrupt reappearance in the seventies as part of a highly aggressive and invasive sexuality was made possible by the saturation of press, media, and cinema of the time with neo-Gothic rhetoric and iconography. These provided the evangelical Right with a convenient new formula (and target) for a rhetoric of perversion, sin, and evil. Thus, if Darwin and the evolutionists focused the concerns of religionists earlier in the century, and if communists and infiltrators were the culprits at mid-century, in the waning years of the century homosexuals, portrayed as diabolic and demonic, became the apocalyptic agents of national collapse. Satan is "the author of this lifestyle," screamed a protestor at the Arlington Library.[70] Gays and lesbians are the "most pernicious evil today," says the Reverend Lou Sheldon, president of the Traditional Values Coalition.[71]

The sexual monster in its most recent form was perhaps first delineated during Anita Bryant's "Save Our Children, Inc." campaign. In 1977 Bryant organized a successful effort in Dade County, Florida, to repeal a civic ordinance prohibiting discrimination against homosexuals in employment, housing, and public accommodations. Bryant's highly publicized action was one among many that would lend credence, a few years hence, to the consolidation of "the monster figure of the pedophile stranger-abductor."[72] In *Bound and Gagged,* Laura Kipnis observes that "pedophilia is the new evil empire of the domestic imagination: . . . it seems to occupy a similar metaphysical status [as communism] as the evil of all evils."[73] As an "archetypal scene of horror," it became the perfect repository for animus against the hated homosexual, whose social visibility rendered him or her immune to less dramatic tactics.[74]

III. *In Hoc Signo* Frenzy

There is a kind of fanaticism in the love of country which could be called a cult of the hearth . . . and it is especially for its religious content that it merits even more the name fanaticism.

Voltaire, *Encyclopédie*[75]

There are numerous evangelical groups whose "holy war" against homosexuals seems so maniacal and so, well, *Gothic* that it bears examination.[76] The rhetoric could be, and often seems to be, imported from another world—perhaps a video one—so socially disconnected is it from any of the cautious political correctness that customarily damps down political debate. Fred Phelps, for example, pastor of the Westboro Baptist Church in Topeka, Kansas, came to media prominence after the pistol-whipping of Matthew Shepard. He is not shy of announcing his—or his congregation's—intent.

As stated on their Web page (GODHATESFAGS.COM), the church's macabre mission is, among other things, to picket the funerals of dead homosexuals. Partly as a response to the publicity he gained at the Shepard funeral, Phelps branched out to speak in other causes, although he continued to picket funerals for homosexuals. Inveighing against the Human Rights Campaign's Millennium March on Washington, Phelps wrote, "The fags are touting this orgy of lies and insanity as the largest gathering of perverts in history!" The march, he said, would be a "habitation of devils." [77]

Phelps makes no claims for originality here; he merely recycles material from the same religiously Gothic cupboards that provided Cotton Mather with ammunition against the spurious "habitation of witches" in Salem in 1693. In the witch hysteria that ensued, dozens of persons arrested and at least twenty (mostly women) were convicted and killed.[78] The formula incantations that Phelps finds useful are centuries old, and this is partly my point. Despite a breast-beating reliance upon the inerrancy of the Bible, these eager evangelists bolster their convictions with a different inerrancy altogether, weaving their disorderly conclusions into the dense slipknot of prejudicial trope and metaphor. The sturdy opaqueness of Gothic formula adds heft to the vituperation of these self-styled "Old-Time religionists." Once paired with emotional pathology or gender incompetence, in the evangelical press homosexuals are now likely to be inflated by demonic, Gothic, or other supernatural agency. When demonic agents fail to satisfy, more sturdily human denigration occurs. Homosexuals are said to be "like," in the words of a professional football player, "liars, cheaters, backstabbers and malicious people." [79] A high-standing Congressional official compares them to "kleptomaniacs" or "persons with alcohol and sex addiction." [80] Indeed, not even the sky seems the limit. Pat Robertson, for example, blamed an influx of gays (visiting Orlando's Disney World) for the inclement weather and wildfires affecting the state. Robertson remarked on his "700 Club" broadcast: "A condition like this [homosexuals in the community] will bring about the destruction of your nation. It'll bring about terrorist bombs. It'll bring earthquakes, tornadoes, and possibly a meteor." [81]

In keeping with the millennial energy circulating not too distantly in these accounts, the reports, bulletins, speeches, and articles of fundamentalist groups on this topic (and, to be fair, on many other subjects as well) is crazily apocalyptic—clotted by lumpen nuclear imagery, Edenic reference, and cheap sci-fi image. The centrality of the homosexual to these narratives leads one to conclude that he or she is useful precisely because the offense of their presence enables the apocalypse to play itself out. A few examples will suffice to show the narrow, mantra-like range of reference: "We are witnessing the Administration's moral meltdown," Robert Knight (Family Research Council) says of Bill Clinton, after Rev. Troy Perry—a gay-identified clergyman associated with the gay Metropolitan Community Church—was included in an ecumenical breakfast at the White House.[82] In another instance, Paul Cameron remarks that "AIDS is a guardian . . . sent . . . about forty years ago to destroy Western civilization unless we change our sexual ways."[83] Typically apocalypse is construed as a crisis of gender, in which effeminized men bring on Satan's minions: "As man is reduced in stature, all hell will break loose," says Robert Knight. "We'll see a breakdown in social organization, with more drug use, more disease, more unwanted pregnancies. You're mainstreaming dysfunction."[84] Considering Robertson's comment earlier about the homosexual's pronounced effect on weather, it is nonetheless clear that however weak and unmanned these creatures are, they nonetheless are symbolically very powerful.

At other times the narrative seems evenhanded in its mix of contemporary deviancy and criminality: "If we discovered that being a serial killer or a sociopath was genetic, . . . we certainly would not allow him to act up his serial killing or sociopathological disposition."[85] In *Using Murder,* Philip Jenkins argues that the genre of the serial-killer panic was used to discredit gains made by homosexuality in public spaces. Paul Cameron makes the criminal/deviancy association more directly, Gothically and graphically: gays "who practice oral sex verge on consuming raw human blood."[86] Such associations, of course, are standard boilerplate, enduring fantasies of degradation. They were once employed about early Christians, and have been sturdily consistent throughout history, most recently circulating around Dahmer and Cunanan.[87] However, again Phelps raises the volume. If one death is good, many is better and *all* is terrific. He gleefully conflates apocalypse with genocide. The jeremiad that results exhausts the reader long before the end is reached, and it is almost Lovecraftian in its linguistic excess:

> Conceiving the militant homosexual movement to pose the greatest threat to the survival of this nation, and that the government in all its branches (including the courts) is caving in to this anti-majoritarian law-trained pervert elite with their specious arguments couched in the inapposite language of civil rights law, and that the churches . . . are likewise crumbling to their junk theology and snake oil pitchman rhetoric which is nothing but heretical sophistry—Westboro Baptist Church has determined to act. The Destroyer of Sodom is not dead. If the same conditions prevail, God's wrath will destroy America just as it did Sodom and Gomorrah in

1898 BC. . . . THE REAL CHURCH-BURNERS ARE FAGS! (Westboro Baptist Church press release, 30 June 1996; emphasis in original)

The primary effect of the Gothic idiom is to destroy language by de-
priving it of significant reference. This, in turn, effectively removes action
or person so characterized from moral evaluation. Expostulations of unspeakability thus signal a commensurate moral failure. Accordingly, while
apocalyptic texts are densely *moralistic* in their need to reach closure, the
morality they preach recedes in the distance. In other words, while closure
is part of the defining form of apocalyptic narrative, as we see with Phelp's
version of it, the form comes undone as the words trip over themselves in
a mad panic to end. The moral collapse Phelps fears he enacts in textual
overreaching. As a result sense is entirely evacuated. The words are never
enough, and so every closure necessitates a new beginning.

Gothic formula patterns forget and erase; they piece together formula
prejudice. Surely similar observations can be made about the reckless wash
of words used to deny, repudiate, condemn, taint, tar and contaminate
homosexuals, the rush of which results in a clotted speech void of significant content. Such a speech act is, then, more akin to an assault with words
than a mode of address or speech. "The Gay Agenda" published in 1998
by the Christian Coalition of Maine exemplifies this process. So remarkable was the text that reviews of it were forced into competitive verbal
pyrotechnics: "The piece of hate literature that Paul Volle, Mark Finks and
others have produced in the form of political advertising, however, goes
beyond the bounds of taste, fairness and rational dialogue."[88] Almost as if
it were trying to keep up with the escalating linguistic violence, the *Portland Press Herald* adapts for its own purposes the purple coloration it la-
ments, charging that "The Gay Agenda" was a "Product of sick minds.
May not be suitable for civilized society . . . homophobic . . . unsolicited,
unsubstantiated and unadulterated filth . . . vile and ill-formed . . . hateful
smut . . . 16 pages of pure, homophobic hatred."[89]

With only minor changes, then, a catalogue of horrible intimacies, a
Gothic iconography of blood and pain, deviltry and devil-spawn, become
the moralized invective of many Christian apologists. An earlier chapter
discussed the way erotic investments occlude moralizing literature. In
evangelical polemics we see how a rhetoric of hateful rectitude, Gothic in
cadence and linguistic effect, finds sanctioned entry into civic discourse,
where it passes unacknowledged in speeches, religious documents, ads, and
polemic of all kinds. As Fred Botting observes, "The effects of the literature of terror, the thrills, violence and unspeakable encounters, push to-

wards the limits of language, outside words: Language is doubled in a stressful reflection on itself." [90] Critics as diverse as George Steiner, Elaine Scarry, and Paul Oppenheimer chart the corrosive ethical and social consequences of the diminution, corruption or elimination of language. [91] The furious energy registered in these drive-by shouts reminds one of the magic implicitly contained in the verbal act itself; the spell of language is contained in its nearly magic potency to effect what it says. In Phelps's diatribe cited earlier, for example, we see acted out an anxiety distributed more widely in the very form of Gothic speech itself—the fear that the magic is gone, lost, evacuated. Beneath the fulmination lurks the anxiety that language, finally, is not much more than purposeless sound and fury.

Nonetheless, such violence is arguably as significant—perhaps more so—as assaults that are physical in nature. Groups that elsewhere advocate quarantining AIDS patients in "cities of refuge" (Traditional Values Coalition), even "extermination" (Paul Cameron), achieve a similar violent removal, unobserved, by quarantining populations in language. Such language, however, only provides a sanctioned way of addressing a different fantasy altogether: "Unless we get medically lucky, in three or four years, one of the options discussed will be the extermination of homosexuals." [92] When one considers, as Laura Kipnis documents, that citizens can be jailed for the contents of their fantasies, one wonders how such rhetoric is legal, let alone defensible. [93] Fred Phelps responds, however, with refreshing candor, "You can't preach the Bible without preaching hatred." Phelps was speaking at Lynchburg about the "kissy-pooh stuff Falwell is putting out." [94] It is easy for the homosexual man or woman to see Phelps coming from a distance and to avoid him; on the contrary, it is less easy to deflect Dr. Laura Schlessinger's baleful, malign altruism which would attribute the fault of homosexuality to biology. As Senator Allan Spear of Minnesota remarked at a Minneapolis rally protesting Phelps, "What many of us face every day is not so blatant as that, but hate wrapped up in the face of Minnesota Nice." [95] One might propose that niceness and civility prompt the fractured fury of Fred Phelps or Paul Cameron. That is, the lascivious catalogues of immoralities detailed by *The Lambda Report*—a newsletter designed, as its subtitle suggests, to "Monitor . . . the Homosexual Agenda in American Politics and Culture" [96]—and their Gothic incoherencies are made possible by the unavailability of other public discourse. The war being conducted here—to use Buchanan's expression—is between the public address of homosexuality in *law* and *custom,* or its deflection into a para-discourse—the genre, as Kate Ellis reminds us, for things that "aren't supposed to exist." [97]

Silence is built into the genre in another form, as well. Many commentators decry media violence and its effects upon viewers and readers, while remaining oblivious to their rhetoric—the use of which, in John Aravosis's phrase, "amounts to a loaded gun."[98] Richard Cohen observes that "the same politicians who assert a connection between . . . violence in the media and violence in society" are the ones who "see no connection between their own rhetoric and incident after incident of gays being assaulted or . . . killed."[99] Cardinal Joseph Ratzinger, for instance, bemoans the violence against homosexuals even while he sees such actions as "understandable" and "expected." The cynic might respond, Well, yes—understandable by the well-meaning Catholic who would pick up Ratzinger's "Letter to the Bishops of the Catholic Church on the Pastoral Care of Homosexual Persons" (1986) hoping to learn from it how Catholics should act and feel.[100]

In "The Nurture of the Gothic," William Veeder comments that the "policing function of discourses damage[s] persons by damaging language."[101] An anonymous editorial "header" on Wired Strategies, a political Internet consulting source, clarifies how this works: "It is simply not possible to constantly preach the inhumanity of man, then blithely skulk away when principle meets practice. It is simply not moral to give a child a gun, then feign ignorance when someone gets hurt."[102] In other words, why fulminate if no response is expected? And the response desired, as Phelps, Cameron, Robertson, Falwell, Ratzinger, and Buchanan say, almost explicitly, is the removal or elimination of certain kinds of persons from public space. The more usual word for the action they have in mind is genocide. What action might they expect, then, if not the one they announce by indirection?

I wish to emphasize, however, that the violence of this Gothic Christian discourse signals not so much the collapse of grammar as the excess of meanings made possible by the discourse itself. The homosexual monster, occasion of such threat, is so monstrous because it pointedly derives from the discourse that would repudiate it. Unquestionably, in the terms of which it was first conceived, the homosexual is a nexus of confusions, crossings, and transgressions. Like sodomy, for which it is a convenient if inaccurate stand-in, homosexuality poses a vast symbolic geography of illegality, unnaturality, and hellishness: "abnormal, wrong, unnatural and perverse"—in the words of Oregon's Ballot Measure 9.[103] Pat Robertson, for example, demonstrates the category-scrambling typical of these invectives when he argues that "many of those people involved in [sic] Adolf Hitler were Satanists, many of them were homosexuals, the two things seem to go together, it is a pathology it is a sickness." [104] Robertson does make one thing clear. What seems evident though not always stated is the demonstrable *mutuality* of the conjunction we have been following. The demonic and the angelic, the hellish and horrible do "seem to go together," as Robertson himself acknowledges, although perhaps not for the reasons he suggests. Robertson's association of Satan and gender-deviancy echoes the use made of similar images by Phelps, and before him, by Cotton Mather, and before him, by a tradition of witch-staking. All three examples share a common insistence: hidden witches signify social perversity, perhaps, but more importantly, they announce *heresy* as well. What we are tracing here is the formation, and the confirmation, of ideology. The coherence and continuity of *this* tradition of preaching representation is as deep as it is disallowed. Why should Christian authority need witches and homosexuals? Why is Jesus not "man enough" to handle the debate alone?

There is no question but that the "homosexual monster" was deeply offensive to the Christians outside the Arlington Library and to those who picketed in Dade County, and that the homosexual remains a source of outrage to Phelps and other Christian groups. [105] Offense, in this case, is not uncomplicated, however, and in fact may be a positive sign. Homosexuality is more deeply rooted than this phobia, or perhaps fetish, might suggest, since it is also significantly implicated in the formation of Christian doctrine itself. Arguably, as a category homosexuality derives from basic Judeo-Christian ideological beliefs—a point made by numerous theologians, social historians, and literary critics. [106] The argument can be summarized in this fashion: As systematic theologies went about the business of constructing the Holy and defining its ancillary, the Natural, the reverse was also made possible. The unholy—an abstraction, to be sure—could be imagined and demonstrated in examples of the socially perverse and unnatural. [107] Freud's use of the term "perversion" developed independently of the word's original religious meanings, and of course at a much later date. Freud would not have been primarily interested in its theological usage, although it is this moralized notion of evil/perversion/sin that now disrupts current understandings of the word. Tracing the word back beyond Freud, for example, Jonathan Dollimore writes that the "tradition indebted to Augustine" offers "a perspective whose complex inheritance will help identify the sexual pervert as a modern incarnation of evil." [108] As perhaps "*the* pervert" in the Christian exemplary mode—the homosexual (like the witch) is the scapegrace; both obligingly perform nonreproductive sexual deviancy as moral show. [109]

In the way they perform deviancy to the scandalized eye, homosexuals underscore the complicated rite of deviancy through which transgression becomes necessary to Christian governance.[110] Sin must be "flaunted" in order to exercise its pedagogical effect. If "all hell will break loose" when "man is reduced in stature," the contrary is true, as well. Hell will be contained and dysfunction eliminated to the extent that homosexuals are paradoxically both visible as well as repressed. That is, homosexuals can only trigger social dismay to the extent *that* they are visible in their monster-face. For this reason they must be constantly massaged into scrutiny by means of legal, moral, and medical discourse.[111] Cohen observes that "scandal makes sexual ideology palatable in narrative form."[112] As a necessary buttress to the regulatory work of sexual ideology, encapsulated most cogently within the economic terms of family values, homosexuals *must* be pinioned in the public gaze, their deviancy presumed for its normalizing effects.[113]

This is why Christ's bloody, pained body needs the parallel pained bodies of Matthew Shepard, the witch in Salem, and other monstrous examples of transgression to underwrite it—a truism as old as Kenneth Anger's use of the life of Christ in *Scorpio Rising*. The problem, however, is that these representations are unstable, as we saw with Susan Smith and here with Matthew Shepard. In the poisonously benign view of Christian altruism, the gender-failed homosexual and the fallen woman equally provide occasions for liberal demonstrations of showy love and sympathy. Nonetheless, these Christian ministrations do not preclude a heavy dollop of hate as well; the hapless female becomes the malevolent witch, while the ingénue Matt becomes the queer-boy fag. In the rite of deviancy, sacramentally underwriting Christian culture, the sanctifying cross—always the holy antidote in Gothic rites of monster-staking—does not eliminate the monster. To the contrary, the cross *guarantees* that the monster it faces down is, and must be, visible.[114]

IV. What Isn't "Supposed to Exist." [115]

I began this chapter by observing the sometimes symbiotic relationship between religious piety and Gothic terror. Fear does not oppose belief; it is its other face. Stephen King remarks, directly, that "without belief, there is no terror."[116] The taboo homosexual body and the redemptive Christic body are deeply implicated in the representations of the other. Surely without the unflagging Christian sponsorship the homosexual receives, he or she would be out of work—no longer on the public representational dole, as it were. In late-modern Christianity each image supports the other in the conflict of twin gazes, transcendent and worldly, as *eros* and *sanctos* build upon the other. Katharine Park writes that

. . . we often forget the central role played by religious and ultimately theological commitments in American homophobia and the construction of AIDS in the United States, where 41 percent of people identify them- selves as born-again Christians and 32 percent believe every word of the Bible to be literally true. [117]

It is important to understand, however, in reverse, the importance of the homosexual in the formation of modern Christian identity. This is surely the motive behind John Paul II's recent comment about the offensiveness of homosexuality. While Christian discourse is of many minds about many things, the body of believers is still generally of one mind about homo- sexuals. It is this consensus of exclusion that numerous church leaders, Pope included—worried about shrinking numbers of believers—bank upon. Thus, even if homosexuals didn't exist, they would have to be in- vented, if for no other reason than to consolidate opinion on other matters. Further, without the symbolically abject body of the homosexual, as Mark Jordan makes clear, complex patterns of Christian rhetoric and practice would be suddenly evacuated of meaning. Jordan opens *The Silence of Sodom* with an unnamed pope contemplating lifting the ideological silence on homosexuality in the church. Jordan wittily comments that even if this were to happen, nothing could change. The homosocial system in which this binary has existed is so long-standing that its effects thoroughly en- tangle dogma as well as pastoral practice.[118] But Jordan observes that the reverse might also happen. Perhaps the correction would change every- thing, and *that* is the problem: "A subject that Catholic theologians cannot discuss . . . except with thunder, derision, or disgust is not a subject on which Catholic theology is ready to speak." [119]

Thunder, derision, disgust: Jordan alerts us to conditions we have seen before where language must be evacuated of meaning in order for the melo- drama of speechlessness to achieve its full, Gothic effect. Provoking such doubled effects of repression and reactivation is central to Christian dis- course and history. One could further argue that the church needs to main- tain its interest in licensing transgression—being its sole identifying agent for example. Maybe church structures *are* Gothic, in that they make visible things that aren't supposed to exist—like sin, for instance. As St. Paul argues, the law creates the sin, not the reverse. Judith Butler remarks similarly that "juridical power inevitably 'produces' what it claims merely to represent."[120] Ecclesiastical structures of dogma and representation exploit this categorical imperative to its fullest. To paraphrase St. Paul and Judith Butler in this con- text, the enunciating of the law makes possible a space in which a certain kind of love can be situated, precisely in order that it NOT speak. Why? In order that profit—rhetorical, emotional, and ideological, as well as economic and spiritual—can be made from that fact.[121]

Nonetheless, it takes no great skill to elicit shock, anger, and outrage. This is Terrence McNally's not very original point, surely, in *Corpus Christi*. McNally's "body of Christ" itemizes not only the scandal of Christianity but the scandal set resolutely against it in contemporary evangelical politics. His drama about a gay Christ and his disciples was much ballyhooed, picketed by religious groups who acted without ever reading the play.[122] Similar effects of outrage also circulate around Robert Mapplethorpe's work, or Andres Serrano's "Piss Christ," or, more recently, the elephant-dung-spattered image of Mary in the Brooklyn museum; possibly the same can be said for the winged fairies outraged by uncharitable Christians, or an aged Pope scandalized by a city of (visible) homosexuals—many of them Catholic, and probably among them more than a few priests.[123] What appears under the sign of outrage to be self-evident blasphemy is, from another perspective, a sign of deep reverence as well.

Monsters draw upon aspects of the fear/awe producing energy of the sacred and taboo, often in ways we do not expect. Patterns of belief and disbelief, representations of the awe-ful and the awful, can bear a significant resemblance to each other. What we are left with, then, is a dense, knotted figure, a vexing cross and a vexed crossing. Sentimental Christianity's fretting at the twinned male bodies of the crucified Jesus and the vilified homosexual uncovers the scandalous double bind contained in the very heart of Christianity. As Dreyfuss observes, "The Christian right succeeds by tapping into America's deep ambivalence toward homosexuality."[124] More accurately, the Christian right succeeds by tapping into the ambivalence deep within Christianity itself regarding bodies and the various systems employed to control their pleasures, as well as to interpret their pains.

This is the bind which a politically astute, erotophobic Christianity—liberal as well as conservative—is always trying to undo, the crossing it is desperate to uncross and so is always redoing: the linkage of transcendence and transgression; the Janus-faced vision of the man who (for religion) died a monstrous death and the men who (in religious discourse) live as visible monsters. From both directions, each is engaged in a ritual dying that means to redress, maybe even rewrite, a religious authority that is deeply fissured and divided against itself. The historical moment is of such ominous portent that language fails, leaving only a *signo,* a sign, to mark its presence. This melodrama of obsessive gesturing presumes a language so violent that words no longer signify. The crucifix is a multifaceted religious image; yet stripped of its complexity as *marturon,* it morphs into the comic-book sketch of the monster, uncannily similar. We are soul-deep in the Gothic.

This realization brings us, perhaps not to closure, at least to a place to end. Through all the political wars fought over the dead body hanging upon it, the cross is a mute exposition of monstrous trauma not limited to any given age. At stake is a system of traditional belief whose iconography, imagery, and rhetoric exploits the body as totem of the spiritual, yet whose practice voids that spirituality and erases the body in taboo—a "dimity" Christianity, ashamed, in Dickinson's words, of "freckled Human Nature" (poem no. 401). Interesting questions remain. For as Leo Steinberg and others document, the study of how Jesus became the Christ is a matter of history as well as theology, involving material practices that would one day be associated with the Gothic, as well.[125] From either direction erasure of the body had further consequences, notably in a diminution of language used to describe that body. Why, for example, at this period such minute attention is given to suffering and pain deserves to be explored. How, in other words, has a religious discourse become, in the fullest sense of the word, academic? Why is the study of masochism, and the gender-bending it suggests, so popular a topic in literary studies?[126] In *Nightmare on Main Street,* Mark Edmundson argues the presence of an S-M cultural motif throughout late twentieth-century American representational culture. Edmundson's insights need to be extended.

In an era whose rhetorical horizons (the transcendent) are the languages of abuse, victimization and therapeutic self-help (a form of spiritual violence), the image of the crossed man signals the deification of the victim. At the same time, that image authorizes a self-effacement that has long been the rhetorical centerpiece in the power dynamic of Christian altruism. That is, sentimentalities of love disguise a mechanics of power—as do the display of guilt and the staging of expiatory scenes of confession.[127] Matthew Shepard, who disappeared into a system of representation, had spent what little life he had in a religious system likewise designed to make him disappear. Transgression and perversion participate in the Divine Economy, not as surplus, but as essential currency.

Conclusion

The bound man, handed over to the state for exemplary capital punishment: the criminal recouped as Christ. Matthew Shepard, bound to a fence, handed over for exemplary vigilante violence—recouped as angelic queer, virginal. In an uncanny parallel to Catholicism's devotion to the

Virgin Mary, Matthew was erased from the body and its pains altogether. These images run the risk of swamping in excess. Yet of course to read the perverse implications of this body is to read against the grain of sentimental Christianity, which tosses the *monstrum* out, leaving just the bathos of a simpering Jesus, my best friend. Theologically Jesus who is *The Christ* is a hybrid—a bodied and bloodied God. In both its aspects of body and blood the image circulates a mixture of taboo, religiousness (blood, historically), monstrousness, as well as legal criminality.[128] Indeed, we have here, as Updike calls it, the scandal of the Incarnation in which transcendence, bodied forth in Word and flesh, becomes, instead, a scandal marked *by* transgressive bodies. A theology of the Incarnation gives way to a demonology of the flesh—in whose repudiations, of course, lingers the desire.[129]

Finally, it can be argued that homosexuality is too "monstrous to be tolde" because its categories, definitions and meanings "proced[ed] from a Christian brest."[130] It is this surplus of meaning that constitutes the Gothic dimension of Christianity, making it, in its own way, monstrous—an effect which can be called the religious pornogothic. By reason of the intensity it focuses upon displayed bodies, such a system is politically useful. The position of the cross in public buildings in this predominately Christian environment is apocalyptic in a significantly ironic way: its bones and blood a constant reminder of judgment against the banal culture that would forget both. The apocalyptic quality of the cross is the judgment it keeps making, even against those who wield it. The cross is the omen, the *monstrum:* it is, finally, promiscuous in meaning, because it contains them all. It is the greatest *monstrum* of all.

At its most empty it becomes the inverted face of a moralized love whose chastisement is both threat and promise of redemption. Such conflict can signal a promising new avenue of resistance, as gay angels stand guard at the grave of Matthew Shepard: "The cultural task for gays now is the restoration of institutional sites for awe. Traditionally, religion has provided the home for awe."[131] The resistance of course is open to all, gay or straight. Matthew, the monster, like Jesus, reminds us, finally, by warning us to remember who we are, *marturon,* but *Milagro,* as well. We are witness, and thus, memory. As the angel says to Prior in *Millennium Approaches:* "You are all fabulous creatures."[132] And so we are—relics, of a sort, holy gifts: monstrous and revelatory, ever dreadful.

Monster, you are an abomination. I love you.

Juliette, Marquis de Sade

You are all fabulous creatures, each and every one.

Tony Kushner, *Angels in America*, part 2, *Perestroika*

COMMON WEAL, COMMON WOE

This book has examined how narrative images of reprisal, scandal, and silence are coded into the tight slipknot prejudices of the monster spectacle, popularly available as social anodyne in a glut of TV and cinema, and freely dispensed in the drive-by shouting of political speech. At many different levels of cultural discourse, private fear is mapped into public duty. The danger here: While politics exploits entertainment methods, it succumbs as well to its expectations.

Those who are nominated as monsters may be coded as foreign or outlandish, but rarely are they alien. Despite the protestations of shock and alarm accompanying these narratives, the simple fact is that we *know* the monster intimately. Perhaps worse, the monster *is* us: bone of our bone, wish of our wish, or even ourselves, slightly out of focus—or maybe frighteningly focused. Monsters are less *agents* of social collapse than *announcers* that the collapse has already occurred. He or she dramatizes the collapse of social boundaries, while hiding from view the particular linguistic and social usages by which those boundaries are fabricated. One genre answers another, as it were. "Whoever did this . . . must have been some kind of monster," says the brother of a man killed in a string of unsolved murders in the Tidewater area.[1] The speaker's concern, rather, is aimed at one of us—at anyone who might think such things, or God forfend, might take action upon those thoughts.[2] Why make monsters? As ongoing displays of atrocity in this rational century demonstrate, definitions of the human no longer seem self-assured. Monstrosity inheres, as Arendt famously said, in the banality of evil, not in its exceptionality. The various deviant or criminal lives that we have examined—however ineptly rendered as "truth" for erotic or moral pay—are, in the end, cobbled together rather desperately to keep us from observing larger patterns of civic fragmentation. Indeed, the energy invested in disguising from ourselves the fragmentariness reflects a prior troubling. That is, definitions of the human are themselves often little more than formula, beneath which there is "nothing there." The sentimental *desiderata* of liberal rhetoric will always be put at risk, then, discomfited by actual individuals, since living persons rarely perform civility well, and never all the time.

So, if monsters must be stitched together bit by bit, the bricolage of a society's rhetorical debris and political repudiations, it is only because citizens likewise must be carefully designed, normalized with care to exacting specifications. We become "persons" only by submitting to the unceasing attentions of culture, its vigilant and repetitive urgings, its relentless managements of body and gesture. Citizens must be subjected: "educated in the emotional lexicon of his society."[3] Such an observation might seem basic, even trite. However, it is often overlooked. Take, for example, the contentious but often contentless debate in which proponents "for life" denounce abortion in violent polemics (and sometimes practice)—all the while demanding death-on-call in the form of capital punishment. Since ambivalence is coded into most social norms, it should not surprise us that despite a facile support of "life," not all lives are equally reverenced and respected. Clearly, certain lives are more valued than others.[4] This very ambiguity increases, rather than decreases, the social fury expended in the pursuit of monsters: monsters are those who test the lines, those who fail to stay within the bounds of neighborliness—the ones who, for whatever reason, we no longer want. These civil escapees are those persons (or class of persons) who prompt the fear that culture's managed emotional care might not, after all, be perfect. Monsters cannot be allowed to live because they allow our slip to show.

Despite what the mindlessly plotted narratives tell us, then, monsters do not erupt into our safe and secure lives from someplace else. Rather, they emerge *from* within the constraints of our imagined selves. Monstrosity writes out as a public text the social incoherency of identity. The monster is already a metaphor, a place of suture in the public body, and monster making is "the making of a human."[5] Jeffrey Dahmer's example—his desperate need for love, and his literalness in pursuing intimacy—is instructive. Dahmer's mistake was to make visible the seams where his—and our—identity comes undone, at the vexed place where our desire teaches us how to be (the word says it all) consumers. What's worse, we hardly recognized Dahmer, although we should have. In class, caste, and color (the metaphors by which an Anglo culture defines the acceptably human), Dahmer found sanctuary. White, male, young, he was able to hide within the trappings of expected normalcy. In other words, his closet held; he passed. Yet his successful passing—now used in both senses in which Dahmer "passed"—provokes anxiety because we know that others like him exist. What prompts our fear is that *their* visibility is never assured, while on the other hand, our *invisibility* can never be guaranteed. We can never hide far enough away from the suspicion that normalcy is, after all, a put-on, or, perhaps, a take-off, a riff and joke. Finally, Dahmer's life (like Andrew Cunanan's, in this respect) needs to be read against its pervasive white, or "civilized," grain. Such a reading shows their monstrosity as indicting the racial and homophobic society that arguably made them possible, and which continues to reproduce Dahmer's (in particular) Gothic image for all manner of spoken and unspoken needs.

Whatever their particular features and historical specifics, the monsters of the social life share a common fate in the civic dramaturgy of spectacle and expiation by which they are ritually made visible. How, after all, does one make a monster? Repudiate, deny, unname, degrade: "People try to make us nonhuman so they feel OK about degrading us," remarked a college friend of Matt Shepard.[6] The language of monstrosity is as promiscuous as the monsters themselves. The killers of Matt Shepard were, to liberal-minded folk, "monsters." Wyoming governor Jim Geringer called the protesting Christians "a bunch of wingnuts."[7] "You're nothing, you're trash, you're garbage," cried one of the mourners at Shepard's funeral to a bearded protestor, who responded in kind: "Your life is filth, like a dog's life."[8] From the opposing side, however, homosexuals were monsters: "Fags Burn in Hell" and "God Hates Fags," helpfully note signs waved by a Baptist Christian congregation. Robert A. Bernstein writes that "it was obvious the monster ["dread" of homosexuals and lesbians] existed only in my imagination."[9]

But Bernstein's statement is of course not true, or only partially true. If the monster existed only in the imagination, Dahmer would be alive, and maybe the men he killed would be as well. Likewise, while much jocular commentary was offered up about Jerry Falwell's campaign against the "homosexual" Teletubby doll, no one commented upon the pernicious interlocking of Falwell's particular points—purse, purple dress, triangle antenna, effeminate voice.[10] Three out of the four points are specifically gendered. Is this particular configuration so firm as American categories of deviancy that it passes unexamined? To this same point, an editorial in *Planet Out,* an online gay news agency, noted that Matthew Shepard's diminutive size (5'2", 120 lbs.) made him "too close to the popular mythical stereo-types," and thus "a target for homophobes." [11] There is nothing in the least *mythical,* then, about these stereotypes that made him the target for uncom-promising fury. The same thing could be said, although in reverse, when press reports began circulating as "news" the rumor that the youths re-sponsible for the Columbine High School killings were gay. Are the for-mulas of homicidal deviancy already that fixed? How hold and stake a monster best? The most oppressive chains we cast are those spells—words—by which we nominate and transfix people in categories of like-ness and deviancy. The power to name and identify; to establish legitimacy and thus to create deviancy and to legalize it as criminality—this is true power. When we wish to do violence and don't want to leave marks, words are nice, and will suffice.

Kempton writes about Susan Smith that her "derangement appears to be the awful and all-but-incurable madness peculiar to those who carry their ideas to their logical conclusions." [12] However, whether bombing churches, pro-life clinics, city buildings, or cultists reserves, or sending bombs through the mail, Smith's madness—if it is one, is well distributed in the population, and takes the form so often of vigilante, self-help vio-lence. In the case of the boy in San Francisco who awoke in a hospital, beaten, to find "Fag" carved upon his body, words were the violence of choice, his body the place where they were written and where they would be remembered forever. Ask Jerry Falwell or Patrick Buchanan or Pat Robertson or William Dannemeyer or Jesse Helms—although there is no particular need to specify individuals. These in their own way merely con-spire with a cultural order that instructs them to make us afraid and then hands them the tools to do so. Announcing the culture war, they point out, name, and stake the monsters—all for the greater good.

The destruction of the Capitol in *Independence Day* makes a pleasant symbolic cameo; however, as the rest of the film makes clear, it is more than allegory. Culture wars are rarely fought in the capitols. The most important wars are fought over those whose dead bodies are not socially valued and so can be easily disposed: gays in Colorado and AIDS-sick per-sons, gay or straight, anywhere; immigrants in California; persons who let down the public sense of themselves. Still, such persons deserve at least a nod of sympathy. Like Victor's creature facing off the maddened crowd beneath the burning windmill, these hapless monsters are trapped as much by our individual and collective need for systems of reprisal as by the social ineptnesses (sometimes criminal, sometimes merely existential) that make them candidates for negative attention in the first place.

Why else are they candidates? As genocide in Nazi Germany, or its moral equivalent in the evangelical Right's "holy war" against homosexuals, or Dahmer and the recent crop of celebrity monsters in the United States attest, one's position as a "subject" is never stable. Each of us is always, in some secret or perhaps less secret way, falling short of the socially ideal self. This is the monster's role—to justify the violence, the blood, the effacement: to make a worthy sacrifice of the otherwise brutish, even banal social necessity of violence that is already so much a part of civility. It is important to keep in mind, then, that however monstrous, the rough beasts slouching toward us on TV and in newspaper are the image and likeness in which the human—that frail creature—is likewise made. As Augustine reminds us, "A monstrous man is nonetheless a man." And from the reverse, as Aristotle argues in *De Generationes, all* individuals are by definition monstrous, deviations from the norm. Patrick Buchanan and Stephen King, weaving political and literary fictions, respectively, from different points in the political spectrum, are at pains to remind us of this fact.[13] The monster's most grievous affront is that he or she holds us to our duty.

Maybe this is why monstrous persons seem poised—destined perhaps—to touch our lives at every crucial civic boundary or crossing, like the guardian angels of old, or sacraments and rites of passage. It might be argued, in fact, that the monster is *supposed* to teach us precisely this banal point—that the neighborhood *has* limits and that when we reach the place where the monster stands guard, we have arrived to the place beyond which, humanly, we dare not go. The monster's message is one of negation: flaming sword to hand, the monster guards just that contested boundary of the human we would occasionally think to challenge—or which, even more frequently, seems to be collapsing. So this brings us round to where we began, in my prologue, "What the Angel Said": For of course, viewed this way monsters *are* angels, messengers from on high: undoing us, as Rilke suggests, with the possibility of transcendence. And maybe this is why, again, the ritual cry, "Be not afraid!" For surely we must be in any such encounter with ourselves.

NOTES

Prologue

1. See Harold Bloom, *Omens of Millennium: The Gnosis of Angels, Dreams, and Resurrection* (New York: Riverhead Books, 1996).

2. See Maria Damon, "Angelology, Things with Wings," in *Mass Culture and Everyday Life,* ed. Peter Gibian (New York: Routledge, 1997), 205–211. In *Religion in Greece and Rome* (New York: Harper, 1959), H. J. Rose argues that early beliefs of the daimon "inevitably grew . . . [and] all manner of further complications being introduced, until it passed into the angelology and demonology of Christian speculators" (110ff.). See Sophy Burnham, *A Book of Angels: Reflections on Angels Past and Present and True Stories of How They Touch Our Lives* (New York: Ballantine, 1990); Joan Webster Anderson, *Where Angels Walk: True Stories of Heavenly Visitors* (New York: Ballantine, 1993); Charlie W. Shedd, *Brush of an Angel's Wing* (Ann Arbor, MI: Servant Publications, 1994). See *Time* (27 December 1993): 55–56.

3. For Titian's various Annunciations, see Harold Wethey, *The Paintings of Titian: Complete Edition* (London: Phaidon, 1975); also see Lorenzo Lotto, *The Annunciation* (New York: McGraw-Hill, 1963), and Bernard Berenson, *The Italian Painters of the Renaissance* (Ithaca: Cornell University Press, 1980). I am indebted to my first real professor, Sylvano Votto, S.J., for these references; about Lotto's *Annunciation,* Fr. Votto writes, "If you want an image of terror, look at the Lotto piece: the look on the virgin's face, the way she stretches her hand, the screeching cat, fur straight up, horrid in the Latin sense of *horreo,* I bristle. That is a monstrous annunciation" (correspondence).

4. Or perhaps we are, as my study argues indirectly. Tony Kushner's angel in *Angels in America* are profoundly no-nonsense creatures, speaking in poly-pronouns to convey majesty. See *Angels in America: A Gay Fantasia on National Themes,* part 1, "Millennium Approaches" (New York: Theater Communications Group, 1993). More in keeping with the collapse of dread and awe I am tracing, in his *Nightmare on Main Street: Angels, Sadomasochism, and the Culture of Gothic,* Mark Edmundson observes the erasing of any distinction between the two in the "fiction of the serial killer as an avenging angel" (Cambridge, Mass.: Harvard University Press, 1997), 29.

5. Edmundson, *Nightmare,* 77. For his reading of *Forrest Gump,* see 78–82. Gump's world is "the ostensible inverse of Freddy Krueger's and Hannibal Lecter's, where you're guilty when you sin, and guilty when you don't" (78–79).

6. As William James observes: "Gods are conceived to be first things in the way of being and power. They overarch and envelop, and from them there is no escape." William James, *The Varieties of Religious Experience: A Study in Human Nature,* ed. and with an introduction by Martin E. Marty (New York: Penguin, 1982), 54 and passim, esp. lecture 1, "Religion and Neurology," and lecture 7, "The Sick Soul."

7. Will H. Rockett, *Devouring Whirlwind: Terror and Transcendence in the Cinema of Cruelty* (New York: Greenwood Press, 1988), 9. Indeed, in a filiopietistic examination of St. Augustine's theology, a candidate for a degree in Sacred Theology writes that Augustine's discussions of fear would make a volume "of considerable size," but that Augustine "is interested in fear only as another aspect of love." John Selner, *Teaching of St. Augustine on Fear as a Religious Motive* (S.T.D. diss., Baltimore: St. Mary's University, 1937), xvi.

8. Marilyn Stasio, "Night of the Living, and Unliving, Dead." *New York Times,* 3 October 1999, late edition, 4.

9. André Haynal, "From Priest to Philosopher: The Origins of a Concept," in *Fanaticism: A Historical and Psychoanalytical Study,* by André Haynal, Miklós Molnár, and Gérard de Puymège, trans. Linda Butler Koseoglu (New York: Schocken Books, 1983), 18.

10. See Regina M. Schwartz, *The Curse of Cain: The Violent Legacy of Monotheism* (Chicago: University of Chicago Press, 1997). Schwartz writes, "We secularists have barely begun to acknowledge the biblical influence, confidently, and I think mistakenly, believing that a sharp division has been achieved between the premodern sacred worldview and the modern secular one. But sacred categories of thought have not just disappeared. They have lingered into the modern world where they are transformed into secular ones" (6). I have also made this point. See Ingebretsen, *Maps of Heaven, Maps of Hell: Religious Terror as Memory from the Puritans to Stephen King* (Armonk, N.Y.: M. E. Sharpe, 1996). See also Leonard Wolf, "In Horror Movies, Some Things Are Sacred," *New York Times,* 4 April 1976, Sunday Arts and Leisure section, 1, 19.

11. Marcia Clark wore an angel pin into the O. J. Simpson trial; reportedly it took Judge Lance Ito seven hours to decide whether she could keep it. See Ginny Carroll, "How to Run a Textbook Trial, *Newsweek* (7 August 1995): 23.

12. David Smith and Sandra Leicester, *Hug the Monster: How to Embrace Your Fears and Live Your Dreams* (Kansas City: Andrew and McMeel, 1996); advertisement, *Wired* (December 1998): 154.

13. Engels to Marx, letter 214, 27 October 1890 (Karl Marx and Frederick Engels, *Selected Correspondence, 1846–1895,* trans. Dona Torr [New York: International Publishers, 1942], 482).

14. After I wrote this, I happened upon Paul Oppenheimer, who observes the "widespread decline of the influence of organized religion, but not of its images and metaphors, which continue to serve as a shorthand for contemporary emotional states," *Evil and the Demonic: A New Theory of Monstrous Behavior* (New York: New York University Press, 1996), 41.

Introduction

1. *Time* (3 May 1999).

2. In Aristotle, *teras* refers to a child with what we might call birth defects. One popular Greek dictionary (Liddell and Scott) has this: "*teras:* a sign, wonder, marvel. Lat. *portentum, prodigium.* In Homer, esp. of signs from heaven. II. In concrete sense, a monster."

3. John Block Friedman, *The Monstrous Races in Medieval Art and Thought* (Cambridge, Mass.: Harvard University Press, 1981), 179. Even Seneca (4 B.C.–A.D. 65) observes that "unnatural progeny we destroy; we drown even children who at birth are weakly or abnormal. Yet it is not anger, but reason, that separates the harmful from the sound." *Moral Essays,* trans. J. W. Basore (Cambridge, Mass.: Harvard University Press, 1963), 145.

4. In *Wonders and the Order of Nature, 1150–1750* (New York: Zone Books, 1988), Lorraine Daston and Katharine Park find "three separate complexes of interpretations and associated emotions—horror, pleasure, and repugnance" associated with the monstrous birth (176).

5. *Prodigium* "seems to be the ancient synonym to *monstrum.* It refers to an unnatural event, creature or person portending a disaster. . . . Cicero is fond of using *prodigium* and *monstrum* together, perhaps because *prodigium* adds a nuance to *monstrum*" (Dr. Martin D. Snyder, Ph.D., personal communication).

6. Such language is not outdated. "Freak of nature" and "monster" are still used to describe anomalous births. See "The Only Disability to Fear Is a Closed Mind," in which Mary Kenny reflects upon the crisis of thalidomide births in the sixties. *Sunday Telegraph,* 24 December 1995, 2.

7. Popularly, the etymology of the word "monster" derives from the Latin *monstrare,* to show (with cognate forms *demonstrate* and *remonstrate*), as well as *monere,* to warn. Through the tradition both usages shadow each other. The OED cites Chaucer using "monstre" as marvel in 1374, while "monstre" as misshapen is cited in 1300 (vol. 6). To show, to warn: as the etymological burden of these phrases suggests, bodily anomaly *signified;* difference—whether lack or superfluity, whether too many or too much, hand, toe, finger, or other bodily member, for instance—demanded interpretation. Lack as well excess needed positioning in a mental geography of meaning. The word's complicated etymology suggests a long and sometimes convoluted history of events *contra naturam,* whether *portentum, prodigium,* or *ostentum.* Each, in differing ways, signified the ominous, something from which a detriment is expected, and something which deviates from the norm (Friedman, *Monstrous Races,* 110ff.). Thanks go to Dr. Martin Snyder, Ph.D., for his helpful discussions in these areas.

8. Gary Indiana, *Three Month Fever* (New York: HarperCollins, 1999).

9. Susan Stewart, *On Longing: Narratives of the Miniature, the Gigantic, the Souvenir, the Collection* (Baltimore: Johns Hopkins University Press, 1984), esp. "The Imaginary Body," 104–31.

10. In addition, the prodigious sexual claims made for Clinton clearly are meant to enfold him into the repudiative genre of the exceptional body, whose powers signified a commensurate moral failure; see R. I. Moore, *The Formation of a Persecuting Society* (Oxford: Blackwell, 1987), esp. 46–50, on the leper; Saul Brody, *The Disease of the Soul: Leprosy in Medieval Literature* (Ithaca: Cornell University Press, 1974), esp. chaps. 3 and 4; Claude Quétal, *History of Syphilis,* trans. Judith Braddock and Brian Pike (Baltimore: Johns Hopkins University Press, 1990); on blacks and other bodies, see Cindy Patton, *Sex and Germs: The Politics of AIDS* (Boston: South End Press, 1985). For a more general study, see Sander L. Gilman, *Sexuality: An Illustrated History* (New York: John Wiley and Sons, 1989), passim.

11. Susan Stewart, *Crimes of Writing: Problems in the Containment of Representation* (Durham, N.C.: Duke University Press, 1994), 242.

12. James Kincaid, foreword to *Of Men and Monsters: Jeffrey Dahmer and the Construction of the Serial Killer,* by Richard Tithecott (Madison: University of Wisconsin Press, 1997), ix.

13. For an example of one scapegoating drama, see Jon Tinker, ed., *Blaming Others: Prejudice, Race, and Worldwide AIDS* (London: The Panos Institute, 1988).

14. For Gingrich's remarks about Clinton, see Deborah Barfield and Elaine S. Povich, "Tangled in Tape: Committee to Decide Today If Evidences Goes to Public," *Newsday,* 17 September 1998, A5.

15. The *Frankfurter Allegmeine* uses the expression: "The public 'undressing' of a human being—irrespective of his position—is not justice, but instead is a punishment that has been abolished in states where the rule of law prevails." See "The Starr Report," *St. Louis Post-Dispatch,* 16 September 1998, B7.

16. Friedman, *Monstrous Races,* 109. H. J. Rose, in *Religion in Greece and Rome* (New York: Harper, 1959), writes, "A belief in omens was and continued to be universal among the general run of people throughout antiquity; indeed such a belief is by no means dead in our own day" (35). Monsters provided a means of reading the gods, understanding the cosmos by detailing in small its every aspect. The fabulous and exceptional interpreted the real and the mundane by demonstrating its limit—as well as, on occasion, by offering it implicit critique, sometimes both at once, as in this sixteenth-century example: "I will ascribe the causes of this hideous monster to God alone," writes a German medical writer Jakob Rueff about the famous monstrous birth of Krakow in 1540 (Daston and Park, *Wonders,* 193).

17. Sir Richard C. Jebb, ed., *Oedipus Tyrannus, Sophocles: The Plays and Fragments, with Critical Notes, Commentary, and Translation in English Prose* (Amsterdam: Servio, 1963), 53.

18. Rose, *Religion in Greece and Rome,* 233ff.

19. See André Haynal, "From Priest to Philosopher: The Origins of a Concept," in *Fanaticism: A Historical and Psychoanalytical Study,* by André Haynal, Miklós Molnár, and Gérard de Puymège, trans. Linda Butler Koseoglu (New York: Schocken Books, 1983), p. 17.

20. "Monster Culture (Seven Theses)," in *Monster Theory: Reading Culture,* ed. Jeffrey Jerome Cohen (Minneapolis: University of Minnesota Press, 1996); citations from pp. 4, 6, 7, 12. It may not be an easy matter, then, to sort out the origin of the word "monster" from the efflorescence of accrued meanings, connotations, and implications. The breadth of its history can be indicated by its bibliographies: it can be considered in its biological history, from Aristotle to Paré. See Friedman, *Monstrous Races;* Wilson, *Signs and Portents: Monstrous Births from the Middle Ages to the Enlightenment* (New York: Routledge, 1993); Ambroise Paré, *On Monsters and Marvels,* trans. Janis L. Pallister (Chicago: University of Chicago Press, 1982), from which venue it slips into Renaissance use as metaphor of human as well as imaginative possibility, a use perhaps typified by Shakespeare's Caliban: Dennis Todd, *Imagining Monsters: Miscreations of the Self in Eighteenth-Century England* (Chicago: University of Chicago Press, 1995); Marie-Hélène Huet, *Monstrous Imagination* (Cambridge, Mass.: Harvard University Press, 1993); David Williams, *Deformed Discourse: The Function of the Monster in Mediaeval Thought and Literature* (Montreal: McGill-Queen's University Press, 1996). The framing of the monster as a normal function of nature gives us the convoluted double history of exhibitionism and scientistic collection (Daston and Parks, *Wonders*) from Erasmus onward to the freak show of the nineteenth century, and thus latterly Fiedler, *Freaks,* Bogdan, *Freak Show,* and Thomson, *freakery;* most recently the word has been repositioned as a conceptual, rather than directly evaluative, tool, in what might be called the theoretical politics of postmodernism. See Bahktin's development of the grotesque body, as well as Foucault's groundbreaking *The Order of Things: An Archeology of the Human Sciences* (New York: Vintage, 1970). See, to this end, how biological and Gothic use inform postmodernity in the cyborg—and, further, postmodern feminist politics: see Donna J. Haraway, "The Promises of Monsters: A Regenerative Politic for Inappropriate/d Others," in *Cultural Studies,* ed. Lawrence Grossberg, Cary Nelson, Paula A. Treichler (New York: Routledge, 1992), 295–337; also Chris Hables Gray, ed., *The Cyborg Handbook* (New York: Routledge, 1995). Conceptually, as a tool for "reading culture," see, as cited, Cohen, *Monster Theory.* So compelling is the use that John O'Neill's *Five Bodies: The Human Shape of Modern Society* (Ithaca: Cornell University Press, 1985) seems lacking. O'Neill explores "the World's Body," "the Body Politic," "Social Bodies," and "Medical Bodies"—"the Monstrous Body," not discussed, seems an oversight.

21. Mike Farrell, "Forgo [*sic*] the Monster Test for True Justice," *Los Angeles Times,* 15 January 1998, Column Left, Home edition, B9.

22. Lauren Berlant, *The Anatomy of National Fantasy: Hawthorne, Utopia, and Everyday Life* (Chicago: University of Chicago Press, 1991), 5. See, too, Mark Seltzer, *Serial Killers: Death and Life in America's Wound Culture* (New York: Routledge, 1998). In his index, under "Fantasy," he lists "Fantasy, and violence . . . and pornography." See also, he suggests, "Public fantasy; Public/private divide."

23. Slavoj Zizek, "Grimaces of the Real, or When the Phallus Appears," *October* 58 (fall 1991): 44–68. Judith Halberstam, in *Skin Shows: Gothic Horror and the Technology of Monsters* (Durham: Duke University Press, 1995), paraphrasing Kaja Silverman, defines suture in cinematic theory: "The spectator . . . experiences suture first by acknowl-

edging a wound [what "is denied access to upon the screen"] and then by ignoring the wound by allowing the narrative to cover the wound with fiction, a fiction that the spectator must utterly believe in" (153).

24. The ages of Exploration and Conquest witnessed a public fascination with strange peoples and habits as never before. Monstrous races, once wondrous, were not useful as justification for a variety of political rhetorics of exploration and conquest, aspects of which inform Shakespeare's complex portrayal of Caliban in *The Tempest*. On the one hand Caliban casts a long shadow backward to a Plinean fascination with those who lived on the edge of the world; on the other, Caliban is Shakespeare's "monster child," the issue of the witch Sycorax. The alien-child Caliban exploits the belief that monstrosity was a product of his mother's desire, which by definition signaled inappropriate longing. Finally, however, as subject to the authority of those who colonize him, Caliban dramatizes not his monstrosity, but theirs.

25. See OED, vol. 6, "Monstrify," v. "To render monstrous; to pervert."

26. Monstrosity came to signify not only the unusual and maybe mythical, but additionally, and sometimes separately, human morals lapsed or exceptional. Suetonius, for example, writing his history of the Caesars, makes such a separation: "So much for Caligula as emperor. We must now tell of his career as a monster." In other cases visuality is reconceived as monstrous in order to demonstrate presumed internal deficiency. Thomas More thus demonizes Richard III by retrofitting him at birth with a "deformed body" that was in this way "a readable text" (cited in Cohen, *Monster Theory,* 9).

27. Commenting on Seamus Heaney's *Beowulf,* P. J. Kavanaugh notes that Heaney's rendition of "monsters overcome (and overcoming)" can be read as an "allegory of the soul in its struggle with inevitable evil." See "Monsters and Dragons," *Spectator* (16 October 1999): 56–57.

28. The appeal of the Plinean peoples, says Friedman, "was based on such factors as fantasy, escapism, . . . and . . . fear of the unknown. If the monstrous races had not existed, it is likely that people would have created them" (24). See, also, more currently, Colbert I. King, "How Monsters Are Born," *Washington Post,* 20 February 1999. In a discussion of the racially motivated slaying of James Byrd, Jr., in Texas, King writes that monsters are born "out of an unhealthy mixture" of racially centered alienation, fear, and anger (A19).

29. Singer Michael Jackson was also demonized in this currently fashionable way. For one evaluation of the present mood, see James R. Kincaid, in *Salon,* "Is This Child Pornography? American Photo Labs Are Arresting Parents as Child Pornographers for Taking Pictures of Their Kids in the Bath" (31 January 2000). On the James R. Porter case, see Paul Wilkes, "Unholy Acts," *New Yorker* 69 (7 June 1993): 62–79. To the point of this book, however, Mark Edmundson's commentary in *Nightmare on Main Street: Angels, Sadomasochism, and the Culture of Gothic* (Cambridge: Harvard University Press, 1997) locates responsibility for pedophilia "in some measure" in "the ban on priestly sex, combined with the church's narrow attitudes toward sex in general" (59). Nowhere does he examine the gothicized system of representation in which the Church is, historically, a gothicized site, haunted by ghosts and spirits, even as it seems to haunt others. See Edmundson, 57ff.

30. For the use made of Willie Horton in Michael Dukakis's presidential campaign, see Kathleen Hall Jamieson, *Dirty Politics: Deception, Distraction, and Democracy* (New York: Oxford University Press, 1992). For the use made of Greg Louganis, see Barbara Walters's lubricious interview with him (24 February 1995, ABC's *20/20*) on the occasion of the publication of his memoirs, *Breaking the Surface;* for the AIDS monster, see, especially although not exclusively, James Kinsella, *Covering the Plague: AIDS and the American Media* (New Brunswick, R.I.: Rutgers University Press, 1989); Cindy Patton, *Inventing AIDS* (New York: Routledge, 1990); Simon Watney, *Policing Desire: Pornography, AIDS, and the Media* (Minneapolis: University of Minnesota Press, 1987); Douglas Crimp, ed., *AIDS: Cultural Analysis, Cultural Activism* (Cambridge, Mass.: MIT Press, 1988).

31. The recurrent fear of our children, a staple of sixties horror, returns via a projection of violence onto youth. A few years ago Hal Crowther ended his post-Halloween diatribe about violence in popular culture by focusing on the children; "lock them up at night" he writes, or "face the devil's dawn when one of them will be standing in the doorway with a cleaver" ("I Dismember Mama," *Independent Weekly,* 7 November 1990, 6). See Donna Britt, "Young Monsters R U.S.," *Washington Post,* 27 March 1998, B1.

32. George Lakoff and Mark Johnson, *Metaphors We Live By* (Chicago: University of Chicago Press, 1980), 62.

33. Indeed, Hollywood itself becomes the monster; see Claudia Puig, "Hollywood Examines Its Soul: Worried about Censorship, Leaders Debate How to Uncreate a Monster," *USA Today,* 7 June 1999, cover story, D1. See also Joseph Natoli, *Speeding to the Millennium: Film and Culture, 1993–1995* (Albany: State University of New York Press, 1998).

34. Sigmund Freud, *Civilization and Its Discontents,* v. 21 of *The Standard Edition of the Complete Psychological Works of Sigmund Freud* (hereinafter *Standard Edition*), trans. and ed. James Strachey (London: Hogarth Press, 1961), 114.

35. Franco Moretti, "Dialectic of Fear," in *Signs Taken for Wonders: Essays in the Sociology of Literary Forms,* trans. Susan Fischer, David Forgacs, and David Miller (London: Verso, 1988), 88.

36. Its use *as* government can be documented in "The Line Forms Here," *The National Journal's CongressDaily,* 4 March 1999, online a.m. edition. Former chairman of the House Ways and Means Committee Dan Rostenkowski referred to the balanced budget constitutional amendment as a "monster." See "Hill Briefs," *National Journal's Congress-Daily,* 11 May 1992 (online).

37. Sign carried protesting the inclusion of a gay newspaper in a Virginia library. See Lou Chibbaro, Jr., "Emotional Hearing in Fairfax over the *Blade,*" *Washington Blade* (19 March 1993): 6.

38. See Tom Teepen, "Gingrich Chooses God as His New Political Ally," *Atlanta Journal-Constitution,* 18 May 1999, Home edition. "Gingrich's visions remain pretty much as they always have been—of liberal academic, political and media elites who menace the country like monsters from a nightmare" (A11). Brian Lowry writes,

"Given the power of any 'Save our children' theme, virtually no one from the major parties dares challenge this view [decrying sex and violence on TV]"; see "The Campaign Speech You Will Never Hear," *Los Angeles Times,* 7 December 1999, Home edition, 1.

39. *Newsweek* (31 July 1995): 65.

40. Sedgwick writes that "the labeling of a particular force as 'ignorance' seems to place it unappealably in a demonized space on a never quite explicit ethical schema" (*Epistemology of the Closet* [Berkeley: University of California Press], 7).

41. Walter Benjamin, *Illuminations,* ed. and with an introduction by Hannah Arendt, trans. Harry Zohn (New York: Schocken Books, 1968); René Girard, *Violence and the Sacred,* trans. Patrick Gregory (Baltimore: Johns Hopkins University Press, 1977); Peter Gay, *The Cultivation of Hatred* (New York: W. W. Norton, 1993).

42. Freud, *Civilization and Its Discontents,* 115.

43. Dea Birkett, "Monsters with Human Faces," *Guardian* "Weekend Page," 27 September 1997, TT22.

44. "The Secret Tapes," *ABC PrimeTime* with Diane Sawyer, 19 November 1997.

45. Not so in literature and the Gothic more generally, where monsters to the contrary are notable for their volubility. The same can be said, too, for the fairy tale, in which good girls are generally mute, bad ones excessive talkers. See Jack Zipes, ed., *Don't Bet on the Prince: Contemporary Feminist Fairy Tales in North America and England* (Aldershot: Gower, 1986); also Maria Tatar, *The Hard Facts of the Grimms' Fairy Tales* (Princeton: Princeton University Press, 1987).

46. James Curtis, Whale's biographer, writes that he "invested the central character . . . with human qualities." It is more apt to say that Karloff's portrayal of the lumpen creature elicited sympathy, which Whale then had to undermine. See Jan Herman, "Making Monsters Matter," *Los Angeles Times,* 1 August 1998, Orange County edition, Calendar section, F1.

47. According to Roger Shattuck, "Watching [Ted Bundy's interview on 'Inside Edition,' following his execution earlier that day], some people had the feeling that Bundy had survived his own death, that the monster had come back to haunt us through an electronic afterlife" (*Forbidden Knowledge: From Prometheus to Pornography* [New York: St. Martin's Press, 1996], 260).

48. Mary Schmich, writing in the *Chicago Tribune,* 25 July 1997, 1.

49. Nancy Gibbs and Timothy Roche, "The Columbine Tapes," *Time* (20 December 1999): 42.

50. Ibid., 51. See also Bill Hewitt, "Horror and Outrage," *People* (3 May 1999): 94–102.

51. See, among others, Patrick Cook, "Monsters in the Closet: Homosexuality and the Horror Film," *Journal of Popular Film and Television* (fall 1999); Richard Dyer, *Now You See It: Studies on Lesbian and Gay Film* (New York: Routledge, 1990), and "Coming Out as Going In: The Image of the Homosexual as a Sad Young Man," in *The Matter of Images: Essays on Representations* (New York: Routledge, 1993), 73–92. Also,

Harry Crowley, "'Homicidal Homosexual': The Media Left Their Mark; Cunanan Will Be Remembered Foremost as a Gay Killer," *Advocate* (2 September 1997): 24. Crowley cites a former president of the National Lesbian and Gay Journalists Association: "My visceral sense is that the coverage says gayness is all about sex, that sex is perverted and leads to horrible murder."

52. A point Nina Auerbach makes in *Our Vampires, Ourselves* (Chicago: University of Chicago Press, 1995).

53. "Is it a surprise society produces monsters?" *USA Today,* 13 August 1999, A16: After inveighing against "the decline in morality" the article concludes, "It takes a village to raise a murderer."

54. See Crowley, "'Homicidal Homosexual.'"

55. For one, Richard Hofstadter, *Anti-Intellectualism in American Life* (New York: Alfred A. Knopf, 1964).

56. "Inhumation" is Leo Steinberg's term, see *The Sexuality of Christ in Renaissance Art and in Modern Oblivion* (New York: Pantheon Books, 1983).

57. For a contemporary revision of this idea, see Arthur Saltzman, "Avid Monsters: The Look of Agony in Contemporary Literature," *Twentieth Century Literature* (summer 1999): 236–52.

58. "Every real man, that is, every mortal animal that is rational, however unusual to us may be the shape of his body, or the color of his skin, or the way he walks, or the sound of his voice, and whatever the strength, portion or quality of his natural endowments, is descended from the single first-created man." Augustine, *The City of God,* vol. 5, bk. 16, chap. 8, ed. Vernon J. Bourke (New York: Doubleday Image Books, 1958).

Chapter One

1. Slipping its linguistic niche, the word signifies the "irregular," as well as the "unnatural" and "mannerless." Respectively, see these texts: George M. Eberhart, *Monsters: Including Bigfoot, Many Water Monsters, and Other Irregular Animals* (New York: Garland, 1983); Daniel Cohen, *Monsters, Giants, and Little Men from Mars: An Unnatural History of the Americas* (Garden City, N.Y.: Doubleday, 1975), and *A Natural History of Unnatural Things* (New York: E. P. Dutton, 1971); Ted Hughes, *Nessie: The Mannerless Monster* (London: Faber and Faber, 1964).

2. See John Block Friedman, *The Monstrous Races in Medieval Art and Thought* (Cambridge, Mass.: Harvard University Press, 1981). For a discussion of monsters and ideology, see Lorraine Daston and Katharine Park, *Wonders and the Order of Nature, 1150–1750* (New York: Zone Books, 1988); John Knox, "The First Blast of the Trumpet against the Monstrous Regiment of Women" (1558); Alan Fotheringham, "Children of a monster society," *Maclean's* (13 December 1993): 64. President Truman addressed the "monstrous conspiracy" of communism (cited in Timothy Melley, *Empire of Conspiracy: The Culture of Paranoia in Postwar America* [Ithaca: Cornell University Press, 2000],

9). Marx's *Communist Manifesto* opens with an image of a Gothic monster stalking rational and civilized Europe: "A specter is haunting Europe" (Karl Marx and Frederick Engels, *The Communist Manifesto: A Modern Edition,* introduction by Eric Hobsbawm [London: Verso, 1998], 35). Freud's explorations of the political life of civilizations uses similar tropes. The Unconscious haunting the house of Reason or troubling its dreams, is, as numerous commentators observe, "homologous" to the Gothic: psychoanalysis is "a late Gothic story." See Maggie Kilgour, *The Rise of the Gothic Novel* (New York: Routledge, 1995), 221; also Peter Brooks, *Psychoanalysis and Storytelling* (Cambridge, Mass.: Blackwell, 1994).

3. See Freud, "The Ego and the Id," vol. 19, *Standard Edition,* 55–56.

4. "Monster of an All-Star Game," *USA Today,* 13 July 1999, cover story; for the Y2K reference, "Apocalypse? Not Now," *Boston Globe,* 20 July 1999, City edition, A14; for the "monster who roamed the earth in [the coach's] body," see Terence Moore, "Can't Coach 'em Like They Used To," *Atlanta Journal-Constitution,* 24 August 1999, F3; for "party monster" see Betsy Sherman, "Party . . . Challenges Senses, Spirit," *Boston Globe,* 16 July 1999, C6; for bad metaphors, see Paul Johnson, "Block That Metaphor," *Spectator* (9 January 1999): 21; for monstrous metros, see Lyndsey Layton, "Metro Vows Improvement in 60 Days," *Washington Post,* 11 August 2000, 1.

5. See Anne Williams's definition of allegory: "In allegory, the reader is aware, conscious, of reading a text designed to embody, to incarnate, an abstraction. . . . The allegorist personifies the speaking subject as totalitarian overlord of a language who directs and manipulates his world according to a priori thoughts" *Art of Darkness: A Poetics of Gothic* (Chicago: University of Chicago Press, 1995), 81–82.

6. Freud, *Civilization and Its Discontents,* vol. 21, *Standard Edition,* 115. Aristotle writes that "anyone who does not take after his parents is really in a way a monstrosity, since in these cases Nature has in a way strayed from the generic type" (*Generation of Animals,* trans. A. L. Peck [Cambridge, Mass.: Harvard University Press, 1963], bk. 4, 401).

7. Corey Robin cites Hobbes as the "master theorist of fear and its role in political matters" ("Why Do Opposites Attract?: Fear and Freedom in the Modern Political Imagination," in *Fear Itself: Enemies Real and Imagined in American Culture,* ed. Nancy Lusignan Schultz [West Lafayette, Ind.: Purdue University Press, 1999], 3). Hobbes argues, in Roelofs's words, that "the original contract creating the commonwealth is itself born of fear . . . and it is best preserved by the capacity of the sovereign, by the sheer terror of his ways, to hold us all in awe." See Mark H. Roelofs, "Hobbes, Liberalism, and America," in *Liberalism and the Modern Polity: Essays in Contemporary Political Theory,* ed. Michael J. Gargas McGrath (New York: Marcel Dekker, 1978), 132. See esp. "Of Commonwealth," chap. 17 in *Leviathan: or the Matter, Forme and Power of a Commonwealth, Ecclesiasticall and Civil,* ed. Michael Oakeshott (Oxford: Basil Blackwell, 1946).

8. As Corey Robin writes, "modern theorists persistently have expressed . . . that fear may lie at the very heart of human selfhood" (Robin, "Why Do Opposites Attract?" 4). See also David M. Kennedy, "Culture Wars: The Sources and Uses of Enmity in American History," in *Enemy Images in American History,* ed. Ragnhild Fiebig-von Hase

and Ursula Lehmkuhl (Providence, R.I.: Berghahn Books, 1997), 339−56; and Judith N. Shklar, "The Liberalism of Fear," in *Liberalism and the Moral Life,* ed. Nancy L. Rosenblum (Cambridge, Mass.: Harvard University Press, 1989), 21−38.

9. See Sam B. Girgus, ed., *The American Self: Myth, Ideology, and Popular Culture* (Albuquerque: University of New Mexico Press, 1981), esp. 5−43: Sacvan Bercovitch, "The Rites of Assent: Rhetoric, Ritual, and the Ideology of American Consensus."

10. Nina Auerbach, *Our Vampires, Ourselves* (Chicago: University of Chicago Press, 1995), 3.

11. At a few removes my argument incorporates insights derived from Mikhail Bakhtin's work on bodily grotesquery, although even the word grotesque derives, as I will observe, from an older vocabulary of the sacred. See Bakhtin's *Rabelais and His World,* trans. Helene Iswolsky (Cambridge, Mass.: MIT Press, 1968); and *Dialogic Imagination,* ed. Michael Holquist (Austin: University of Texas Press, 1981).

12. Yi-fu Tuan, *Landscapes of Fear* (New York: Pantheon Books, 1979), 182.

13. See Peter Stallybrass and Allon White, *The Politics and Poetics of Transgression* (London: Methuen, 1985). In Robert K. Martin and Eric Savoy, eds., *American Gothic: New Interventions in a National Narrative* (Iowa City: University of Iowa Press, 1998), Martin defines poetics as "a tropics, a recurring turn of language" (3).

14. See, for example, Elaine Showalter, *Hystories: Hysterical Epidemics and Modern Culture* (New York: Columbia University Press, 1997); and Barbara Ehrenreich, *Blood Rites: Origins and History of the Passions of War* (New York: Metropolitan, 1997). Also, Richard Hofstadter's "The Paranoid Style in American Politics," in *The Paranoid Style and Other Essays* (New York: Knopf, 1965); as well as Richard Hofstadter and Michael Wallace, eds., *American Violence: A Documentary History* (New York: Alfred A. Knopf, 1970). Philip Jenkins, *Using Murder: The Social Construction of Serial Homicide* (New York: Aldine de Gruyter, 1994), and *Pedophiles and Priests: Anatomy of a Crisis* (New York: Oxford University Press, 1996). David Sonenschein, *Pedophiles on Parade,* vol. 2, *The Popular Imagery of Moral Hysteria* (San Antonio, Tex: D. Sonenschein, 1998).

15. Michel Foucault, *Discipline and Punish: The Birth of the Prison,* trans. Alan Sheridan (New York: Pantheon, 1977); also Pieter Spierenburg, *The Spectacle of Suffering: Executions and the Evolution of Repression: From a Preindustrial Metropolis to the European Experience* (Cambridge, U.K.: Cambridge University Press, 1984). Wendy Lesser, *Pictures at an Execution* (Cambridge, Mass.: Harvard University Press, 1993). Patrick McGowen, "Punishing Violence, Sentencing Crime," in Armstrong and Tennenhouse, *The Violence of Representation: Literature and the History of Violence* (New York: Routledge, 1989), 140−56: "The Violence of Punishment was a language employed by authority to write the message of justice. The afflictions suffered by the body of the condemned were a way of representing lessons" (143).

16. Clifford Geertz, "Religion as a Cultural System," in *Reader in Comparative Religion,* ed. W. Lessa and E. Vogt, 3d ed. (New York: Harper and Row, 1972), 167. Also, see Victor W. Turner's use of ritual in *Dramas, Fields, and Metaphor: Symbolic Action in Human Society* (Ithaca: Cornell University Press, 1974).

17. Nevertheless, the concept of showy pain is as old as Quintilian: "Wherever we

crucify the guilty, the most crowded roads are chosen, where the most people can see and be moved by this fear. For penalties relate not so much to retribution as to their exemplary effect" (cited in Tuan, *Landscapes of Fear,* 176–77). Dr. Johnson agreed: "If they do not draw spectators, they don't answer their purpose" (cited, Tuan, 183).

18. "Eschatological anguish" is taken from the jointly written epilogue to André Haynal, Miklós Molnár, Gérard de Puymège, *Fanaticism: A Historical and Psychoanalytical Study,* trans. Linda Butler Koseoglu (New York: Schocken Books, 1983), 217. But see Frank Kermode's discussion of a similar affect in *The Sense of an Ending: Studies in the Theory of Fiction* (1967; reprint, New York: Oxford University Press, 2000), or Norman Cohn, *The Pursuit of the Millennium: Revolutionary Messianism in Medieval and Reformation Europe and Its Bearing on Totalitarian Movements* (New York: Harper, 1961).

19. This fact has implications in the formation of nationality in Western cultures more generally, as Benedict Anderson argues in *Imagined Communities: Reflections on the Origin and Spread of Nationalism* (1983; revised, New York: Verso, 1991), esp. 19ff. For the way demonization is used as structural support to civic governance, see, for instance, René Girard, *The Scapegoat,* trans. Yvonne Freccero (Baltimore: Johns Hopkins University Press, 1986); René Girard, *Violence and the Sacred,* trans. Patrick Gregory (Baltimore: Johns Hopkins University Press, 1977); Regina M. Schwartz, *The Curse of Cain: The Violent Legacy of Monotheism* (Chicago: University of Chicago Press, 1997); R. I. Moore, *The Formation of a Persecuting Society: Power and Deviance in Western Europe, 950–1250* (Oxford: Blackwell, 1987).

20. Karen Halttunen, *Murder Most Foul: The Killer and the American Gothic Imagination* (Cambridge, Mass.: Harvard University Press, 1998), 58.

21. As the dust settled—or didn't—on the indecisive presidential election of 2000, "wrangling between the Bush and Gore camps [had] taken on a kind of Gothic hue—but with a uniquely Florida twist." See Michael Schaeffer, "Fun and Frolic, It's Florida!" *U.S. News & World Report* (27 November 2000): 37.

22. Two classic studies include Vera Dika, *Games of Terror: Halloween, Friday the 13th, and the Films of the Stalker Cycle* (Rutherford, N.J.: Fairleigh Dickinson University Press, 1990); and John McCarty, *Splatter Movies: Breaking the Last Taboo of the Screen* (New York: St. Martin's Press, 1984).

23. Gabriele Schwab, "The Subject of the Politically Unconscious," in *Politics, Theory, and Contemporary Culture,* ed. Mark Poster (New York: Columbia University Press, 1993), 83–110. See Clifford D. Shearing and Phillip C. Stenning, "From the Panopticon to Disney World: The Development of Discipline," in *Perspectives in Criminal Law,* ed. Anthony N. Doob and Edward L. Greenspan (Toronto: Canada Law Book, 1984). Also John O'Neill, *Plato's Cave: Desire, Power, and the Specular Functions of the Media* (Norwood, N.J.: Ablex, 1991).

24. Sigmund Freud, "The Psychopathology of Everyday Life," vol. 6, *Standard Edition,* 1–279.

25. See Gérard Genette, *Narrative Discourse: An Essay in Method,* trans. Jane E. Lewin (Ithaca: Cornell University Press, 1980).

26. See Fred G. See, *Desire and the Sign: Nineteenth-Century American Fiction* (Baton Rouge: Louisiana State University Press, 1987).

27. Since children will one day become adults, they too are trained into necessary desires, including fear. See, for example, the video title "Alvin and the Chipmunks Meet Frankenstein" or the popular *Bunnicula* series, by Deborah Howe, or Kathleen Stevens's *The Beast in the Bathtub*. See, too, Kevin Baxter, "Kids' Books: Tales Embrace the Fun, Fright of Halloween," *Los Angeles Times,* 31 October 1999, Record edition, 3; R. L. Stine's "Goosebumps" series of fright books for adolescents numbers upwards of sixty, and one hundred are promised. See, among many, Felicia R. Lee, "Who's Afraid of the Pokemon Monster?" (*New York Times,* 24 October 1999, sec. 14, 1). Lee writes, apropos of my subject, "We live in times in which parents are told to fear everything, from squashing their small children by sleeping with them to diminishing their I.Q.'s by parking them in front of the television. The latest scare is that the ubiquitous Pokemon cards invite addiction." See also Meki Cox, "Those 'Pocket Monsters' Spawn a Mini Crime Wave," *Los Angeles Times,* 12 December 1999, Record edition, 54; Bemjamin Fulford, "Monster Mash," *Forbes* (26 July 1999): 54–55.

28. For example, slasher films are now like Hallmark cards, marketed according to the secular high holidays of the calendar: *My Bloody Valentine* (1981); *Mother's Day* (1980); *Prom Night* (1983). Freddy Krueger is fantasy killer, object of parental revenge, and a well-loved child's doll.

29. Measure 9 states categorically that "homosexuality, pedophilia, sadism and masochism" are "abnormal, wrong, unnatural, and perverse." See Didi Herman, *The Antigay Agenda: Orthodox Vision and the Christian Right* (Chicago: University of Chicago Press, 1997), 145.

30. Roger Chartier, cited in Jean Delumeau, *Sin and Fear: The Emergence of a Western Guilt Culture, 13th–18th Centuries,* trans. Eric Nicholson (New York: St. Martin's Press, 1990), 58.

31. Classicist Martin Snyder, Ph.D., observes that *pietas* is "very much a family word," and that it "describes the proper performance of mutual obligations within a family." Snyder notes that state and state religion, in classical Rome, were extrapolations of the Roman family, and that Christianity "narrowed the scope of 'piety' and . . . stripped it of its reciprocity" (personal communication).

32. See, for instance, Dennis L. White's examination of "The Poetics of Horror: More Than Meets the Eye," in *Cinema Journal* 10, no. 2 (spring 1971): 1–18.

33. For an overview of the "sublime" as an organizing category of American thought, see David E. Nye, *American Technological Sublime* (Cambridge, Mass.: MIT Press, 1994), 1–17. More generally, see Vijay Mishra, *The Gothic Sublime* (Albany: State University of New York Press, 1994).

34. Julia Kristeva, *Powers of Horror: An Essay on Abjection,* trans. Leon S. Roudiez (New York: Columbia University Press, 1982), 208.

35. With particular reference to horror, Terry Heller examines Gothic narrative and reader response theory in *The Delights of Terror: An Aesthetics of the Tale of Terror* (Ur-

bana: University of Illinois Press, 1987). For popular culture more widely, see Lawrence W. Levine, "William Shakespeare and the American People: A Study in Cultural Transformation," in *Rethinking Popular Culture: Contemporary Perspectives in Cultural Studies,* ed. Chandra Mukerji and Michael Schudson (Berkeley: University of California Press, 1991).

36. Schwab, "The Subject of the Politically Unconscious," 85.

37. Halttunen, *Murder Most Foul.* Also in this regard, see Priscilla Wald, *Constituting Americans: Cultural Anxiety and Narrative Form* (Durham, N.C.: Duke University Press, 1995); Steven Watts, *The Romance of Real Life: Charles Brockden Brown and the Origins of American Culture* (Baltimore: Johns Hopkins University Press, 1994); Jane Thompkins, *Sensational Designs: The Cultural Work of American Fiction, 1790–1860* (New York: Oxford University Press, 1985); James D. Hart, *The Popular Book: A History of America's Literary Taste* (New York: Oxford University Press, 1950).

38. E. Digby Baltzell explores this point in *The Protestant Establishment: Aristocracy and Caste in America* (London: Secker and Warburg, 1965); also, Levine, "William Shakespeare and the American People"; John S. Gilkeson, *Middle-Class Providence, 1820–1940* (Princeton: Princeton University Press, 1986).

39. See Daniel A. Cohen, *Pillars of Salt, Monuments of Grace: New England Crime Literature and the Origins of American Popular Culture, 1674–1860* (New York: Oxford University Press, 1993); Cohen's argument about the development of indigenous narrative resembles Halttunen's. Chris Baldick tracks the way rhetorics of monstrosity emerged in response to Enlightenment rationality; he also shows how overheated Gothic address became a favored way of speaking about civil unrest during the late seventeenth and early eighteenth centuries. See *In Frankenstein's Shadow: Myth, Monstrosity, and Nineteenth-Century Writing* (Oxford: Clarendon Press, 1987).

40. Halttunen, *Murder Most Foul,* 50.

41. Ibid., 5; Halttunen's italics.

42. Walter Kendrick, *The Thrill of Fear: 250 Years of Scary Entertainment* (New York: Grove Press, 1991), 7. Stephen Prickett spells out one of the consequences: "It was in America, at the very time when the scientific interest in monsters was coming to a climax, that the gothic quest for the dramatic moment or scene was most effectively combined with a metaphysical sense of evil." See *Victorian Fantasy* (Bloomington: Indiana University Press, 1979), 97–98.

43. For a careful delineation of their varieties and differences, see Elisabeth Young-Bruehl, *The Anatomy of Prejudices* (Cambridge, Mass.: Harvard University Press, 1996).

44. Harry S. Stout, *Preaching and Religious Culture in Colonial New England* (New York: Oxford University Press, 1986); David D. Hall, *Days of Wonder, Days of Judgment: Popular Religious Belief in Early New England* (Cambridge, Mass.: Harvard University Press, 1990). For the jeremiad tradition, see Perry Miller, *The New England Mind: From Colony to Province* (1953; reprint, Cambridge, Mass.: Belknap Press of Harvard University Press, 1983). The diary of John Winthrop, first governor of the province, recounts his thoughts about Anne Hutchinson's monstrous issue shortly after her exile from the Massachusetts Bay Colony. See Richard S. Dunn and Laetitia Yeandle, eds., *The Journal of John Winthrop,* abridged ed. (Cambridge, Mass.: Belknap Press of Harvard University

Press, 1996), 141–42; 146–47); also "A Short Story of the Rise, Reign and Ruine of the Antinomians, Familists and Libertines," in *The Antinomian Controversy, 1636–1638,* ed. David D. Hall (Middletown, Conn.: Wesleyan University Press, 1968).

45. Alexis de Tocqueville, *Democracy in America,* trans. George Lawrence, ed. J. P. Mayer (New York: Harper and Row, 1969), 444.

46. Freud, *Civilization and Its Discontents,* 116.

47. Kennedy, "Culture Wars," 342. The passage in Freud's *Civilization and Its Discontents* to which he refers can be found in vol. 21 of the *Standard Edition,* 115–16.

48. Marx and Engels, *Communist Manifesto,* passim. Marx applied the language of horror to the horrific productivities of capitalism: "But capital obtains this ability [its illusory permanence of value] only by constantly sucking in living labour as its soul, vampire-like" (*Grundrisse,* 646; cited in Baldick, *Frankenstein's Shadow,* 129). Baldick notes that the "ghoulish effects" of Marx's thoroughgoing use of Gothic images are "no mere stylistic flourish but a consistent ironic reversal of the bourgeoisie's own myth." (125).

49. George Lakoff and Mark Johnson employ "tactic" in their discussion of metaphor. See *Metaphors We Live By* (Chicago: University of Chicago Press, 1980), 62ff.; also Michael Kowalewski, *Deadly Musings: Violence and Verbal Form in American Fiction* (Princeton: Princeton University Press, 1993).

50. The first Gothic monster in the Anglo "New World" was—thanks to the Puritan determined to eradicate him—a combination of all these: the hellish red demon, alien and undomesticated, pagan, lurking in the woods. Robert Berkhofer's *The White Man's Indian* (New York: Vintage, 1978) cites early Puritan texts which demonize Indians in many of the same terms as contemporary examples. Cotton Mather remarks, in *Wonders of the Invisible World,* that the "Swarthy Indians" (85) were kin to the "small Black man," the devil (Boston, 1862; 80). J. Edgar Hoover, beginning forty years before the serial killer panic, claimed that "depraved human beings, more savage than beasts, are permitted to rove America almost at will" (J. Edgar Hoover, "How Safe Is Your Youngster?" *American Magazine* 159 [3 March 1955]: 19, 99–103).

51. See Giles Gunn, *The Interpretation of Otherness: Literature, Religion, and the American Imagination* (New York: Oxford University Press, 1979).

52. Joyce Carol Oates, "I Had No Other Thrill or Happiness," *New York Review of Books* (24 March 1994): 52–59.

53. If from one perspective the ambiguous body possessed high moral authority, from long-standing practice the different body also provided a form of entertainment, however distasteful to contemporary sensibility, not dissimilar from the practice of viewing incarcerated mental patients. See Dennis Todd, *Imagining Monsters: Miscreations of the Self in Eighteenth-Century England* (Chicago: University of Chicago Press, 1995); also Rosemarie Thomson, *Freakery: Cultural Spectacles of the Extraordinary Body* (New York: New York University Press, 1997); Leslie Fiedler, *Freaks: Myths and Images of the Secret Self* (New York: Penguin, 1978).

54. Mikhael Elbaz and Ruth Murbach, "Fear in the Face of the Other, Condemned and Damned: AIDS, Epidemics, and Exclusions," in *A Leap in the Dark: AIDS,*

Art, and Contemporary Cultures, ed. Allan Klusacek and Ken Morrison (Montreal: Véhicule Press, 1993), 2.

55. Mark Edmundson, *Nightmare on Main Street: Angels, Sadomasochism, and the Culture of Gothic* (Cambridge, Mass.: Harvard University Press, 1997), 60; Edmundson's italics. Using a rhetoric of monsters to stabilize a disrupted rhetoric of race is a repeated scene in American politics. Thus, while the economics of slavery had made necessary the development of a caste rhetoric as early as precolonial times, the political threat represented by the War Between the States caused an increased hysteria, whose economic incentive was deflected into a different economy, the intimate and sexual. The *New York Daily News* on 4 April 1864 called miscegenation "a real, completely organized, living monster [which] rears its horrible head in our midst *and threatens* to devour society itself" (cited in Forrest Wood, *Black Scare: The Racist Response to Emancipation and Reconstruction* [Berkeley: University of California Press, 1968], 61). The violence of the language signifies, for one thing, that a formal containment of the black sanctioned by law no longer existed, and so, therefore, other forces were brought to bear. See Joan Dayan, "Romance and Race," *The Columbia History of the American Novel,* ed. Emory Elliott (New York: Columbia University Press, 1991), 89–109.

56. See, for instance, Gary Heba, "Everyday Nightmares: The Rhetoric of Social Horror in the *Nightmare on Elm Street* Series," *Journal of Popular Film and Television* (1 September 1995): 106.

57. Freud, vol. 21, *Standard Edition,* 114.

58. Michael Uebel, "Unthinking the Monster: Twelfth-Century Responses to Saracen Alterity," in Jeffrey Jerome Cohen, ed., *Monster Theory: Reading Culture* (Minneapolis: University of Minnesota Press, 1996), 266.

59. Homi K. Bhabha, "The Other Question: The Stereotype and Colonial Discourse," in *The Sexual Subject: A Screen Reader in Sexuality,* collective editorial (New York: Routledge, 1992), 312–31.

60. Eve Kosofsky Sedgwick, *Epistemology of the Closet* (Berkeley: University of California Press, 1990), 13.

61. Roger Shattuck, in *Forbidden Knowledge: From Prometheus to Pornography* (New York: St. Martin's Press, 1996), comments that "the transvaluation of all values [in Sade's writing] does not find a new language; rather, it reinforces the sharp edge of conventional terms [horrible, monstrous, infamous, etc.] to underline the scandal of what is described" (277).

62. "Milwaukee Murders," Alex Prud'Homme, *Time* (12 August 1991): 28.

63. William Veeder, "The Nurture of the Gothic, or How Can a Text Be Both Popular and Subversive?" in Martin and Savoy, *American Gothic,* 21; Veeder's italics.

64. F. Scott Fitzgerald, *The Great Gatsby,* ed. Matthew J. Bruccoli (New York: Simon and Schuster, 1991), 6.

65. Yet as feminist theorists point out, the language of gender itself is hybridic, incoherent, patchwork, a literal production of the copy that then passes for an original. See Teresa de Lauretis, "The Violence of Rhetoric," in *Technologies of Gender: Essays on*

Theory, Film, and Fiction (Bloomington: Indiana University Press, 1987); Judith Butler, *Bodies That Matter: On the Discursive Limits of "Sex"* (New York: Routledge, 1993); this gender-specific text is further scripted, implicated into monstrosity through the trope of the absent or failed mother—a cinematic convention reproduced politically. For body anxiety specific to gender and its social formations, see, among others, Judith Butler, *Gender Trouble: Feminism and the Subversion of Identity* (New York: Routledge, 1990); Marjorie Garber, *Vested Interests: Cross-Dressing and Cultural Anxiety* (New York: Harper-Perennial, 1992), and *Vice Versa: Bisexuality and the Eroticism of Everyday Life* (New York: Simon and Schuster, 1995); Julia Epstein and Kristina Straub, *Body Guards: The Cultural Politics of Gender Ambiguity* (New York: Routledge, 1991).

66. Or, as Jameson argues, following Delueuze and Guatarri, schizophrenic presence is the product of "the fragmenting effects of late consumer capitalism." See Schwab, "The Subject of the Politically Unconscious," 94.

67. Teresa A Goddu, *Gothic America: Narrative, History, and Nation* (New York: Columbia University Press, 1997), 10. For bibliographic studies of American Gothic, see Frederick S. Frank, *Through the Pale Door: A Guide to and through the American Gothic* (Westport, Conn.: Greenwood Press, 1990). See also *The Fantasy Tradition in American Literature: From Irving to LeGuin,* by Brian Attebery (Bloomington: Indiana University Press, 1980). The Gothic, historically, according to one view, emerged as a way of articulating a particular kind of fear, one I will call, for lack of a better word, metaphysical. Leslie Fiedler suggests that in its original forms the Gothic "reveals the 'soul of Europe' in flight from "its own darker impulses"; cited in Victor Sage, *The Gothick Novel: A Casebook* (Basingstoke: Macmillan, 1990), 129.

68. Patrick McGrath, "Transgression and Decay," in *Gothic: Transmutations of Horror in Late Twentieth-Century Art,* ed. Christoph Grunenberg (Cambridge, Mass.: MIT Press, 1997), 155 (italics in original).

69. Director David Cronenberg remarks that the source of horror seems fixed, the fear of "the human body and the fact of aging and death and disease" (cited in McCarty, *Splatter Movies,* 80). The violent body, as well—see Richard Slotkin, famously, *Regeneration through Violence: The Mythology of the American Frontier, 1600–1860* (Middletown, Conn.: Wesleyan University Press, 1973).

70. Specific treatments of American Gothic include Ringe's aesthetic-historical; Gross's sociopolitical; Delamotte's, Williams's, and Ellis's feminist; Goddu's revisionist history. See Leslie Fiedler, *Love and Death in the American Novel* (New York: Dell, 1966); Louis S. Gross, *Redefining the American Gothic: From Wieland to Day of the Dead* (Ann Arbor, Mich.: UMI Research Press, 1989); Donald A. Ringe, *American Gothic: Imagination and Reason in Nineteenth-Century Fiction* (Lexington, Ky.: University Press of Kentucky, 1982); Goddu, *Gothic America;* Edmundson, *Nightmare on Main Street;* Ingebretsen, *Maps of Heaven, Maps of Hell: Religious Terror as Memory from the Puritans to Stephen King* (Armonk, N.Y.: M. E. Sharpe, 1996). For cinema, see Stephen King, *Danse Macabre* (New York: Everest House, 1981); David J. Skal, *The Monster Show: A Cultural History of Horror* (New York: W. W. Norton, 1993), and *Hollywood Gothic: The Tangled Web of "Dracula" from Novel to Stage to Screen* (New York: W. W. Norton, 1990); Philip Davies and Brian Neve, eds., *Cinema, Politics, and Society in America* (New York: St. Martin's Press, 1981).

71. See Garry Wills, *Under God: Religion and American Politics* (New York: Simon and Schuster, 1990); Michael Walzer, *Exodus and Revolution* (New York: Basic Books, 1984); Joseph A. Conforti, *Jonathan Edwards, Tradition, and American Culture* (Chapel Hill: University of North Carolina Press, 1995); R. Laurence Moore, *Selling God: American Religion in the Marketplace of Culture* (New York: Oxford University Press, 1994); Marjorie Garber and Rebecca L. Walkowitz, *One Nation Under God? Religion and American Culture* (New York: Routledge, 1999); Stephen L. Carter, *The Culture of Disbelief: How American Law and Politics Trivialize Religious Devotion* (New York: HarperCollins, 1993).

72. For example, in "From Sects to Sectarianism" the authors of *Fanaticism* (Haynal, Molnár, de Puymège) write, "The tradition of sects in the United States is a deeply rooted one, inseparable from the country's early history and indeed closely linked to its founding myth of the American Dream, a fresh start, recovered purity. The ubiquitous Bible culture, the disenchantment of the consumer society, the bad conscience born of the Vietnam War and the race problem . . . are only the setting for these dramas" (200–201).

73. Victor Sage and others point out how the Gothic's devotion to ghosts suddenly made visible parlayed into mundane life spiritual, even religious issues and concerns during a period of history in which political concerns of property, lineage, and historical stability were likewise deflected into less obvious modes, the literary and the aesthetic. Victor Sage, *Horror Fiction in the Protestant Tradition* (London: Macmillan, 1988).

74. Daniel Snowman and Malcolm Bradbury, "The Sixties and Seventies," in *Introduction to American Studies,* ed. Malcolm Bradbury and Howard Temperley, 3d ed. (London: Longman, 1988), 273. Edmundson writes, in a similar vein, that "suddenly, great masses of Americans who had lived subordinate, secondary lives demanded to be recognized as full citizens, as having as much right to liberty and the pursuit of happiness as the upholders of the box-shouldered, male, heterosexual norm" (*Nightmare,* 64).

75. See John D'Emilio, *Sexual Politics, Sexual Communities: The Making of a Homosexual Minority in the United States,* 2d ed. (Chicago: University of Chicago Press, 1998); John I. Kitsuse, "Coming Out All Over: Deviants and the Politics of Social Problems," *Social Problems* 28 (1980): 1–13; Lynne Segal, *Straight Sex: Rethinking the Politics of Pleasure* (Berkeley: University of California Press, 1994); also John D'Emilio and Estelle B. Freedman, *Intimate Matters: A History of Sexuality in America,* 2d ed. (Chicago: University of Chicago Press, 1987).

76. Vance Packard, *The Hidden Persuaders* (New York: David McKay, 1957); J. Edgar Hoover, *Masters of Deceit: The Story of Communism in America and How to Fight It* (New York: Henry Holt, 1958).

77. Gregory A. Waller, ed., *American Horrors: Essays on the Modern American Horror Film* (Urbana: University of Illinois Press, 1987), 4.

78. Walter Kendrick suggests that a famous anti-comic crusader of the fifties may have been after something other than comics: "Wertham's most horrifying revelation was that America's children formed a tribe that had eluded parental surveillance until he exposed it" (242). See "The New Pornography," in Kendrick, *The Thrill of Fear,*

240ff.; also Thomas Doherty, *Teenagers and Teenpics: The Juvenilization of American Movies in the 1950s* (Boston: Unwin Hyman, 1988). Part of the anxiousness was generational; the kids were privately suspect to their uptight parents, an anxiety evident in what Welch Everman calls "those marvelous teen rebel movies of the fifties," (*Cult Horror Films: From Attack of the 50 Foot Woman to Zombies of Mora Tau* [Secaucus, N.J.: Citadel Press, 1993], 229): *I Was a Teenage Werewolf* (1957); *Teenage Frankenstein* (1958); even—horrors!—*Teenagers from Outer Space* (1959); and *Rebel without a Cause* (1955).

79. Beginning early in the fifties, the cross-fertilization of Eisenhower and Heinlein made for a siege mentality in which bug-eyed creatures articulated social distresses of all sorts, indiscriminately, monstrously mixed, just like the problems they suggested, but never fully addressed: space travel, generational conflict, domestic refitting, racial upset. For example: *It! The Terror from Beyond Space* (1958) and *The Cosmic Monsters* (1958) gave evidence of a post-Sputnik (i.e., post-1957) concern with space. Atomic politics likewise continued to cause anxiety: *The Atomic Monster* (1961) *Them!* (1954), or *The Mysterians* (1958), *The Brain Eaters* (1959). Jack Finney's novel, *The Body Snatchers* (New York: Dell, 1955), turned into film, demonstrates the concern we have been tracking: *Invasion of the Body Snatchers* (1956).

80. Kendrick, likewise, observes that the "magnitude of the comic-book craze, and its extraordinary growth, were scary in themselves. . . . By 1948 . . . about sixty million comics were being bought each month in the United states; the figure had risen to ninety million per month by 1954. The number is astonishing, given that in 1950 the country's total population was about 140 million" (*The Thrill of Fear*, 242). This production did not go unchallenged. Fredric Wertham had been lobbying against the "new pornography" of comic books since 1946; in 1954 he published *Seduction of the Innocent* (New York: Rinehart).

81. Cristoph Grunenberg, "Unsolved Mysteries: Gothic Tales from *Frankenstein* to the Hair-Eating Doll," in Grunenberg, *Gothic,* 165.

82. Skal, *The Monster Show,* 230. From the films *Mole People* (1956), *Island of Doctor Moreau* (1977), *The Swarm* (1978), *Creature from the Black Lagoon* (1955), and *The Slime People* (1959). "A short list, a very short list, would include as representatives of the nuclear imagination alligator people, human flies, colossal man, transport man, she-woman, atomic kid, atomic man, atomic mutant, crab monster, 50 foot woman, giant leeches, puppet people, a beast from 20,000 fathoms, a beast with a million eyes, a blob, cosmic mutants, giant mantis, amphibian monsters, tree monsters, pod people, campus monster, mutant children, mutant parents, giant Gila monster, giant plants, man-eating brains, four-dimensional man, gamma people, giant squid, Godzilla, shrinking man, giant octopus, giant cucumber, killer shrews, magnetic monster, giant sea slugs, pterodactyls, giant tarantula, giant carrot, wasp woman and mineral monster" (Jonathan Lake Crane, *Terror and Everyday Life: Singular Moments in the History of the Horror Film* [Thousand Oaks: Sage Publishers, 1994], 107). See, also, Joseph D. Andriano, *Immortal Monster: The Mythological Evolution of the Fantastic Beast in Modern Fiction and Film* (Westport, Conn.: Greenwood Press, 1999).

83. See Carol J. Clover, "Her Body, Himself: Gender in the Slasher Film," in *Fantasy and the Cinema,* ed. James Donald (London: British Film Institute, 1989), 91–133.

84. Richard Hofstadter, "Reflections on Violence in the United States," in Hofstadter and Wallace, *American Violence,* 7.

85. Janice Radway, "Phenomenology, Linguistics, and Popular Literature," *Journal of Popular Culture* 12 (1973), 96.

86. Walter Kendrick terms the period "history's grandest fit of paranoid dementia" (*The Thrill of Fear,* 241).

87. The romance has been, since Richard Chase's *The American Novel and Its Tradition* (New York: Doubleday, 1957), the "American" genre. However, as Goddu suggests in *Gothic America,* in order to create the ideological space in which its superiority could remain unchallenged, the Gothic, and all persons or places associated with it (the South, Poe, women buried—socially or actually), were dismissed as derivative, secondary, and, ultimately, anti-national. See Joan Dayan, "Amorous Bondage: Poe, Ladies, and Slaves," *American Literature* 66 (1994): 239–73; Toni Morrison, *Playing in the Dark: Whiteness and the Literary Imagination* (Cambridge, Mass.: Harvard University Press, 1992).

88. Judith Wilts, without intending to do so, exploits the Gothic's split religious sensibility: "Dread is the father and mother of the Gothic. Dread begets rage and fright and cruel horror, or awe and worship and shining steadfastness—all of these have human features, but Dread has no face" (*Ghosts of the Gothic: Austen, Eliot, and Lawrence* [Princeton: Princeton University Press, 1980], 5).

89. Mark Edmundson discusses what this split looks like in popular culture; he terms it "one of the modes of facile transcendence" (*Nightmare on Main Street,* 77).

90. For different versions of the psychological, from the most reductive to sophisticated, see Walter Evans, "Monster Movies: A Sexual Theory," *Journal of Popular Film* 2 (fall 1973): 353–65; Kevin Fauteux, "Fear and Trembling at the Movies," *Pastoral Psychology* 36, no. 2 (1987): 84–87; James Twitchell, *Dreadful Pleasures: An Anatomy of Modern Horror* (New York: Oxford University Press, 1985); Crane, *Terror and Everyday Life;* Barbara Creed, *The Monstrous-Feminine: Film, Feminism, Psychoanalysis* (London: Routledge, 1993).

91. Grunenberg, "Unsolved Mysteries," in Grunenberg, *Gothic,* 201.

92. King, *Danse Macabre,* 282. See Thomas S. Frentz and Thomas B. Farrell, "Conversion of America's Consciousness: The Rhetoric of *The Exorcist,*" *Quarterly Journal of Speech* 61, no. 1 (February 1975): 40–47.

93. Noel Carroll argues that *The Exorcist* (text, 1971; film 1973) is crucial to the subsequent mainstream popularity of the horror genre; see *The Philosophy of Horror: Paradoxes of the Heart* (New York: Routledge, 1990), 2–3. Michael Morrison places the date for the Gothic resurgence "roughly from the late 1970's through the early 1990's" ("After the Danse: Horror at the End of the Century," in *A Dark Night's Dreaming: Contemporary American Horror Fiction,* ed. Tony Magistrale and Michael A. Morrison [Columbia: University of South Carolina Press, 1996], 9).

94. Isabel Pinedo, *Recreational Terror: Women and the Pleasures of Horror Film Viewing* (Albany: State University of New York Press, 1997), 2. Similarly, Marina Warner, author of a pair of books on fairy tales (*In a Dark Wood* [New York: Knopf, 1977] and *From the Beast to the Blonde: On Fairy Tales and Their Tellers* [London: Chatto and Windus, 1994]),

says that daily prayers and retreats, "thrilling" stories about saints, and "the discipline of identification with the suffering body of Christ . . . wakened my imagemaking tendencies." See Elizabeth Gleick, "Boo! (Scared Yet?)" *Time* (24 May 1999): 84–86.

95. Pinedo, *Recreational Terror,* 2.

96. Ibid., 5. Burke writes, "If the pain and terror are so modified as not to be actually noxious; if the pain is not carried to violence, and the terror is not conversant about the present destruction of the person . . . [the mind] experiences a 'delightful horror'" (Edmund Burke, *A Philosophical Enquiry into the Origin of Our Ideas of the Sublime and the Beautiful,* ed. Adam Phillips [New York: Oxford University Press, 1990], 123).

97. King, *Danse Macabre,* 41.

98. Alan Lloyd Smith and Victor Sage, "Introduction," in *Modern Gothic: A Reader,* ed. Victor Sage and Allan Lloyd Smith (Manchester: Manchester University Press, 1996), 5.

99. For a study of the development of a media of fear during this period, see Les Daniels, *Living in Fear: A History of Horror in the Mass Media* (New York: Scribner's, 1975). Also, H. Aaron Cohl, *Are We Scaring Ourselves to Death? How Pessimism, Paranoia, and a Misguided Media Are Leading Us toward Disaster* (New York: St Martin's Griffin, 1997); Barry Glassner, *The Culture of Fear: Why Americans Are Afraid of the Wrong Things* (New York: Basic Books, 1999). Glassner argues that "symbolic substitutes" "tap into our moral insecurities" (xxviii).

100. John J. O'Connor, " 'Tales from the Crypt' Raises Ratings for HBO," *New York Times,* 26 June 1991.

101. Peter Gay, *The Cultivation of Hatred* (New York: W. W. Norton, 1993), 6.

102. To take one example, the campaign of fear instigated early in the thirties by J. Edgar Hoover, and which bequeaths to us the ubiquitous pervert, the child molester, was probably as fanciful as the sanctimonious certainties of the neighborhood streets their presence was thought to threaten.

103. William Patrick Day, *In the Circles of Fear and Desire: A Study of Gothic Fantasy* (Chicago: University of Chicago Press, 1985), 191.

104. Eugenia C. DeLamotte, *Perils of the Night: A Feminist Study of Nineteenth-Century Gothic* (New York: Oxford University Press, 1990), vii.

105. Cited in Marshall Blonsky, *American Mythologies* (New York: Oxford University Press, 1992), 361.

106. Mark Seltzer, *Serial Killers: Death and Life in America's Wound Culture* (New York: Routledge, 1998); for psychological and cultural perspectives on the crisis of the ambiguous, see Mary Douglas, *Purity and Danger: An Analysis of Concepts of Pollution and Taboo* (New York: Praeger, 1966); Julia Kristeva, *Powers of Horror: An Essay on Abjection,* trans. Leon S. Roudiez (New York: Columbia University Press, 1982); Iris Marion Young, *Justice and the Politics of Difference* (Princeton: Princeton University Press, 1990), esp. chap. 5.

107. Bill Clinton, responding to Sol Wisenburg before the grand jury, 17 August 1998 (cited in Alan Dershowitz, *Sexual McCarthyism: Clinton, Starr, and the Emerging*

Constitutional Crisis [New York: Basic Books, 1998], 29). See also Jeffrey Toobin, *A Vast Conspiracy: The Real Story of the Sex Scandal That Nearly Brought Down a President* (New York: Random House, 1999), 314.

108. Contemporary American Gothic thus offers interesting parallels to the body-panic civic structures of an earlier century. Nineteenth-century Gothic circulates hysteria around the degenerating and metamorphosing physical body. See Kelly Hurley, *The Gothic Body: Sexuality, Materialism, and Degeneration at the Fin de Siècle* (Cambridge, U.K.: Cambridge University Press, 1996). Contemporary Gothic, on the other hand, interiorizes that panic. Criminalization charts the interior body, obsessing around identities that are always already becoming something else, using metaphors of monstrous bodily deviation to dramatize the mode. See, for example, Charles Winick, ed., *Deviance and Mass Media* (Beverly Hills: Sage, 1978); William G. Staples, *The Culture of Surveillance: Discipline and Social Control in the United States* (New York: St. Martin's Press, 1997); Clinton R. Sanders and Jeff Ferrell, eds., *Cultural Criminology* (Boston: Northeastern University Press, 1995).

109. See, for example, Elizabeth Mehren, "Ex-Priest Gets 18-Year Term for Sex Abuse at 5 Parishes," *Los Angeles Times,* 7 December 1993, A1; "Former Catholic Priest Sentenced to 18 to 20 Years for Sex Crimes," *New York Times,* 7 December 1993.

110. Dahmer acted, an escaped victim said, "like he was the character in *Exorcist III*" (*Los Angeles Times,* 31 January 1992, A4; cited in Richard Tithecott, *Of Men and Monsters: Jeffrey Dahmer and the Construction of the Serial Killer* [Madison: University of Wisconsin Press, 1997], 9).

111. See, for instance, Stephen J. Pfhol, *Images of Deviance and Social Control* (New York: McGraw-Hill, 1985); John Curra, *The Relativity of Deviance* (Thousand Oaks, Calif.: Sage Publications, 2000).

112. Hannah Arendt, *Eichmann in Jerusalem: A Report on the Banality of Evil* (New York: Penguin, 1964), 276. Eichmann himself denied the term "monster" in his statement of defense. Cited in chap. 2.

113. Films such as *The Astounding She Monster* (1959) reflect, while evidencing, places of social as well as semantic discontent. For a taxonomy of prejudice, see Elisabeth Young-Bruehl, *The Anatomy of Prejudices* (Cambridge, Mass.: Harvard University Press, 1996).

114. Matthew Ruben, "Of Newts and Quayles: National-Political Masculinity in the Current Conjuncture," in *Boys: Masculinities in Contemporary Culture,* ed. Paul Smith (New York: Westview Press, 1996), 256.

Chapter Two

1. Ann Rule [Andy Stack, pseud.], *Lust Killer* (New York: Signet, 1983), 166.

2. See Franco Moretti's discussion of rhetorical forms in "Dialectic of Fear": "Rhetorical figures, and the larger combinations which organize long narratives, are thus of a piece with the deep, buried, invisible presuppositions of every world view. . . . (Almost

all emotional language—from 'honey' to 'scum' and beyond—is a long chain of metaphors)." *Signs Taken for Wonders: Essays in the Sociology of Literary Forms,* trans. Susan Fischer, David Forgacs, and David Miller (London: Verso, 1988), 6.

3. David E. Musselwhite, *Partings Welded Together: Politics and Desire in the Nineteenth-Century English Novel* (London: Methuen, 1987), 59; Musselwhite's italics.

4. Terry Heller, *The Delights of Terror: An Aesthetics of the Tale of Terror* (Urbana: University of Illinois Press, 1987). Heller argues the "reenactment of repression" in which culturally forbidden material is elicited through narrative, but re-repressed in terms of the narrative (72, 85). See also Slavoj Zizek, "Grimaces of the Real, or When the Phallus Appears," *October* 58 (fall 1991): 44–68: "The analysis that focuses on the 'ideological meaning' of monsters overlooks the fact that . . . before serving as a vessel of meaning, monsters embody enjoyment qua the limit of interpretation, that is to say, *non-meaning as such*" (64).

5. Gabriele Schwab, "The Subject of the Politically Unconscious," in *Politics, Theory, and Contemporary Culture,* ed. Mark Poster (New York: Columbia University Press, 1993), 86.

6. Moretti, "Dialectic of Fear," 3.

7. For Pol Pot, see Wilson Strand, letter to the editor, *Newsweek* (1 June 1998): 8H. For Stalin, see Edith Milton, "Inside the Creepily Logical Mind of a Monster," *Boston Globe,* 6 June 1999, City edition, N6; also Anthony Olcott, "No Regrets, Comrades," review of *The Autobiography of Joseph Stalin,* by Richard Lourie, *Washington Post,* 18 July 1999, X13. Even Boy Scout founder Robert Baden-Powell comes in for a revisionist drubbing as the "Monster of Mafikeng," because of his alleged mistreatment of blacks in the Boer War. See Dean E. Murphy, "Pinning Demerit Badge on Chief Boy Scout," *Los Angeles Times,* 24 July 1999, Home edition, 1. We will see examples for Smith and Cunanan later in this book. For those who mistreat animals, see Claudia McCue, "Pay Back Monsters," letter to the editor, *Atlanta Journal-Constitution,* 28 September 1999, Final edition, A19. A follow-up letter on the same story decries anonymity in the story: "expose these monsters," the author says; see Jack T. Boling, letter to the editor, *Atlanta Journal-Constitution,* 22 November 1999, A10. For Pinochet, see Ariel Dorfman, "Let Pinochet Back Only on His Deathbed; . . . He's a monster who should face a reckoning before the families of those who were his victims," *Los Angeles Times,* 28 November 1999, Opinion section, Home edition, 5. The president of North Korea, "lately a monster," is said to be "morphing into something less sinister, could be in the process of going straight"[!]. See Mary McGrory, "More Missile Madness," *Washington Post,* 22 June 2000, A3.

8. Karen Halttunen, *Murder Most Foul: The Killer and the American Gothic Imagination* (Cambridge, Mass.: Harvard University Press, 1998); both citations from 46; Halttunen's italics.

9. In *Murder Most Foul,* "The Birth of Horror," Halttunen cites numerous examples: a 1778 murderer killed "in cool blood" (45); in an 1809 narrative the killer was an "unfeeling fiend" (45) or, in 1802, "a fiend-like *foe* to man" (47; author's italics); in a case evocative of James Porter in court, John Battus, convicted of murder and rape,

writes from his prison cell in 1804, "I am fearful you will not have hearts to forgive such a wretched creature, such a monster as I have been" (46).

10. Lorraine Daston and Katharine Park, *Wonders and the Order of Nature, 1150–1750* (New York: Zone Books, 1988), 176.

11. Richard Zoglin, "Manson Family Values," *Time* (21 March 1994): 77.

12. *People* (12 August 1991): 32.

13. Michael D. Kelleher and C. L. Kelleher, *Murder Most Rare: The Female Serial Killer* (Westport, Conn.: Praeger, 1998), x.

14. Howard G. Chua-Eoan, "The Uses of Monsters," *Time* (19 August 1991): 66.

15. *New York Times,* 25 July 1995, A11.

16. Angela Carter, afterword to *Fireworks: Nine Profane Pieces* (London: Quartet, 1974), 122.

17. Richard Tithecott, *Of Men and Monsters: Jeffrey Dahmer and the Construction of the Serial Killer* (Madison: University of Wisconsin Press, 1998); Mark Seltzer, *Serial Killers: Death and Life in America's Wound Culture* (New York: Routledge, 1998). Su C. Epstein explores how the proliferation of serial killers is a fact of cinematic representation: see "The New Mythic Monster," in *Cultural Criminology,* ed. Jeff Ferrell and Clinton R. Sanders (Boston: Northeastern University Press, 1995), 66–79. Epstein's sample extends from 1930–1992. See also Nicola Nixon, "Making Monsters, or Serializing Killers," in *American Gothic: New Interventions in a National Narrative,* ed. Robert K. Martin and Eric Savoy (Iowa City: University of Iowa Press, 1998), 217–36.

18. Tithecott, *Of Men and Monsters,* 4ff.

19. Philip Jenkins, *Using Murder: The Social Construction of Serial Homicide* (New York: Aldine de Gruyter, 1994), 15.

20. David Sonenschein, *Pedophiles on Parade,* vol. 2, *The Popular Imagery of Moral Hysteria* (San Antonio, Tex.: D. Sonenschein, 1998), 52. See Erich Goode and Nachman Ben-Yehuda, eds., *Moral Panics: The Social Construction of Deviance* (Durham: University of North Carolina Press, 1997). Norris R. Johnson defines moral panics as "episodes of collective action in which concern by the press, the public, and public officials to some perceived threat is disproportional to the crucial ideas. . . . Perhaps we need a discussion of scholarly panic, an exaggerated reaction by scholars to popular reaction to issues." See *Social Forces* (1 June 1997): 1514.

21. Jane Caputi writes that serial killers are "celebrated . . . along a cultural gamut including made-for-TV movies, rock 'n' roll songs, horror fanzines, jokes, pornographic magazines, such as Hustler, and extreme sadist publications" (*The Age of Sex Crime* [Bowling Green, Ohio: Bowling Green State University Popular Press, 1987], 1). They are also financially lucrative as games, baseball cards, and such. Ed Christman notes that Red Decibel Records had used a Gacy clown painting in 1993, although Columbia Records refused to market it. PR material for Louisiana rock group Acid Bath says sketches by convicted murderers Richard Ramirez ("the Night Stalker") and Kenneth Bianchi (the Hillside Strangler) were also used. See Ed Christman, "Spec's Closes 'Clean-up' Year," *Billboard* (9 November 1996): 56.

22. From the baseball card collection (how American!) of serial killers, to Gacy's art show, to rock lyrics, bracelets made by convicted serial killers—the least point of connection is enough. The battered 1949 Ford sedan owned by Ed Gein (Hitchcock's original model for *Psycho*) actually went on tour within a year of Gein's 1957 arrest: "See the car that hauled the dead from their graves!" See Paul Anthony Woods, *Ed Gein—Psycho!* (New York: St. Martin's Press, 1995), 155. The name "Ed Gein's Car" was adopted by a postpunk New York hardcore band (156); indeed, as Woods notes, Gein rapidly became the darling of rock groups—the Meteors and Macabre used his portrait for record covers; Gein's "name and bizarre acts have been recalled in countless contemporary songs and lyrics" (158). In this respect, at least in terms of popular grunge and punk music, Gein anticipates the uses to which Charles Manson will later be put—although Manson's poetry was adapted for an album by none other than The Beach Boys (Manson's lyrics to his song "Cease to Exist," became, reworked, "Never Learn Not to Love" on their 1969 album *20/20*). See Ivan Solotaroff, "Charlie Manson Saves the Whales," *Esquire* (February 1992): 78+.

23. Consider for example the furious social energy around pedophilia and its (presumed) agents. Children panics are, like other fear-delivery systems, recurrent; no moment so socially overdetermined can be treated in isolation, although each moment must be considered in its singular context. Not to do so, as David Sonenschein traces in "Child-threatening Figures," is to miss the point of recurrence and be misled by the distraction of the formula (in *Pedophiles on Parade,* 52–74). See, especially, Philip Jenkins, *Moral Panic: Changing Concepts of the Child Molester in Modern America* (New Haven, Conn.: Yale University Press, 1998).

24. Three days before Smith reported her children abducted, Pauline Zile claimed that her child had been taken from her in a flea market. Like Smith, Zile played up a televised appearance, tearfully asking for the return of the child. Less than a day after Smith was charged with murder, Ziles and her husband were charged with murder in Florida.

25. David Van Biema, "Parents Who Kill," *Time* (14 November 1994): 50. The story about Pauline Zile (see note 24, above) is a sidebar: Paul O'Donnell, "Another Suspect Plays Victim," *Newsweek* (14 November 1994): 30.

26. In Dahmer's case, in addition, there is also a slippage from what might be called metaphor to what is presented as fact. Cannibalism is a complicated cultural metaphor, dense with meaning, and it quickly focused the reporting of Dahmer. It has been argued, however, that Dahmer's case was more about a "consumer's" *fantasy* of flesh-eating than Dahmer's actual practice. A book could be written about this theme alone. Some places to begin: Paula Brown and Donald Tuzin, eds., *The Ethnography of Cannibalism* (Washington, D.C.: Society for Psychological Anthropology, 1983); W. Arens, *The Man-Eating Myth: Anthropology and Anthropophagy* (New York: Oxford University Press, 1979); and for a critique of Arens see Peggy Reeves Sanday, *Divine Hunger: Cannibalism as a Cultural System* (Cambridge, U.K.: Cambridge University Press, 1986). Also see Frank Lestringant, *Cannibals: The Discovery and Representation of the Cannibal from Columbus to Jules Verne,* trans. Rosemary Morris (Berkeley: University of California Press, 1997). See also Claude Rawson, "The Horror, the Holy Horror," *Times Literary Supple-*

ment 4935 (31 October 1997): 3–4. Regarding the collapse of taboo and the sacred, see William T. Cavanaugh, *Torture and Eucharist: Theology, Politics and the Body of Christ* (Oxford: Blackwell, 1998). Dahmer made possible a continuation of an already existing public fetish, in which cannibalism serves an array of complex civic emotions. These include, as Rawson says, the "attribution of it to 'others,' whom 'we' wish to defame, conquer, appropriate, or 'civilize' " ("The Horror," 3).

27. Regarding body counts in these narratives: Robert Jay Lifton, "Home from the War: The Psychology of Survival," in *The Vietnam Reader,* ed. Walter Capps (New York: Routledge, 1991). Lifton observes that the body count is the "perfect symbol of America's descent into evil . . . the amount of killing—any killing—becomes the total measure of achievement" (60).

28. For the Rifkin story, see Eugene H. Methvin, "The Face of Evil," *National Review* (23 January 1995): 34–37. Also, Maria Eftimiades, "The Quiet Man," *People* (6 December 1993): 65–72: "He's just plain evil," a mother of one of his victims says. "Joel is simply a gentle young man," a neighbor of thirty years says.

29. See Jack Olsen, *The Misbegotten Son: The True Story of Arthur J. Shawcross* (New York: Dell, 1993).

30. See Zoglin, "Manson Family Values," 77.

31. John Corry, "Decadence Chic," *American Spectator* (1 September 1997): 46–47.

32. Or consider the obscurity of Glen Edward Rogers, whose crimes bear a striking resemblance to Cunanan's, two years later. Rogers was dubbed the Cross-Country Killer for a six-week crime spree. He is accused of killing four women in as many states, and is presently on death row in Florida for a previous killing. His 1995 manhunt came to an end in November. See Evelyn Larrubia, "Death Penalty Recommended for Rogers," *Los Angeles Times,* 7 July 1999, Valley edition, 1.

33. James Alan Fox and Jack Levin, *Overkill: Mass Murder and Serial Killing Exposed* (New York: Plenum Press, 1994), 6.

34. See Harry Summers, writing in review of McNamara's *In Retrospect,* in the *Washington Times,* 1 January 1995. Also see Woody West, "Unforgiven," *The World and I* 10 (1 September 1995): 254.

35. Rheta Grimsley Johnson, *Atlanta Journal-Constitution,* 17 November 1999, Home edition, C2. For Frost, see Lawrance Thompson, *Robert Frost: The Early Years, 1874–1915* (New York: Holt, Rinehart and Winston, 1966). For Clinton, see Christopher Hitchens on C-SPAN, "Washington Forum," 13 January 2000; further citations in chapter 5.

36. John Douglas and Mark Olshaker, *Mindhunter: Inside the FBI's Elite Serial Crime Unit* (New York: Pocket Star Books, 1995), 141–42. See also Robert K. Ressler and Tom Shachtman, *Whoever Fights Monsters* (New York: St. Martin's Paperbacks, 1992), 79.

37. Esther I. Madriz, "Images of Criminals and Victims: A Study on Women's Fear and Social Control," *Gender and Society* 11, no. 3 (June 1997): 342–56.

38. Rodney R. Frazier, letter to the editor, *USA Today,* 30 December 1997, 12A. McVeigh often passes the monster test: see Karla Jennings's letter in the *Atlanta Journal-*

Constitution, 27 June 1997; also "Jury Found McVeigh Didn't Act Like a Monster," *USA Today,* 16 June 1997, 18A.

39. *USA Today,* 24 December 1997, 8A. "Vicious 'monster'" is also the description used of Mark Ballard, in court; see Janan Hanna, "Judge Hears 2 Portraits of Hanover Park Killer," *Chicago Tribune,* 17 September 1999, D edition, 1.

40. "O.J. Simpson and Timothy McVeigh: White America's Monster and Patriot," *New York Amsterdam News,* 17 May 1997, 10.

41. Gary Indiana, *Three Month Fever: The Andrew Cunanan Story* (New York: HarperCollins, 1999), 253.

42. Andy Pawelczak, "Death and the Maiden," *Films in Review* 46, nos. 5–6 (July 1995): 54; Jay Martin, "Force Fields: Abjection Overruled," *Salmagundi* 103 (summer 1994): 234+; Richard Lacayo, "Anatomy of an Acquittal," *Time* (11 May 1992): 31.

43. Kevin Johnson, "Strategy May Save Nichols' Life," *USA Today,* 24 December 1997, 3A.

44. *Exposing Myself,* by Geraldo Rivera, cited in Charles M. Young, "Geraldo Rivera," *Rolling Stone* 769 (18 September 1997): 88–95.

45. Ivor Davis, "Out Of Exile?" *Los Angeles Times Magazine* (January 1995): 90.

46. *Time* (3 May 1999). For Stewart, Rheta Grimsley Johnson apologizes for calling her a "border-stenciling, hydrangea-grafting, mosaic-making, ice sculpture-carving, paint-mixing monster." (*Atlanta Journal-Constitution,* 17 November 1999, Home edition, C2).

47. Metaphors themselves become villainized: Paul Johnson refers to a column in the *New Yorker* that cites examples "which had turned into Frankenstein's monsters and had taken control of their creators." See "Block That Metaphor and Detribalise Yourself, You Flying Pig!" *Spectator* (9 January 1999): 21.

48. *People* (6 December 1993): 65+.

49. Larrubia, "Death Penalty Recommended for Rogers," 1.

50. Joanne Fowler, "One Good Man," *People* (11 August 1997): 56. An acquaintance of Cunanan demurs, however, noting that on the basis of his affectionate manner—"he would put his arm around you and squeeze"—"certainly he wasn't a monster" (see Corry, "Decadence Chic," 46–47).

51. Thomas Fields-Meyer. "Up Front: Odyssey of Violence All His Adult Life, Richard Davis Was a One-Man Crime Wave." *People* (13 May 1996): 44–49.

52. See Johnson, "Strategy May Save Nichols' Life," 3A; Kevin Johnson, "Invoking McVeigh at the Nichols Trial Carries Some Risks," *USA Today,* 10 November 1997, A10; "Lawyers Seek to Polish McVeigh's Image," *Star Tribune,* 15 September 1996, 24A. The biography is by Brandon M. Stickney, *"All-American Monster": The Unauthorized Biography of Timothy McVeigh* (Amherst, N.Y.: Prometheus, 1996).

53. Don Davis, *The Milwaukee Murders: Nightmare in Apt. 213, the True Story* (New York: St. Martin's Press, 1991), 280.

54. *Washington Post,* 7 August 1991, B1.

55. Joel Norris, *Jeffrey Dahmer* (New York: Pinnacle Books, 1992), 8.

56. Ibid., 102.

57. "Creature": Alex Prud'Homme, "Little Flat of Horrors," *Time* (5 August 1991): 26.

58. Cathy Connors, "Dahmer the Cannibal Is Killed," *New York Amsterdam News*, 3 December 1994, PG.

59. Davis, *Milwaukee Murders*, 126.

60. Eugene H. Methvin, "The Face of Evil," *National Review* (23 January 1995): 34.

61. Brian Masters, *Killing for Company: The Story of a Man Addicted to Murder* (New York: Random House, 1993), 20.

62. Maggie Kilgour, *The Rise of the Gothic Novel* (New York: Routledge, 1995), 5.

63. An industry arose out of such narratives, consisting of attempts that tried equally to moralize the event (and invoke a moral denial) as well as to heighten its "curiosity." As Dennis Todd writes, "The sheer volume of this literature of monsters was immense, spanning everything from popular ballads and broadsides to recondite treatises. Some of it was religious, seeking to find in each singular birth a portent or sign. Much of it was of a more profane character, trading off an uncritical fascination in the marvelous, often collected in profusely illustrated, encyclopedic volumes." *Imagining Monsters: Miscreations of the Self in Eighteenth-Century England* (Chicago: University of Chicago Press, 1995), 44.

64. Hayden V. White, *The Content of the Form: Narrative Discourse and Historical Representation* (Cambridge, U.K.: Oxford University Press, 1987). See also Fredric Jameson's "ideology of form": "symbolic messages transmitted to us by the coexistence of various sign systems which are themselves traces or anticipations of modes of production" (*The Political Unconscious: Narrative as a Socially Symbolic Act* (Ithaca: Cornell University Press, 1981), 76.

65. Geoffrey O'Brien notes, for instance, that " . . . a genre that originated in a concern for realism now provides the trappings for the wildest of fantasizing." See *Hardboiled America: The Lurid Years of Paperbacks* (New York: Van Nostrand Reinhold, 1981), 95. See, too, in this regard, Michael Denning, *Dime Novels and Working-Class Culture in America* (London: Verso, 1987).

66. In much the way the pornographic element of the Clinton narrative had to be verbally produced again and again, in anxious awareness that it otherwise could not be "pornographic," despite the constant reference to its visuality. See, in this regard, Susan Stewart's informative essay on the pornographic apparatus of the Meese Commission's report on pornography, "The Marquis de Meese," in *Crimes of Writing: Problems in the Containment of Representation* (Durham, N.C.: Duke University Press, 1994), 235–72.

67. Gerold Frank, *The Boston Strangler* (New York: New American Library, 1966), vii. St. Martin's True Crime Library borrows Frank's stratagem in its marketing. "A Letter to the Reader" inside the front cover of a hastily written life of Andrew Cunanan

proposes that a St. Martin's text is "better than the most terrifying thriller, because it's all true," although a careful read of the text in question leads one to conclude that the contrary is in fact the case; Wensley Clarkson's *Death at Every Stop* (New York: St. Martin's Press, 1997) is no more "true" than the slapdash reportage upon which it is largely based, and which it often closely borrows without citation.

68. *Time* (19 May 1997): 40.

69. *Time* (4 August 1997): 30.

70. Wendy Lesser, *Pictures at an Execution: An Inquiry into the Subject of Murder* (Cambridge, Mass.: Harvard University Press, 1993), 2.

71. Jenkins, *Using Murder,* 15.

72. Henry Lee Lucas could be said to epitomize Jenkins's point here; he is a cottage serial-killer industry in his own right, as much fantasy as fact. He claims to have killed upwards of five hundred people, according to one source, six hundred according to another. Lucas's claims however, have been largely debunked; *Time* reports he "phonied confessions partly to achieve star status" (4 April 1994, 64). Still, he achieves an indirect stardom. *Henry: Portrait of a Serial Killer* is just one of many books, documentaries, and commentaries based upon his life—a life whose status, real or fantasy, is hugely in doubt.

Finally, Jenkins's point is confirmed in the case of Florida killer Aileen Wuornos, in which the conventions of cinematic serial killing shaped the politics and legal reception of her case. Nick Broomfield investigates how—despite her claims to committing murder in self-defense—Wuornos's life was instead massaged into the more economically as well as politically lucrative frame of the serial killer (*Aileen Wuornos: The Selling of a Serial Killer,* a film by Nick Broomfield, cited in Tithecott, *Of Men and Monsters,* 125–26). See Kelleher and Kelleher, *Murder Most Rare,* 71–83.

73. Seltzer, *Serial Killers,* 125.

74. Ibid., 11.

75. 27 February 1989, cited in Roger Shattuck, *Forbidden Knowledge: From Prometheus to Pornography* (New York: St. Martin's Press, 1996), 262.

76. Masters, *Killing for Company,* 195.

77. Elizabeth Mehren, "Ex-Priest Gets 18-Year Term for Sex Abuse at 5 Parishes," *Los Angeles Times,* 7 December 1993, A1.

78. Respectively: *Time* (14 November 1994): 42; Marvin Kitman, "The Criminal Cunanan Coverage," *Newsday,* 3 Aug 1997, The Marvin Kitman Sunday Show, C39; *People* (13 May 1996): 44+.

79. Stephen G. Michaud and Hugh Aynesworth, *The Only Living Witness* (New York: New American Library, 1983), 6, 13, 226.

80. A recent review of Gus Van Sant's 1999 remake of *Psycho,* however, praises Anthony Perkins (Norman Bates in Hitchcock's original) for "add[ing] an unusual and unusually appealing monster to the American Gothic landscape" (Richard Alleva, "Renovations," *Commonweal* [29 January 1999]: 21). Hitchcock's original was modeled on Ed Gein, arrested in Wisconsin in 1957 on multiple charges of murder. The judge presiding

over the trial later wrote it up. See Robert H. Gollmar, *Edward Gein: America's Most Bizarre Murderer* (Delavan, Wis.: C. Hallberg, 1981). Also Harold Schechter, *Deviant: The Shocking True Story of Ed Gein, the Original "Psycho"* (New York: Pocket Books, 1989).

81. Michaud and Aynesworth, *The Only Living Witness,* 7.

82. Davis, *Milwaukee Murders,* 41.

83. *Time* (4 April 1994): 64–66.

84. *USA Today,* 13 May 1997, 3A.

85. Mary Noel, *Villains Galore: The Hey-day of the Popular Story Weekly* (New York: Macmillan, 1954), 33.

86. *New York Times,* 16 February 1992, 24. "Halley's Comet" (*Dahmer: Mystery of the Serial Killer,* A&E, 1993), hoping to explain thereby Dahmer's "sudden" appearance on the scene, rather than his periodicity, since he elsewhere called him "unique." Boyle's metaphor at least recalls the earlier meaning of monstrous, as it would have been applied in the seventeenth century to such things as comets, as a "wonder" or a "prodigy."

87. Robert K. Ressler and Tom Shachtman, *I Have Lived in the Monster: A Report from the Abyss* (New York: St. Martin's Press, 1977), 65.

88. This is why Shelley's *philosophe,* the creature put together by Victor Frankenstein, is not in the conventional sense a monster; in other words, he speaks. Chris Baldick notes that "a simple word-tally shows 'monster,' with 27 appearances, to have won by a short head from 'fiend' (25), followed by 'daemon' (18), 'creature' (16), 'wretch' (15), and 'devil' (80); 'being' (4) and 'ogre' (1). See *In Frankenstein's Shadow: Myth, Monstrosity, and Nineteenth-Century Writing* (Oxford, U.K.: Clarendon Press, 1987), 10, note 1.

89. Ressler and Shachtman, *I Have Lived in the Monster,* 95.

90. Ressler and Shachtman, *Whoever Fights Monsters,* 97.

91. Lesser, *Pictures at an Execution,* 2.

92. Kathey Painko, to her daughter outside the North Valley Jewish Community Center in Los Angeles, where a gunman shot three boys and two adults. The child had asked the mother if the police were trying to catch a monster. "Perspectives," *Newsweek* (23 August, 1999): 17.

93. Cited in Shattuck, *Forbidden Knowledge,* 264.

94. Martin, "Force Fields," 234ff.

95. See "Getting Away with Serial Murder," *Wall Street Journal,* 23 July 1997, A18.

96. Ressler is well respected as an FBI agent. Since the middle seventies he has positioned himself as one of the "experts" most knowledgeable about the serial killer representational "epidemic." Indeed, Ressler claims credit for coining the expression "serial killer"—derived, he said, from "the serial adventures we used to see on Saturday at the movies." See Ressler and Shachtman, *Whoever Fights Monsters,* 29–30.

97. Ressler and Shachtman, *I Have Lived in the Monster,* 46.

98. Ibid., 51.

99. Ibid.

100. Ibid., 46.

101. Jenkins, *Using Murder,* 112−13. See, for example, "A True Discourse Declaring the Damnable Life and Death of One Stubbe Peeter. A Most Wicked Sorcerer. Who in the Likeness of a Wolf Committed Many Murders." In *A Lycanthropy Reader: Werewolves in Western Culture,* ed. Charlotte F. Otten (Syracuse, N.Y.: Syracuse University Press, 1986). Here the point must be made that Ressler and Jenkins sidestep the point; even in 1589 natural killings are cloaked in a metaphysics of the supernatural. Rule, in *Lust Killer,* cites Ressler making similar genre leaps (328).

102. Eve Kosofsky Sedgwick, *The Coherence of Gothic Conventions,* rev. ed. (New York: Arno, 1980), 13.

103. Nixon, "Making Monsters," 217.

104. Ressler and Shachtman, *Whoever Fights Monsters,* 89.

105. Robert D. Keppel, with William J. Birnes, *Signature Killers* (New York: Pocket Books, 1997), xix.

106. Moira Martingale, in *Cannibal Killers,* calls Fish "the archetypal bogey-man of [*sic*] whom parents warn their children" (*Cannibal Killers: The History of Impossible Murderers* [New York: St. Martin's Paperbacks, 1993], 45−46).

107. Ann Rule, *The Stranger Beside Me* (New York: New American Library, 1981), 170.

108. Anne E. Schwartz, *The Man Who Could Not Kill Enough: The Secret Murders of Milwaukee's Jeffrey Dahmer* (Secaucus, N.J.: Carol Publishing Group, 1992), 152.

109. Ibid.

110. Fox and Levin, *Overkill,* 15.

111. Seltzer, *Serial Killers,* 127.

112. Michaud and Aynesworth, *The Only Living Witness,* 6.

113. Rule, *The Stranger Beside Me,* xv.

114. Masters, *Killing for Company.* Cited in Joyce Carol Oates, "I Had No Other Thrill or Happiness," *New York Review of Books* 41, no. 6 (24 March 1994): 57.

115. David Williams, *Deformed Discourse: The Function of the Monster in Mediaeval Thought and Literature* (Montreal: McGill-Queen's University Press, 1996), 10.

116. Seltzer, *Serial Killers,* 126.

117. Stephen King, *Carrie* (New York: Signet, 1973), 133.

118. Indiana, *Three Month Fever,* xvii. "If Milosevic is Hitler, then the planet is thick with such monsters" (Nick Gillespie, "Fuhrer Furor," editorial, *Reason Magazine* 31, no. 2 (June 1999): 5−6. But according to Pat Buchanan, Hitler *is* a monster; see the exchange between Norman Podheretz and Buchanan in the *Wall Street Journal,* 25 October 1999: Podheretz, "Buchanan and Anti-Semitism"; Buchanan's letter to the editor, "Free at Last," *Wall Street Journal,* 5 November 1999, A19; and Podheretz's response, "A Willful Blindness," *Wall Street Journal,* 8 November 1999, A51. Also Robert Dallek, "Pat Buchanan's Revisionist Fantasy," *Washington Post,* 19 October 1999, Final edition, A19.

119. Seltzer, *Serial Killers,* 10.

120. Such explains the *National Enquirer*'s need, in September 2000, to run the headline, "Baby-killer Pregnant by Prison Guard." We are not yet finished with Susan Smith. See, for instance, the follow-up story in a Canadian-based tabloid: Mike Foster, "Susan Smith Beaten Again in Jail," *Weekly World News,* 16 January 2001, 89.

121. Tim Purtell, in "The Shock Troops," notes that Davis took "a month to research and write the Dahmer book" (*Entertainment Weekly* [4 March 1994]): 23.

122. Davis, *Milwaukee Murders,* 145.

123. A similar rush to narrative closure, with barely a pause for legal nuance, tracked Cunanan. For example, a report on a proposed ABC film about Cunanan— within a week of his death—describes "Andrew Cunanan, the alleged serial killer whose victims included fashion designer Gianni Versace." See "ABC Planning Film on Alleged Serial Killer," *Los Angeles Times,* 30 July 1997, Home edition, D1, 6.

124. Carol Morello, "School Shooting Trial to Begin," *USA Today,* 9 June 1998, 2A.

125. Michaud and Aynesworth, *The Only Living Witness,* 274.

126. Steve Lopez, "In Snow, in Ice, in Rain, One Mother's Trip," *Time* (8 February 1999): 45.

127. Josephine McDonagh, "Do or Die: Problems of Agency and Gender in the Aesthetics of Murder," in *New Feminist Discourses: Critical Essays on Theories and Texts,* ed. Isobel Armstrong (New York: Routledge, 1992), 223.

128. Daniel A. Cohen, *Pillars of Salt, Monuments of Grace: New England Crime Literature and the Origins of American Popular Culture, 1674–1860* (New York: Oxford University Press, 1993), 251.

129. See, for example, Gerald Posner, "In Search of the Real Boston Strangler," *Talk* (October 2000): 112–18, 160–63.

130. Frank, *Boston Strangler,* 321.

131. Schwartz, *The Man Who Could Not Kill Enough,* 39.

132. See Linda K. Fuller, "Super Bowl Speak: Subtexts of Sex and Sex Talk in America's Annual Sports Extravaganza," in *Sexual Rhetoric: Media Perspectives on Sexuality, Gender, and Identity,* ed. Meta G. Carstarphen and Susan C. Zavoina (Westport, Conn.: Greenwood Press, 1999), 161–73.

133. Joel Norris, *Serial Killers.*

134. Masters, *Killing for Company,* 26.

135. Barbara Ehrenreich explores the religious derivation of the scapegoat and the "sacred" quality of state-sanctioned violence in "Sacred Meat." See *Blood Rites: Origins and History of the Passions of War* (New York: Metropolitan, 1997), 23–35.

136. André Haynal, Miklós Molnár, and Gérard de Puymège, *Fanaticism: A Historical and Psychoanalytical Study,* trans. Linda Butler Koseoglu (New York: Schocken Books, 1983), 140. In classic images of Satan one sees this tendency toward the collapse of two different schemata of repudiation; in representations the demonic often convey a

visible stigma of beastliness, in the satyr-like presentation of the latter (the demonic, historically), and the potent dehumanization of the former (sins carried by the goat were, necessarily, real and human). See Jeffrey Burton Russell, *The Devil: Perceptions of Evil From Antiquity to Primitive Christianity* (Ithaca: Cornell University Press, 1977). Also, Gerald Messadié, *A History of the Devil,* trans. Marc Romano (New York: Kodansha International, 1996).

137. Working from a Lacanian, psychoanalytical perspective, Julia Kristeva defines abjection in similar ways, as threat and desire alike. The abject is "something rejected from which one does not part, from which one does not protect oneself as from an object. Imaginary uncanniness and real threat, it beckons to us and ends up engulfing us" (*Powers of Horror: An Essay on Abjection,* trans. Leon S. Roudiez [New York: Columbia University Press, 1982], 4).

138. For instance, the language endures, even as specifics change. As noted earlier, Robert Berkhofer's *The White Man's Indian: Images of the American Indian From Columbus to the Present* (New York: Knopf, 1978) cites early Puritan texts which demonize Indians in many of the same terms as contemporary examples of that rhetoric in other contexts. See J. Edgar Hoover, "How *Safe* is Your Youngster," *American Magazine* 159 (3 March 1957): 19, 99−103.

139. Joseph Grixti, "Consuming Cannibals: Psychopathic Killers as Archetypes and Cultural Icons," *Journal of American Culture* 18, no. 1 (spring 1995): 91, 90.

140. David L. Scruton, ed., introduction to *Sociophobics: The Anthropology of Fear* (Boulder, Co.: Westview Press, 1985), 10.

141. René Girard, *Violence and the Sacred,* trans. Patrick Gregory (Baltimore: Johns Hopkins University Press, 1977), 8.

142. King, *Danse Macabre,* 442−43.

143. Mark Edmundson, *Nightmare on Main Street: Angels, Sadomasochism, and the Culture of Gothic* (Cambridge, Mass.: Harvard University Press, 1997), 61.

144. Wendy Lesser, *Pictures at an Execution,* 20.

145. Rule, *Lust Killer,* 166.

146. See related note 45, chapter 3. Also, Ann Rule, who testifies to the number of "young women who had 'fallen in love' with Bundy" (*The Stranger Beside Me,* 415). Also see the Geraldo show on "the mind of serial killers and the women who love them" (29 March 1993; cited in Tithecott, *Of Men and Monsters,* 105); and "Ted Bundy's Sermon," in Shattuck, *Forbidden Knowledge,* 259−67.

147. Michaud and Aynesworth, *The Only Living Witness,* 253.

148. 18 April 1993.

Chapter Three

1. Colin Wilson and Damon Wilson, *The Killers Among Us,* book 2, *Sex, Madness, and Mass Murder* (New York: Warner Books, 1997), 228.

2. Similarly, *People Magazine*'s cover story on the two Littleton killers focused upon their presumed homosexuality. Bill Hewitt, "Sorrow and Outrage" (3 May 1999): 94–102.

3. Gary Indiana, *Three Month Fever* (New York: HarperCollins, 1999), xiii.

4. Lee Edelman, "Tearooms and Sympathy, or The Epistemology of the Water Closet," in *The Lesbian and Gay Studies Reader*, ed. Henry Abelove, Michèle Aina Barale, and David M. Halperin (New York: Routledge, 1993), 559.

5. Carol J. Clover, *Men, Women, and Chain Saws: Gender in the Modern Horror Film* (Princeton: Princeton University Press, 1992), 27.

6. See, for example, Paul Wells, "The Invisible Man: Shrinking Masculinity in the 1950s Science Fiction B-Movie," in *You Tarzan: Masculinity, Movies, and Men,* ed. Pat Kirkham and Janet Thumim (New York: St. Martin's Press, 1993). See Harry M. Benshoff, *Monsters in the Closet: Homosexuality and the Horror Film* (New York: Manchester University Press, 1997). Rhona Berenstein, *Attack of the Leading Ladies: Gender, Sexuality, and Spectatorship in Classic Horror Cinema* (New York: Columbia University Press, 1996). Jonathan Lake Crane's *Terror and Everyday Life: Singular Moments in the History of the Horror Film* (Thousand Oaks, Calif.: Sage Publications, 1994), and Barbara Creed's *The Monstrous-Feminine: Film, Feminism, Psychoanalysis* (London: Routledge, 1993), examine the gendered political implications of the genre.

7. As Carol J. Clover writes, "The appointed ancestor of the slasher film is Hitchcock's *Psycho*" (*Men, Women, and Chain Saws,* 23). Walter Kendrick considers the commercial development of the splatter film, with its origins partly derived from formula horror, in *The Thrill of Fear: 250 Years of Scary Entertainment* (New York: Grove Press, 1991), 235ff. Diana Fuss, "Monsters of Perversion: Jeffrey Dahmer and *The Silence of the Lambs,*" in *Media Spectacles,* ed. Marjorie Garber, Jann Matlock, and Rebecca L. Walkowitz (New York: Routledge, 1993), 181–205.

8. See Harry Crowley, *Advocate,* 2 September 1997, 24.

9. James Levin, *The Gay Novel: The Male Homosexual Image in America* (New York: Irvington Publishers, 1983); David Bergman, *Gaiety Transfigured: Gay Self-Representation in American Literature* (Madison: University of Wisconsin, 1991); Matthew Ruben, "Of Newts and Quayles: National-Political Masculinity in the Current Conjuncture," in *Boys: Masculinities in Contemporary Culture,* ed. Paul Smith (New York: Westview Press, 1996); Stephen Cohan, *Masked Men: Masculinity and the Movies in the Fifties* (Bloomington: Indiana University Press, 1997).

10. Barbara Ehrenreich, in *The Hearts of Men: American Dreams and the Flight from Commitment* (New York: Anchor, 1983), writes that during the period of the fifties and beyond, the "image of the irresponsible male . . . blurred into the shadowy figure of the homosexual. So great was the potential overlap between the sexually 'normal,' but not entirely successful man, and the blatant homosexual that the psychoanalyst Lionel Ovesey had to create a new category—'pseudohomosexuality'—to absorb the intermediate cases" (24).

11. Edelman, "Tearooms and Sympathy," 553–54.

12. Cohan, *Masked Men,* x.

13. William Strauss and Neil Howe, *Generations: The History of America's Future, 1584 to 2069* (New York: Morrow, 1991). I am indebted to Mark Smith for directing me to this illuminating text.

14. Robert J. Corber, *Homosexuality in Cold War America: Resistance and the Crisis of Masculinity* (Durham, N.C.: Duke University Press, 1997), 2.

15. Edelman, "Tearooms and Sympathy," 556.

16. See, for example, the use of this term in "The Homosexual in America," *Time*'s "essay" for 21 January 1966 (40–41).

17. Vito Russo, *The Celluloid Closet: Homosexuality in the Movies* (New York: Harper and Row, 1981), 107.

18. Tracy D. Morgan, "Pages of Whiteness: Race, Physique Magazines, and the Emergence of Public Gay Culture," in *Queer Studies: A Lesbian, Gay, Bisexual, and Transgender Anthology,* ed. Brett Beemyn and Mickey Eliason (New York: New York University Press, 1996), 280–97.

19. Simon Watney, *Policing Desire: Pornography, AIDS, and the Media* (Minneapolis: University of Minnesota Press, 1987), 26.

20. Edward Alwood, *Straight News: Gays, Lesbians, and the News Media* (New York: Columbia University Press, 1996), 1.

21. Peter Michelson, *Speaking the Unspeakable: A Poetics of Obscenity* (Albany: State University of New York Press, 1993), 25. Stephan Cohan makes passing note of the incendiary public reaction to the conclusions reached by these documents (*Masked Men,* 57ff.).

22. Among other causes for alarm, Kinsey's research documented widespread homosexual activity among adult American men, as well as an age-related decline in male biological function. See C. A. Tripp, *The Homosexual Matrix* (New York: McGraw-Hill, 1975), for a review of the furor attending the Kinsey Report (232–40).

23. Helen Mayer Hacker, "The New Burdens of Masculinity," *Marriage and Family Living* 19 (1957): 227–33. "And it is axiomatic in the social context within which this representation occurs that a masculinity subject to questioning is no masculinity at all" (Edelman, "Tearooms and Sympathy," 565).

24. Cited in James Twitchell, *Preposterous Violence: Fables of Aggression in Modern Culture* (New York: Oxford University Press, 1989), 143.

25. Barbara and Peter Wyden, *Growing Up Straight: What Every Thoughtful Parent Should Know about Homosexuality* (New York: Stein and Day, 1968), 48.

26. Typically the association was used to criticize parenting and the adequacy of home-life—particularly maternal. As Diane Johnson argues, "Theories regarding the father's role have come and gone, but mothers remain—insecure, daunted, and blamed, their children's behavior problems laid entirely at their door" ("My Blue Heaven," *New York Review of Books* [16 July 1998]: 15). In Frank's *The Boston Strangler,* for example, authorities are warned that "special attention should be paid to persons suffering from a paranoia of mother-hate" (31). Years later, Ressler can likewise announce that serial killing is "induced by faulty parenting" (cited in Don Davis, *The Milwaukee Murders: Night-*

mare in Apt. 213, the True Story [New York: St. Martin's Press, 1991], 171). Concern over the collapsed family figures more prominently in the fantasy-ridden eighties. As Susan Jeffords comments, "gender cults" of the eighties—the men's movement, for one—made sweeping claims linking private and public. Robert Bly argued the "unmistakable decline" of the United States, which he "attributes to the increasing power of women" and the parallel "diminishment of the father." Cited in Susan Jeffords, *Hard Bodies: Hollywood Masculinity in the Reagan Era* (New Brunswick, N.J.: Rutgers University Press, 1994), 9.

27. Ann Rule's Jerry Brudos had a domineering mother and "seldom saw his father"; see *Lust Killer* (New York: Signet, 1983), 21. Twenty-five years later, self-proclaimed "expert" on serial killers Robert Ressler hardly advances the argument. Of the thirty-six serial killers he has studied, suggests Ressler, "most of them had single-parent homes, and those who didn't had dysfunctional families, cold and distant fathers, inadequate mothers. We are creating a poor environment for raising normal, adjusted young males" (cited in Anastasia Toufexis, "Dances with Werewolves," *Time* [4 April 1994]: 64).

28. Jesse Green, "Gays and Monsters," *New York Times Magazine* (13 June 1999): 14.

29. Cited in "The Mind of the Mass Murderer," *Time* (27 August 1973): 57. Despite the inevitable slide into blaming "faulty parenting" (Robert K. Ressler and Tom Shachtman, *Whoever Fights Monsters* [New York: St. Martin's Press, 1977], 166), part of the confusions inhere within gender myths themselves. Jane Caputi takes note of a pervasive attitude when she argues that the hatred of women used sometimes to explain serial killers actually masks male "deep and abiding fear of each other" (*The Age of Sex Crime* [Bowling Green, Ohio: Bowling Green State University Popular Press, 1987], 150).

30. For the association of violence as a particular gendered practice, see Caputi, *The Age of Sex Crime;* Deborah Cameron and Elizabeth Frazer, *The Lust to Kill: A Feminist Investigation of Sexual Murder* (New York: New York University Press, 1987), which text, McDonagh argues, focuses "upon these representations that work toward the construction of a violent masculinity." See Josephine McDonagh, "Do or Die: Agency and Gender in the Aesthetics of Murder," in *New Feminist Discourses: Critical Essays on Theories and Texts,* ed. Isobel Armstrong (London: Routledge, 1992), 223.

31. See, for example, Carol J. Clover, "Her Body, Himself: Gender in the Slasher Film," in *Fantasy and the Cinema,* ed. James Donald (London: British Film Institute, 1989), 91–133. In *Killers Among Us,* Colin and Damon Wilson, for example, expostulate that the torture associated with "sex crime" would be found "incomprehensible" by "normal males"—"even those who find it easy enough to understand a multiple rapist" (3).

32. Davis, *Milwaukee Murders,* 80

33. Brian Masters, "Dahmer's Inferno," *Vanity Fair* (November 1991): 189.

34. Ressler and Shachtman, *Whoever Fights Monsters,* 77. See, too, Colin and Damon Wilson, whose killers Glatman and Gein are each referred to as a "mother's boy" (*Killers Among Us,* 284, 292). Further, and more curiously, the Wilsons, père and fils,

write that Gein "was a sexually normal man—his mother's undivided attention had not turned him into a homosexual—but he was frightened of women, and not very attractive to them" (293). In "Tearooms and Sympathy," Edelman observes that "if momism is the theory, then homosexuality is the practice, for it is seen as enacting the destabilization of borders, the subversion of masculine identity from within, that momism promotes" (568).

35. Ressler, *Whoever Fights Monsters*, 81.

36. "Lawyers Seek to Polish McVeigh's Image," *Star Tribune*, 15 September 1996, 24A.

37. See Su C. Epstein, "The New Mythic Monster," in *Cultural Criminology*, ed. Jeff Ferrell and Clinton R. Sanders (Boston: Northeastern University Press, 1995), 66–79. Epstein notes the proliferation of cinematic serial killers, in a survey that extends from 1930–1992. Also, see Nicola Nixon, "Making Monsters, or Serializing Killers," in *American Gothic: New Interventions in a National Narrative*, edited by Robert K. Martin and Eric Savoy (Iowa City: University of Iowa Press, 1998), 217–36.

38. Philip Jenkins, *Using Murder: The Social Construction of Serial Homicide* (New York: Aldine de Gruyter, 1994), 177.

39. Green, "Gays and Monsters," 13. Such links are customarily made. In "We Like to Watch," a discussion of Voyeur Television, James Poniewozik observes that if you are gay and "coming out" on TV and announce that you have "a secret," you "better have a severed head in your luggage" (*Time* [26 June 2000]: 61).

40. Brian Massumi observes this about the "fear-producing mechanisms" crucial to the period: "The media-induced public conviction during the early to mid 1980s that violent crime throughout America was rising at epidemic proportions (despite statistics to the contrary, also reported in the media) enabled Ronald Reagan to expand police powers beyond anything Richard Nixon could have dreamed of" ("Everywhere You Want to Be," in *The Politics of Every Day Fear*, ed. Brian Massumi [Minneapolis: University of Minnesota Press, 1993], ix; 26). For the decreasing crime rate, see "Crime Drops in '97; Murders Are at 30-Year Low," from the Associated Press: "The highlight was the decline in the number of murders, . . . 7 percent below the figure for 1996 and 26 percent below the 1993 figure" (*New York Times*, 23 November 1998, Online edition).

41. Jenkins, *Using Murder*, 184. Jenkins notes that the "serial murder panic should thus be seen as at least in part a covert assault on the gay movement and gay political rights" (*Using Murder*, 186).

42. Fuss, "Monsters of Perversion," 182.

43. Bundy, Dahmer, and Gacy appear on T-shirt, Internet, trading card, and board game. Gacy's clown paintings, as well as sketches by Bianchi and Ramirez, grace CD wrappers. Jonathan Lake Crane notes the release of the game *Serial Killer*, devised by a pen-pal friend of John Wayne Gacy (suggested price, $49.95). The game comes packaged in a body bag (Crane, *Terror and Everyday Life*, 156, note 14). See also *Serial Killers and Mass Murders* (Forestville, Calif.: Eclipse, 1992)—a set of fifty-five "true crime trading cards," featuring pictures, bios, and criminal tally.

44. Maureen Orth, "The Versace Killings," *Vanity Fair* (September 1997): 268–75, 329–36.

45. In general the sexual life of straight killers is glossed over for the violence, as was Bundy's erotic interest in the women he killed (while women's erotic interest in Bundy was played up). In *The Stranger Beside Me* (New York: New American Library, 1981), Ann Rule discusses the erotic appeal Bundy held for many women (esp. 170, 270, and passim). The courtroom was "jammed with pretty young women" (Rule, 354); see, too, Joyce Carol Oates, "I Had No Other Thrill or Happiness," *New York Review of Books* (24 March 1994): 52–59, (esp. 55). In Cunanan's case, to the contrary, the sexual material often eclipsed the violence either attendant upon or associated with it.

46. See for example, Rule's *Lust Killer* and Richard T. Pienciak's *Mama's Boy: The True Story of a Serial Killer and His Mother* (New York: Dutton, 1996). In both instances the killers are married, although each seriously fails normal straight gender expectations, which both titles suggest. One has only to compare the coverage of Ted Bundy, in the middle to late seventies, to Rule's *Lust Killer* (1983), to see how straightness was no longer so straight. When compared to earlier portrayals of Ted Bundy, Rule's description of Brudos—a less well-known killer who followed Bundy some years later—shows the first signs of a change in attitudes; thus, even by 1983, straightness was no longer as straight as it had once been—a change that would become more pronounced in subsequent narratives of killers, straight or gay.

47. Written in 1983, for example, Rule's *Lust Killer* anticipates the historical moment, still some years ahead, where the mere thought of joining homosexuality and domesticity (in the demand for "gay marriage") will become a political provocation resulting in the 1994 so-called Defense of Marriage Act. Her title perhaps unintentionally raises that other pathology, those who "kill for love." Whether as practiced by Andrew Cunanan or Susan Smith or Jeffrey Dahmer, love is apparently not so simple as the records would have us believe. For the (male) masochism of love as it is romantically construed, see Carol Siegel, *Male Masochism: Modern Revisions of the Story of Love* (Bloomington: Indiana University Press, 1995), esp. 1–17.

48. Frank's *The Boston Strangler* is percipient. While the expression "serial killer" is never used, the utility of Frank's text is that it prepares a reading constituency willing to entertain such a person in their imaginative lives; it helps craft the "romance of crime"—which, as Joyce Carol Oates observes, is "purely that—a romance, a fiction" ("No Other Thrill or Happiness," 58). Frank's is one of the narratives of public mayhem and civil crime that, like *The Exorcist,* or further back, Stevenson's "Dr. Jekyll and Mr. Hyde," might be said to have instituted a genre of copycat readers, if not killers. The development of the voyeur, the watching, desiring subject as responsible citizen, begins.

49. Queer visibility, however, was evidenced more as a straight anxiety and fantasy than in the "deviants" themselves, who for the most part were accommodatingly invisible, except for the periodic excursions into their shadow world by the always-interested straight press. Alternately alarmed and titillating reports like *The Seventh Man* (Jess Stearn, 1961) and *Growing Up Straight* (Wyden and Wyden, 1968) kept homosexuals breathlessly on public lips, if not always in public eyes. Coverage in—for example—

Time ("The Homosexual in America," 21 January 1966) and *Look* (Jack Star, "The Sad, 'Gay' Life," 10 January 1967) cast homosexuals as cultural misfits, perverts, and criminals.

50. Capote takes care to situate his pair of killers as heterosexual; nonetheless, Capote will draw attention to the less dominant of the two, Perry, for, among other things, the "intensity" of his male relations (see 34–36) and his guitar playing. In addition, Dick, the "totally masculine" of the two killers (Perry's term, 102), consistently demasculinizes Perry in his address: "honey" (30); "O.K. Sugar" (37); "Sure, honey" (82).

51. Andrew Ross, *No Respect: Intellectuals and Popular Culture* (New York: Routledge, 1989), 173; emphasis in original.

52. For Gothic as narrative mode, see, particularly, Judith Halberstam, *Skin Shows: Gothic Horror and the Technology of Monsters* (Durham, N.C.: Duke University Press, 1995); Anne Williams, *Art of Darkness: Poetics of Gothic* (Chicago: University of Chicago Press, 1995); Kelly Hurley, *The Gothic Body: Sexuality, Materialism, and Degeneration at the Fin de Siècle* (Cambridge, U.K.: Cambridge University Press, 1996).

53. The FBI's Edwin Cogswell, cited in *USA Today,* 13 May 1997, 3A. "He could be anywhere"—a phrase repeated verbatim by law enforcement agents in different cities (see Associated Press, 11 May 1997).

54. Transcript, "All Things Considered," National Public Radio, 24 July 1997.

55. Cited in Tony Perry and Judy Pasternak, "Cunanan Doesn't Fit Serial Killer Mold," *Los Angeles Times,* 20 July 1997, Orange County edition, A1.

56. The most outrageous example of this makeover is, to my mind, Maureen Orth, who terms the Cunanan search the "greatest failed manhunt in American history" although her topic, clearly, requires a very specific kind of man—the lurid life of the homosexual. David Blake, in "Dead Man Walking," reviews Orth. She "cites some of the most clueless representations of the gay community." "In her attempt to conjure a lethal subculture that fosters Cunanan's values, Orth selectively combs the gay world and conflates her 'findings' into sensational generalizations that not so subtly encompass all gay men" (*Advocate* [13 April 1999], 77, 78, 79). Maureen Orth, *Vulgar Favors* (New York: Delacorte Press, 1999).

57. Diane Sawyer, "Family Matters," *ABC PrimeTime Live* (16 August 1997).

58. In death he was identified by a thumbprint found on a coin he had pawned a few days previously.

59. Jonathan Dollimore, *Sexual Dissidence: Augustine to Wilde, Freud to Foucault* (New York: Oxford University Press, 1991), 230.

60. Michelson, *Speaking the Unspeakable,* 16.

61. Chua-Eoan, "Dead Men Tell No Tales," 30.

62. Reuters news service, 7 May 1997.

63. Ibid., 10 May 1997.

64. *Newsday,* 11 May 1997, A19.

65. Richard Lacayo, *Time* (28 July 1997): 28.

66. Andrew Phillips, "The Cunanan Enigma," *Maclean's* (4 August 1997): 32.

67. David Punter, *The Literature of Terror: A History of Gothic Fictions from 1765 to the Present Day* (London: Longmans, 1980), 14, 423.

68. Elizabeth Napier, *The Failure of Gothic: Problems of Disjunction in an Eighteenth-Century Literary Form* (New York: Oxford University Press, 1987), 29.

69. Indiana, *Three Month Fever,* xviii.

70. Halberstam, *Skin Shows,* 3.

71. Craig Schneider, "The Versace Slaying: Fatal Designs," *Atlanta Journal-Constitution,* 16 July 1997, A7.

72. *Progressive* 61, no. 9 (September 1997): 41.

73. Patrick Rogers, et al., "Blood Trail Fugitive Andrew Cunanan Posed as a Class Act," *People* (7 July 1997): 53.

74. Tony Perry, "Fugitive a Surprising Suspect," *Los Angeles Times,* 16 May 1997, Home edition, A3.

75. Amy Bernstein, "Reinvention, the American Way," *U.S. News & World Report* (4 August 1997): 7.

76. Chua-Eoan, "Dead Men Tell No Tales," 30–32.

77. "News in Brief," *Atlanta Journal-Constitution,* 9 May 1997, C2.

78. Perry, "Fugitive a Surprising Suspect."

79. Ibid.

80. Indiana, *Three Month Fever,* xiii. For example, Wensley Clarkson's hasty pastiche of Andrew Cunanan (*Death at Every Stop* [New York: St. Martin's Press, 1997]) was available within weeks of Cunanan's death; it takes its form and content, very obviously, from the press reports which the author duplicates, sometimes verbatim. The subtitle of Clarkson's book, on the book's cover, reads "The True Story of Serial Killer Andrew Cunanan—the Man Who Murdered Designer Gianni Versace." That same book as listed in *Books in Print* reads, "The True Story of *Alleged Gay* Serial Killer Andrew Cunanan—the Man Accused of Murdering Designer Gianni Versace." The italicized words are additions.

81. Schneider, "The Versace Slaying."

82. Eve Kosofsky Sedgwick, *Tendencies* (Durham, N.C.: Duke University Press, 1993), 221–22.

83. In *Hard-core: Power, Pleasure, and the "Frenzy of the Visible"* (Berkeley: University of California Press, 1989), Linda Williams calls this expectation the "girl/girl number." For examples of the time, see the voyeurism of Stearn's *The Grapevine* (1964) and *The Seventh Man* (1961), for instance. Currently, Tom Reichert, Kevin R. Maly, and Susan C. Zavoina, "Designed for (Male) Pleasure: The Myth of Lesbian Chic in Mainstream Advertising," in *Sexual Rhetoric: Media Perspectives on Sexuality, Gender, and Identity,* ed. Meta G. Carstarphen and Susan C. Zavoina (Westport, Conn.: Greenwood Press, 1999), 123–34.

84. "Fugitive 'Gay' Killer Strikes in New Jersey," Reuters news service, 10 May 1997.

85. Maria Puente and Lori Sharn, "Murder Suspect Eluding Manhunt," *USA Today,* 13 May 1997, 3A.

86. *ABC World News This Morning,* 24 July 1997.

87. Brian Lowry, "ABC Planning Film on Alleged Serial Killer," *Los Angeles Times,* 30 July 1997, Record edition, D1, 6. One person connected with the project explained, "This is a serial killer that's front-page headline news. I assume that the public's interested and fascinated in what makes these people tick."

88. Puente and Sharn, "Murder Suspect Eluding Manhunt."

89. Ibid.

90. The link between homosexuality, and a perverse intelligence, added to aggression and killing, is fictionally presented in Thomas Harris's Hannibal Lecter, but as Tithecott notes there are other forces at work; see the chapter "The Serial Killer and the Powers of Intelligence," in his book *Of Men and Monsters: Jeffrey Dahmer and the Construction of the Serial Killer* (Madison: University of Wisconsin Press, 1997), 145–49. Numerous reports commented upon Cunanan's "genius," his ability with languages, his being "well-read." *People* (7 July 1997), noting the emptiness of Cunanan's life, said that he "read" during the days to fill up the hours.

91. Noel Carroll, *The Philosophy of Horror; or, Paradoxes of the Heart* (New York: Routledge, 1990), 182.

92. Anticipating my discussion of the mechanics of scandal in a subsequent chapter, see, William A. Cohen, *Sex Scandal: The Private Parts of Victorian Fiction* (Durham, N.C.: Duke University Press, 1996).

93. John R. Engen, "Questions at Start of Fatal Trail," *Newsday,* 14 May 1997, A4.

94. Perry and Pasternak, "Cunanan Doesn't Fit Serial Killer Mold."

95. Ibid.

96. Chua-Eoan, "Dead Men Tell No Tales," 30–32.

97. Tony Perry, "Fugitive a Surprising Suspect," *Los Angeles Times,* 16 May 1997, A3.

98. Chua-Eoan, "Dead Men Tell No Tales," 31.

99. Ibid., 32.

100. Douglas Crimp, ed., "How to Have Promiscuity in an Epidemic," in *AIDS: Cultural Analysis, Cultural Activism* (Cambridge, Mass.: MIT Press, 1988).

101. Andrew Phillips, et al., "Murder in Miami," *Maclean's* (28 July 1997): 22.

102. Engen, "Questions at Start of Fatal Trail."

103. *Time* (27 August 1973): 56.

104. See Crimp, introduction to *AIDS: Cultural Analysis, Cultural Activism.* Also, see Mikhael Elbaz and Ruth Murbach, "Fear in the Face of the Other, Condemned and Damned: AIDS, Epidemics, and Exclusions," in *A Leap in the Dark: AIDS, Art, and Contemporary Cultures,* edited by Allan Klusacek and Ken Morrison (Montreal: Véhicule Press, 1993), 1–9; Barbara Park, "Kimberly Bergalis, AIDS, and the Plague Metaphor," in Garber, Matlock and Walkowitz, *Media Spectacles,* 232–53.

105. *USA Today,* 13 May 1997, 3A.

106. Perry, "Fugitive a Surprising Suspect."

107. The queer-as-loaded-gun script, while as old as Hitchcock's *Rope,* was retrieved and refitted for the eighties in Gaetan Dugas ("Patient Zero")—in what Ellis Hanson calls "the very Dracula of AIDS" (cited in Fuss, 332). Hanson refers to Randy Shilts's documentary narrative of the early AIDS years in the United States, *And the Band Played On* (New York: St. Martin's Press, 1987). See Ellis Hanson, "Undead," in *Inside/Out: Lesbian Theories, Gay Theories,* ed. Diana Fuss (New York: Routledge, 1991), 324–40.

108. Phillips, et al., "Murder in Miami."

109. Hugh Davies, "Killer's Last Stand on Indian Creek," *Daily Telegraph,* 25 July 1997, 18.

110. John McCormick and Evan Thomas, "A Lethal Road Trip," *Newsweek* (19 May 1997): 52. *Time*'s riff on this, written before Cunanan's death, though dated *after* it, is as follows: "Openly gay as a teenager, he once showed up at a school function in a red patent-leather jumpsuit that he said was a gift from his *much* older date" (Lacayo [28 July 1997]: 33; italics mine).

111. Perry and Pasternak, "Cunanan Doesn't Fit Serial Killer Mold."

112. While Dahmer may only have fantasized his cannibal interest, another killer— Gary "The Bishop" Heidnik—seems to have been the real item. Although he was actively killing only four years before Dahmer, he is hardly a household name. See Oates, "No Other Thrill or Happiness," 54. For a discussion of Dahmer's willingness to assume the role of cannibal, see Tithecott, *Of Men and Monsters,* esp. 65–67. Forensic specialists downplayed Dahmer's—and the media's—interest in cannibalism. Milwaukee Police Chief Philip Arreola said directly that "the evidence is not consistent" with Dahmer's claims (cited in Tithecott, 66).

113. Perry and Pasternak, "Cunanan Doesn't Fit Serial Killer Mold."

114. See Corber, *Homosexuality in Cold War America.* Stephen Cohan writes, "The virulent repression of homosexuality following the war is a rather telling index of the entire culture's conversion to a middle-class sexual ideology" (*Masked Men,* xiv).

115. Perry and Pasternak, "Cunanan Doesn't Fit Serial Killer Mold."

116. Ibid.

117. Homi K. Bhabha, "The Other Question: The Stereotype and Colonial Discourse," in *The Sexual Subject: A* Screen *Reader in Sexuality,* collective editorial (New York: Routledge, 1992), 318.

118. Benedict Anderson, *Imagined Communities: Reflections on the Origin and Spread of Nationalism* (1983; revised, London: Verso, 1991), 188, 35–36.

119. Thomas, "Facing Death," 22.

120. Edelman, "Tearooms and Sympathy," 559.

121. See, for example, Crimp, "How to Have Promiscuity in an Epidemic."

122. "By infusing the spark of life into a novel, [Shelley] let loose a murderous being, a *homicidal text* that kills those nearest to it" (Robert Olorenshaw, "Narrating the Monster: From Mary Shelley to Bram Stoker," in *Frankenstein, Creation, and Monstrosity,* ed. Stephen Bann [London: Reaktion Books, 1994], 164).

123. This accounts, I think, for the genocidal fantasies swirling around the case, such as the one attributed to John Walsh, the host of *America's Most Wanted* and *Entertainment Tonight.* On the July 24 edition of *ET* he remarked: "[Cunanan] crossed the line from killing gay people for revenge and started killing innocent bystanders" ("GLAADLines," 25 August 1997, www.glaad.org, Web page for the Gay and Lesbian Alliance Against Defamation). Or the veiled edge of *Vanity Fair's* title, already referenced: "On the Trail of the Gay Serial Killer" (cover, September 1997). Or the July 29 editorial by Bill Morrison in *Rolla Daily News:* "According to news reports, Cunanan's killing spree involved homosexual people he probably had had past relationships with. Which leads me to wonder, where's the downside to this story?" ("GladAlert," 1 August 1997, www.glaad.org).

124. *USA Today,* 13 May 1997, 3A.

125. Perry and Pasternak, "Cunanan Doesn't Fit Serial Killer Mold."

126. Hugh Davies, "Killer's Last stand on Indian Creek."

127. Miami Beach Police Chief Richard Barreto, *ABC World News This Morning,* 24 July 1997.

128. Lacayo, *Time* (28 July 1997). The subsequent story on Cunanan, by Chua-Eoan ("Dead Men Tell No Tales"), disparages this claim (see 28). *Time's* consistently lurid coverage of the case is, as noted, remarkable. The two issues immediately following Cunanan's death are noteworthy for the amount of sheer speculative, tendentious moralizing, and ostensibly guileless bad taste: "The murder scene [referring to finding Trail's body] was an investigator's dream" (28 July 1997). Later, referring to Cunanan's death, *Time* magazine can mystifyingly write that Cunanan tries "to destroy the only [face] he has left in order to remain forever masked in mystery"—and, four paragraphs later, reverse itself: "As for his face, one source said it still bore a resemblance to the photos in his wanted posters" (4 August 1997, 30–31). When one considers that confirmation of the body's identification depended upon a thumbprint, as Miami Beach Police Chief Richard Barreto reported to NPR ("All Things Considered," 24 July 1997) it is clear that *Time* has its own fiction, figured out in the metaphors of theater, visuality, and scene that clutter the story's first two paragraphs. In both issues metaphors of the theater ("coup de théâtre") and horror show ("pulp fiction") indicate the framing paradigm; Cunanan's life is read back into *Pulp Fiction* in much the same way that Dahmer's life was read back into (choose one) *The Exorcist* or *The Silence of the Lambs.* See *Time* (4 August 1997): 30.

129. Clover, *Men, Women, and Chain Saws,* 47.

130. Carol J. Clover, "Her Body, Himself," 117.

131. Marvin Kitman, "The Criminal Cunanan Coverage," *Newsday,* 3 August 1997, The Marvin Kitman Sunday Show, C39.

Chapter Four

1. Kathie Lee Gifford, "Life with Regis and Kathie Lee"; cited in Peter Johnson and Alan Bash, "Child-Death Case Grabs Talk Shows, Newsmags," *USA Today,* 7 November 1994, 3.

2. See the chapter "Marriages as Happy Endings" in Judith Perkins, *The Suffering Self: Pain and Narrative Representation in the Early Christian Era* (New York: Routledge, 1995). Perkins demonstrates that the work of convincing readers about the joys of marital relations is not, indeed, a recent development of late-evangelical American politics, nor even of Western industrial ideology more broadly conceived.

3. Sr. Helen Prejean reverses the strategy of attorney Pope: "I'll acknowledge the evil Pat has done and make very clear that I in no way condone his terrible crime, but I'll try to show that he is not a monster but a human being like the rest of us in the room." *Dead Man Walking: An Eyewitness Account of the Death Penalty in the United States* (New York: Vintage Books, 1993), 62.

4. See Philippe Ariès, *Centuries of Childhood: A Social History of Family Life,* trans. Robert Baldick (New York: Vintage Books, 1965); Maria W. Piers, *Infanticide: Past and Present* (New York: W. W. Norton, 1978); William L. Langer, "Infanticide: A Historical Survey," *History of Childhood Quarterly* 1, no. 3 (1974). Also Peter C. Hoffer and N.E.H. Hull, *Murdering Mothers: Infanticide in England and New England, 1558–1803* (New York: New York University Press, 1981). In American popular literatures, see Daniel A. Cohen, *Pillars of Salt, Monuments of Grace: New England Crime Literature and the Origins of American Popular Culture, 1674–1860* (New York: Oxford University Press, 1993); also Andy Tucher, *Froth and Scum: Truth, Beauty, Goodness, and the Ax Murder in America's First Mass Medium* (Chapel Hill: University of North Carolina, 1994).

5. Matthew Ruben, "Of Newts and Quayles: National-Political Masculinity in the Current Conjuncture," in *Boys: Masculinities in Contemporary Culture,* ed. Paul Smith (New York: Westview Press, 1996), 258.

6. "The Remoteness That Betrays Desire," *Times Literary Supplement* (11 July 1997): 6.

7. Nancy Armstrong argues that such nationalizing narrative arises out of the novelistic impulse itself. In *Desire and Domestic Fiction: A Political History of the Novel* (New York: Oxford University Press, 1987), she shows how domestic fiction produces a consciousness "so important to the stability of capitalist society," and that "writing that constituted the self as such was a primary agent to history" (191). For a specific treatment of American domesticity in the constructing and critiquing of women's roles, see Kathleen Anne McHugh, *American Domesticity: From How-to Manual to Hollywood Melodrama* (New York: Oxford University Press, 1999).

8. Ted Bundy interview with James Dobson in Florida State Prison, February 1989; cited in James Alan Fox and Jack Levin, *Overkill: Mass Murder and Serial Killing Exposed* (New York: Plenum Press, 1994), 73. See also Roger Shattuck, *Forbidden Knowledge: From Prometheus to Pornography* (New York: St. Martin's Press, 1996), 264.

9. Christoph Grunenberg, "Unsolved Mysteries: Gothic Tales from *Frankenstein* to the Hair-Eating Doll," in *Gothic: Transmutations of Horror in Late Twentieth Century Art,* ed. Christoph Grunenberg (Cambridge, Mass.: MIT Press, 1997), 176–175 [*sic;* pagination reversed]. Vivian Sobchack sums up the anxiety: "A man's home in bourgeois patriarchal culture is no longer his castle" ("Bringing It All Back Home: Family Economy and Generic Exchange," in *American Horrors: Essays on the Modern American Horror Film,* ed. Gregory Waller [Urbana: University of Illinois Press, 1987], 177).

10. Judith Halberstam, *Skin Shows: Gothic Horror and the Technology of Monsters* (Durham, N.C.: Duke University Press, 1995), 167.

11. Anne Williams, *Art of Darkness: A Poetics of Gothic* (Chicago: University of Chicago Press, 1995), 95.

12. Rick Bragg, "Union, S.C., Is Left a Town Torn Asunder," *New York Times,* 24 July 1995, A8.

13. Nina Auerbach, *Our Vampires, Ourselves* (Chicago: University of Chicago Press, 1995), 206, note 51.

14. See also Elisabeth Bronfen, *Over Her Dead Body: Death, Femininity, and the Aesthetic* (New York: Routledge, 1992); B. Bassein, *Women and Death: Linkages in Western Thought and Literature* (Westport, Conn.: Greenwood Press, 1984).

15. *New York Times,* 30 July 1995; the word appeared again a day later in *Newsweek* (31 July 1995).

16. *Newsweek* (31 July 1995): 65. See also *Newsweek's* earlier report in which "crowds that once agonized for Smith jeered her" (14 November 1994): 28.

17. See Leonce Gaiter, "American Mantra: Blame the Black Man," *New York Times,* 12 November 1994, A21.

18. Lorrie Grant. "Smith Jury to Hear Testimony in Penalty Phase of Trial," Reuters news service, 23 July 1995.

19. The photograph of the dead JonBenet Ramsey's hand on the cover of *Globe* magazine organizes similar effects. JonBenet Ramsey was found dead in her home on December 26, 1996. Ken Harrell, "Little Beauty Tortured to Death," *Globe* (21 January 1997): 24–36.

20. Carol Karlsen, *The Devil in the Shape of a Woman: Witchcraft in Colonial New England* (New York: Vintage Books, 1989). For the Gothic vectoring of this unnatural woman, the failed or absent mother, see Susan Wolstenholme, who writes that "Gothic-marked narratives always point to the space where the absent mother might be" (*Gothic (Re)Visions: Writing Women as Readers* [Albany: State University of New York Press, 1993], 151); see especially her chapter "Exorcizing the Mother." Also see Bram Dijkstra, *Idols of Perversity: Fantasies of Feminine Evil in Fin-De-Siècle Culture* (New York: Oxford University Press, 1986); Marie-Hélène Huet explores the accustomed pathological link posited between the imagination and gender in *The Monstrous Imagination* (Cambridge, Mass.: Harvard University Press, 1993); Barbara Creed examines the spectatorial male gaze that creates the feminine Monster in *The Monstrous-Feminine: Film, Feminism, Psy-*

choanalysis (London: Routledge, 1993); see also Carol J. Clover, "Her Body, Himself: Gender in the Slasher Film," in *Fantasy and the Cinema,* ed, James Donald (London: British Film Institute, 1989): 91–133.

21. Walter Kendrick, *The Thrill of Fear: 250 Years of Scary Entertainment* (New York: Grove Press, 1991), 19.

22. James Twitchell, *Preposterous Violence: Fables of Aggression in Modern Culture* (New York: Oxford University Press, 1989), 98.

23. Discussing the JonBenet Ramsey case, Diana York Blaine underscores the difficulty of announcing the possibility that there "could be some national interest in the sexuality of children" ("Necrophilia, Pedophilia, or Both?: The Sexualized Rhetoric of the JonBenet Ramsey Murder Case," in *Sexual Rhetoric: Media Perspectives on Sexuality, Gender, and Identity,* ed. Meta G. Carstarphen and Susan C. Zavoina (Westport, Conn.: Greenwood Press, 1999), 52. Specific to the point of this chapter, John Douglas asks, for instance, "What kind of monster could abduct, molest, and/or take the life of an innocent child?" A few lines later he answers his own question, calling "sexual predators . . . the lowest of life forms" (John Douglas and Mark Olshaker, *Journey into Darkness* [New York: Pocket Star Books, 1997], 123). Douglas spends a chapter extolling the work of the National Center for Missing and Exploited Children (founded in 1984, he observes, under the "mandate" of "that year's Missing Children Act" [122]).

24. Murray Kempton, *Newsday,* 28 June 1995, A15. Kempton might have had little control over the title of the essay, although in terms of content the title is consistent with Kempton's remarks.

25. See District Attorney Christopher Darden's statement to the jury in the Simpson trial: "Like many public men . . . they have a private side, a private life, a private face. And that is the face we will expose to you in this trial, the other side of O. J. Simpson, the side you never met before." Darden lists the "faces" of Simpson as "batterer, a wife beater, an abuser, a controller . . . the face of Ron's and Nicole's murderer" (cited in Jeffrey Toobin, *The Run of His Life: The People v. O. J. Simpson* [New York: Random House, 1996], 244). See also Marcia Clark, with Teresa Carpenter, *Without a Doubt* (New York: Penguin, 1997).

26. One reason for this is that Simpson's public identity is already in place, already constituted as fantasy by virtue of his celebrity. To that extent, that role is held separate from his domestic life. Whether this is a result of the operations of the "star" system or because of the operations of gender blindness in public discourse is not clear.

27. Marc Peyser and Ginny Carroll, "Southern Gothic on Trial," *Newsweek* (17 July 1995): 29; Rick Bragg, "Focus on Susan Smith's Lies and a Smile," *New York Times,* 25 July 1995, A11.

28. *Newsweek* headline (17 July 1995); Abbe Smith, "Women and the Law," *Boston Globe,* 27 February 1995, 15.

29. Written by *People* magazine reporter Maria Eftimiades (18 January 1995). The phrase is also a *Newsweek* cover (14 November 1994). In the subsequent murder of Jon-Benet Ramsey, motherhood similarly came under fire. See especially Blaine, "Necrophilia, Pedophilia, or Both?"

30. Title of a *Los Angeles Times* article by Lynn Smith and Elizabeth Mehren, 5 November 1994, A1; see also *Boston Globe,* 5 November 1994, 1. Also, Bonnie Miller Rubin, "Why Did She Do It?" *Chicago Tribune,* 15 November 1994, sec. 5, 1.

31. Robert Davis, *USA Today,* 4 November 1994, A3.

32. "All Things Considered," National Public Radio, 4 November 1994.

33. In a different case, an editorial about the Ramsey case addresses the parental subtext: "We don't know whether her parents were involved. But the bigger question is: Why is it so easy to think so?" Rochelle Riley, "Case against Killer of JonBenet Must Be Tight," Gannet news service, 5 February 1997, ARC.

34. Bella English, *Boston Globe,* 5 Nobember 1994, 1.

35. Ray Recchi, "The Greatest Pain," *Atlanta Journal-Constitution,* 11 November 1994, A19.

36. Put more bluntly, the politics of marriage have always been about securing public space, while its sentimentalizing has been about insuring a fantasy of the private. By enshrining courtly love (traditionally extramarital—and thus extra*political*) as the chivalric ideal, the romance of love has, historically, rarely impinged upon the material and political realities which, in Western patriarchal society, keep marriage pragmatically necessary. See R. Howard Bloch, *Medieval Misogyny and the Invention of Western Romantic Love* (Chicago: University of Chicago Press, 1991).

37. The problem of wife-killing, for example, doubly compounds the crisis of private intimacy by marking it, essentially, as no longer a private matter. Rather, it becomes a public crisis, uncovering as it does the theme of ownership still very much intended by the theory of marriage. That is, so long as she is alive, the wife is a form of property, owned you might say by the state in whose name the marriage contract is issued. The wife is on loan as it were to the husband, who, by laws of coverture, "covered" her with his legal presence. The husband could treat her as he would, often with little penalty. It is only in death, ironically, that the wife becomes a "person." The startling dichotomy, for example, can be seen by positioning Simpson's proven but uncharged violence against his wife—a recording of Nicole's calling a 911 help line exists—against the alleged but legally adjudicated murder.

38. Certain metaphors—e.g. the angel in the house, vulnerability, positioning of the virile as "outside" and protecting, the feminine hapless and entrapped—are customary tropes of "Marital Gothic" (Michelle A. Masse, *In the Name of Love: Women, Masochism, and the Gothic* [Ithaca: Cornell University Press, 1992], 25). See also Juliann Fleenor, ed., *The Female Gothic* (Montreal: Eden Press, 1983), especially Kay J. Mussell, "'But Why Do They Read Those Things?': The Female Audience and the Gothic Novel" (57–68).

39. "Why Are We Shocked When Mothers Kill Their Children?" *USA Today,* 19 April 1995, A13.

40. Halberstam, *Skin Shows,* 18.

41. Philip Jenkins, *Using Murder: The Social Construction of Serial Homicide* (New York: Aldine de Gruyter, 1994), 3.

42. A *US News and World Report* a few weeks after the verdict underscores this judicial/representational blind spot. It argues a statistic noted earlier, that "mothers kill their children about 600 times a year in the United States." The report further observes how "Pop culture has glorified violent women" (*Thelma and Louise* and Lorena Bobbitt are provided as examples). The essay never mentions fathers, or the possibility of fathers killing their children, or the routine glorification of violent men (Steven V. Roberts, "The Murderer Who Was Too Pathetic to Kill," Outlook, *US News and World Report* (7 August 1995): 8–9.

43. See the *New York Times,* 5 May 1995, A20: "Bias Issue Is Raised in Child Killer's Fate." "The report raises questions concerning equal treatment by Prosecutor Tommy Pope; he is seeking the death penalty for Smith, but had allowed a father guilty of smothering his son to negotiate a plea agreement." See also Blanche McCrary Boyd ("Who Killed Susan Smith?" *The Oxford American* [August/September 1996]: 34–42), who discusses this case. "Pope let Richard Darnell Haynes plead guilty for manslaughter, sentencing him to eight years in prison" (37). In another case a man who "slammed [his girlfriend's infant son] against the side of his crib" was charged with second-degree murder. See Ching-Ching Ni, Lauren Terrazzano, and Soraya Sarhaddi Nelson, "Toddler Fatally Slammed; Mother's Boyfriend Arrested," *Newsday,* 18 May 1997, A8.

44. *Washington Post,* 28 June 1999, A22.

45. *Atlanta Journal-Constitution,* 12 July 1995, A12.

46. These range from homosexuals who don't know how to be men, to serial killers and other civic miscreants who likewise lack this essential but mysterious knowledge.

47. Ann Rule [Andy Stack, pseud.], *Lust Killer* (New York: Signet, 1983), 233.

48. Boyd, "Who Killed Susan Smith?" 38.

49. *Time* (14 November 1994): 50

50. Another case in Oregon in 1983 sounds formulaically close to Smith's fabricated story of racial assault; similarly, so did the example of a young father who reported his daughter kidnapped, and then pleaded for her return before confessing he had buried her. See "They Don't Have to Kill Children," *Atlanta Inquirer,* 22 July 1995, 4.

51. See "The Trial of Darlie Routier," *ABC PrimeTime Live* (23 July 1997).

52. *Newsday,* 2 September 1996, A5.

53. David Van Biema, "Parents Who Kill," *Time* (14 November 1994): 50. More recently, we have the case of Louise Woodward, accused, and found guilty, of killing an infant in her care. See George Will, Sam Donaldson, and Cokie Roberts, "The Prosecution's Stance on Au Pair Case," *ABC This Week* (2 November 1997). Nonetheless, even in this case, attention was diverted from Woodward to the child's parents.

54. Tracy Wilson, "Parents Go on Trial in Death of Toddler," *Los Angeles Times,* 18 November 1997, Ventura County edition, 1.

55. *Time* (14 November 1994): 42.

56. "All Things Considered," National Public Radio, 5 November 1994. "The vast majority of child abductions are committed by a family member, often a divorced

parent who takes a child in violation of a custody agreement. Numbering 354,000 a year, these make up the bulk of the cases featured in the mailings and on 'missing' posters" (Richard Laliberte, "Missing Children: The Truth, the Hype, and What You Must Know," *Redbook* [1 February 1998]: 77–79, 110).

57. *Time* (14 November 1994): 50. The report adds, however, that in 1992 another "1,100 children died from abuse or neglect" (50). "All Things Considered" cites a Justice Department figure that "57% of the children who are murdered" in the United States "are killed by a parent" (4 November 1994). An op-ed piece in the *New York Times* writes, "Americans kill their children in horrifying numbers. . . . At least five children are killed by parents or their caretakers every day" (Paul Mones, "Life and Death and Susan Smith," 28 July 1995, A27). The article "Capital Report: Looking to Stop Child Killing," notes that between 1980 and 1994, 900 children were killed, and of these "288 were *killed* by parents, and 58 were slain by other family members" (*Cleveland Call and Post,* 8 May 1997; emphasis in original).

58. Mary Noel, *Villains Galore: The Heyday of the Popular Story Weekly* (New York: Macmillan, 1954), 1.

59. *USA Today,* 12 December 1994; *Boston Globe,* 28 December 1994, abstract; "South Carolina Murders Still Stun the Nation," "All Things Considered," National Public Radio, 4 November 1994.

60. *Atlanta Journal-Constitution,* 6 November 1994, sec. C, p. 1, col. 1.

61. Mones, "Life and Death and Susan Smith."

62. Adler, "Innocents Lost," 26.

63. Nancy Gibbs, "Death and Deceit," *Time* (14 November 1994): 42.

64. After drafting this chapter I read Mark Edmundson's description of "Apocalyptic Gothic" (*Nightmare on Main Street: Angels, Sadomasochism, and the Culture of Gothic.* Cambridge [Mass.: Harvard University Press, 1997], 77ff.).

65. Howard Kurtz, "Gingrich Already at War with Media," *Washington Post,* reprinted in the *Philadelphia Inquirer,* 20 November 1994, A6. Gingrich responds in a lengthy letter; see the *Wall Street Journal,* 18 November 1994.

66. Miriam Longino, "The End of INNOCENCE," *Atlanta Journal-Constitution,* 9 July 1995, M1.

67. See Charles Sennott, "Southern Secrets," *Boston Globe,* 28 December 1994, 1.

68. Bragg, "Union, S.C."

69. "All Things Considered," National Public Radio, 5 November 1994.

70. Frank Rich, "Beverly Russell's Prayers," *New York Times,* 2 August 1995, A19.

71. *Newsweek* (17 July 1995): 29; *Newsweek* (14 November 1994): 29.

72. In the JonBenet Ramsey case (which has preoccupied news and media since December 1996 and is yet unsolved), many accounts lay blame at the parents'—and particularly her mother's—feet. See, for instance, Diane Freeman, "JonBenet Ramsey's Parents Deny Role in Her Murder," Reuters news service, 1 May 1997; "Mom Wrote on

JonBenet Pad," *Newsday,* 2 July 1997, A19. See Bill Hewitt, "Stalemate Eleven Weeks and Counting," *People* (24 March 1997): 108. Discussing this case, Diana York Blaine writes that the "ludicrous conclusions" about Patty, the girl's mother, "permit us to heap blame on the woman who is violated, thereby ignoring the agency of men, an omission that is necessary for our sexually stratified culture to retain its structure" ("Necrophelia, Pedophilia, or Both?" 56).

73. "Help the Women Drug Users," *Philadelphia Inquirer,* 14 September 1990, 21A.

74. Longino, "The end of INNOCENCE."

75. *Newsweek* (17 July 1995): 29.

76. *Newsweek* (7 August 1995): 20; *New York Times,* 24 July 1995.

77. Gibbs, "Death and Deceit," 42.

78. Ann Jessie Van Sant, *Eighteenth-Century Sensibility and the Novel: The Senses in Social Context* (Cambridge, U.K.: Cambridge University Press, 1993), 5. See, in particular, her chapter "Locating Experience in the Body: The Man of Feeling" (98–115). See, too, Laura Hinton, who, in *The Perverse Gaze of Sympathy: Sadomasochistic Sentiments from "Clarissa" to "Rescue 911"* (Albany: State University of New York Press, 1999), examines the "Failed Mirror of Sympathy" and what becomes, more properly, the mode of sensation and excess of sentiment.

79. The death of Matthew Shepard, for example, rapidly escalated into scenes of civic grief, but also, in some instances, to scenes of civic violence, as happened in Manhattan following the announcement of his murder.

80. Marianne Noble, "An Ecstasy of Apprehension: The Gothic Pleasures of Sentimental Fiction," in *American Gothic: New Interventions in a National Narrative,* ed. Robert Martin and Eric Savoy (Iowa City: University of Iowa Press, 1998), 164.

81. Hinton, *The Perverse Gaze of Sympathy,* 11.

82. Bill Hewitt, "Tears of Hate, Tears of Pity," *People* (13 March 1995): 76–80.

83. Adler, "Innocents Lost," 28.

84. Abstract, 6 November 1994.

85. *Newsweek* (17 July 1995): 29.

86. Rheta Grimsley Johnson, "May We Never Come to Expect Worst of Mothers," *Atlanta Journal-Constitution,* 6 November 1994, C1.

87. Longino, "The end of INNOCENCE."

88. Peyser and Carroll, "Southern Gothic on Trial."

89. Chris Burritt, "Around the South: The Susan Smith Trial," *Atlanta Journal-Constitution,* 11 July 1995, C8.

90. Tom Morganthau, "Will They Kill Susan Smith?" *Newsweek* (31 July 1995): 65.

91. See Boyd, "Who Killed Susan Smith?" 38. *People* magazine (13 March 1995), has a version of this confession, referred to in the text—although it edits out the last, possibly extenuating phrase—"to protect us all from any grief or harm" (82).

92. Matthew Ruben, "Of Newts and Quayles," 257–58.

93. And which, in September 2000, is still circulating, as the *National Enquirer* trumpets, "Baby-Killer Pregnant in Jail by Prison Guard."

94. Gibbs, "Death and Deceit," 42.

95. Dennis Todd, *Imagining Monsters: Miscreations of the Self in Eighteenth-Century England* (Chicago: University of Chicago Press, 1995), 156.

96. *Newsday*, 28 June 1995, A15.

97. James W. Carey, "The Dark Continent of American Journalism," in *Reading the News: A Pantheon Guide to Popular Culture*, ed. Robert Karl Manoff and Michael Schudson (New York: Pantheon Books, 1986), 147.

98. David Punter, "Problems of Recollection and Construction: Stephen King," in *Modern Gothic: A Reader*, ed. Victor Sage and Allan Lloyd Smith (Manchester, U.K.: Manchester University Press, 1996), 122.

99. *New York Times*, 24 July 1997, A8.

100. For example, in study after study, readers are told that serial killers came, *en masse* and suddenly, "from nowhere," and that they "rove America," or, alternately, they "roam the streets and countrysides of America in search of victims." See "Murderers, Bombers Indict Death Sentence," *Minnesota Daily via U-Wire*, 27 January 1998; they "stalk and kill and wait . . . and stalk and kill again and wait" (Rule, *Lust Killer*, 229, ellipse in text). John Wayne Gacy said that he "trawl[ed] down the streets and stalk[ed] young boys and slaughtered them" (in Robert K. Ressler and Tom Shachtman, *I Have Lived in the Monster: A Report from the Abyss* [New York: St. Martin's Press, 1997], 77). They are a consequence, it is urged, of collapsing civic and moral structures of the kind providing the nostalgia backdrop of the Smith narrative. See, for example, John Douglas's polemic "For the Children," (121–61) where he notes the "urgency surrounding their [Staffers at the National Center for Missing and Exploited Children] mission" (in *Journey into Darkness*, 121).

101. Ann Douglas, *The Feminization of American Culture* (New York: Knopf, 1977).

102. Maggie Kilgour, *The Rise of the Gothic Novel* (New York: Routledge, 1995), 108.

103. Ibid., 99.

104. Robert Ressler, quoted on a 1994 episode of *20th Century*, "America's Serial Killer Epidemic."

105. See the *Protection of Children from Sexual Predators Act of 1998*, which continues a history of legislative collapse around child abduction and serial killing. See "Legislative History of P.L. 105-314," *Congressional Index Service*, 98-PL105-314, 30 October 1998. See Steven A. Egger, *Serial Murder: An Elusive Phenomenon* (Westport, Conn.: Praeger, 1990), 44–46, 192.

106. Frank Rich, "The Mother Next Door," *New York Times*, 13 November, 1994, sec. 4, 15.

107. Douglas W. Pryor, *Unspeakable Acts: Why Men Sexually Abuse Children* (New York: New York University Press, 1996), 255.

108. David Sonenschein, on the other hand, notes not so much a crisis of pedophiles in society as "the pedophilia *of* popular culture," specifically, "the eroticization of youth by the conventional world itself . . . interests excessively denied and vigorously scapegoated" (*Pedophiles on Parade,* vol. 2, *Popular Imagery of Moral Hysteria* [San Antonio, Tex.: D. Sonenschein, 1998], 29). Susan Bordo, similarly, citing a 1958 review of *Lolita,* remarks, "Humbert is all of us." She then comments, "The unconfronted secret of our culture is surely not childhood sexuality . . . but the adult eroticization of children" (*Chronicle of Higher Education,* 24 July 1998, B7, 8). Similarly, see John Leonard, "The New Puritanism: Who's Afraid of Lolita? (We Are)," *Nation* (24 November, 1997): 11–15. Diana York Blaine offers, she says, a "shocking proposition"—that "the eroticization of children's bodies and our overwhelming fear of natural death leave us fascinated with the case of JonBenet Ramsey" ("Necrophilia, Pedophilia, or Both?" 51). The eroticized child reshapes the fantasy of domesticity. Sentimental narratives no longer need find ways of displaying the dying child, as in Dickens. Rather, the new subjectivity undresses them—or rather, redresses them as sexual adults. Ramsey is an example, first by her parents' actions and then, by the consequent fantasies of readers around her and the always-already threat to the child. See James R. Kincaid, *Child-loving: The Erotic Child and Victorian Culture* (New York: Routledge, 1992); and his "Is This Child Pornography?" (*Salon* <www.salon.com>, January 2000).

109. Ann Hulbert, "Home Repairs: Parents, Work and the Durability of the Family," *New Republic* (16 August 1993): 26–32.

110. David J. Skal, *The Monster Show: A Cultural History of Horror* (New York: W. W. Norton, 1993).

111. This may explain why a history of "abuse" in Smith's case seems offered as exoneration, while in Dahmer's case, abuse, when it arises, does so not to exonerate, but as confirmatory reason, the "primary cause of his crime" (Fox and Levin, *Overkill,* 78). Jurors in the Smith case, for example, remarked that there "are a lot more people in this case who should have been punished who weren't." Another juror said about Smith, "I don't know if she ever realized she was sick or not" (*Newsday,* 29 July 1995, A4).

112. See Josephine McDonagh, "Do or Die: Problems of Agency and Gender in the Aesthetics of Murder," in *New Feminist Discourses: Critical Essays on Theories and Texts,* ed. Isobel Armstrong (London: Routledge, 1992), 222. Pertinent to this topic is Michael D. and C. L. Kelleher, *Murder Most Rare: The Female Serial Killer* (Westport, Conn.: Praeger, 1998), esp. ix–xii.

113. Another way of considering the shifting valences of these cases is to ask the question about Cunanan and Dahmer that lurked behind the questions of Ramsey and the two Smith boys: Is the domesticity of Cunanan and Dahmer of a different sort? Recall Oprah's question: "Are you raising a Jeffrey Dahmer?" Diane Sawyer's interview with Andrew Cunanan's family a few weeks after his death attempts a sentimental makeover in the terms which we are exploring; this nineties Donna Reed unit becomes, in Sawyer's phrase "a family reeling in horror" ("Family Matters," *ABC PrimeTime Live,* 16 August 1997). In the earlier Dahmer case, Lionel Dahmer will attempt a similar domestic rehabilitation effort in *A Father's Story* (New York: William Morrow, 1994); he chides himself for not spending time with his boy Jeff, though in reports and TV inter-

views the boy's natural mother, Joyce, is singled out for use of medications during her pregnancy, while his stepmother, Shari, is characterized by Geraldo as "a wicked step-mother" (Richard Tithecott, *Of Men and Monsters: Jeffrey Dahmer and the Construction of the Serial Killer* [Madison, Wis.: University of Wisconsin Press, 1997], 44). A submerged issue here is the oblique reference Dahmer's birth (thirty years previously), drugs, and the thalidomide frights.

114. An editorial in the *Washington Post* entitled "Killer Mom" takes umbrage at the explicit gendering distinctions accorded to such cases. The editorial notes that "we seem to have a way of treating baby killers more gently than other murderers. It is a pattern that we have seen locally, where a woman was sentenced to weekends in jail for three years for killing her infant daughter." After listing a few other cases, the editorial remarks, "It is as though these babies are something less than real people and killing them is something less than real murder." See "Killer Mom," *Washington Post*, 2 July 1999, A26.

115. Similar judgments pass as unexceptional at another register, too. In *Scandal: The Crisis of Mistrust in American Politics* (New York: Random House, 1991), Suzanne Garment writes, apropos of judging the morality of the (male) politician, "Does it make a difference whether the wife is a saint or a monster?" (196). Dads, on the other hand, face stigma for economic, rather than sexual, failing; e.g., "deadbeat dad."

116. Matthew Ruben, "Of Newts and Quayles," 255.

117. Robert Bly's *Iron John: A Book about Men* (New York: Random House, 1990) is probably the locus classicus of the genre. From a different perspective, see Mark Simpson, *Male Impersonators: Men Performing Masculinity* (London: Cassell, 1994).

118. See Rhona J. Berenstein, *Attack of the Leading Ladies: Gender, Sexuality, and Spectatorship in Classic Horror Cinema* (Columbia, N.Y.: Columbia University Press, 1996). In this regendering of the monster, however, Shelley was again in the lead. Victor Frankenstein sets about making a creature whose "lustrous black" hair and "pearly" teeth (Bantam edition, 52) seem to hint at a feminizing code confirmed, rather than de-nied, by the creature's general powerlessness over the basic essentials—including repro-duction—of its life. For a specific discussion of the genesis of *Frankenstein*, see Ellen Moers, *Literary Women* (London: Women's Press, 1978); "Horror's Twin: Mary Shelley's Monstrous Eve," in *The Madwoman in the Attic: The Woman Writer and the Nineteenth-Century Literary Imagination*, by Sandra Gilbert and Susan Gubar (New Haven: Yale University Press, 1979), 213–47.

119. Masse, *In the Name of Love*, 41.

120. These various narratives function, then, as analogues perhaps of the horror film—"a form of modern defilement rite" by which the symbolic order casts out "all that threatens its stability, particularly the mother and all that her universe signifies. In this sense, signifying horror involves a representation of, and a reconciliation with, the maternal body" (Creed, *The Monstrous-Feminine*, 14).

121. See Kate Ellis, "Monsters in the Garden: Mary Shelley and the Bourgeois Family," in *The Endurance of Frankenstein: Essays on Mary Shelley's Novel*, ed. George Le-vine and U. C. Knoepflmacher (Berkeley: University of California Press, 1979), 123–42.

Nina Auerbach likewise argues that a generation of movie vampires is familial, and thus monstrous: "The heart and horror of *Horror of Dracula* [is] the family" (*Our Vampires, Ourselves,* 124).

122. Cited in Henry A. Giroux, *Disturbing Pleasures: Learning Popular Culture* (New York: Routledge, 1994), 41.

Chapter Five

1. Quoted in "Perspectives," *Newsweek* (21 December 1998): 15.

2. Kenneth Starr's rejoinder to presidential lawyer David E. Kendall. Kendall questioned Starr in the presence of the House Impeachment Committee. See "Excerpts from Starr's Questioning by the President's Personal Lawyer David E. Kendall," *New York Times,* 20 November 1998, <www.nytimes.com>.

3. See Susan Bordo, "True Obsessions: Being Unfaithful to 'Lolita,'" *Chronicle of Higher Education,* 24 July 1998, B7–8.

4. Mark Seltzer, *Serial Killers: Death and Life in America's Wound Culture* (New York: Routledge, 1998), 138. For broader treatments of mass culture, see Patrick Brantlinger, *Bread and Circuses: Theories of Mass Culture as Social Decay* (Ithaca: Cornell University Press, 1985); Andrew Ross, *No Respect: Intellectuals and Popular Culture* (New York: Routledge, 1989); Todd Gitlin, *The Whole World Is Watching* (Berkeley: University of California Press, 1980).

5. Seltzer, *Serial Killers,* 64–65.

6. Laura Hinton writes, "The reproduction of sentiment calls forth images of femininity, sympathy, and virtuous moral feeling. But the reproduction of sentiment also relies upon a visual power structure that is gendered male, and a sympathetic spectator whose 'sentiments' are sadomasochistic" (*The Perverse Gaze of Sympathy: Sadomasochistic Sentiments from Clarissa to Rescue 911* [Albany: State University of New York Press, 1999], 2).

7. For a detailed and foreboding account of what happens when fantasy collapses into politics, see Laura Kipnis, *Bound and Gagged: Pornography and the Politics of Fantasy in America* (New York: Grove Press, 1996).

8. See Patricia Joyner Priest, *Public Intimacies: Talk Show Participants and Tell-All TV* (Cresskill, N.J.: Hampton Press, 1995); Richard Schickel, *Intimate Strangers: The Culture of Celebrity* (New York: Fromm International, 1985).

9. "Just When You Thought TV Couldn't Squeeze In Another Talk Show," Noel Holston, *Star Tribune,* 18 September 1995, 1E. See Philip Rieff, *The Triumph of the Therapeutic: Uses of Faith after Freud* (1966; reprint, Chicago: University of Chicago Press, 1987).

10. To this general point, see Nancy Armstrong and Leonard Tennenhouse, "Representing Violence; or, How the West Was Won," in *The Violence of Representation: Literature and the History of Violence,* ed. Armstrong and Tennenhouse (London: Routledge, 1989), 1–26. They suggest that "writing is not so much about violence as a form of violence in its own right."

11. Bateman's compulsive accumulation of facts and knowledge of human bodies, like Starr's in this respect, has its historical precedents in the pre-Cartesian preoccupation with bodily interiors as sites of human identity. The body's interior, writes Elaine Scarry, "confirms the truth." See "Donne: 'But Yet the Body Is His Booke,'" in *Literature and the Body,* ed. Elaine Scarry (Baltimore: John Hopkins University Press, 1988), 77. See, too, the way discourse informally returns us to the body: "body of knowledge," "Anatomy of Melancholy," "Anatomy of Criticism," etc.

12. Pierre Bourdieu discusses the "implicit pedagogy" of the body as a social epistemology, in *Outline of a Theory of Practice,* trans. Richard Nice (Cambridge, U.K.: Cambridge University Press, 1977), 94. See Mary Douglas, *Natural Symbols: Explorations in Cosmology* (New York: Pantheon, 1980); Bryan Turner, *The Body and Society: Explorations in Social Theory* (Oxford: Blackwell, 1984).

13. Joshua Gamson, *Freaks Talk Back: Tabloid Talk Shows and Sexual Nonconformity* (Chicago: University of Chicago Press, 1998), 13; later in the book he returns to this point: "Indeed, talk shows in general, through the unabashed pursuit of the entertaining moment, make high, personalized, thinned-out drama out of deeper social divisions, cultural anxieties, and political struggles" (212). For a history of the talk show, see Brian G. Rose, "The Talk Show," in *TV Genres: A Handbook and Reference Guide,* ed. Brian G. Rose (Westport, Conn.: Greenwood Press, 1985); Paolo Carpignano et al., "Chatter in the Age of Electronic Reproduction: Talk Television and the 'Public Mind,'" *Social Text,* nos. 25–26 (1990); also Vicki Abt and Mel Seesholtz, "The Shameless World of Phil, Sally, and Oprah: Television Talk Shows and the Deconstructing of Society," *Journal of Popular Culture* 28, no. 1 (1994); Jane Shattuc, *The Talking Cure: TV Talk Shows and Women* (New York: Routledge, 1997); Gini Graham Scott, *Can We Talk?: The Power and Influence of Talk Shows* (New York: Insight Books, 1996); Donal Carbaugh, *Talking American: Cultural Discourses on Donahue* (Norwood, N.J.: Ablex Publishing, 1989).

14. Jonathan Lake Crane, *Terror and Everyday Life: Singular Moments in the History of the Horror Film* (Thousand Oaks, Calif.: Sage Publications, 1994), 141.

15. See, to this point, Stephen Moore, *God's Gym: Divine Male Bodies of the Bible* (New York: Routledge, 1996).

16. See Jurgen Habermas's foundational discussion of the private and "public sphere," in *The Structural Transformation of the Public Sphere,* trans. Thomas Burger (Cambridge: MIT Press, 1991).

17. For a discussion of the grotesque body, see Peter Stallybrass and Allon White, *The Politics and Poetics of Transgression* (London: Methuen, 1986). See Robert Bogdan, *Freakshow: Presenting Human Oddities for Amusement and Profit* (Chicago: University of Chicago Press, 1988).

18. Elaine Hadley, *Melodramatic Tactics: Theatricalized Dissent in the English Marketplace, 1800–1885* (Stanford, Calif.: Stanford University Press, 1995). The scandalizing body, no matter how weak it appears, is nonetheless a powerful body, just as the monster is, likewise, still, accorded a trace of awe. The police who arrested Dahmer and then sought his autograph demonstrated this interesting calculus, holding mastery over him while subjecting themselves to him. These police were thus guilty of a displacement

fairly typical of these cases of outrage, by which writing acts are exchanged for sex acts, or better, in which sex acts are transformed into writing acts (a maneuver which seems on the whole different from pornographic representation but which is not); that is, the production of narratives of the private reinforce a movement that would, in a visual context, be called pornographic.

19. Similarly, "in a culture in which images of body parts are so heavily eroticized the victim [of rape] who speaks of violation may be experienced as speaking pornographically" (Emilie Buchwald, Pamela R. Fletcher and Martha Roth, eds., *Transforming a Rape Culture* [Minneapolis: Milkweed Editions, 1993], 66; cited in Patricia E. O'Connor, "Discourse of Violence," *Discourse and Society* 6, no. 3 [July 1995]: 313).

20. For some general studies on the politics of talk, see Howard Kurtz, *Hot Air: All Talk, All the Time* (New York: Times Books, 1996); Wayne Munson, *All Talk: The Talkshow in Media Culture* (Philadelphia: Temple University Press, 1994).

21. See, especially, John B. Thompson, "Scandal and Social Theory," in *Media Scandals: Morality and Desire in the Popular Culture Marketplace,* ed. James Lull and Stephen Hinerman (New York: Columbia University Press, 1997), 34–64.

22. See, for instance, the popular studies *Scandal! An Encyclopaedia,* Colin Wilson and Donald Seaman (London: Weidenfeld and Nicolson, 1986); and *The Book of Modern Scandal: From Byron to the Present Day* (London: Weidenfeld and Nicolson, 1995). More serious studies include Andrei S. Markovits and Mark Silverstein, eds., *The Politics of Scandal: Power and Process in Liberal Democracies* (New York: Holmes and Meier, 1988); Suzanne Garment, *Scandal: The Culture of Mistrust in American Politics* (New York: Times Books, 1991); also Sally Engle Merry, "Rethinking Gossip and Scandal," in *Fundamentals,* vol. 1 of *Toward a General Theory of Social Control,* ed. Donald Black (Orlando, Fla.: Academic Press, 1984). Also Victor Turner, *The Ritual Process: Structure and Anti-Structure* (1966; reprint, Ithaca: Cornell University Press, 1979).

23. For the way an older moralizing impulse reads sexual conduct as the sacramental, visible sign of communal orthodoxy, see David D. Hall, *Worlds of Wonder, Days of Judgment: Popular Religious Belief in Early New England* (New York: Knopf, 1989). Also Edmund S. Morgan's foundational essay, "The Puritans and Sex," *New England Quarterly* 25 (December 1942): 591–607; see also his *Visible Saints: The History of a Puritan Idea* (New York: New York University Press, 1963). Susan Harding, "The Born-Again Telescandals," in *Culture/Power/History: A Reader in Contemporary Social Theory,* ed. Nicholas B. Dirks, Geoff Eley, and Sherry B. Ortner (Princeton: Princeton University Press, 1994).

24. Garment, *Scandal,* 2.

25. Ibid., 66.

26. When Patrick Buchanan announced his candidacy to replace Mr. Clinton, he found it rhetorically compelling to install Clinton within this mystical/religious framework, calling him "our own Elmer Gantry" and accusing him of "desecration of the temples of our civilization." "Text of Buchanan's Speech," AP Online, 25 October 1999. The bibliography addressing American Christian nationalism is extensive; see note 71 in chapter 1.

27. Garment, *Scandal,* 5–10.

28. See, in particular, Michael Colacurcio, *Doctrine and Difference: Essays in the Literature of New England* (New York: Routledge, 1997); also David Leverenz, *The Language of Puritan Feeling* (New Brunswick: Rutgers University Press, 1980); also John Winthrop, "A Short Story of the Rise, Reign and Ruine of the Antinomians, Familists and Libertines," in *The Antinomian Controversy, 1636–1638: A Documentary History,* ed. David D. Hall (Middletown, Conn.: Wesleyan University Press, 1968), 199–310.

29. Garment, *Scandal,* 14.

30. James Lull and Stephen Hinerman, "The Search for Scandal," in Lull and Hinerman, *Media Scandals,* 3. Roger Shattuck, discussing Pasolini's *Salo,* argues that the "power" of commodification is distilled "in the form of calculated provocation and scandal" (*Forbidden Knowledge: From Prometheus to Pornography* [New York: St. Martin's Press, 1996], 251). In other words, scandal, far from being an exception to the daily rhythms of popular culture, is its defining moment.

31. Paul Soukup, "Church, Media, and Scandal," in Lull and Hinerman, *Media Scandals,* 230.

32. Susan Smith, for example, appeared on *ABC Good Morning America, NBC Today,* and *CBS This Morning* to continue her stump speech about her children; later that same day she was arrested. Donahue and Maury Povich will air from Union, as did Oprah Winfrey; see *USA Today,* 7 November 1994, 3.

33. Thompson, "Scandal and Social Theory," 41.

34. Steven Cohan and Linda Shires, *Telling Stories: A Theoretical Analysis of Fiction* (London: Routledge, 1988), 149.

35. Elaine Scarry observes that "physical pain has no voice, but when it at last finds a voice, it begins to tell a story, and the story that it tells" is invariably a story of the "embeddedness of the political and perceptual complications" of pain, and that "whatever pain achieves, it achieves in part through its unsharability, and it ensures this unsharability through its resistance to language" (*The Body in Pain: The Making and Unmaking of the World* [New York: Oxford University Press, 1985], 3, 4). Pain, then, is unspeakable—beyond either the possibility of speech or its permission.

36. The resulting confusion of pleasures and guilt prompts the representational speechlessness to which scandal invariably moves. That is, it is part of the rubric of scandal that feelings be confused and that words fail. Indeed language *must* fail in order to signify; and in order that the prophylactic melodrama of the unspeakable might inhabit the place vacated by language.

37. Laura Mulvey, "Visual Pleasure and Narrative Cinema," *Screen* 16, no. 3 (autumn 1975): 14.

38. See Page Dubois, *Torture and Truth* (London: Routledge, 1991); Edward Peters, *Torture* (New York: Basil Blackwell, 1985).

39. See Hinton, *The Perverse Gaze of Sympathy;* also Kaja Silverman, *Male Subjectivity at the Margins* (New York: Routledge, 1992); and David Savran, *Taking It Like a Man: White Masculinity, Masochism, and Contemporary American Culture* (Princeton: Princeton University Press, 1998).

40. See Joshua Gamson, *Claims to Fame: Celebrity in Contemporary America* (Berkeley: University of California Press, 1994).

41. Hadley, *Melodramatic Tactics,* 31. Matthew Tinkcom writes that Kenneth Anger's *Hollywood Babylon* reads cinematic history of Hollywood as "a history in which stardom and scandal are closely linked and, indeed, constitute one another within the ideological field of popular culture." ("Scandalous! Kenneth Anger and the Prohibitions of Hollywood History," in *OUT Takes: Essays on Queer Theory and Film,* ed. Ellis Hanson [Durham, N.C.: Duke University Press, 1999], 277).

42. Cited in Lull and Hinerman, "The Search for Scandal," 1. Bennett, and the public-interest group "Empower America," argue the degenerative implications of talk shows. Speaking for that organization, Connecticut senator Joseph Lieberman said the entertainment industry "degrad[es] our culture and ultimately threaten[s] our children's future" through "sexual deviancy" and "constant hyperemotional confrontations" (cited in Gamson, *Freaks Talk Back,* 9).

43. Cited in Perry Miller, ed., *The American Puritans: Their Prose and Poetry* (Garden City, N.Y.: Doubleday, 1956), verse 58, 289.

44. See, for example, Jeffrey Toobin, *A Vast Conspiracy: The Real Story of the Sex Scandal that Nearly Brought Down a President* (New York: Random House, 1999).

45. Jonathan Alter, "Clinton's Houdini Act," *Newsweek* (9 February 1998): 21.

46. See Deborah Barfield and Elaine S. Povich, "Tangled in Tape: Committee to Decide Today if Evidence Goes to Public," *Newsday,* 17 September 1998, A5. Christopher Hitchens likewise referred to Clinton as a monster, on C-SPAN, "The Washington Journal" (13 January 2000). *Le Monde* refers to the Starr Report like this: "The legal process of a nation that claims to lead the world has given birth to a monster." See "The Starr Report," *St. Louis Post-Dispatch,* 16 September 1998, B7. Patrick Buchanan, in his bid to seek the presidential nomination of the Reform Party, comes very close to aligning Clinton with the monster; he quotes John Quincy Adams, claiming that America "goes not abroad in search of *monsters* to destroy." A few lines later Buchanan refers to "Mr. Clinton, whose desecration of the temples of our civilization. . . ." AP Online, "Text of Buchanan's Speech," 25 October 1999. In "Clinton Saga Is Lose-Lose Choice for U.S.," David Corn considers the charges laid against Clinton, allegations of his sexual misconduct and perjury. If this is true, "then Clinton is a monster cad of reckless proportion." *Newsday,* 23 January 1998, A43. Dick Morris, former associate of Clinton, nicknamed him "The Monster" because of his temper—see Carol Innerst, "The Bewitching of David Brock," *Washington Times,* 27 October 1996, 31. See "Revelations Prompt Morris Resignation as Clinton Adviser," *National Journal's CongressDaily,* 29 August 1996, online edition.

47. A book remains to be written about Clinton's exhibitionist tendencies—his need for what Richard Lacayo calls "remorse ops" ("What Makes Clinton a Survivor?" *Time* [21 September 1998]: 74–75). He was still confessing two years later, at the brink of the Democratic National Convention.

48. Deborah Zabarenko, "Sleaze Takes Precedence over Impeachment Pomp," Reuters news service, 12 January 1999.

49. See Judith Butler on one of the chief allegorical anxieties circulating here. She writes that if "men are said to 'have' the phallus symbolically, their anatomy is also a site marked by having lost it; the anatomical part is never commensurable with the phallus itself." *Bodies That Matter: On the Discursive Limits of "Sex"* (New York: Routledge, 1993), 85.

50. Seltzer, *Serial Killers,* 35.

51. Cotton Mather, *Wonders of the Invisible World* (Boston: Smith, 1862), 101.

52. John B. Judis, "Washington Possessed," *New Republic* (25 January 1999). Judis writes that "the Republican impeachment drive belongs to a peculiar paradigm, dating back to the Puritans, in which political action becomes so thoroughly intermingled with moral and religious preoccupations."

53. See "Excerpts from Starr's Questioning," cited above. One of the problems facing Mather, in hindsight, was his absence from the trials themselves. Kendall grills Starr likewise for being absent from the grand jury investigations he himself instigated.

54. John M. Broder, "Attack by the President's Lawyer at Length Ruffles a Cool Witness," *New York Times,* 20 November 1998, <www.nytimes.com>.

55. President Clinton, responding to the prosecutor at the Paula Jones deposition, cited in Alan Dershowitz, *Sexual McCarthyism: Clinton, Starr, and the Emerging Constitutional Crisis* (New York: Basic Books, 1998), 29.

56. Eric Pooley, "High Crimes? Or Just a Sex Cover-Up?" *Time* (21 September 1998): 35–40.

57. Nancy Gibbs, "We, the Jury," *Time* (21 September 1998): 28.

58. Ibid., 30.

59. Pooley, "High Crimes?" 35.

60. Howard Kurtz, "Larry Flynt, Investigative Pornographer," *Washington Post,* 19 December 1998, C1.

61. Ibid.; also see Zabarenko, "Sleaze Takes Precedence." Zabarenko writes that "Flynt's announcement was a media event covered by outlets ranging from the tabloid talk show 'Rivera Live' . . . to the mainstream CNN, to C-SPAN, the cable network that covers Congress."

62. William Booth, "How Larry Flynt Changed the Picture," *Washington Post,* 11 January, 1999, C1.

63. Al Kamen, "Navy's Columbia Roast," *Washington Post,* 28 September 1998, A23.

64. A black-bordered box below the letter repeats the admonition to parents. Philip J. Trounstine, "The Starr Report," *San Jose Mercury News,* 13 September 1998, insert, 1–12.

65. Both letters can be found in *Time* (12 October 1998): 10. The remark about government-issued pornography raises the issue of the Meese Commission Report on Pornography, which, as Stewart notes, was extraordinarily popular.

66. Throughout these comments I follow Peter Michelson's usage of obscenity and pornography. He writes that he uses "obscenity in the Greek sense of bringing onstage what is customarily kept offstage" (xi); while pornography "is the representation of sexuality so as to make its obscenity conspicuous, to the point of evoking its transgression of conventional taboos" (xii). See *Speaking the Unspeakable: A Poetics of Obscenity* (Albany: State University of New York Press, 1993).

67. Howard Fineman and Mark Hosenball, "Out of Control," *Newsweek* (28 September 1998): 10.

68. Susan Stewart, *Crimes of Writing: Problems in the Containment of Representation* (Durham, N.C.: Duke University Press, 1994), 241.

69. Of course, in one way the Starr Report wasn't "pornography," at least in terms of its economics, since on the Web the Report was completely free sex for all but the most media-blinkered or resolutely offline. Indeed, the "grim, long-running sex farce in Washington" was, while it ran, a chief national export, as demonstrated by the headline status awarded it by the *International Herald Tribune* and other European presses (Sylviane Gold, "One Place Sex Is Seldom Taken Seriously," *New York Times,* 27 June 1999, Late edition, 5). See, for example, "The Starr Report," cited above (*St. Louis Dispatch,* 16 September, 1998, B7), for a brief overview of European coverage.

70. Stewart, *Crimes of Writing,* 242.

71. Ann Barr Snitow, "Mass Market Romance: Pornography for Women Is Different," in *Passion and Power: Sexuality in History,* ed. Kathy Peiss and Christina Simmons, with Robert A. Padgug (Philadelphia: Temple University Press, 1989), 269–270.

72. Ibid., 270.

73. Anne Williams, *Art of Darkness: A Poetics of Gothic* (Chicago: University of Chicago Press, 1995), 4.

74. See, for example, a history of such production in Gail Kern Paster, *The Body Embarrassed: Drama and the Disciplines of Shame in Early Modern England* (Ithaca: Cornell University Press, 1993).

75. ". . . others argue all [Starr] proved in the end was his own willingness to humiliate the President and horrify the public with a report so gratuitously detailed and pornographic that it warranted warning stickers and a plain brown wrapper." Gibbs, "We, The Jury."

76. Ibid.

77. Jonathan Alter, "Shaming the Shameless," *Newsweek* (28 September 1998): 16.

78. For a discussion of the various discourses in which "public" and "private" define categories, see *Public and Private in Thought and Practice: Perspectives on a Grand Dichotomy,* ed. Jeff Weintraub and Krishan Kumar (Chicago: University of Chicago Press, 1996).

79. Al Kamen, "They Asked, He Told," *Washington Post,* 3 February 1999, A15.

80. Dershowitz, *Sexual McCarthyism,* 7.

81. See Michael J. Colacurcio, "The Woman's Own Choice," in Colacurcio, *Doctrine and Difference.*

82. Dershowitz, *Sexual McCarthyism,* 210.

83. Arthur Miller, editorial, "Our Bloodless Coup," *Nation* (11 January 1999): <www.thenation.com>.

84. See John D'Emilio and Estelle B. Freedman, *Intimate Matters: A History of Sexuality in America,* second edition (Chicago: University of Chicago Press, 1998). Also, Carol F. Karlsen, *The Devil in the Shape of a Woman: Witchcraft in Colonial New England* (New York: Vintage Books, 1989).

85. Colacurcio, *Doctrine and Difference,* 210.

86. Indeed, although the framing of sex as *the* moral moment of public electioneering is often associated with Gary Hart's abortive campaign for the presidency, it is much older than that. Winthrop's Journal reminds us that Richard Bellingham, briefly governor of the Massachusetts Bay Colony, faced charges of inappropriate sex that resulted in his being removed from office in 1642 (see Dunn and Yaendle, *The Diary of John Winthrop,* 192 ff.). Colacurcio argues that Hawthorne's use of the historical name is significant; see "The Woman's Own Choice." On Hart, see Garry Wills, *Under God: Religion and American Politics* (New York: Simon and Schuster, 1990), 41–50.

87. Howard Kurtz discusses the changing, but unchanging, nature of the media involvement with such scenes. See "Larry Flynt and the Barers of Bad News," *Washington Post,* 20 December 1998, F1.

88. Clinton to Donna Shalala, Health and Human Services Secretary. Gibbs, "We, the Jury," 31.

89. For some of this history, see David D. Hall, *Worlds of Wonder, Days of Judgment: Popular Religious Belief in Early New England* (New York: Knopf, 1989)—esp. for the "sacramental" quality of the confessional (187 ff.).

90. D'Emilio and Freedman, *Intimate Matters,* 9.

91. Ibid., 11.

92. In addition, confession also justified the legal apparatus; thus no matter how heavy the penance, properly confessed sinners who "participated in the rituals of punishment" (ibid., 22) would be reinstated to the community as "respectable members" without problem. In contrast, those who refused to undergo public confession could be excommunicated from their congregation" (ibid., 23). For a current American example of the successful confession, see Jimmy Swaggart's moment of public abjection. See Soukup, "Church, Media, and Scandal," 236.

93. William Bennett, *Washington Post,* 26 October 1995, C8. Similarly, see Shattuck, *Forbidden Knowledge,* whose frontispiece is an enclosed line of text: "Parents and teachers should be aware that Chapter VII does not make appropriate reading for children and minors."

94. Gibbs, "We, the Jury," 33.

95. Pooley, "High Crimes?" 35.

96. ABC *20/20*, "Starr Speaks Out," 25 November 1998. Sawyer provokes Starr by saying, "So to the people who say you're a prude, you're a puritan, you're the sex police, you say what?"

97. Lynette Clemetson and Pat Wingert, "Clinton on the Couch," *Newsweek* (28 September 1998): 15.

98. Garment, *Scandal*, 14.

99. Shattuck argues that "books devoted to erotic behavior became a graphic demonstration of revolutionary ideas, and also earned good money. This outburst of pornography served as a vehicle for attacks on religion, the monarchy, and the aristocracy." (see "The Divine Marquis," in *Forbidden Knowledge,* esp. 286ff.).

100. Lynn Avery Hunt, ed., *The Invention of Pornography: Obscenity and the Origins of Modernity, 1500–1800* (New York: Zone Books, 1993), 18–19.

101. Lynda Nead in fact defines obscenity in many of the terms I used earlier to define the Gothic: "in terms of excess, as form beyond limit, beyond the frame." Lynda Nead, "Getting Down to Basics: Art, Obscenity, and the Female Nude," in *New Feminist Discourses: Critical Essays on Theories and Texts,* ed. Isobel Armstrong (London: Routledge, 1992). See Laurence O'Toole, *Pornocopia, Porn, Sex, Technology, and Desire* (London: Serpent's Tail, 1998).

102. From a slightly different perspective, see Susan Stewart, who argues that "pornography and the public discourse on pornography have the same comparative logic" ("The Marquis de Meese," in *Crimes of Writing,* 235–72). See, also, Angela Carter, *The Sadeian Woman and the Ideology of Pornography* (New York: Pantheon Books, 1978).

103. Garment, *Scandal*, 98.

104. Laura Grindstaff writes, "The analogy to pornography [talk shows] is both deliberate and fitting. The climax of most sex scenes in film and video porn, the money shot is the moment of orgasm and ejaculation offering incontrovertible 'proof' of a man's . . . 'real' sexual excitement and prowess. Pornography thus performs a kind of low-brown ethnography of the body, part of the documentary impulse Williams (1989) calls 'the frenzy of the visible.' Like pornography, daytime talk is a narrative of explicit revelation where people 'get down and dirty' and 'bare it all' for the pleasure, fascination, or repulsion of viewers" ("Producing Trash, Class, and the Money Shot: A Behind-the-Scenes Account of Daytime TV Talk Shows," in Lull and Hinerman, *Media Scandals,* 167).

105. Speaking with reference to the Andrew Cunanan loop, Gary Indiana, *Three Month Fever: The Andrew Cunanan Story* (New York: HarperCollins, 1999), 244.

106. To this point, of course, see Frank Kermode, *The Genesis of Secrecy: On the Interpretation of Narrative* (Cambridge, Mass.: Harvard University Press, 1979).

107. Starr's success harkens back to an earlier public condemnation of pornography, the Meese Commission Report, and the fact, as Stewart notes, "that the report itself has become a pornographic best seller" (*Crimes of Writing,* 237).

108. From the perspective of the cultural order, interactions around the monster gave tacit permission for the exercise of a range of otherwise unacknowledgable emotions, many of which would be destabilizing to a social order: spectacles of sex, warning, threat, economic profit, moral lesson, repudiation, licensed transgression, and public pornographies. For history of nineteenth-century American freak shows, see Bogdan, *Freakshow;* also Leslie Fiedler, *Freaks: Myths and Images of the Secret Self* (New York: Anchor Books, 1978).

109. Rosemarie Garland Thomson, ed., *Freakery: Cultural Spectacles of the Extraordinary Body* (New York: New York University Press, 1996), 1. Thomson uses the term "extraordinary body" to refer, in particular, to handicapped or disabled bodies, apart from the social handicapping I am suggesting here.

110. William A. Cohen, *Sex Scandal: The Private Parts of Victorian Fiction* (Durham, N.C.: Duke University Press, 1996), 3.

111. Victor's creature in Mary Shelley's *Frankenstein* provides an example with wider significance, as Botting observes. "Often described as 'unnamable,' the monster is given many names, though no *one* name fixes his identity in a single and unified position of subject or object" (Fred Botting, *Making Monstrous: Frankenstein, Criticism, Theory* [Manchester: Manchester University Press, 1991], 16.

112. See *Struggles and Triumphs; or, Forty years' recollections of P. T. Barnum,* ed. Carl Bode (Harmondsworth, U.K.: Penguin, 1981); Neil Harris, *Humbug: The Art of P. T. Barnum* (Boston: Little, Brown, 1973).

Chapter Six

1. For instance, the National Coalition of Anti-Violence Programs notes a dramatic increase in anti-gay offenses in selected areas of the country; while the same source noted that the calendar year 1997–1998 saw a 242 percent increase in the number of hate group offenders in the United States. According to the FBI, 7,755 bias-motivated incidents were reported to them in 1998; 4,321 were motivated by racial bias; 1,390 by religious; 1,260 by sexual orientation; 754 by ethnicity or national origin bias; 25 by disability bias; 5 by multiple bias. See National Center for Victims of Crime, <www.nvc.org/stats/hc.htm>.

2. See Nancy Lusignan Schultz, ed. *Fear Itself: Enemies Real and Imagined in American Culture* (West Lafayette, Ind.: Purdue University Press, 1999); and David M. Kennedy, "Culture Wars: The Sources and Uses of Enmity in American History," in *Enemy Images in American History,* ed. Ragnhild Fiebig-von Hase and Ursula Lehmkuhl (Providence, R.I.: Berghahn Books, 1997).

3. John Leo, "Why Ruin a Good Story?" *US News and World Report* (5 May 1997): 17.

4. For a discussion of the Tawana Brawley incident, see "Brawley Defamation Suit Goes to Court, *Law Street Journal* (21 November 1997): <www.lawstreet.com>.

5. The Smith case distilled these formulas with particular American resonance. Laura Hinton observes that the prosecution "may have emphasized the master and slave aspects of the heterosexual romance," although its parallel attempt to "repress the master and slave story of American racism . . . notoriously failed" (*The Perverse Gaze of Sympathy: Sadomasochistic Sentiments from Clarissa to Rescue 911* [New York: State University of New York Press, 1999], 10).

6. *Newsweek* (14 November 1994): 29.

7. *New York Times,* 24 July 1995, A8.

8. Cited in the introduction (by Fiebig-von Hase) to Fiebig-von Hase and Lehmkuhl, *Enemy Images,* 15.

9. Ibid., 6.

10. See Jeff Cohen and Norman Solomon, *Adventures in Medialand: Behind the News, Beyond the Pundits* (Monroe, Me.: Common Courage Press, 1993); Neil Postman, *Amusing Ourselves to Death: Public Discourse in the Age of Show Business* (New York: Penguin, 1986); Howard Kurtz, *Media Circus: The Trouble with America's Newspapers* (New York: Dover, 1973).

11. Paula Chin and Civia Tamarkin, "Up Front: The Door of Evil" ("The unimaginable horror in apartment 213 leaves a shaken city wondering about the serial killer in its midst"), *People* (12 August 1991): 32.

12. "McVeigh—from Model Soldier to Bomber," Reuters news service, 13 June 1997.

13. Brandon M. Stickney, *"All-American Monster": The Unauthorized Biography of Timothy McVeigh* (Amherst, N.Y.: Prometheus, 1996). Also, Richard A. Serrano, *One of Ours: Timothy McVeigh and the Oklahoma City Bombing* (New York: Norton, 1998); Mark S. Hamm, *Apocalypse in Oklahoma: Waco and Ruby Ridge Revenged* (Boston: Northeastern University Press, 1997).

14. Caroline Hendrie, "Abuse by Women Raises Its Own Set of Problems," *Education Week* 18, no. 14 (2 December 1998): 15.

15. "Ex-Priest in Massachusetts Sentenced to 18–20 Years in Prison for Sexual Abuse," *Washington Post,* 7 December 1993, A7.

16. See Paul Wilkes, "Unholy Acts," *New Yorker* 69 (7 June 1993): 62–79. About the moral panic of priests and sex, and more specifically, priests and children, see Philip Jenkins, *Pedophiles and Priests: Anatomy of a Contemporary Crisis* (New York: Oxford University Press, 1996). Jenkins deconstructs the representational crisis around priest pedophilia in a way that would surely be useful reading. Mark Edmundson, in *Nightmare On Main Street: Angels, Sadomasochism, and the Culture of Gothic* (Cambridge, Mass.: Harvard University Press, 1997), offers a naive discussion of Wilkes's *New Yorker* article. He notes that the "ban on priestly sex, combined with the church's narrow attitudes toward sex in general, could be in some measure responsible for priests' indulgence in pedophilia" (59). The representational factors he neglects, and which he himself uses, are to the point of this book.

17. Blanch McCrary Boyd, "Who Killed Susan Smith?" *Oxford American* (August/September 1996): 36.

18. Garry Wills, "It's His Party," *New York Times Magazine* (11 August 1966): section 6, 37, 58.

19. Debbi Wilgoren, "Another Ex-Altar Boy Reports P.G. Priest Abused Him," *Washington Post,* 11 February 1995, C1.

20. Peter Stallybrass and Allon White, *The Politics and Poetics of Transgression* (London: Methuen, 1986).

21. Susan Sontag's observation regarding sci-fi films of the fifties is still appropriate: "Another kind of satisfaction these films supply is extreme moral simplification—that is to say, a morally acceptable fantasy where one can give outlet to cruel or at least amoral feelings ("The Imagination of Disaster," in *Against Interpretation and Other Essays* [New York: Farrar, Straus and Giroux, 1966], 215).

22. Joseph Grixti, "Consuming Cannibals: Psychopathic Killers as Archetypes and Cultural Icons." *Journal of American Culture* 18, no. 1 (spring 1995): 90.

23. Michael Levenson, "The Nayman of Noland," *New Republic* (6 July 1987): 34.

24. See William E. Dannemeyer, *Shadow in the Land: Homosexuality in America* (San Francisco: Ignatius Press, 1989).

25. Atlanta Braves pitcher John Rocker, interviewed in a Christmas-week *Sports Illustrated,* decried New York for its "foreigners," wondering how "the hell did they get here?" Rocker also took aim at the Number 7 train, comparing it to "Beirut"; imagine, he said, sitting "next to some kid with purple hair next to some queer with AIDS right next to some dude who just got out of jail for the fourth time right next to some 20-year-old mom with four kids. It's depressing" (see Jeff Pearlman, "At Full Blast," *CNN Sports Illustrated Online* [23 December 1999]: <sportsillustrated.cnn.com>).

26. R. I. Moore, *The Formation of a Persecuting Society: Power and Deviance in Western Europe, 950–1250* (Oxford: Blackwell, 1987), 5; Moore's emphasis.

27. "A History of Hatred: Suspect in Gay Slaying Known for Hostility," *Times Herald Record,* 6 March 1999, <www.th-record.com>.

28. *Time,* Milosevic cover (5 April 1999).

29. Roger Bromley argues that "genre" expectations—"a specialized diction, imagery, and system of metaphors increasingly 'unitary' in its structure"—influence the construction of social, and thus personal, memory (see *Lost Narratives: Popular Fictions, Politics, and Recent History* [New York: Routledge, 1988], 5). See also W. Russell Neuman, Marion R. Just, and Ann N. Crigler, *Common Knowledge: News and the Construction of Political Meaning* (Chicago: University of Chicago Press, 1992); Jerome Bruner, *Acts of Meaning* (Cambridge, Mass.: Harvard University Press, 1990); Livia Polanyi, *Telling the American Story: A Structural and Cultural Analysis of Conversational Storytelling* (Cambridge, Mass.: MIT Press, 1989).

30. Elizabeth Bird and Robert W. Dardenne, "Myth, Chronicle and Story," in

Media, Myths, and Narratives: Television and the Press, ed. James W. Carey (Los Angeles: Sage, 1988), 69.

31. Benedict Anderson argues, "Both the newspaper and its fictional correlate the novel invent or perhaps more properly furnish the modern conception of being in the world. . . . The novel and the newspaper make it possible to imagine a secular community," *Imagined Communities* (London: Verso, 1993), 35.

32. Thus, rather than being an account arrived at *after* the fact, the narrative *creates* the occasion it unfolds, creates what it assumes merely to order. Hayden White addresses this point, noting that experientially nothing "present[s] itself . . . in the form of well-made stories, with central subjects, proper beginnings, middles, and ends" ("The Value of Narrativity in the Representation of Reality," in *On Narrative,* ed. W. J. T. Mitchell [Chicago: University of Chicago Press, 1981], 23).

33. David Sonenschein, *Pedophiles on Parade,* vol. 2, *The Popular Imagery of Moral Hysteria* (San Antonio, Tex.: D. Sonenschein, 1998), 33; Noam Chomsky, *Necessary Illusions: Thought Control in Democratic Societies* (Boston: South End Press, 1989). See, too, Christopher Shea, "Americans More United in Social Views," *Chronicle of Higher Education,* 17 January 1997, A17.

34. Jeffrey Jerome Cohen, "Monster Culture (Seven Theses)," the introduction to *Monster Theory: Reading Culture,* ed. Jeffrey Jerome Cohen (Minneapolis: University of Minnesota Press, 1996), 17.

35. "Moral politics": a phrase adapted from Ellen Willis, "Down With Compassion," *New Yorker* (30 September 1996).

36. Stephen King, *Danse Macabre* (New York: Everest House, 1981), 368.

37. Putting his name in for nomination as president in the 2000 U.S. election, Patrick Buchanan's address touched all these all these triggers of trauma. See Ron Fournier, "Buchanan Announces White House Bid," AP Headlines, 2 March 2000.

38. King, *Danse Macabre,* 58, 51.

39. Howard Fineman, "Extreme Measures," *Newsweek* (4 March 1996): 22.

40. Alan Brinkley, "A Swaggering Tradition," *Newsweek* (4 March 1996): 29.

41. George W. Bush campaign ad (11 September 2000).

42. See, for example, Michael Barton, "Journalistic Gore: Disaster Reporting and Emotional Discourse in the *New York Times,* 1852–1956," in *An Emotional History of the United States,* ed. Peter N. Stearns and Jan Lewis (New York: New York University Press, 1998).

43. "A 1993 study by the American Association of University Women found the worst type of sexual harassment for students is 'being called gay.' It said 86 percent of students would rather be targeted any other way—including getting hit—than called gay" (Robert D. Davila, "Schools Losing Tolerance for Anti-Gay Harassment," *Sacramento Bee,* 10 September 1998).

44. Patricia E. O'Connor, "Discourse of Violence," *Discourse and Society* 6, no. 3 (July 1995): 309.

45. One researcher commented, "Scientific data shows that homophobic behavior

in society begins with inflammatory statements. . . . These people [religious leaders] don't actually commit violence, but they do trigger it, more or less" (see "Wyoming Death Has National, Local Impact," *Auburn Plainsman via U-WIRE,* 23 October 1998. The executive director of GLAAD, speaking at a press conference the day after Shepard's death, said, "If you think homophobic advertisements like those which ran in our newspapers this summer ["ex-gay ads" sponsored by Family Research Council] are devoid of repercussions—think again. These ads give people permission to hate."

46. Wyoming governor Jim Geringer, in response to the slaying of Matthew Shepard; cited in a letter to the U.C. Irvine community by Ron Wilson, Assistant Executive Vice Chancellor, University of California, Irvine (16 October 1998). My sincere thanks to Jay Kent Lorenz, of the Visual Studies Program at Irvine, for bringing this, and other related materials, to my attention.

47. "Images of Criminals and Victims: A Study on Women's Fear and Social Control," *Gender and Society* 11, no. 3 (June 1997).

48. See Wills, "It's His Party," 37, 58. See Robert Ivie, "Speaking 'Common Sense' about the Soviet Threat: Reagan's Rhetorical Stance," *Western Journal of Speech Communication* 48, no. 1 (winter 1984): 39–50.

49. Kennedy, "Culture Wars," 356. For Milosevic, *Time* (5 April 1999). For another example, see the description of Zeljko Raznatovic, charged with crimes against humanity by the International War Crimes tribunal; Peter Klebnikov, "Encounters with a Monster," *Playboy* (October 1999): 50, 150.

50. For Jesse Helms, see Dewayne Wickham, "Helms' Wish to Punish AIDS Sufferers Is Irrational," Gannett news service, 6 July 1995; Ruth Larson, "Helms Takes Aim At Pro-Gay Programs," *Washington Times,* 30 January 1995, 4. Elizabeth Birch, executive director of the Human Rights Campaign Fund, comments in this article about Helms's "anti-gay obsession." Also, Eric Bates, "What You Need to Know about Jesse Helms," *Mother Jones* (15 May 1995): 56+.

51. Bob Edwards, "Thoughts on Playing the 'Race Card.'" National Public Radio, morning edition, 4 October 1995.

52. A phrase adapted from Philip Jenkins, *Using Murder: The Social Construction of Serial Homicide* (New York: Aldine de Gruyter, 1994), 15.

53. Cited in Liz McMillen, "The Importance of Storytelling: A New Emphasis by Law Scholars," *Chronicle of Higher Education,* 26 July 1996, A10.

54. Ibid.

55. Under the pressure of entertainment narrative expectations, for example, discourses of law and justice find themselves folded into a prior system of exchange. Steven Starks, for example, argues that crime-oriented TV drama has changed "the public's perception of lawyers, the police, and the legal system" (cited in Richard Stack, "Prime Time Crime: Television's Influence on Public Understanding of the Criminal Justice System," *Mid-Atlantic Almanack* 4 [1995]: 77). "Infotainment" or "Docudrama" are now, themselves, genres. As Stack notes, "Since 1958, almost one-third of all entertainment shows have been about crime. Such programming was a mainstay of popular radio broadcasting even before the advent of TV" (76). Also see W. Russel Gray, "Supralegal

Justice: Are Real Juries Acting Like Fictional Detectives?" *Journal of American Culture* 21, no. 1 (spring 1998): 1–5. Also, Lawrence M. Friedman, "Law, Lawyers and Popular Culture," *Yale Law Journal* 98 (July 1989): 1579–1606. See also Peter Brooks and Paul Gewirtz, eds., *Law's Stories: Narrative and Rhetoric in the Law* (New Haven: Yale University Press, 1996); for the pressure to narrative, see W. Lance Bennett and Martha S. Feldman, *Reconstructing Reality in the Courtroom: Justice and Judgment in American Culture* (New Brunswick: Rutgers University Press, 1981), esp. 3, 9.

56. Boyd, "Who Killed Susan Smith?" 42.

57. We have seen how the media sponsorship of Susan Smith emerged from within a set of narrative formulas about sex, intimacy, and motherhood that have a long *economic* history *as* representation. Laura Hinton discusses the Smith narrative in *The Perverse Gaze of Sympathy;* she writes, "Novels may imitate life, but life also imitates novels. The Susan Smith murder trial is but a recent case in point in the reproduction of sentiment through its visual monitor of sympathy. This has been an excessive reproduction since the mid-eighteenth century" (2).

58. Boyd, "Who Killed Susan Smith?" 38.

59. Steven V. Roberts, "The Murderer Who Was Too Pathetic to Kill," *US News and World Report* (7 August 1995), 8–9.

60. Numerous reports took umbrage at the portrayal of "America's bogeymen," a term used by Ron Kuby. See Michael Alexander, "She Broke Our Hearts," *Newsday,* 5 November 1997, A4/5; Leonce Gaiter, "American Mantra: Blame the Black Man," *New York Times,* 12 November 1994, A21. Also, DeWayne Wickham, "Blame-a-Black Refrain Is No Joking Matter," *USA Today,* 7 November 1994, A13; Barbara Vobejda, "Smith's Kin Apologize to Blacks," *Washington Post,* 9 November 1994, A8. Firewalling racial difference in the terms of monstrosity is an American commonplace. See Thomas Dixon's *The Clansman: An Historical Romance of the Ku Klux Klan* (1905), for example (and the D. W. Griffith classic derived from it, *Birth of a Nation*): "A single tiger-spring and the black claws of the beast sank into the soft white throat and she was still" (Dixon, *Clansman,* 304). Teresa Goddu opens *Gothic America* with Richard Wright's realization that the "thrilling horror stories" he found in the comics insert of a white supremacist paper were intimately connected to the paper's ideology (see *Gothic America: Narrative, History, and Nation* [New York: Columbia University Press, 1997], 1–3). O. J.'s darkened photograph on the cover of *Time* thus recalls a long foreground of judiciously engineered hate in American representation of the black, a point made almost fifty years earlier by James Baldwin in a critique of Wright's *Native Son.* See "Many Thousands Gone," *James Baldwin: Collected Essays* (New York: Library of America, 1998). Further, the issue of miscegenation, never *quite* spoken, circulated around Smith as well as around Simpson; their transgressive bodies and the fragility of personal relations they signified, were used to control—coerce, elicit?—allegiance to certain presumed cultural norms.

61. One observer notes the collusion of discourse, genre as well as medium: "The strategies of the documentary and the action-adventure were both subsumed into the live feed" (John Taylor, "Murder, the Ultimate Art Form," *Esquire* 122 [1 September 1994]: 76+).

62. *People* (8 August 1991): 32.

63. Within a week of Dahmer's arrest, *Time*'s feature story is archly titled "Little Flat of Horrors" (5 August 1991: 26).

64. 12 September 1991.

65. One that has already been largely written; see Richard Tithecott, *Of Men and Monsters: Jeffrey Dahmer and the Construction of the Serial Killer* (Madison: University of Wisconsin Press, 1997).

66. Editorial, *Atlanta Journal-Constitution,* 5 August 1991, A13.

67. Killers learn their lines as often from television as TV takes its scripts from the killers. Dahmer's transcribed confession to the Milwaukee police became the basis for ABC's *Day One* reenactment of his arrest (18 April 1993). The already vexed line between the theatrical and the real was further blurred, then, when a reviewer critiqued Dahmer's confessions—rather than the show itself—for sounding "like a third-rate . . . script in Hollywood" (*Los Angeles Times,* 4 August 1991, A22).

68. References to the televisual, unlike the "fictional" mode of the dramatic, are meant to *confirm* the *real* while deflecting away from the ideological frame, the personal agency designing the representation. What Kathleen Hall Jamieson calls the "evocative power of television's visual grammar" gives the televisual a deceptively mimetic authority. See *Dirty Politics: Deception, Distraction, and Democracy* (New York: Oxford University Press, 1992). TV, in other words, operates by a degree of convincibility, if not of accuracy or believability. Ann Rule, for instance, writes about Ted Bundy, "Not even a television script could make [certain coincidences] believable" (*The Stranger Beside Me* [New York: New American Library, 1981], 155).

69. *Day One* transcript, 18 April 1993.

70. As suggested, Gothic borrowings from cinematic technique are common; sometimes, however, the borrowing is evocative, implicit rather than a direct riff. Consider the A&E Network's "biography" of Jeffrey Dahmer, with its clear visual reminder of the prologue to *The Texas Chainsaw Massacre,* a black-and-white display with narrated voice-over: "This program chronicles the crimes of serial killer Jeffrey Dahmer, the description of which some viewers may find disturbing. Viewer discretion is advised."

71. *Newsweek* (17 July 1995).

72. Chin and Tamarkin, "The Door of Evil," 32.

73. "McVeigh: From Model Soldier to Bomber," Reuters news service, 13 June 1997.

74. According to this position, the yet-to-be child within the womb warrants more legal security than the fully formed, though flawed human beings they become. Newspaper children (that is, those created for representational use), children in the womb, like other fantasies of children, have almost infinite symbolic pliability. These "pre-children" (as one bumper sticker has it) can be molded to suit any program. Again, sentimental and horror balance, and fulfill, each other's plot requirements.

75. *USA Today,* 16 June 1997, 18A.

76. A letter to the editor, responding to *U.S. News & World Report* coverage of the bombing of a U.S. military vessel, makes this point: "[*U.S. News & World Report*] used

careless and offensive words in referring to the victims of the terrorist attack on the USS Cole as 'U.S. sailors being blown to bits.' . . . I find this sort of graphic, cartoonish language to be very disrespectful to the sailors who tragically lost their lives. . . ." (Stuart Baker, letter to the editor, *U.S. News & World Report* [20 November 2000], 8).

77. Bill Johnson, "Student's Death Holds Lesson for US." *Rocky Mountain (Denver) News,* 14 October 1998, 6A.

78. Emily Gurnon, "Specter of Hate in 2 Assaults on Youths," *San Francisco Examiner,* 14 February 1999, <www.sfgate.com>.

79. Postman, *Amusing Ourselves to Death,* 8. A few pages earlier he observes the "dissolution of public discourse in America and its conversion into the arts of show business" (5).

80. In a review of Jon Turney's *Frankenstein's Footsteps: Science, Genetics, and Popular Culture,* Edward Tenner makes a similar observation: "Turney argues convincingly that the monster metaphor impedes clear thinking and debate on issues of biotechnology. . . . In the finest traditions of unintended consequences, scientists themselves now invoke the monster metaphor to chill discussion of risks by imputing vulgar fears to opponents and critics" (*Wilson Quarterly* 22 [22 September 1998]: 101–2.

81. Paul Oppenheimer, *Evil and the Demonic: A New Theory of Monstrous Behavior* (New York: New York University Press, 1996), 154.

82. Whale's biographer, James Curtis, remarks, however, that "it was Whale who recognized that giving the monster human qualities would ultimately win the sympathy of the audience." See Jan Herman, "Making Monsters Matter," *Los Angeles Times,* 1 August 1998, Orange County edition, Calendar section, 1. Although he has no voice and so cannot ask directly for our sympathy, nonetheless viewers see the creature's too-real human terror visible in Karloff's wide eyes and gaping mouth; the creature's terror is evident in his desperation—although he is voiceless, these do not elicit, overmuch, the viewer's sympathy.

83. *USA Today,* 16 June 1997, 18A.

84. See George Lakoff and Mark Johnson, *Metaphors We Live By* (Chicago: University of Chicago Press, 1980), 62ff.

85. In *Dreadful Pleasures: An Anatomy of Modern Horror* (New York: Oxford University Press, 1985), James B. Twitchell suggests that horror films are like other formula rituals which provide the social neophyte with information he or she needs. In particular, Twitchell notes the target age group for many of the horror films and suggests the films are about sorting out the complexities of reproduction. They are "fables of sexual identity" (7). This language is very similar to Peter Gay's definition of national rhetoric as "fables of aggression."

86. Again, let me refer to back to James Whale's wonderful blueprint for making monsters. In *Frankenstein* (1931), there is a sequence in which the creature plays with a young girl on the bank of the river. She throws a flower into the water, and he imitates her action, throwing *her* into the water; in his childlike simplicity the creature assumes that the girl, pretty and flower-like, will also float like the flower. In the penultimate version of the film, Whale shows the creature reaching for the girl, and then the scene

cuts to the father carrying the drowned girl into the town, where the townspeople are celebrating a wedding. The inevitable result follows, and the creature—as childlike as the girl whose death he is accidentally guilty of—is marked for death at the hands of a mob. Whale cut the scene of the creature reaching for the girl because, like Karloff's voice, the gesture too visibly demonstrates the creature's innocence.

87. Pearlman, "At Full Blast."

88. The Columbia Correctional Institution in Portage, Wisconsin, is equipped with "a glass-enclosed central-command station with twenty-eight video views of the facility" (*Newsweek* [3 February 1992]: 50). See, also, Walter C. Farrell, Jr., and James H. Johnson, "Back to the Future: The Death (Execution) of Jeffrey Dahmer," *New York Voice, Inc.,* 4 January 1995.

89. Stephanie Saul, "Authorities ID Dahmer Killer," *Newsday,* 30 November 1994, A4.

90. *Newsday,* 29 November 1994.

91. Stephanie Saul, "Dahmer Slain," *Newsday,* 29 November 1994, A3. On the other hand, according to the *Progressive* editorial "Let Them Eat Values," "It doesn't matter how hideous Dahmer's crimes were. He was not sentenced to death; he was sentenced to life in prison. And the prison failed to do its job in seeing that the sentence of the court was carried out" (*Progressive* 59 [1 January 1995]: 10, 12).

92. *New York Times,* 29 November 1994, A1.

93. Cathy Connors, "Dahmer the Cannibal Is Killed," *New York Amsterdam News,* 3 December 1994, 50.

94. *Newsweek* (7 August 1995): 23.

95. Rick Bragg, "Susan Smith Verdict Brings Relief to Town," *New York Times,* 30 July 1995, A16. But notorious prisoners often face violence, sometimes in their own person, sometimes because of symbolic displacement. This is especially true in cases of those who have faced the "particicution" of monstrosity. Albert DeSalvo, who claimed to be the Boston Strangler, was killed in prison; recently James Earl Ray came under attack; Warren Bass, convicted of raping and murdering Heidi Goldberg, had his throat cut in the prison yard. See Donald P. Myers, "The Murderer," *Newsday,* 8 June 1994, B5.

96. Norma Jean White, letter to the editor, *St. Louis Post-Dispatch,* 21 June 1997, 36. White continues: "McVeigh says her son is not the monster the media has portrayed him to be. When he is incarcerated, that's exactly who some of his fellow inmates will be—perverts, murderers, rapists. McVeigh is a nice-looking young man; he will be prime prey for many inmate predators."

97. Peter Hamill, *Newsday,* 30 November 1994, A33.

98. Twitchell, *Dreadful Pleasures,* 100.

99. Thomas Fields-Meyer, "Odyssey of Violence," *People* (13 May 1996): 44+. The same essay cites Klaas, again, about Davis, "The sun has come up, and the vampire's got nowhere to hide."

100. S.S. Prawer, *Caligari's Children: The Film as Tale of Terror* (Oxford: Oxford University Press, 1980), 110. One critic takes note of the devaluation by arguing the

"sublime terror that accompanies the epochal failure of society . . . has not, especially in the case of the 1950s creature film, been represented in holy enough language" (Jonathan Lake Crane, *Terror and Everyday Life: Singular Moments in the History of the Horror Film* [Thousand Oaks, Calif.: Sage Publications, 1994], 102).

101. Barbara Creed, *The Monstrous-Feminine: Film, Feminism, Psychoanalysis* (London: Routledge, 1993), 11.

102. Richard Zoglin, "Manson Family Values," *Time* (21 March 1994): 77.

103. Dudley Wilson, *Signs and Portents: Monstrous Births from the Middle Ages to the Enlightenment* (New York: Routledge, 1993), 194.

Chapter Seven

1. "Every angel is terrible." Cited in Martin E. Marty, "Beauty and Terror: Rapture in Art and the Sacred," *Image*, no. 17 (Fall 1997): 72.

2. "John Paul expressed what he called 'bitterness for the insult' of having the festival 'during the grand Jubilee of the year 2000 and for the offense to Christian values in a city that is so dear to the heart of Catholics all over the world.'"

3. See Edward J. Ingebretsen, *Maps of Heaven, Maps of Hell: Religious Terror as Memory from the Puritans to Stephen King* (Armonk, N.Y.: M. E. Sharpe, 1996). For a similar argument, see Regina M. Schwartz, *The Curse of Cain: The Violent Legacy of Monotheism* (Chicago: University of Chicago Press, 1997); also Ellis Hanson, *Decadence and Catholicism* (Cambridge, Mass.: Harvard University Press, 1997); Julia Kristeva, in *Powers of Horror: An Essay on Abjection,* trans. Leon S. Roudiez (New York: Columbia University Press, 1982), writes that the "abject is edged with the sublime. It is not the same moment on the journey, but the same subject and speech bring them into being" (11).

4. Stephen Greenblatt, "Mutilation and Meaning," in *The Body in Parts: Fantasies of Corporeality in Early Modern Europe,* ed. David Hillman and Carla Mazzio (New York: Routledge, 1997), 224.

5. See Nigel Spivey, "Christ and the Art of Agony," *History Today* (August 1999): on <www.britannica.com>.

6. Accounts of this moment in Constantine's history vary. The Christian apologist Lactantius writes that Constantine received instructions in a dream to paint the Christian sign on his troops' shields. Eusebius, with apparent authority from Constantine himself, gives the more traditional account of the vision in the heavens, the cross with the words "In this sign, conquer." See Lactantius, *De Mortibus Persecutorum,* ed. and trans. J. L. Creed (New York: Clarendon Press, 1984); Timothy D. Barnes, *Constantine and Eusebius* (Cambridge, Mass.: Harvard University Press, 1981).

7. Chris Bull and John Gallagher, *Perfect Enemies: The Religious Right, the Gay Movement, and the Politics of the 1990s* (New York: Crown Publishers, 1996), 2.

8. In a letter written to a cellmate's wife, Aaron McKinney writes that when he learned Matthew Shepard was gay, he "flipped out and began to pistol whip the f——

with my gun." (Kevin Vaughan, "Suspect 'Flipped Out,' Beat Shepard, Letters Say," *Denver Rocky Mountain News,* 7 April 1999, <insidedenver.com>.

9. The two bicyclists who found Shepard thought he "was a scarecrow or manne-quin because of the way he was sprawled on the fence." ("Gay Student Clings to Life after Savage Beating," CNN Interactive (10 October 1998): <www.cnn.com/US>.

10. Aaron McKinney, ibid.

11. Earlier accounts place the time at twelve hours; see "Victim of Anti-Gay Attack in Wyoming Clings to Life," CNN Interactive (11 October 1998): <www.cnn.com/US>. Later accounts move the time back. An October 13 report, the day after Shepard's death, puts the time at eighteen hours. See "Did Shepard's Accused Killers Attack Before?" Channel 3000 (Madison) News (13 October 1998): <www.channel3000.com>.

12. The names have become achingly familiar over the years: Billy Jack Gaither, the Alabama man viciously beaten with an axe, covered with kerosene, and then set afire. See "Billy Jack Gaither's Life and Death," editorial, *New York Times,* 9 March, 1989. James Byrd, Jr., a disabled Texas man, chained behind a pickup and dragged to death. See AP news service, "Cops: Gay Slaying Followed Advance," 4 March 1999. Teena Brandon, a 21-year-old woman who passed as a man, and who was beaten, raped, and murdered by two men. See David Ansen, "Walk Like a Man, Talk Like a Man," *Newsweek* (11 October 1999).

13. See "Anti-Gay Group Plans to Protest Funeral," *Casper Star Tribune,* 13 Octo-ber 1998, <www.trib.com/CST>.

14. The same groups faced off at the court hearing in which Russell Henderson pleaded guilty to kidnapping and murder. See Patrick O'Driscoll, "Emotions Still High in Shepard Case," Patrick O'Driscoll, *USA Today,* 5 April 1999, <www.usatoday.com>.

15. See Marty, "Beauty and Terror," 72–83.

16. Kristeva, *Powers of Horror,* 207ff.

17. David J. Skal, *The Monster Show: A Cultural History of Horror* (New York: W. W. Norton, 1993), 313.

18. Garry Wills, "The Tragic Pope," *New York Review of Books* 41, no. 21 (22 De-cember 1994): 6. Theologians argued that the atonement of the human race was accom-plished by virtue of the paradox inherent in the Incarnation. That is, only a transgressive body—one that violates categories, and so by definition monstrous—could overcome the transgression wrought in human nature by the monstrousness of sin. In *Deformed Discourse: The Function of the Monster in Mediaeval Thought and Literature* (Montreal: McGill-Queen's University Press, 1996), for example, David Williams discusses this point in connection with a mediaeval conflation of the Oedipus and Christ stories: "Just as the Greek myth recognized the basic monstrosity of human beings and expressed it through the image of paradox and enigma, the Christian mediaeval text extends this perception to God Himself and so makes of the human monster a reflection of the ultimate mon-ster, God" (266).

19. John Updike, "Hawthorne's Creed," *Hugging the Shore: Essays and Criticism*

(New York: Alfred Knopf, 1983), 76–77. See "The 'Offence' of the God-Man: Kierkegaard's Way of Faith," *Times Literary Supplement* (27 March 1937): 229–30. In terms of its theology, the monstrous Incarnation was a matter of record through the medieval ages. Yet despite the attempts of orthodox readings to erase the offense, the stigmata of scandal surrounding Jesus constantly edged him into an epistemology of the monstrous in both its meanings of marvelous as well as horrible. This was a fairly standard association. In 1412, for instance, Hoccleve asks, "Was it not eek a monstre as in nature yat god I-bore was of a virgine?" (*De Reg. Princ.* 344, *OED,* vol. 6, p. 1036).

20. A book remains to be written upon the Gothic frame of the Testaments. That Matthew implicitly recognizes the monstrous implications of Jesus can be seen in his otherwise incomprehensible remark that Jesus' birth "troubled all of Jerusalem."

21. See Joachim Guhrt, "Offence, Scandal, Stumbling Block," in *The New International Dictionary of New Testament Theology,* ed. Colin Brown, 4 vols. (Grand Rapids: Zondervan, 1975–78), vol. 2: 705–10.

22. John P. Meier, *A Marginal Jew: Rethinking the Historical Jesus,* vol. 1, *The Roots of the Problem and the Person* (New York: Doubleday, 1991), 8. See too, J. P. M. Walsh, S.J., *The Mighty from Their Thrones: Power in the Biblical Tradition* (Philadelphia: Fortress Press, 1987). Walsh argues that for Paul, the cross symbolizes Jesus' "identification with those . . . under a curse" (161ff.).

23. The body in pain has a long history of double-representation in Christian theology, first as sign of sin, but in addition, as a sign of grace. The leper and the syphilitic, in particular, were thus ambiguously designated. See Saul Brody, *The Disease of the Soul: Leprosy in Medieval Literature* (Ithaca: Cornell University Press, 1974), esp. chaps. 3 and 4. See Claude Quétal, *History of Syphilis,* trans. Judith Braddock and Brian Pike (Baltimore: Johns Hopkins University Press, 1990); Susan Sontag, *AIDS and Its Metaphors* (New York: Farrar, Straus, Giroux, 1989); also Sander L. Gilman, "AIDS and Syphilis: The Iconography of Disease," in *AIDS: Cultural Analysis, Cultural Activism,* ed. Douglas Crimp (Cambridge, Mass.: MIT Press, 1988), 87–107; Alfred W. Crosby, "New Diseases," in *A Leap in the Dark: Aids, Art, and Contemporary Cultures,* ed. Allan Klusacek and Ken Morrison (Montreal: Véhicule Press, 1993), 10–15.

24. Kristina Campbell, "In Spite of Opposition, the *Blade* Will Remain in Fairfax Libraries," *Washington Blade* (26 March 1993): 8; Lou Chibbaro, Jr., "Emotional Hearing in Fairfax over the *Blade,*" *Washington Blade* (19 March 1993): 6.

25. Production Journal, *Dracula,* cited in Ingebretsen, *Maps of Heaven,* xxvi.

26. Norman Cohn, "Le Diable au Coeur," review of *The Origin of Satan,* by Elaine Pagels, *New York Review of Books* 42, no. 14 (21 September 1995): 20. In a different context, Pagels herself remarks, "Demonization is one of the plagues of religious tradition because [one is] dealing with an intense rhetoric intensified to the voltage of the divine" (quoted in David Remnick, "The Devil Problem," *New Yorker* [3 April 1995]: 64). The rite of scapegoating, which is part of this dynamic, predates Christianity, of course, although Christian organizational models have focused and heightened the deadly zeal of its effects.

27. Dr. Martin D. Snyder, correspondence.

28. See John A. T. Robinson, *The Body: A Study in Pauline Theology* (London: SCM Press, 1952).

29. Spivey, "Christ and the Art of Agony."

30. *Skandalizo*, gr., cause to be caught or to fall; See David McCracken, *The Scandal of the Gospels: Jesus, Story, and Offense* (New York: Oxford University Press, 1994), 194.

31. Spivey, "Christ and the Art of Agony."

32. My use of the word "rewrite" in this context is intentional, since, as Greenblatt argues, both Jewish and Christian exegetical practices are suffused with textuality, and might even be said to offer a textual spirituality: "For Jews, God manifested himself principally in a text, the Torah, but for Christians, God's flesh was itself a text, written upon with universal characters." (223). Devotion to the Sacred Heart of Jesus is such a holdover. See Greenblatt, "Mutilation and Meaning," 221–42.

33. See the extensive puns throughout Scripture aligning the rock of Christ as "foundation" and the "stone of stumbling and a rock of offense" (1 Peter 2:8). While Paul in Corinthians celebrates this scandal, he does so only in the interests of managing its stigma; his conventionally religious, not to say pharisaical, habits leave him uncomfortable with the implications of this socially shameful death.

34. Indeed, coming to terms with the scandal of the Cross and Christ's obvious mortality precipitated a crisis of management as old as the Council of Chalcedon (James Twitchell, *Preposterous Violence: Fables of Aggression in Modern Culture* [New York: Oxford University Press, 1989], 28ff.). It was the Trullan Synod in Constantinople (A.D. 692) that finally lifted the authoritative ban on representations of Christ's body. Until then, representations of Jesus' death tacitly ignored the body by substituting a lamb, a dove, or other symbol. This tactic likewise had the effect of bypassing the riddle of Jesus' mortality: how could the body of God suffer? How could the suffering of immortality be humanly represented? What were the implications of this suffering for Christian doctrine about the omnipotence of God? The history of Christianity is scarred by battles over the exact nature of Christ's body, its capabilities, needs, and desires. From Christ's cry of despair in the Garden, to his "I Thirst" on the cross, his mortality was ever in sight, if not exactly in question. Twitchell observes that the most "visually arresting" part of the Christ passion has been his suffering as a man, "given the progressive increase in violence to Christ as he was reimaged from the stoic mystic in the late Middle Ages to the suffering human in the Renaissance" (*Preposterous Violence*, 23–24).

35. Cardinal James Hickey, *Washington Catholic Standard* (13 November 1997): 5. Apropos of this point is Annie Dillard's remark about the Bible itself, "Why did they spread this scandalous document [the Bible] before our eyes? If they had read it . . . they would have hid it" (*An American Childhood*, cited in McCracken, *The Scandal of the Gospels*, 69).

36. Joy Dickinson, "Service Memorializes Slain Gay Student," *Dallas Morning News*, 19 October 1998, 15A. This is not to say that such imagery was exclusive to Shepard. The mother of a man allegedly killed by Andrew Cunanan suffered, in her

words, "a worse death than Christ." See John McCormack and Evan Thomas, "A Lethal Road Trip," *Newsweek* (19 May 1997): 52.

37. Coleman Cornelius, "In Face of Hate, a Call for Peace," *Denver Post,* 17 October 1998, <www.denverpost.com>.

38. The Hate Crimes Prevention Act, proposed a year earlier by President Clinton, was just then moving through the Senate, coming to a vote the day of Shepard's funeral. The act failed to pass. The director of Empire State Pride Agenda sees Shepard's death as "a catalyst for renewed activism." The image of the scarecrow on the fence became part of a fraternity float, in a homecoming parade a few blocks from where Shepard lay near death in a Fort Collins hospital. The straw-haired scarecrow on the float was labeled, in black spray paint, "I'm Gay." On the manikin's back was painted, "Up My Ass." Fraternity officials suspended seven members, saying they acted "independently." See "Homophobia Often Found in Schools, Data Show," *New York Times,* 14 October 1998, Late edition, A19. See also People for the American Way, *Hostile Climate: Report on Anti-Gay Activity* (Washington, D.C.: PFAW Foundation, 1999), 99–100.

39. Robert Brustein, "McNally on the Cross," review of "Corpus Christi," by Terrence McNally, *New Republic* (30 November 1998).

40. Melanie Thernstrom, "The Crucifixion of Matthew Shepard," *Vanity Fair* (March 1999).

41. But see Steven D. Moore, *God's Gym: Divine Male Bodies of the Bible* (New York: Routledge, 1996), and Regina Schwartz, *The Curse of Cain: The Violent Legacy of Monotheism* (Chicago: University of Chicago, 1997). Especially pertinent to this chapter is her section on "God the Father and Homosexuality," 106–19.

42. That is to say, Jesus is constantly perceived as *giving* scandal (here understood as breach of religious protocol), as evidenced in things he did and the people with whom he associated. Numerous Scripture scholars note that Jesus regularly provoked scandal pedagogically, intending to cause shock, and then a change of heart. Indeed, Jesus is a scandal because, as McCracken observes, Yahweh is the prior stumbling block in the Hebrew Bible. See McCracken, *The Scandal of the Gospels,* viii; John Dominic Crossan, *Cliffs of Fall: Paradox and Polyvalence in the Parables of Jesus* (New York: Seabury Press, 1980) From a specific gay and lesbian perspective, see Robert Goss, *Jesus Acted Up: A Gay and Lesbian Manifesto* (San Francisco: HarperCollins, 1993). See, too, John H. Yoder, *The Politics of Jesus* (Grand Rapids, Mich.: William B. Eerdmans, 1972).

43. Averil Cameron, *Christianity and the Rhetoric of Empire: The Development of Christian Discourse* (Berkeley: University of California Press, 1991), 14.

44. Erving Goffman, *Stigma: Notes on the Management of Spoiled Identity* (Englewood Cliffs, N.J.: Prentice Hall, 1963).

45. Quoted in Gary Delsohn and Sam Stanton, "I'm Guilty of Obeying the Laws of the Creator," *Salon.com* (8 November 1999): <www.salon.com>. In this same article, the director of the Center on Hate and Extremism comments, "Many of these people are influenced by Bible passages that they perceive to give them complete license to murder gays because it's a sin."

46. See Brigette Cazelles, introduction to *Images of Sainthood in Medieval Europe,* ed. Renate Blumenfeld-Kosinski and Timea Szell (Ithaca: Cornell University Press, 1991), 2.

47. The saint or holy one becomes the "exemplar," whose suffering is morally instructive. Peter Brown, "The Saint as Exemplar," *Representations* 1 (1983): 1–25.

48. A year later, the prominent gay publication the *Advocate* revisited the drama of Matthew Shepard; see "Matthew Shepard One Year Later" (12 October 1999).

49. Cited in Robert Dreyfuss, "The Holy War on Gays," *Rolling Stone,* no. 808 (18 March 1999): 41.

50. See, for example, the *Advocate* editorial commentary on the one-year anniversary of Shepard's death: "[Matthew] was a gentle young man with a loving family and close friends" (*Advocate,* 12 October 1999, 37). See, too, Robert Black, "Shepard Remembered as 'Gentle Spirit,' " *Boston Globe,* 31 March 1999, online edition.

51. Thernstrom, "The Crucifixion of Matthew Shepard," 209, 210.

52. Goffman, *Stigma.*

53. Non-churchgoing Ronald Reagan typifies how Biblical appeal provides a loose antidote for all manner of civil woes: "I've found that the Bible contains an answer to just about everything and every problem that confronts us, and I wonder sometimes why we don't recognize that one book could solve a lot of problems for us." Ronald Reagan, in a news conference on 21 February 1985, cited in Lucia Folena, "Figures of Violence," in *The Violence of Representation: Literature and the History of Violence,* ed. Nancy Armstrong and Leonard Tennenhouse (York: Routledge, 1989), 229–30. The problem-solving to which Reagan refers begins, of course, with the solutions made possible by misspeaking, the various potentials of which this book explores. Only fastidious attention given to (non)language makes possible the intense and sudden wind shear of the pogrom, witch-hunt, or hate crime.

54. Candice Hughes, "Pope Denounces Gay Pride Parade," AP Online, 7 July 2000. Robert Knight and Peter LaBarbera, discussed in this chapter, also weigh in, for once approving of the Catholic position. See "Calculated to Provoke: Gay Cultural Warriors Threaten Church," *Washington Times,* 2 August 2000, A21. About the general conflict between the church and the gay march, see also Richard L. Wentworth, "New Battle at Rome Colosseum," *Christian Science Monitor,* 3 July 2000, 6. The Pontiff's remarks are all the more ironic considering the fourteen-part series of reflections on homosexuality and Christianity published in 1997 in *L'Osservatore Romano.* In the last of the series, Jean-Louise Bruges, of the International Theological Commission, advises those who minister to homosexuals to "overcome his fears and perhaps repress his opposition or even the repulsion that homosexuality inspires in him more or less consciously." See Philip Pullella, "Vatican Newspaper Urges Church Respect for Gays," Reuters news service, 24 April 1997.

55. Didi Herman, *The Anti-Gay Agenda: Orthodox Vision and the Christian Right* (Chicago: University of Chicago Press, 1997), 59, 61.

56. Thomas Laqueur observes that "serious talk about sexuality is inevitably about the social order that it both represents and legitimates" ("Of Language and the Flesh," in *Making Sex: Body and Gender from the Greeks to Freud* [Cambridge, Mass.: Harvard University Press, 1990], 11).

57. John Lichfield, "Buchanan: The Nightmare Scenario," *Independent,* 22 February 1996, 17.

58. Among very many good essays on this topic, see Dennis Altman, "AIDS and the Reconceptualization of Homosexuality," in Klusacek and Morrison, *A Leap in the Dark,* 32–43.

59. A few years following the 'birth" of Gay Rights as a political movement in the June 1969 police action at the Stonewall Bar in Manhattan, the American Psychiatric Association removed homosexuality from its *Diagnostic and Statistical Manual of Mental Disorders* (DSM III, 1973).

60. Dreyfuss, "The Holy War on Gays," 39.

61. Similarly, in *Perfect Enemies,* Bull and Gallagher note how the Christian evangelical and the gay liberation movements face each other as "diametrically opposed voting blocks"; a page later, in a noteworthy shift of discourse, they observe that "gay activists and religious conservatives have long had the unmistakable feel of smoldering archenemies" (2, 3).

62. Cited in Dreyfuss, "The Holy War on Gays," 39.

63. Bull and Gallagher, *Perfect Enemies,* 22.

64. Marshall Kirk and Hunter Madsen, *After the Ball: How America Will Conquer Its Fear and Hatred of Gays in the '90s* (New York: Plume, 1989), 144.

65. *New York Post* (24 May 1983), cited in the *New Republic* (18 March 1996): 17. Falwell, quoted in Bull and Gallagher, *Perfect Enemies,* 26.

66. Jeff Cohen and Norman Solomon, "Gay Rights and News 'Balance,'" in *Adventures in Medialand: Behind the News, Beyond the Pundits* (Monroe, Me.: Common Courage Press, 1993), 106.

67. Anti-homosexual rhetoric continued to serve Patrick Buchanan in his 2000 election year bid as the presidential nominee from the Reform party. At a news conference at the Reform Party Convention, Buchanan issued a statement denouncing "rampant homosexuality" as "a sign of cultural decadence and moral decline." See Thomas B. Edsall, "Reform Party Convention Is Split, *Washington Post,* 11 August 2000, 6. In an October 3 visit to Vermont, Buchanan called homosexuality an "unnatural and immoral lifestyle" (see Kara Fox, "Reform Party: Pat Buchanan," *Washington Blade* [20 October 2000]: 25).

68. Fox, "Reform Party: Pat Buchanan."

69. For the use of gender/horror motifs, and their appropriation to the discourse of homosexual stigma, see Rudi C. Bleys, *The Geography of Perversion: Male-to-Male Sexual Behavior outside the West and the Ethnographic Imagination, 1750–1918* (New York: New York University Press, 1995).

70. Kristina Campbell, "Dozens Turn Out to Protest the *Blade* at Fairfax Library," *Washington Blade* (23 April 1993): 6.

71. Cited in Bull and Gallagher, *Perfect Enemies,* 266.

72. Laura Kipnis, *Bound and Gagged: Pornography and the Politics of Fantasy in America* (New York: Grove Press, 1996), 6.

73. Ibid., 5.

74. Ibid., 6. Elements of this predatory sexual creature are of ancient origin; it can be found in the tales of Hansel and Gretel and the witch, for instance, and American variants have a long history in the United States. See David Sonenschein, "Child-Threatening Figures," in *Pedophiles on Parade,* vol. 2, *The Popular Imagery of Moral Hysteria* (San Antonio, Tex.: D. Sonenschein, 1998), 52–74. The current bogey is entangled with that other domestic terrorist, the serial killer. These are actually, as well as politically, linked; see the House Committee, the Serial Killer and Child Abduction Unit, for instance). As Gayle Rubin remarks in "Thinking Sex," the "current wave of erotic terror has reached deepest into those areas bordered in some way, if only symbolically, by the sexuality of the young" (7). Rubin expands on this in "Sexual Politics, the New Right, and the Sexual Fringe," in *The Age Taboo: Gay Male Sexuality, Power, and Consent,* ed. Daniel Tsang (Boston: Alyson Publications, 1981), 108–15.

75. Vol. 18, 333. Cited in Haynal, André, Miklós Molnár, Gérard de Puymège, "From Priest to Philosopher," in *Fanaticism: A Historical and Psychoanalytical Study,* trans. Linda Butler Koseoglu (New York: Schocken Books, 1983), 31.

76. In 1996, for example, a group of local Christian right-wing groups formed an "anti-homosexual network" (Dreyfuss, "The Holy War on Gays," 38). The group, calling itself the National Pro-Family Forum, included Pat Robertson's Christian Coalition, the American Family Association, and James Dobson's Focus on the Family, as well as perhaps ten or twelve other like-minded Christian groups. The *Wired Strategies* Web site samples the rhetoric, for instance, of the Traditional Values Coalition, the Family Research Council, Pat Robertson, Jerry Falwell, Ex-Gay Ministries, the Christian Coalition of Maine, the National Association for Research and Treatment of Homosexuality, the American Family Association, the Claremont Institute, Colorado for Family Values, Americans for the Truth about Homosexuality.

77. Rhonda Smith, "Phelps Announces Plans," *Washington Blade* (14 April 2000): 18.

78. For example, a September 1966 press release on the death of Leni Wylliams announced that the church would picket the memorial service. Phelps used Wylliams's funeral to issue his own jeremiad, warning that the sodomite lifestyle guarantees Hell. He wrote that "the *Kansas City Star* Fag Rag writing tributes, and his fellow perverts dancing and singing in his honor, will not buy one drop of water to cool Leni's tongue where he likely now is" (from a similarly overwrought Web site; see www.godhatesfags.com). Phelps employs a rhetorical prejudice as old as the eleventh century: "The Jews . . . are sinful, greedy, Hell-bound, money-grubbing sodomites; and they have dedicated their synagogue to be a gay and lesbian propaganda mill and recruiting depot, soliciting young

people to sodomy" (Westboro Baptist Church press release, 7 September 1998). When the suggestion was made that one, or both, of the boys implicated in the Littleton killings were gay, Phelps stalwartly showed up at their funerals. Phelps also announced he would picket the funeral of a man killed in a Virginia gay bar, 30 September 2000. See "Roanoke Gunman Shoots Seven," *Washington Blade* (29 September 2000): 10.

79. Reggie White, Green Bay Packers defensive end, interviewed by Peggy Wehmeyer on ABC's *20/20* (27 April 1998). These remarks followed almost verbatim a 25 March speech made by White in the Wisconsin Assembly. See People for the American Way, *Hostile Climate,* 231, 232.

80. Trent Lott, Associated Press, 15 June, 1998. In a June 15 taped interview on "The Armstrong Williams Show," Senate Majority Leader Lott said homosexuality was a problem "just like alcohol . . . or sex addiction . . . or kleptomaniacs" (see People for the American Way, *Hostile Climate,* 12).

81. Cited in Ibid., 117. See Urvashi Vaid, *Virtual Equality: The Mainstreaming of Gay and Lesbian Liberation* (New York: Anchor Books, 1995). In July 1998, the National Pro-Family Forum started the Truth In Love campaign, whose initiating discourse of sympathy and compassion emphasized that homosexuals "can change" and that ex-gays "have walked out of homosexuality into sexual celibacy or even marriage" (Robert Dreyfuss, "The Holy War on Gays," 39).

82. Web site for People for the American Way, <www.pfaw.org>, information retrieved 25 February 1999.

83. Cited by Mark E. Pietrzyk, *News-Telegraph* (10 March 1995): <www.wired strategies.com/cameron.html>.

84. Cited in Dreyfuss, "The Holy War on Gays," 39, 40.

85. American Family Association, "Homosexuality in America: Exposing the Myths," a Homosexual Agenda resource, <www.afa.net>.

86. Paul Cameron, "Medical Consequences of What Homosexuals Do," Family Research Institute, <www.biblebelievers.com/Cameron2.html>. "The typical sexual practices of homosexuals are a medical horror story," says Paul Cameron, and his projective fiction is something out of Lovecraft, a horror of the body and its collapsing boundaries: "exchanging saliva, feces, semen and/or blood . . . drinking urine, ingesting feces and experiencing rectal trauma."

87. "Some early persecutors of the Christians in Rome" suggested "that their 'holy supper' was a cannibalistic rite." See Nigel Spivey, "Christ and the Art of Agony," 5. For an additional perspective, see William T. Cavanaugh, *Torture and Eucharist: Theology, Politics, and the Body of Christ* (Oxford: Blackwell, 1998).

88. *Portland Press Herald,* 29 October 1998, cited in "Anti-Gay Quotes from the Christian Coalition of Maine's Paul Volle," <www.wiredstrategies.com/cc.html>.

89. *Portland Press Herald,* 30 October 1998, cited in ibid.

90. Fred Botting, *Making Monstrous: Frankenstein, Criticism, Theory* (Manchester: Manchester University Press, 1991), 27.

91. Addressing this point, and appropriate to the narratives of Shepard, Edward

Peters, in *Torture* (New York: Basil Blackwell, 1985), observes that the "victim's discourse presents unique difficulties to interpretation, since strictly speaking the point of victimization is to strip the victim of its voice and to deny its subjectivity through violence" (198). See, too, Elaine Scarry, *The Body in Pain: The Making and Unmaking of the World* (New York: Oxford University Press, 1985); George Steiner, *Language and Silence: Essays on Language, Literature, and the Inhuman* (New York: Atheneum, 1967); Paul Oppenheimer, *Evil and the Demonic: A New Theory of Monstrous Behavior* (New York: New York University Press, 1996).

92. Paul Cameron, cited by Mark E. Pietrzyk, *News-Telegraph* (10 March 1995): <www.wiredstrategies.com/hate.html>. Rev. Lou Sheldon is also featured on Wired Strategies: "Reverend Louis Sheldon of the Traditional Values Coalition has come out in favor of quarantining AIDS patients in what he calls 'cities of refuge'" (Mark E. Pietrzyk, *News-Telegraph* [10 March, 1995]: <www.wiredstrategies.com/sheldon.html>. For an overview of the rhetoric and the action, see People for the American Way, *Hostile Climate*. Nor are "fringe" groups alone responsible: William F. Buckley writes, "Everyone detected with AIDS should be tattooed in the upper fore-arm, to protect common-needle users, and on the buttocks, to prevent the victimization of other homosexuals" ("Identify All the Carriers," *New York Times,* 18 March 1986, A27).

93. Kipnis, *Bound and Gagged.*

94. People for the American Way, *Hostile Climate,* 221.

95. Ibid., 158.

96. See Herman, *The Anti-Gay Agenda,* 78–79.

97. Kate Ferguson Ellis, *The Contested Castle: Gothic Novels and the Subversion of Domestic Ideology* (Urbana: University of Illinois Press, 1989), 7.

98. John Aravosis, "Anti-Gay Rhetoric Chronicled on New Web Site," Wired Strategies (7 December 1998): <www.wiredstrategies.com/hate.html>.

99. Richard Cohen, "An Anti-Gay Party," *Washington Post,* 17 August 1999, A15.

100. Cardinal Joseph Ratzinger and the Congregation for the Doctrine of the Faith, "Letter to the Bishops of the Catholic Church on the Pastoral Care of Homosexual Persons" (1986); its Latin title is more sharply indicative of its tenor, "Homosexualitatis problema" (Acta Apostolicase Sedis 79 [1987]: 543–54).

101. William Veeder, "The Nurture of the Gothic, or How Can a Text Be Both Popular and Subversive?" in *American Gothic,* ed. Robert K. Martin and Eric Savoy (Iowa City: University of Iowa Press, 1998), 14.

102. <www.wiredstrategies.com/hate.html>.

103. See Mark D. Jordan, *The Invention of Sodomy in Christian Theology* (Chicago: University of Chicago Press, 1997).

104. "Satanists and Homosexuals," cited in Wired Strategies, <www.wiredstrategies .com/robertson.html>. A version of Robertson's statement is also posted by People for the American Way; see "Anti-Gay Politics and the Religious Right," <www.pfaw.org/ issues/right/rtvw.antigay.shtml>. This is not the first time that Robertson linked the demonic with homosexuality/lesbianism. To this point Mary Douglas's observation about

witchcraft is apt: "witchcraft beliefs are essentially a means of clarifying and affirming social definition"; and "witchcraft sharpens definition where roles are ill-defined" (*Natural Symbols: Explorations in Cosmology* [New York: Pantheon, 1982], xxv, xxx). Witchcraft and homosexuality both derive their origins from within Christianity itself. Arguably the role each "sharpens" is that presumably "natural" one undergirding the *form* to which the Incarnation itself is irreducibly bound, the bodied form to which we apply the term—not always skillfully—of gender.

105. See, in particular, Herman, *The Anti-Gay Agenda;* also Bull and Gallagher, *Perfect Enemies.*

106. See John Boswell, *Christianity, Homosexuality, and Social Tolerance: Gay People in Western Europe from the Beginning of the Christian Era to the Fourteenth Century* (Chicago: University of Chicago Press, 1980). Mark Jordan explores how a limited geographical Old Testament reference becomes an extensive moral cartography in *The Invention of Sodomy.* R. I. Moore complements Boswell from a different perspective; see *The Formation of a Persecuting Society: Power and Deviance in Western Europe, 950–1250* (Oxford: Blackwell, 1987). J. Michael Clark, for example, observes that "the inordinate valuing of heterosexual men and male sexuality entered western consciousness simultaneously with the earliest beginnings of Judaeo-Christianity" (see "Patriarchy, Dualism, and Homophobia: Marginalization as Spiritual Challenge," in *Homophobia and the Judaeo-Christian Tradition,* ed. Michael L. Stemmeler and J. Michael Clark [Dallas: Monument Press, 1990], 51). Particular to contemporary Catholic practice, and following to some extent Moore's work, see Mark Jordan, *The Silence of Sodom: Homosexuality in Modern Catholicism* (Chicago: University of Chicago Press, 2000); Tom Fox, *Sexuality and Catholicism* (New York: George Braziller, 1995); John McNeil, *The Church and the Homosexual,* 4th rev. ed. (Boston: Beacon, 1993).

107. See Michael Goodich, "Sodomy in Ecclesiastical Law and Theory," *Journal of Homosexuality* 1, no. 4 (1976): 427–34; Albert R. Jonsen and Stephen Toulmin, *The Abuse of Casuistry: A History of Moral Reasoning* (Berkeley: University of California Press, 1988); Pim Pronk, *Against Nature?: Types of Moral Argumentation Regarding Homosexuality,* trans. John Vriend (Grand Rapids, Mich.: William B. Eerdmans, 1993). Augustine, for example, early undertook the task of exploring the idea of evil, with the purpose in mind of absolving the Deity of any complicity with it. As Dollimore wittily remarks, such attempts were bound to fail, and thanks to Augustine's efforts, "perversion and deviation become lodged at the heart of those contradictions which were to haunt Christianity" and which "have the happy consequence of making God rather than Satan the ultimate or original pervert" (Jonathan Dollimore, *Sexual Dissidence: Augustine to Wilde, Freud to Foucault* [New York: Oxford University Press, 1991], 146).

108. Ibid., 143.

109. Family Research Council spokesman Steven Schwalm explicitly positioned the furor over Shepard's murder, and the ensuing call for hate-crime legislation: "Hate crimes laws have nothing to do with perpetrators of violent crime and everything to do with silencing political opposition. . . . It would criminalize pro-family beliefs" (cited in NewsPlanet Staff, "Shepard as Cause Celebre," *PlanetOut* (13 October 1998): <www.planetout.com/news/article.html?1998/10/13/2>.

110. On the one hand a rhetoric of altruism must negotiate a complex terrain; an announced "care" for the homosexual produces a rhetoric of altruism, concern, even "love." See, for example, the Truth In Love campaign sponsored by religious right groups to "push[ ] a scientifically discredited treatment into the mainstream mailings" (People for the American Way, *Hostile Climate,* 7), On the other hand, the tainted and problematic body elicits a countering language of abjection and repudiation—although, as Kristeva might argue, taboo would be more proper in this case since what is being produced is a rather more complicated *engagement* with, rather than abjection of, the homosexual presence.

111. Thus, in the Catholic Church, for instance, the various attempts to foreclose on New Ways Ministry (a Catholic gay educational group) at Georgetown University were ingenuous. Like the now fifteen-year old suppression of the gay-friendly Dignity chapters in Catholic churches, the subject speaks all the more loudly for the efforts repeatedly taken to quiet it. See, for example, Timothy Dlugos, "A Cruel God: The Gay Challenge to the Catholic Church," *Christopher Street* 4, no. 2 (September 1979): 20–39; Jeannine Gramick and Pat Furey, eds., *The Vatican and Homosexuality: Reactions to the "Letter to the Bishops of the Catholic Church on the Pastoral Care of Homosexual Persons"* (New York: Crossroad, 1988); Robert Nugent and Jeannine Gramick, eds., *A Challenge to Love: Gay and Lesbian Catholics in the Church* (New York: Crossroad, 1983).

112. William A. Cohen, *Sex Scandal: The Private Parts of Victorian Fiction* (Durham, N.C.: Duke University Press, 1996), 111.

113. See Robert A. Orsi, " 'Mildred, Is It Fun to Be a Cripple?': The Culture of Suffering in Mid-Twentieth-Century American Catholicism," in *Catholic Lives, Contemporary America,* ed. Thomas J. Ferraro (Durham, N.C.: Duke University Press, 1997), 19–64.

114. See Peter Stallybrass and Allon White, *The Politics and Poetics of Transgression* (London: Methuen, 1986). Specific to the American Christianity/homosexuality confrontation, see, for example, George Grant and Mark A. Horne, *Legislating Immorality: The Homosexuality Movement Comes Out of the Closet* (Chicago: Moody Press, 1993); George Grant, ed., *Gays in the Military: The Moral and Strategic Crisis* (Franklin, Tenn.: Legacy Communications, 1993); George Grant and Mark A. Horne, *Unnatural Affections: The Impuritan Ethic of Homosexuality in the Church* (Franklin, Tenn.: Legacy Communications, 1991); Tony Marco, *Gay Rights: A Public Health Disaster and Civil Wrong* (Ft. Lauderdale, Fla.: Coral Ridge Ministries, 1992); William Dannemeyer, *Shadow in the Land: Homosexuality in America* (San Francisco: Ignatius Press, 1989).

115. Ellis, *The Contested Castle,* 7.

116. Stephen King, *Danse Macabre* (New York: Everest House, 1981), 261.

117. Katharine Park, "Kimberly Bergalis, AIDS, and the Plague Metaphor," in *Media Spectacles,* ed Marjorie Garber, Jann Matlock, and Rebecca L. Walkowitz (Routledge: New York, 1993), 239. Park cites the Gallup Poll for 1991.

118. Jordan, *The Silence of Sodom,* 5–6. Garry Wills, in *Papal Sin: Structures of Deceit* (New York: Doubleday, 2000), writes that "many observers suspect that John Paul

II's real legacy to his Church is a gay priesthood. (cited in Tad Szulc, "Challenging the Church," *Washington Post Book World* [4–10 June 2000], 3).

119. Jordan, *The Silence of Sodom,* 3.

120. Judith Butler, *Gender Trouble: Feminism and the Subversion of Identity* (New York: Routledge, 1990), 2.

121. A conference, for example, concerned with the "problem" of homosexual visibility in American public life, managed, nonetheless, to keep the homosexual visible as a problem as well as justification for the conference. Even the title suggests the bifurcation of its intentions: "Homosexuality and American Public Life" (Georgetown University Conference Center, June 19–21, 1997). John Richard Neuhaus noted that the conference was intended to "break the silence on what for many has become a taboo subject"; he draws attention to the "organized insurgency in our public life" of the "homosexual impulse." *Silence, taboo; insurgency, impulse:* Neuhaus seems oblivious to his part in orchestrating the melodrama of visibility in the very terms by which he denounces it. See John Richard Neuhaus, "Love, No Matter What," *First Things,* no. 76 (October 1997): 81–82.

122. See, for instance, Patrick Pacheco, "Furor over New Play, Its Cancellation," *Los Angeles Times,* 28 May 1998, Calendar section, 47. One reviewer suggested that the play's sexual subtext guaranteed that the play would be remembered, even if not for its quality (which this reviewer thought it lacked).

123. Peter Steinfels discusses an exhibit in Seattle that features "nuns, a pope, oral sex, Jesus hanging from a cross of penises, a pedophilic priest in flagrante delicto and pages of the Bible defaced with satanic marks." See "Defining the Sacred and the Profane," *New York Times* (16 May 1998).

124. Dreyfuss, "The Holy War on Gays," 40.

125. Leo Steinberg, *The Sexuality of Christ in Renaissance Art and in Modern Oblivion* (New York: Pantheon Books, 1983).

126. And does masochism merely confirm a practice of manhood that is, after all, validated as chivalry? See Carol Siegel, *Male Masochism: Modern Revisions of the Story We Love* (Bloomington: Indiana University Press, 1995). For Material Christianity, see Elizabeth McKeown, "It's Hard to Say," review of *Material Christianity: Religion and Popular Culture in America,* by Colleen McDannell (New Haven, Conn.: Yale University Press), 1995; review published in *American Quarterly* (September 1997).

127. Mimi White, *Tele-Advising: Therapeutic Discourse in American Television* (Chapel Hill: University of North Carolina Press, 1992).

128. See William Gaines's publishing house, "Education Comics," later "Entertaining Comics"—one of which included *Picture Stories from the Bible.* Twitchell, commenting on one of these stories, observes the following: "Inside are eight pages of Jesus being flagellated, Jesus on the cross, Jesus dripping blood. [William Gaines's son] vastly expanded the business by adding a profitable run of action, crime, and horror comics" (*Preposterous Violence,* 144). Indeed, even in religious expression the body in pain is theologically deconstructive; as Kenneth Dutton writes, "Apart from the Damned, only

three portrayals of the unclad human body exercised the imagination of the medieval mind: Adam and Eve, the crucified Christ and St. Sebastian" (*The Perfectible Body: The Western Ideal of Male Physical Development* [New York: Continuum, 1995], 60).

129. Such unstableness of reference is evident in the tradition; see Carlin A. Barton, "Savage Miracles: The Redemption of Lost Honor in Roman Society and the Sacrament of the Gladiator and the Martyr," *Representations* 45 (1994): 41–71. One can conclude that contemporary representations of the eroticized and ecstatic body claim authority from an unacknowledged, although not invisible, traditional hermeneutic of the visionary and confessing body. In this way, through a literary trope of inversion the ecstatic body, in hagiographic tradition the symbol and occasion of the sacred, becomes in turn the Body *as* sexualized *and* sublime, these inversions confirming each other; see the work of de Sade, Genet, Rechie, for example.

130. Cited in Wilson, *Signs and Portents,* 43.

131. Richard Mohr, *Gay Ideas: Outing and Other Controversies* (Boston: Beacon Press, 1992), 6.

132. Tony Kushner, *Angels in America,* part 1, *Millennium Approaches* (New York: Theatre Communications Group, 1993).

Coda

1. Chris Bull, "Into the Shadows," *Washington Post Magazine* (29 June 1997): 11.

2. Peter Sutcliffe, so-called Yorkshire Ripper, for example, justified his killings by saying "I were just cleaning up streets" (cited in Josephine McDonagh, "Do or Die: Problems of Agency and Gender in the Aesthetics of Murder," in *New Feminist Discourses: Critical Essays on Theories and Texts,* ed. Isobel Armstrong [London: Routledge, 1992], 233).

3. Hildred Geertz, cited in *Sociophobics: The Anthropology of Fear,* ed. David L. Scruton (Boulder, Col.: Westview Press, 1986), 13.

4. Indeed, some states seem engaged in a race to see how many capital deaths they can issue. Eve Kosofsky Sedgwick writes, "It *is* difficult to experience from the vantage point of one's own bodily illness and need, all the brutality of a society's big and tiny decisions, explicit and encoded ones, about which lives have or have not value. Those decisions carry not only institutional and economic but psychic and . . . somatic consequences. A thousand things make it impossible to mistake the verdict on queer lives and on women's lives, as on the lives of those who are poor or not white" ("Queer and Now," in *Tendencies* [Durham, N.C.: Duke University Press, 1993], 16). A 14-year-old high school freshman, studying at home one semester because of harassment at school, said, "Kids would start calling me 'gay,' and the teacher wouldn't do anything about it. I'd start thinking, 'OK, is someone going to come beat me up now?'" (Emily Gurnon, "Specter of Hate in 2 Assaults on Youth," *San Francisco Examiner,* Sunday, 14 February 1999). Robert Dreyfuss writes that FBI statistics for 1997, for instance, listed "1,102 reported hate crimes linked to sexual orientation, mostly aimed at gay males. The Na-

tional Coalition of Anti-Violence Programs gives a figure of 2,445" ("The Holy War on Gays," *Rolling Stone* [18 March 1999]: 41).

5. Judith Halberstam, *Skin Shows: Gothic Horror and the Technology of Monsters* (Durham, N.C.: Duke University Press, 1995), 32.

6. Coleman Cornelius, "In Face of Hate, a Call for Peace," *Denver Post,* 17 October 1998, <www.denverpost.com>.

7. "Anti-Gay Group Plans to Protest Funeral," *Casper Star Tribune,* 13 October 1998, <www.trib.com/CST>.

8. Mike A. Soraghan, "Activists, Protesters Trade Views Outside Church," *Denver Post,* 17 October 1998, <www.denverpost.com>.

9. Robert A. Bernstein, "A 'Monster' Only Imagined, Not Real," *Chicago Tribune,* 27 October 1988, sec. 1, 23.

10. "Parents Alert: Tinky Winky Comes Out of the Closet," *National Liberty Journal* (February): <www.liberty.edu/chancellor/nlj/feb99/politics2.htm> Falwell later denied any such comments, although he was featured on CBS's *This Morning* with GLAAD executive director Joan M. Garry, February 12. *Newsweek,* the next week, queried why Falwell "outed only one kid icon. Bert and Ernie, Peppermint Patty, Batman and Robin, Timon and Pumbaa—they've all been rumored to be gay. And Snow White and the Seven Dwarfs!" says writer Paul Rudnick. ("Seven Men Living in One Cottage Sounds Like Fire Island to Me," *Newsweek* [22 February, 1999]: Newsmakers, 55).

11. NewsPlanet Staff, "Shepard as Cause Celebre," *PlanetOut* (13 October 1998): <www.planetout.com/news/article.html?1998/10/13/2>.

12. Murray Kempton, "A Mother's Shame," *Newsday,* 28 June 1995, A15.

13. "Anyone who does not take after his parents is really in a way a monstrosity, since in these cases Nature has in a way strayed from the generic type" (*Generation of Animals,* trans. A. L. Peck [Cambridge, Mass.: Harvard University Press, 1963], book 4, 401).

SELECTED BIBLIOGRAPHY

Books and Journals

Abt, Vicki, and Mel Seesholtz. "The Shameless World of Phil, Sally and Oprah: Television Talk Shows and the Deconstructing of Society," *Journal of Popular Culture* 28 (summer 1994): 171–91.

Altman, Dennis. "AIDS and the Reconceptualization of Homosexuality." In *A Leap in the Dark: AIDS, Art, and Contemporary Cultures,* edited by Allan Klusacek and Ken Morrison, 32–43. Montreal: Véhicule Press, 1992.

Alwood, Edward. *Straight News: Gays, Lesbians, and the News Media.* New York: Columbia University Press, 1996.

American Psychiatric Association. *Diagnostic and Statistical Manual of Mental Disorders.* 3d rev. ed. Washington, D.C.: American Psychiatric Association, 1987.

Anderson, Benedict. *Imagined Communities: Reflections on the Origin and Spread of Nationalism.* 1983; revised, London: Verso, 1991.

Arendt. Hannah. *Eichmann in Jerusalem: A Report on the Banality of Evil.* New York: Penguin, 1964.

Aristotle. *Generation of Animals.* Translated by A. L. Peck. Cambridge, Mass.: Harvard University Press, 1963.

Armstrong, Nancy, and Leonard Tennenhouse, eds. *The Violence of Representation: Literature and the History of Violence.* New York: Routledge, 1989.

Arnheim, Rudolf. "A Note on Monsters." In *Toward a Psychology of Art: Collected Essays.* Berkeley: University of California Press, 1972.

Auerbach, Nina. *Our Vampires, Ourselves.* Chicago: University of Chicago Press, 1995.

Augustine of Hippo. *The City of God.* Edited and with an introduction by Vernon J. Bourke. New York: Doubleday Image Books, 1958.

Baldick, Chris. *In Frankenstein's Shadow: Myth, Monstrosity, and Nineteenth-Century Writing.* Oxford, U.K.: Clarendon Press, 1987.

Barton, Carlin A. "Savage Miracles: The Redemption of Lost Honor in Roman Society and the Sacrament of the Gladiator and the Martyr." *Representations* 45 (1994): 41–71.

Berenstein, Rhona J. "Spectatorship-as-Drag: The Act of Viewing and Classic Horror

Cinema." In *Viewing Positions: Ways of Seeing Film,* edited by Linda Williams, 231–69. New Brunswick, N.J.: Rutgers University Press, 1995.

Berlant, Lauren. *The Anatomy of National Fantasy: Hawthorne, Utopia, and Everyday Life.* Chicago: University of Chicago Press, 1991.

Bhabha, Homi K. "The Other Question: The Stereotype and Colonial Discourse." In *The Sexual Subject: A* Screen *Reader in Sexuality,* collective editorial, 312–31. New York: Routledge, 1992.

Blaine, Diana York. "Necrophilia, Pedophilia, or Both?: The Sexualized Rhetoric of the JonBenet Ramsey Murder Case." In *Sexual Rhetoric: Media Perspectives on Sexuality, Gender, and Identity,* edited by Meta G. Carstarphen and Susan C. Zavoina, 51–62. Westport, Conn.: Greenwood Press, 1999.

Bleys, Rudi C. *The Geography of Perversion: Male-to-Male Sexual Behavior outside the West and the Ethnographic Imagination, 1750–1918.* New York: New York University Press, 1995.

Blonsky, Marshall. *American Mythologies.* New York: Oxford University Press, 1992.

Blumenfeld-Kosinski, Renate, and Timea Szell, eds. *Images of Sainthood in Medieval Europe.* Ithaca: Cornell University Press, 1991.

Bogdan, Robert. *Freakshow: Presenting Human Oddities for Amusement and Profit.* Chicago: University of Chicago Press, 1988.

Boswell, John. *Christianity, Homosexuality, and Social Tolerance: Gay People in Western Europe from the Beginning of the Christian Era to the Fourteenth Century.* Chicago: University of Chicago Press, 1980.

Botting, Fred. *Making Monstrous: Frankenstein, Criticism, Theory.* Manchester: Manchester University Press, 1991.

Bromley, Roger. *Lost Narratives: Popular Fictions, Politics, and Recent History.* New York: Routledge, 1988.

Brooks, Peter. *The Melodramatic Imagination.* New Haven: Yale University Press, 1995.

Bull, Chris, and John Gallagher. *Perfect Enemies: The Religious Right, the Gay Movement, and the Politics of the 1990s.* New York: Crown Publishers, 1996.

Burke, Edmund. *A Philosophical Enquiry into the Origin of Our Ideas of the Sublime and the Beautiful,* edited by Adam Phillips. New York: Oxford University Press, 1990.

Butler, Judith. *Bodies That Matter: On the Discursive Limits of "Sex."* New York: Routledge, 1993.

———. *Gender Trouble: Feminism and the Subversion of Identity.* New York: Routledge, 1990.

Cameron, Averil. *Christianity and the Rhetoric of Empire: The Development of Christian Discourse.* Berkeley: University of California Press, 1991.

Cameron, Deborah, and Elizabeth Frazer. *The Lust to Kill: A Feminist Investigation of Sexual Murder.* New York: New York University Press, 1987.

Capote, Truman. *In Cold Blood: A True Account of a Multiple Murder and Its Consequences.* New York: Random House, 1965.

Caputi, Jane. *The Age of Sex Crime*. Bowling Green, Ohio: Bowling Green State University Popular Press, 1987.

———. "The New Founding Fathers." *Journal of American Culture* 13 (fall 1990): 1–12.

Carey, James W. "The Dark Continent of American Journalism." *Reading the News: A Pantheon Guide to Popular Culture,* edited by Robert Karl Manoff and Michael Schudson, 146–96. New York: Pantheon Books, 1986.

———. *Media, Myths, and Narratives: Television and the Press*. Los Angeles: Sage, 1988.

Carroll, Noel. *The Philosophy of Horror; or, Paradoxes of the Heart*. New York: Routledge, 1990.

Carter, Angela. *Fireworks: Nine Profane Pieces*. London: Quartet, 1974.

Caruth, Cathy. *Unclaimed Experience: Trauma, Narrative, and History*. Baltimore: Johns Hopkins University Press, 1996.

Cavanaugh, William T. *Torture and Eucharist: Theology, Politics, and the Body of Christ*. Oxford: Blackwell, 1998.

Chancer, Lynn. *Sadomasochism in Everyday Life: The Dynamics of Power and Powerlessness*. New Brunswick, N.J.: Rutgers University Press, 1992.

Clark, J. Michael. "Patriarchy, Dualism, and Homophobia: Marginalization as Spiritual Challenge." In *Homophobia and the Judaeo-Christian Tradition,* edited by Michael L. Stemmeler and J. Michael Clark. Dallas: Monument Press, 1990.

Clarkson, Wensley. *Death at Every Stop: The True Story of Serial Killer Andrew Cunanan—the Man Who Murdered Designer Gianni Versace*. New York: St. Martin's Press, 1997.

Clover, Carol J. "Her Body, Himself: Gender in the Slasher Film." In *Fantasy and the Cinema,* edited by James Donald, 91–133. London: British Film Institute, 1989.

———. *Men, Women, and Chain Saws: Gender in the Modern Horror Film*. Princeton, N.J.: Princeton University Press, 1992.

Cohan, Stephen. *Masked Men: Masculinity and the Movies in the Fifties*. Bloomington: Indiana University Press, 1997.

Cohan, Steven, and Linda Shires. *Telling Stories: A Theoretical Analysis of Fiction*. London: Routledge, 1988.

Cohen, Daniel A. *Pillars of Salt, Monuments of Grace: New England Crime Literature and the Origins of American Popular Culture, 1674–1860*. New York: Oxford University Press, 1993.

Cohen, Jeff, and Norman Solomon. *Adventures in Medialand: Behind the News, Beyond the Pundits*. Monroe, Me.: Common Courage Press, 1993.

Cohen, Jeffrey Jerome. "Monster Culture (Seven Theses)." Introduction to *Monster Theory: Reading Culture,* edited by Jeffrey Jerome Cohen. Minneapolis: University of Minnesota Press, 1996.

Cohen, William A. *Sex Scandal: The Private Parts of Victorian Fiction*. Durham, N.C.: Duke University Press, 1996.

Cohn, Norman. "Le Diable au Coeur." Review of *The Origin of Satan,* by Elaine Pagels. *New York Review of Books* (21 September 1995): 18–20.

Colacurcio, Michael. *Doctrine and Difference: Essays in the Literature of New England.* New York: Routledge, 1997.

Conforti, Joseph A. *Jonathan Edwards, Religious Tradition, and American Culture.* Chapel Hill: University of North Carolina Press, 1995.

Conrich, Ian. "Seducing the Subject: Freddy Krueger, Popular Culture, and the *Nightmare on Elm Street* Films." In *Trash Aesthetics: Popular Culture and Its Audience,* edited by Deborah Cartmell, I. Q. Hunter. Heidi Kay, Imelda Whelehan, 118–31. London: Pluto Press, 1997.

Cooper, Emmanuel. *Fully Exposed: The Male Nude in Photography.* 2d ed. New York: Routledge, 1995.

Corber, Robert J. *Homosexuality in Cold War America: Resistance and the Crisis of Masculinity.* Durham, N.C.: Duke University Press, 1997.

Crane, Jonathan Lake. *Terror and Everyday Life: Singular Moments in the History of the Horror Film.* Thousand Oaks, Calif.: Sage Publications, 1994.

Creed, Barbara. *The Monstrous-Feminine: Film, Feminism, Psychoanalysis.* London: Routledge, 1993.

Crimp, Douglas. "How to Have Promiscuity in an Epidemic." In *AIDS: Cultural Analysis, Cultural Activism,* edited by Douglas Crimp. Cambridge, Mass.: MIT Press, 1988.

Dahmer, Lionel. *A Father's Story.* New York: William Morrow, 1994.

Damon, Maria. "Angelology, Things with Wings." *Mass Culture and Everyday Life,* edited by Peter Gibian, 205–11. New York: Routledge, 1997.

Dannemeyer, William. *Shadow in the Land: Homosexuality in America.* San Francisco: Ignatius Press, 1989.

Daston, Lorraine, and Katharine Park. *Wonders and the Order of Nature, 1150–1750.* New York: Zone Books, 1998.

Davenport-Hines, Richard. *Gothic: Four Hundred Years of Excess, Horror, Evil, and Ruin.* New York: North Point Press, 1999.

Davis, Don. *The Milwaukee Murders: Nightmare in Apt. 213, the True Story.* New York: St. Martin's Press, 1991.

Day, William Patrick. *In the Circles of Fear and Desire: A Study of Gothic Fantasy.* Chicago: University of Chicago Press, 1985.

DeLamotte, Eugenia C. *Perils of the Night: A Feminist Study of Nineteenth-Century Gothic.* New York: Oxford University Press, 1990.

Delumeau, Jean. *Sin and Fear: The Emergence of a Western Guilt Culture, 13th–18th Centuries.* Translated by Eric Nicholson. New York: St. Martin's Press, 1990.

D'Emilio, John, and Estelle B. Freedman. *Intimate Matters: A History of Sexuality in America.* 2d ed. Chicago: University of Chicago Press, 1997.

Dershowitz, Alan. *Sexual McCarthyism: Clinton, Starr, and the Emerging Constitutional Crisis.* New York: Basic Books, 1998.

Dickstein, Morris. *Gates of Eden: American Culture in the Sixties.* Cambridge, Mass.: Harvard University Press, 1997.

Dlugos, Timothy. "A Cruel God: The Gay Challenge to the Catholic Church." *Christopher Street* 4, no. 2 (September 1979): 20–39.

Dollimore, Jonathan. *Sexual Dissidence: Augustine to Wilde, Freud to Foucault.* New York: Oxford University Press, 1991.

Donald, James, ed. *Fantasy and the Cinema.* London: British Film Institute, 1989.

Douglas, John, and Mark Olshaker. *Mindhunter: Inside the FBI's Elite Serial Crime Unit.* New York: Pocket Star Books, 1995.

———. *Journey into Darkness.* New York: Pocket Star Books, 1998.

Douglas, Mary. *Natural Symbols: Explorations in Cosmology.* New York: Pantheon, 1982.

Dutton, Kenneth. R. *The Perfectible Body: The Western Ideal of Male Physical Development.* New York: Continuum, 1995.

Lee Edelman. "Tearooms and Sympathy, or The Epistemology of the Water Closet." *The Lesbian and Gay Studies Reader,* edited by Henry Abelove, Michèle Aina Barale, and David M. Halperin, 553–74. New York: Routledge, 1993.

Edmundson, Mark. *Nightmare on Main Street: Angels, Sadomasochism, and the Culture of Gothic.* Cambridge, Mass.: Harvard University Press, 1997.

Elbaz, Mikhael, and Ruth Murbach. "Fear in the Face of the Other, Condemned and Damned: AIDS, Epidemics, and Exclusions." In *A Leap in the Dark: AIDS, Art, and Contemporary Cultures,* edited by Allan Klusacek and Ken Morrison. Montreal: Véhicule Press, 1993.

Ellis, Kate Ferguson. *The Contested Castle: Gothic Novels and the Subversion of Domestic Ideology.* Urbana: University of Illinois Press, 1989.

Epstein, Su C. "The New Mythic Monster." In *Cultural Criminology,* edited by Jeff Ferrell and Clinton R. Sanders, 66–79. Boston: Northeastern University Press, 1995.

Ericson, Richard V., Patricia M. Baranek, and Janet B. L. Chan. *Visualizing Deviance: A Study of News Organization.* Toronto: University of Toronto Press, 1987.

Everman, Welch. *Cult Horror Films: From Attack of the 50 Foot Woman to Zombies of Mora Tau.* Secaucus, N.J.: Citadel Press, 1993.

Ferrell, Jeff, and Clinton R. Sanders, "Culture, Crime, and Criminology." In *Cultural Criminology,* 3–25. Boston: Northeastern University Press, 1995.

Fiedler, Leslie. *Freaks: Myths and Images of the Secret Self.* New York: Anchor Books, 1978.

Fiedler, Leslie. *Love and Death in the American Novel.* New York: Dell, 1966.

Fishkin, Shelley Fisher. *From Fact to Fiction: Journalism and Imaginative Writing in America.* Baltimore: Johns Hopkins University Press, 1985.

Fishman, Mark. *Manufacturing the News*. Austin: University of Texas Press, 1980.

Fitzgerald, F. Scott. *The Great Gatsby*. Edited by Matthew J. Bruccoli. New York: Simon and Schuster, 1991.

Foucault, Michel. *Discipline and Punish: The Birth of the Prison*. Translated by Alan Sheridan. New York: Pantheon, 1977.

Fox, James Alan, and Jack Levin. *Overkill: Mass Murder and Serial Killing Exposed*. New York: Plenum Press, 1994.

Fox, Tom. *Sexuality and Catholicism*. New York: George Braziller, 1995.

Frank, Gerold. *The Boston Strangler*. New York: New American Library, 1966.

Friedman, John Block. *The Monstrous Races in Medieval Art and Thought*. Cambridge, Mass.: Harvard University Press, 1981.

Freud, Sigmund. *Civilization and Its Discontents*. Vol. 21 of *The Standard Edition of the Complete Psychological Works of Sigmund Freud*, translated and edited by James Strachey. London: Hogarth Press, 1961.

Freud, Sigmund. *The Ego and the Id*. Vol. 19 of *The Standard Edition*.

Freud, Sigmund. *The Psychopathology of Everyday Life*. Vol. 6 of *The Standard Edition*, 1–279.

Fuller, Linda K. "Super Bowl Speak: Subtexts of Sex and Sex Talk in America's Annual Sports Extravaganza." In *Sexual Rhetoric: Media Perspectives on Sexuality, Gender, and Identity*, edited by Meta G. Carstarphen and Susan C. Zavoina, 161–73. Westport, Conn.: Greenwood Press, 1999.

Fuss, Diana. "Monsters of Perversion: Jeffrey Dahmer and *The Silence of the Lambs*." In *Media Spectacles*, edited by Marjorie Garber, Jann Matlock, and Rebecca L. Walkowitz, 181–205. New York: Routledge, 1993.

Gamson, Joshua. *Freaks Talk Back: Tabloid Talk Shows and Sexual Nonconformity*. Chicago: University of Chicago Press, 1998.

Garment, Suzanne. *Scandal: The Culture of Mistrust in American Politics*. New York: Times Books, 1991.

Gay, Peter. *The Cultivation of Hatred*. New York: W. W. Norton, 1993.

Geertz, Clifford. "Religion as a Cultural System." In *Reader in Comparative Religion*, edited by W. Lessa and E. Vogt. 167–78. 3d ed. New York: Harper and Row, 1972.

Geertz, Hildred. Cited in David L. Scruton, "The Anthropology of an Emotion." In *Sociophobics: The Anthropology of Fear*, edited by David L. Scruton, 13. Boulder, Col.: Westview Press, 1985.

Girard, René. *Violence and the Sacred*. Translated by Patrick Gregory. Baltimore: Johns Hopkins University Press, 1977.

Giroux, Henry A. *Disturbing Pleasures: Learning Popular Culture*. New York: Routledge, 1994.

Goddu, Teresa A. *Gothic America: Narrative, History, and Nation*. New York: Columbia University Press, 1997.

Goffman, Erving. *Stigma: Notes on the Management of Spoiled Identity.* Englewood Cliffs, N.J.: Prentice-Hall, 1963.

Goodich, Michael. "Sodomy in Ecclesiastical Law and Theory." *Journal of Homosexuality* 1, no. 4 (1976): 427–34.

Gramick, Jeannine, and Pat Furey, eds. *The Vatican and Homosexuality: Reactions to the "Letter to the Bishops of the Catholic Church on the Pastoral Care of Homosexual Persons."* New York: Crossroad, 1988.

Grant, George, ed. *Gays in the Military: The Moral and Strategic Crisis.* Franklin, Tenn.: Legacy Communications, 1993.

Grant, George, and Mark A. Horne. *Legislating Immorality: The Homosexual Movement Comes Out of the Closet.* Chicago: Moody Press, 1993.

———. *Unnatural Affections: The Impuritan Ethic of Homosexuality in the Church.* Franklin, Tenn.: Legacy Communications, 1991.

Greenblatt, Stephen. "Mutilation and Meaning." In *The Body in Parts: Fantasies of Corporeality in Early Modern Europe,* edited by David Hillman and Carla Mazzio. New York: Routledge, 1997.

Grixti, Joseph. *Terrors of Uncertainty: The Cultural Contexts of Horror Fiction.* London: Routledge, 1989.

———. "Consuming Cannibals: Psychopathic Killers as Archetypes and Cultural Icons." *Journal of American Culture* 18, no. 1 (spring 1995): 87–96.

Gross, Louis S. *Redefining the American Gothic: From Wieland to Day of the Dead.* Ann Arbor, Mich.: UMI Research Press, 1989.

Grunenberg, Christoph. "Unsolved Mysteries: Gothic Tales from *Frankenstein* to the Hair Eating Doll." In *Gothic: Transmutations of Horror in Late Twentieth Century Art,* edited by Christoph Grunenberg, 213–158 [*sic;* pagination reversed]. Cambridge, Mass.: MIT Press, 1997.

Hacker, Helen Mayer. "The New Burdens of Masculinity." *Marriage and Family Living* 19 (1957): 227–33.

Hadley, Elaine. *Melodramatic Tactics: Theatricalized Dissent in the English Marketplace, 1800–1885.* Stanford, Calif.: Stanford University Press, 1995.

Halberstam, Judith. *Skin Shows: Gothic Horror and the Technology of Monsters.* Durham, N.C.: Duke University Press, 1995.

Halttunen, Karen. *Murder Most Foul: The Killer and the American Gothic Imagination.* Cambridge, Mass.: Harvard University Press, 1998.

Hanson, Ellis. *Decadence and Catholicism.* Cambridge, Mass.: Harvard University Press, 1997.

Haraway, Donna J. "The Promises of Monsters: A Regenerative Politics for Inappropriate/d Others." In *Cultural Studies,* edited and with an introduction by Lawrence Grossberg, Cary Nelson, and Paula A. Treichler, 295–337. New York: Routledge, 1992.

Haynal, André, Miklós Molnár, and Gérard de Puymège. *Fanaticism: A Historical and*

Psychoanalytical Study. Translated by Linda Butler Koseoglu. New York: Schocken Books, 1983.

Head, Thomas. *Hagiography and the Cult of Saints: The Diocese of Orléans, 800–1200.* Cambridge, U.K.: Cambridge University Press, 1990.

Heller, Terry. *The Delights of Terror: An Aesthetics of the Tale of Terror.* Urbana: University of Illinois Press, 1987.

Herman, Didi. *The Anti-Gay Agenda: Orthodox Vision and the Christian Right.* Chicago: University of Chicago Press, 1997.

Hinton, Laura. *The Perverse Gaze of Sympathy: Sadomasochistic Sentiments from Clarissa to Rescue 911.* Albany: State University of New York Press, 1999.

Hobbes, Thomas. *Leviathan; or, The Matter, Forme and Power of a Commonwealth, Ecclesiasticall and Civil.* Edited and with an introduction by Michael Oakeshott. Oxford: Basil Blackwell, 1946.

Hofstadter, Richard. "The Paranoid Style in American Politics." In *The Paranoid Style and Other Essays.* New York: Knopf, 1965.

Hofstadter, Richard, and Michael Wallace, eds. *American Violence: A Documentary History.* New York: Alfred A. Knopf, 1970.

Hoover, J. Edgar. *Masters of Deceit: The Story of Communism in America and How to Fight It.* New York: Henry Holt, 1958.

Hostile Climate: Report on Anti-Gay Activity. Washington, D.C.: People for the American Way Foundation, 1999.

Huet, Marie-Hélène. *Monstrous Imagination.* Cambridge, Mass.: Harvard University Press, 1993.

Hunt, Lynn Avery, ed. *The Invention of Pornography: Obscenity and the Origins of Modernity, 1500–1800.* New York: Zone Books, 1993.

Hurley, Kelly. *The Gothic Body: Sexuality, Materialism, and Degeneration at the Fin de Siècle.* Cambridge, U.K.: Cambridge University Press, 1996.

Indiana, Gary. *Three Month Fever: The Andrew Cunanan Story.* New York: HarperCollins, 1999.

Ingebretsen, Edward J. *Maps of Heaven, Maps of Hell: Religious Terror as Memory from the Puritans to Stephen King.* Armonk, N.Y.: M. E. Sharpe, 1996.

———. "Staking the Monster: A Politics of Remonstrance." *Religion and American Culture* 8, no. 1 (January 1998): 91–116.

Jackson, Rosemary. *Fantasy: The Literature of Subversion.* London: Methuen, 1981.

James, William. *The Varieties of Religious Experience: A Study in Human Nature.* Edited by Martin E. Marty. New York: Penguin, 1982.

Jameson, Fredric. *The Political Unconscious: Narrative as a Socially Symbolic Act.* Ithaca: Cornell University Press, 1981.

Jamieson, Kathleen Hall. *Dirty Politics: Deception, Distraction, and Democracy.* New York: Oxford University Press, 1992.

Jeffords, Susan. *Hard Bodies: Hollywood Masculinity in the Reagan Era.* New Brunswick, N.J.: Rutgers University Press, 1994.

Jenkins, Philip. *Using Murder: The Social Construction of Serial Homicide.* New York: Aldine de Gruyter, 1994.

Jones, F. L., ed. *The Letters of Mary Shelley.* Norman: University of Illinois, 1946.

Jonsen, Albert R., and Stephen Toulmin. *The Abuse of Casuistry: A History of Moral Reasoning.* Berkeley: University Of California Press, 1988.

Jordan, Mark D. *The Invention of Sodomy in Christian Theology.* Chicago: University of Chicago Press, 1997.

———. *The Silence of Sodom: Homosexuality in Modern Catholicism.* Chicago: University of Chicago Press, 2000.

Kappeler, Suzanne. *The Pornography of Representation.* Cambridge, U.K.: Polity Press, 1986.

Karlsen, Carol F. *The Devil in the Shape of a Woman: Witchcraft in Colonial New England.* New York: Vintage Books, 1989.

Kelleher, Michael D., and C. L. Kelleher. *Murder Most Rare: The Female Serial Killer.* Westport, Conn.: Praeger, 1998.

Kendrick, Walter. *The Thrill of Fear: 250 Years of Scary Entertainment.* New York: Grove Press, 1991.

Kennedy, David M. "Culture Wars: The Sources and Uses of Enmity in American History." In *Enemy Images in American History,* edited by Ragnhild Fiebig-von Hase and Ursula Lehmkuhl, 339–56. Providence, R.I.: Berghahn Books, 1997.

Keppel, Robert D., with William J. Birnes. *Signature Killers.* New York: Pocket Books, 1997.

Kerekes, David, and David Slater. *Killing for Culture: An Illustrated History of Death Film from Mondo to Snuff.* London: Creation Books, 1993.

Kilgour, Maggie. *The Rise of the Gothic Novel.* New York: Routledge, 1995.

Kincaid, James R. *Child-loving: The Erotic Child and Victorian Culture.* New York: Routledge, 1992.

King, Stephen. *Carrie.* Garden City, N.Y.: Doubleday, 1974.

———. *Danse Macabre.* New York: Everest House, 1981.

Kipnis, Laura. *Bound and Gagged: Pornography and the Politics of Fantasy in America.* New York: Grove Press, 1996.

Kirk, Marshall, and Hunter Madsen. *After the Ball: How America Will Conquer Its Fear and Hatred of Gays in the '90s.* New York: Plume, 1989.

Koontz, Dean. *The Door to December.* New York: Signet, 1994.

Kristeva, Julia. *Powers of Horror: An Essay on Abjection.* Translated by Leon S. Roudiez. New York: Columbia University Press, 1982.

Kurtz, Howard. *Media Circus: The Trouble with America's Newspapers.* New York: Dover, 1973.

Kushner, Tony. *Angels in America;* part 1, *Millennium Approaches;* part 2, *Perestroika.* New York: Theatre Communications Group, 1993, 1994.

Lakoff, George, and Mark Johnson. *Metaphors We Live By.* Chicago: University of Chicago Press, 1980.

Laqueur, Thomas. *Making Sex: Body and Gender from the Greeks to Freud.* Cambridge, Mass.: Harvard University Press, 1990.

Lesser, Wendy. *Pictures at an Execution: An Inquiry into the Subject of Murder.* Cambridge, Mass.: Harvard University Press, 1993.

Levin, Jack, and J. A. Fox. *Mass Murder: America's Growing Menace.* New York: Plenum Press, 1985.

Lifton, Robert Jay. "Home from the War: The Psychology of Survival." In *The Vietnam Reader,* edited by Walter Capps. New York: Routledge, 1991.

Lull, James, and Stephen Hinerman. "The Search for Scandal." In *Media Scandals: Morality and Desire in the Popular Culture Marketplace,* edited by James Lull and Stephen Hinerman. New York: Columbia University Press, 1997.

McCracken, David. *The Scandal of the Gospels: Jesus, Story, and Offense.* New York: Oxford University Press, 1994.

McDonagh, Josephine. "Do or Die: Problems of Agency and Gender in the Aesthetics of Murder." In *New Feminist Discourses: Critical Essays on Theories and Texts,* edited by Isobel Armstrong, 222–37. London: Routledge, 1992.

McGrath, Patrick. "Transgression and Decay." In *Gothic: Transmutations of Horror in Late Twentieth-Century Art,* edited by Christoph Grunenberg, 155–151 [*sic;* pagination reversed]. Cambridge, Mass.: MIT Press, 1997.

McNeil, John. *The Church and the Homosexual,* 4th rev. ed. Boston: Beacon, 1993.

Madriz, Esther I. "Images of Criminals and Victims: A Study on Women's Fear and Social Control." *Gender and Society* 11, no. 3 (June 1997): 342–56.

Maltby, Richard. "Made for Each Other: The Melodrama of Hollywood and the House Committee on Un-American Activities, 1947." In *Cinema, Politics and Society in America,* edited by Philip Davies and Brian Neve. New York: St. Martin's Press, 1981.

Martin, Jay. "Force Fields: Abjection Overruled." *Salmagundi* 103 (summer 1994): 234+.

Martin, Robert K., and Eric Savoy, eds. *American Gothic: New Interventions in a National Narrative.* Iowa City: University of Iowa Press, 1998.

Marx, Karl, and Frederick Engels. *The Communist Manifesto: A Modern Edition.* With an introduction by Eric Hobsbawm. London: Verso, 1998.

Masse, Michelle A. *In the Name of Love: Women, Masochism, and the Gothic.* Ithaca: Cornell University Press, 1992.

Massumi, Brian. "Everywhere You Want to Be." In *The Politics of Everyday Fear,* edited by Brian Massumi, 3–37. Minneapolis: University of Minnesota Press, 1993.

Masters, Brian. "Dahmer's Inferno." *Vanity Fair* (November 1991): 183–269.

Masters, Brian. *Killing for Company: The Story of a Man Addicted to Murder.* New York: Random House, 1993.

Masters, Brian. *The Shrine of Jeffrey Dahmer.* London: Coronet Books, 1993.

Mather, Cotton. *Wonders of the Invisible World.* Boston: J. R. Smith, 1862.

Meier, John P. *A Marginal Jew: Rethinking the Historical Jesus,* vol. 1, *The Roots of the Problem and the Person.* New York: Doubleday, 1991.

Michaud, Stephen G., and Hugh Aynesworth. *The Only Living Witness.* New York: New American Library, 1983.

Michelson, Peter. *Speaking the Unspeakable: A Poetics of Obscenity.* Albany: State University of New York Press, 1993.

Miller, Perry. *The American Puritans: Their Prose and Poetry.* New York: Doubleday, 1956.

Mohr, Richard. *Gay Ideas: Outing and Other Controversies.* Boston: Beacon Press, 1992.

Moore, R. I. *The Formation of a Persecuting Society: Power and Deviance in Western Europe, 950–1250.* Oxford: Blackwell, 1987.

Moretti, Franco. "Dialectic of Fear." *Signs Taken for Wonders: Essays in the Sociology of Literary Forms.* Translated by Susan Fischer, David Forgacs, and David Miller. London: Verso, 1988.

Messadié, Gerald. *A History of the Devil.* Translated by Marc Romano. New York: Kodansha International, 1996.

Mulvey, Laura. "Visual Pleasure and Narrative Cinema." *Screen* 16, no. 3 (autumn 1975): 6–18.

Murdoch, Iris. *A Severed Head.* New York: Avon Books, 1961.

Musselwhite, David E. *Partings Welded Together: Politics and Desire in the Nineteenth-Century English Novel.* London: Methuen, 1987.

Napier, Elizabeth. *The Failure of Gothic: Problems of Disjunction in an Eighteenth-Century Literary Form.* New York: Oxford University Press, 1987.

Nead, Lynda. "Getting Down to Basics: Art, Obscenity, and the Female Nude." In *New Feminist Discourses: Critical Essays on Theories and Texts,* edited by Isobel Armstrong, 199–221. London: Routledge, 1992.

Neuhaus, John Richard. "Love, No Matter What." *First Things,* no. 76 (October 1997): 81–82.

Nietzsche, Friedrich. *Thus Spake Zarathustra.* Translated by Thomas Common. New York: Boni and Liveright, 1917.

Nixon, Nicola. "Making Monsters, or Serializing Killers." In *American Gothic: New Interventions in a National Narrative,* edited by Robert K. Martin and Eric Savoy, 217–36. Iowa City: University of Iowa Press, 1998.

Noble, Marianne. "An Ecstasy of Apprehension: The Gothic Pleasures of Sentimental Fiction." In Martin and Savoy, *American Gothic,* 163–82.

Noel, Mary. *Villains Galore: The Hey-day of the Popular Story Weekly.* New York: Macmillan, 1954.

Norris, Joel. *Jeffrey Dahmer*. New York: Pinnacle Books, 1992.

———. *Serial Killers: The Growing Menace*. New York: Doubleday Dolphin, 1988.

O'Brien, Geoffrey. *Hardboiled America: The Lurid Years of Paperbacks*. New York: Van Nostrand Reinhold, 1981.

Olorenshaw, Robert. "Narrating the Monster: From Mary Shelley to Bram Stoker." In *Frankenstein, Creation, and Monstrosity,* edited by Stephen Bann. London: Reaktion Books, 1994.

Olsen, Jack. *The Misbegotten Son: The True Story of Arthur J. Shawcross*. New York: Dell, 1993.

Oppenheimer, Paul. *Evil and the Demonic: A New Theory of Monstrous Behavior*. New York: New York University Press, 1996.

Orsi, Robert A. "'Mildred, Is It Fun to Be a Cripple?': The Culture of Suffering in Mid-Twentieth-Century American Catholicism." In *Catholic Lives, Contemporary America,* edited by Thomas J. Ferraro, 19–64. Durham, N.C.: Duke University Press, 1997.

Packard, Vance. *The Hidden Persuaders*. New York: David McKay, 1957.

Park, Katharine. "Kimberly Bergalis, AIDS, and the Plague Metaphor." In *Media Spectacles,* edited by Marjorie Garber, Jann Matlock, and Rebecca L. Walkowitz, 232–44. Routledge: New York, 1993.

Perkins, Judith. *The Suffering Self: Pain and Narrative Representation in the Early Christian Era*. New York: Routledge, 1995.

Perkins, Michael. *The Secret Record: Modern Erotic Literature*. New York: William Morrow and Sons, 1976.

Peters, Edward. *Torture*. New York: Basil Blackwell, 1985.

Pinedo, Isabel. *Recreational Terror: Women and the Pleasures of Horror Film Viewing*. Albany: State University of New York Press, 1997.

Poster, Mark, ed. *Politics, Theory, and Contemporary Culture*. New York: Columbia University Press, 1993.

Postman, Neil. *Amusing Ourselves to Death: Public Discourse in the Age of Show Business*. New York: Penguin, 1986.

Prawer, S. S. *Caligari's Children: The Film as Tale of Terror*. Oxford: Oxford University Press, 1980.

Prejean, Sr. Helen. *Dead Man Walking: An Eyewitness Account of the Death Penalty in the United States*. New York: Vintage Books, 1993.

Pronk, Pim. *Against Nature?: Types of Moral Argumentation Regarding Homosexuality*. Translated by John Vriend. Grand Rapids, Mich.: William B. Eerdmans, 1993.

Pryor, Douglas W. *Unspeakable Acts: Why Men Sexually Abuse Children*. New York: New York University Press, 1996.

Punter, David. *The Literature of Terror: A History of Gothic Fictions from 1765 to the Present Day*. London: Longmans, 1980.

———. "Problems of Recollection and Construction: Stephen King." In *Modern Gothic: A Reader,* edited by Victor Sage and Allan Lloyd Smith, 121–40. Manchester, U.K.: Manchester University Press, 1996.

Quétel, Claude. *History of Syphilis.* Translated by Judith Braddock and Brian Pike. Baltimore: Johns Hopkins University Press, 1990.

Radway, Janice. "Phenomenology, Linguistics, and Popular Literature." *Journal of Popular Culture* 12 (1978): 88–98.

Ratzinger, Cardinal Joseph. "Letter to the Bishops of the Catholic Church on the Pastoral Care of Homosexual Persons" (1986); "Homosexualitatis problema" (Acta Apostolicase Sedis 79 [1987]: 543–54).

Remnick, David. "The Devil Problem." *New Yorker* (3 April 1995).

Ressler, Robert K., and Tom Shachtman. *I Have Lived in the Monster: A Report from the Abyss.* New York: St. Martin's Press, 1977.

———. *Whoever Fights Monsters.* New York: St. Martin's Paperbacks, 1992.

Robin, Corey. "Why Do Opposites Attract?: Fear and Freedom in the Modern Political Imagination." In *Fear Itself: Enemies Real and Imagined in American Culture,* edited by Nancy Lusignan Schultz. West Lafayette, Ind.: Purdue University Press, 1999.

Robinson, John A. T. *The Body: A Study in Pauline Theology.* London: SCM Press, 1952.

Rockett, Will H. *Devouring Whirlwind: Terror and Transcendence in the Cinema of Cruelty.* New York: Greenwood Press, 1988.

Roelofs, Mark H. "Hobbes, Liberalism, and America." In *Liberalism and the Modern Polity: Essays in Contemporary Political Theory,* edited by Michael J. Gargas McGrath, 119–42. New York: Marcel Dekker, 1978.

Rose, H. J. *Religion in Greece and Rome.* New York: Harper and Row, 1959.

Ross, Andrew. *No Respect: Intellectuals and Popular Culture.* New York: Routledge, 1989.

Ruben, Matthew. "Of Newts and Quayles: National-Political Masculinity in the Current Conjuncture." In *Boys: Masculinities in Contemporary Culture,* edited by Paul Smith, 255–91. New York: Westview Press, 1996.

Rubin, Gayle. "Sexual Politics, the New Right, and the Sexual Fringe." In *The Age Taboo: Gay Male Sexuality, Power, and Consent,* edited by Daniel Tsang, 108–15. Boston: Alyson Publications, 1981.

Rule, Ann. *The Stranger Beside Me.* New York: New American Library, 1981.

Rule, Ann [Andy Stack, pseud.]. *Lust Killer.* New York: Signet, 1983.

Russell, Jeffrey Burton. *The Devil: Perceptions of Evil From Antiquity to Primitive Christianity.* Ithaca: Cornell University Press, 1977.

Russo, Vito. *The Celluloid Closet: Homosexuality in the Movies.* New York: Harper and Row, 1981.

Sage, Victor. *Horror Fiction in the Protestant Tradition.* London: Macmillan, 1988.

———, ed. *The Gothick Novel: A Casebook.* Basingstoke: Macmillan, 1990.

Sage, Victor, and Allan Lloyd Smith, eds. *Modern Gothic: A Reader*. Manchester, U.K.: Manchester University Press, 1996.

Sanders, Clinton R., and Jeff Ferrell, eds. *Cultural Criminology*. Boston: Northeastern University Press, 1995.

Scarry, Elaine. *The Body in Pain: The Making and Unmaking of the World*. New York: Oxford University Press, 1985.

———. "Donne: 'But Yet the Body Is His Booke.'" In *Literature and the Body*, edited by Elaine Scarry. Baltimore: John Hopkins University Press, 1988.

Schlesinger, Arthur M., Jr. *The Vital Center: The Politics of Freedom*. 1949; reprint, New York: DaCapo Press, 1988.

Shklar, Judith N. "The Liberalism of Fear." In *Liberalism and the Moral Life*, edited by Nancy L. Rosenblum, 21–38. Cambridge, Mass.: Harvard University Press, 1989.

Schoell, William. *Stay Out of the Shower: 25 Years of Shocker Films, Beginning with "Psycho."* New York: Dembner Books, 1985.

Schultz, Nancy Lusignan, ed. *Fear Itself: Enemies Real and Imagined in American Culture*. West Lafayette, Ind.: Purdue University Press, 1999.

Schwab, Gabriele. "The Subject of the Politically Unconscious." In *Politics, Theory, and Contemporary Culture*, edited by Mark Poster, 83–110. New York: Columbia University Press, 1993.

Schwartz, Anne E. *The Man Who Could Not Kill Enough: The Secret Murders of Milwaukee's Jeffrey Dahmer*. Secaucus, N.J.: Carol Publishing Group, 1992.

Schwartz, Regina M. *The Curse of Cain: The Violent Legacy of Monotheism*. Chicago: University of Chicago Press, 1997.

Scruton, David L. "The Anthropology of an Emotion." In *Sociophobics: The Anthropology of Fear*, edited by David L. Scruton, 7–24. Boulder, Col.: Westview Press, 1985.

Sedgwick, Eve Kosofsky. *The Coherence of Gothic Conventions*. Rev. ed. New York: Arno, 1980.

———. *Epistemology of the Closet*. Berkeley: University of California Press, 1990.

———. "Queer and Now." In *Tendencies*, 1–20. Durham, N.C.: Duke University Press, 1993.

Seltzer, Mark. *Serial Killers: Death and Life in America's Wound Culture*. New York: Routledge, 1998.

Shanks, Hershel. *Jerusalem: An Archeological Biography*. New York: Random House, 1995.

Shattuck, Roger. *Forbidden Knowledge: From Prometheus to Pornography*. New York: St. Martin's Press, 1996.

Showalter, Elaine. *Sister's Choice: Tradition and Change in American Women's Writing*. New York: Oxford University Press, 1994.

Siegel, Carol. *Male Masochism: Modern Revisions of the Story of Love*. Bloomington: Indiana University Press, 1995.

Simpson, Mark. *Male Impersonators: Men Performing Masculinity*. London: Cassell, 1994.

Skal, David J. *The Monster Show: A Cultural History of Horror.* New York: W. W. Norton, 1993.

———. *Hollywood Gothic: The Tangled Web of "Dracula" from Novel to Stage to Screen.* New York: W. W. Norton, 1991.

Snitow, Ann Barr. "Mass Market Romance: Pornography for Women Is Different." In *Passion and Power: Sexuality in History,* edited by Kathy Peiss and Christina Simmons, with Robert A. Padgug, 259–76. Philadelphia: Temple University Press, 1989.

Snowman, Daniel, and Malcolm Bradbury. "The Sixties and Seventies." In *Introduction to American Studies,* edited by Malcom Bradbury and Howard Temperley. 3d ed. London: Longman, 1998.

Sonenschein, David. *Pedophiles on Parade,* vol. 1, *The Monster in the Media.* San Antonio, Tex.: D. Sonenschein, 1998.

———. *Pedophiles on Parade,* vol. 2, *The Popular Imagery of Moral Hysteria.* San Antonio, Tex.: D. Sonenschein, 1998.

Sophocles. "Oedipus Tyrannus." In *Oedipus Tyrannus, Sophocles: The Plays and Fragments, with Critical Notes, Commentary, and Translation in English Prose,* edited and translated by Sir Richard C. Jebb. Amsterdam: Servio, 1963.

Stallybrass, Peter, and Allon White. *The Politics and Poetics of Transgression.* London: Methuen, 1986.

Staples, William G. *The Culture of Surveillance: Discipline and Social Control in the United States.* New York: St. Martin's Press, 1997.

Stearn, Jess. *The Sixth Man.* New York: Doubleday, 1961.

———. *The Grapevine: A Report on the Secret World of the Lesbian.* New York: Doubleday, 1964.

Steiner, George. *Language and Silence: Essays on Language, Literature, and the Inhuman.* New York: Atheneum, 1967.

Steinberg, Leo. *The Sexuality of Christ in Renaissance Art and in Modern Oblivion.* New York: Pantheon Books, 1983.

Stemmeler, Michael L., and J. Michael Clark, eds. *Homophobia and the Judaeo-Christian Tradition.* Dallas: Monument Press, 1990.

Stewart, Susan. *Crimes of Writing: Problems in the Containment of Representation.* Durham, N.C.: Duke University Press, 1994.

———. *On Longing: Narratives of the Miniature, the Gigantic, the Souvenir, the Collection.* Baltimore: Johns Hopkins University Press, 1984.

Stickney, Brandon M. *"All-American Monster": The Unauthorized Biography of Timothy McVeigh.* Amherst, N.Y.: Prometheus, 1996.

Strauss, William, and Neil Howe. *Generations: The History of America's Future, 1584 to 2069.* New York: Morrow, 1991.

Tatar, Maria. *The Hard Facts of the Grimms' Fairy Tales.* Princeton: Princeton University Press, 1987.

Thompson, John B. "Scandal and Social Theory." In *Media Scandals: Morality and Desire in the Popular Culture Marketplace,* edited by James Lull and Stephen Hinerman. New York: Columbia University Press, 1997.

Thomson, Rosemarie Garland, ed. *Freakery: Cultural Spectacles of the Extraordinary Body.* New York: New York University Press, 1996.

Tithecott, Richard. *Of Men and Monsters: Jeffrey Dahmer and the Construction of the Serial Killer.* Madison: University of Wisconsin Press, 1997.

Tocqueville, Alexis de. *Democracy in America.* Translated by George Lawrence, edited by J. P. Mayer. New York: Harper and Row, 1969.

Todd, Dennis. *Imagining Monsters: Miscreations of the Self in Eighteenth-Century England.* Chicago: University of Chicago Press, 1995.

Toobin, Jeffrey. *A Vast Conspiracy: The Real Story of the Sex Scandal that Nearly Brought Down a President.* New York: Random House, 1999.

Tripp, C. A. *The Homosexual Matrix.* New York: McGraw-Hill, 1975.

Tropp, Martin. *Images of Fear: How Horror Stories Helped Shape Modern Culture (1818–1918).* Jefferson, N.C.: McFarland and Co., 1990.

Tuan, Yi-fu. *Landscapes of Fear.* New York: Pantheon Books, 1979.

Tucher, Andie. *Froth and Scum: Truth, Beauty, Goodness, and the Ax Murder in America's First Mass Medium.* Chapel Hill: University of North Carolina Press, 1994.

Tudor, Andrew. *Monsters and Mad Scientists: A Cultural History of the Horror Movie.* Cambridge, Mass.: Blackwell, 1989.

Twitchell, James. *Preposterous Violence: Fables of Aggression in Modern Culture.* New York: Oxford University Press, 1989.

Uebel, Michael. "Unthinking the Monster: Twelfth-Century Responses to Saracen Alterity." In *Monster Theory: Reading Culture,* edited by Jeffrey Jerome Cohen, 265–91. Minneapolis: University of Minnesota Press, 1996.

Updike, John. "Hawthorne's Creed." In *Hugging the Shore: Essays and Criticism,* 76–77. New York: Alfred Knopf, 1983.

Vaid, Urvashi. *Virtual Equality: The Mainstreaming of Gay and Lesbian Liberation.* New York: Anchor Books, 1995.

Veeder, William. "The Nurture of the Gothic, or How Can a Text Be Both Popular and Subversive?" In *American Gothic,* edited by Robert K. Martin and Eric Savoy, 20–39. Iowa City: University of Iowa Press, 1998.

Waller, Gregory, ed. *American Horrors: Essays on the Modern American Horror Film.* Urbana: University of Illinois Press, 1987.

Walsh, S.J., J. P. M. *The Mighty from Their Thrones: Power in the Biblical Tradition.* Philadelphia: Fortress Press, 1987.

Watney, Simon. *Policing Desire: Pornography, AIDS, and the Media.* Minneapolis: University of Minnesota Press, 1987.

Wells, Paul. "The Invisible Man: Shrinking Masculinity in the 1950s Science Fiction B-

Movie." In *You Tarzan: Masculinity, Movies, and Men,* edited by Pat Kirkham and Janet Thumin, 181–99. New York: St. Martin's Press, 1993.

Wertham, Fredric. *Seduction of the Innocent.* New York: Rinehart, 1954.

White, Hayden V. *The Content of the Form: Narrative Discourse and Historical Representation.* Cambridge, U.K.: Oxford University Press, 1987.

Wigglesworth, Michael. "The Day of Doom." In *The American Puritans: Their Prose and Poetry,* edited by Perry Miller. Garden City, N.Y.: Doubleday, 1956.

Williams, Anne. *Art of Darkness: A Poetics of Gothic.* Chicago: University of Chicago Press, 1995.

Williams, David. *Deformed Discourse: The Function of the Monster in Mediaeval Thought and Literature.* Montreal: McGill-Queen's University Press, 1996.

Williams, Linda. *Hard-Core: Power, Pleasure, and the "Frenzy of the Visible."* Berkeley: University of California Press, 1989.

Wills, Garry. *Papal Sin: Structures of Deceit.* New York: Doubleday, 2000.

Wilson, Colin, and Damon Wilson. *The Killers Among Us,* book 2, *Sex, Madness, and Mass Murder.* New York: Warner Books, 1997.

Wilson, Dudley. *Signs and Portents: Monstrous Births from the Middle Ages to the Enlightenment.* New York: Routledge, 1993.

Winter, Kari J. *Subjects of Slavery, Agents of Change: Women and Power in Gothic Novels and Slave Narratives, 1790–1865.* Athens: University of Georgia Press, 1992.

Woods, Paul Anthony. *Ed Gein—Psycho!* New York: St. Martin's Press, 1995.

Wyatt, Justin. "The Stigma of X: Adult Cinema and the Institution of the MPAA Ratings System." In *Controlling Hollywood: Censorship and Regulation in the Studio Era,* edited by Matthew Bernstein, 238–63. New Brunswick: Rutgers University Press, 1999.

Wyden, Peter, and Barbara. *Growing Up Straight: What Every Thoughtful Parent Should Know about Homosexuality.* New York: Stein and Day, 1968.

Zipes, Jack, ed. *Don't Bet on the Prince: Contemporary Feminist Fairy Tales in North America and England.* Aldershot: Gower, 1986.

Zizek, Slavoj. "Grimaces of the Real, or When the Phallus Appears," *October* 58 (fall 1991): 44–68.

Press Coverage

Acer, Kevin. "Abolish Death Penalty." *USA Today,* 16 June 1997, 18A.

Adams, Noah. "Search for Missing Boys in South Carolina Continues." All Things Considered, National Public Radio, 2 November 1994.

———. "Three Children in America Killed Each Day by a Parent." All Things Considered, National Public Radio, 4 November 1994.

Adams, Noah, and Robert Siegel. "South Carolina Murders Still Stun the Nation." All Things Considered, National Public Radio, 4 November 1994.

Adler, Jerry. "Innocents Lost." Newsweek (14 November 1994): 26–30.

Advertisement. Washington Post Book World (28 April 1996): 2.

Alleva, Richard. "Renovations." Commonweal (29 Jan 1999): 21–22.

Alexander, Michael. "She Broke Our Hearts: Hoaxes Tap Racial Fears; Criminal Stereotypes Play Well." Newsday, 5 November 1994, A4.

Alter, Jonathan. "Clinton's Houdini Act." Newsweek (9 February 1998): 21.

———. "Shaming the Shameless." Newsweek (28 September 1998): 16.

Anderson, Kenneth. "The Remoteness That Betrays Desire." Times Literary Supplement (11 July 1997): 6–7.

Anonymous. "Apocalypse? Not Now." Boston Globe, 20 July 1999, A14.

Anonymous. "Billy Jack Gaither's Life and Death." Editorial. New York Times, 9 March 1989.

Anonymous. "Dip into the Future, Far as Cyborg Eye Can See: and Wince." Economist 346, No. 8049 (3 January 1998): 81–83.

Anonymous. "The End?" Economist 350, no. 8106 (13–19 Feb. 1999): 17–18.

Anonymous. "Excerpts from Starr's Questioning by the President's Personal Lawyer David E. Kendall," New York Times, 20 November 1998, <www.nytimes.com>.

Anonymous. "For Nichols, No Sympathy but Also No Death Penalty." Editorial. USA Today, 24 December 1997, 8A.

Anonymous. "Fugitive 'Gay' Killer Strikes in New Jersey—Police." Reuters news service, 10 May 1997.

Anonymous. "Cops: Gay Slaying Followed Advance." AP news service, 4 March 1999.

Anonymous. GLAADLines (25 August 1997): <www.glaad.org>.

Anonymous. GLAADAlert (1 August 1997): <www.glaad.org>.

Anonymous. "Homophobia Often Found in Schools, Data Show." New York Times, 14 October 1998, A19.

Anonymous. "The Homosexual in America. Time (21 January 1966): 40–41.

Anonymous. "Is It a Surprise Society Produces Monsters?" USA Today, 13 August 1999, 16A.

Anonymous. "Lawyers Seek to Polish McVeigh's Image." Star Tribune, 15 September 1996, 24A.

Anonymous. "The Line Forms Here." CIS Congressional Universe (4 March 1999).

Anonymous. "Matthew Shepard One Year Later." Advocate (12 October 1999).

Anonymous. "McVeigh: From Model Soldier to Bomber." Reuters news service, 13 June 1997.

Anonymous. "The Mind of the Mass Murderer." Time (27 August 1973): 56–57.

Anonymous. "Missing Person." *Atlanta Journal-Constitution,* 9 May 1997, Nation in Brief, C2.

Anonymous. "Mom Wrote on JonBenet Pad." *Newsday,* 2 July 1997, A19.

Anonymous. "Monster of an All-Star Game." *USA Today,* 13 July 1999, A1.

Anonymous. "The Monsters Next Door." *Time* cover (3 May 1999).

Anonymous. "More Talk, Less News." *Atlanta Journal-Constitution,* 7 June 1997, A10.

Anonymous. "Murder Charges Filed in Minnesota Killings." Reuters news service, 7 May 1997.

Anonymous. "Murderers, Bombers Indict Death Sentence." *Minnesota Daily via U-Wire,* 27 January 1998, staff editorial.

Anonymous. "O. J. Simpson and Timothy McVeigh: White America's Monster and Patriot." *New York Amsterdam News,* 17 May 1997, 10.

Anonymous. "The Other Scary Hit of the Summer Was The Many Faces of Andrew Cunanan." *Progressive* 61, no. 9 (September 1997): 41+.

Anonymous. "A Spree Killer Is on the Loose in the USA." *USA Today,* 13 May 1997, 3A.

Anonymous. "The Starr Report." *St. Louis Dispatch,* 16 September 1998, B7.

Anonymous. "Totem Doll Advertisement." *Wired* (December 1998): 154.

Anonymous. "We're Having a Heyday with Horror." *Minneapolis Star Tribune,* 30 October 1997, 16A.

Anonymous. "William Esposito Deputy FBI Director Webwire—Holds News Briefing on the Death of Andrew Cunanan." *Washington Transcript Service,* 24 July 1997.

Applebome, Peter. "What Murder Says about the Society It Exists In." *New York Times,* 29 May 1999, B9.

Associated Press. "Crime Drops in '97; Murders Are at 30-Year Low." *New York Times,* 23 November 1998, <www.nytimes.com>.

Associated Press. "Dangerous Hunt: Wide-Ranging Serial-Killer Suspect Sought." *Newsday,* 11 May 1997, A19.

Barfield, Deborah, and Elaine S. Povich. "Tangled in Tape: Committee to Decide Today If Evidence Goes to Public." *Newsday,* 17 September 1998, A5.

Bates, Eric. "What You Need to Know about Jesse Helms." *Mother Jones* (15 May 1995): 56+.

Baxter, Kevin. "Kids' Books; Tales Embrace the Fun, Fright of Halloween." *Los Angeles Times,* 31 October 1999, 3.

Bennett, William. *Washington Post,* 26 October 1995, C8.

Bernstein, Amy. "Reinvention, the American Way." *U.S. News & World Report* (4 August 1997): 7.

Bernstein, Robert A. "A 'Monster' Only Imagined, Not Real." *Chicago Tribune,* 27 October 1988, sec. 1, 23.

Bertelson, Christine. "Readers Reply to Child Molester." *St. Louis Dispatch,* 31 October 1995, 1B.

Birkett, Dea. "Monsters with Human Faces." *The Guardian,* 27 September 1997, Weekend Page, TT22.

Blake, David. "Dead Man Walking." *Advocate* (13 April 1999): 77.

Boling, Jack T. "Animal Cruelty: Expose Monsters Behind Heinous Acts." Letter to the editor. *Atlanta Journal-Constitution,* 22 Nov 1999, A10.

Booth, Cathy, Kevin Fedarko, and Julie Grace. "Crime: Death at Every Stop; one man, still at large, may be the connection between brutal killings in three different states." *Time* (19 May 1997): 40.

Booth, William. "How Larry Flynt Changed the Picture." *Washington Post,* 11 January 1999, C1.

Bordo, Susan. "True Obsessions: Being Unfaithful to 'Lolita.'" *Chronicle of Higher Education,* 24 July 1998, B7–8.

Boyd, Blanch McCrary. "Who Killed Susan Smith?" *Oxford American.* (August/September 1996): 34–42.

Bragg, Rick. "Focus on Susan Smith's Lies and a Smile." *New York Times,* 25 July 1995, A11.

———. "Sheriff Says Prayer and a Lie Led Susan Smith to Confess." *New York Times,* 18 July 1995, A1, 10.

———. "Susan Smith Verdict Brings Relief to Town." *New York Times,* 30 July 1995, A16.

———. "Union, S.C., Is Left a Town Torn Asunder." *New York Times,* 24 July 1995, A8.

Brinkley, Alan. "A Swaggering Tradition." *Newsweek* (4 March 1996): 28–29.

Broder, John M. "Attack by the President's Lawyer at Length Ruffles a Cool Witness." *New York Times,* 20 November 1998, <www.nytimes.com>.

Brustein, Robert. "McNally on the Cross." Review of "Corpus Christi," by Terrence McNally. *New Republic* (30 November 1998): 34–35.

Buchanan, Patrick. "Free at Last." Letter to the editor. *Wall Street Journal,* 5 November 1999, A19.

Buckley, William F. "Identify All the Carriers." *New York Times,* 18 March 1986, A27.

Bull, Chris. "Into the Shadows: A Detective's Search for a Serial Killer." *Washington Post Magazine* (29 June 1997): 6–11.

Burritt, Chris. "Around the South: The Susan Smith Trial." *Atlanta Journal-Constitution,* 11 July 1995, C8.

———. "'Pain Is Great' as Tots Buried." *Atlanta Journal-Constitution,* 7 November 1994, A1.

Campbell, Kristina. "Dozens Turn Out to Protest the *Blade* at Fairfax Library." *Washington Blade* (23 April 1993): 6.

Carvajal, Doreen. "Better, but Still Not Up to Par." *New York Times,* 9 November 1998, C1.

Chang, Juju, Mark Mullen, and Asha Blake. "Andrew Cunanan Found Dead on House-boat." *ABC World News This Morning* (24 July 1997).

Chin, Paula. "Sins of the Son." *People* (28 March 1994): 38–41.

Chase, Sylvia, Diane Sawyer, and Sam Donaldson. "The Trial of Darlie Routier." *ABC PrimeTime Live* (23 July 1997).

Chibbaro, Lou, Jr. "Emotional Hearing in Fairfax over the *Blade.*" *Washington Blade* (19 March 1993): 6.

Chin, Paula, and Civia Tamarkin. "Up Front: The Door of Evil." *People* (12 August 1991): 32–37.

Connors, Cathy. "Dahmer the Cannibal Is Killed." *New York Amsterdam News,* 3 December 1994, 50.

Corry, John. "Decadence Chic." *American Spectator* (1 September 1997): 46–47.

Cover (O. J. Simpson photo). *Time* (27 June 1994).

Cox, Meki. "Those 'Pocket Monsters' Spawn a Mini Crime Wave." *Los Angeles Times,* 12 December 1999, Record edition, 54.

Crain, Caleb, "Something Wicked This Way Comes." *New York Times Book Review* (6 December 1998): 16.

Christman, Ed. "Spec's Closes 'Clean-up' Year." *Billboard* (9 November 1996): 56.

Chua-Eoan, Howard. "Dead Men Tell No Tales; America's most-wanted man, seen everywhere, ended his life in a houseboat a couple of miles from his last crime scene. Andrew Cunanan's life may be over, but the questions remain." *Time* (4 August 1997): 30–32.

———. "The Uses of Monsters." *Time* (19 August 1991): 66.

Clemetson, Lynette, and Pat Wingert. "Clinton on the Couch." *Newsweek* (28 September 1998): 15.

Cohen, Richard. "An Anti-Gay Party." *Washington Post,* 17 August 1999, A15.

Corn, David. "Clinton Saga Is Lose-Lose Choice for U.S." *Newsday,* 23 January 1998, A43.

Crowley, Harry. " 'Homicidal Homosexual': The Media Left Their Mark; Cunanan Will Be Remembered Foremost as a Gay Killer." *Advocate* (2 September 1997): 24–31.

Dallek, Robert. "Pat Buchanan's Revisionist Fantasy." *Washington Post,* 19 October 1999, Final edition, A19.

Daly, Christopher B. "Ex-Priest Gets 18–20 Years for Sexual Abuse of Youths." *The Washington Post,* 7 December 1993, A1, 7.

Davies, Hugh. "Killer's Last Stand on Indian Creek: Versace Murderer Turns Gun on Himself as His Luck Finally Runs Out." *Daily Telegraph,* 25 July 1997, 18.

Davis, Ivor. "Out of Exile?" *Los Angeles Times Magazine* (January 1995): 90–91.

Davis, Robert. "In S.C., Little Time for Healing." *USA Today,* 12 December 1994, A3.

Dervall, Cheryl, Linda Wertheimer, and Robert Siegel. "Cunanan's Body Found." All Things Considered, National Public Radio, 24 July 1997.

Desowitz, Bill. "Movies: They've Re-created a monster (or Two)." *Los Angeles Times,* 14 November, 1999, 28.

Dickinson, Joy. "Service Memorializes Slain Gay Student," *Dallas Morning News,* 19 October 1998, 15A.

Dorfman, Ariel. "Let Pinochet Back Only on His Deathbed; Chile: He's a monster who should face a reckoning before the families of those who were his victims." *Los Angeles Times,* 28 November 1999, Opinion section, Home edition, 5.

Dreyfuss, Robert. "The Holy War on Gays." *Rolling Stone* (18 March 1999): 38–41.

Driscoll, Amy. "Sources: Cunanan didn't have HIV." *Miami Herald,* 31 July 1997, 1D.

Editorial. *Atlanta Journal-Constitution,* 5 August 1991, A13.

Editorial. "Killer Mom." *Washington Post,* 2 July 1999, A26.

Edsall, Thomas B. "Reform Party Convention Is Split." *Washington Post,* 11 August 2000, 6.

Edwards, Bob. "Thoughts on Playing the 'Race Card.'" National Public Radio, Morning edition, 4 October 1995.

Eftimiades, Maria. "The Quiet Man." *People* (6 December 1993): 65–72.

Engen, John R. "Questions at Start of Fatal Trail." *Newsday,* 14 May 1997, A4.

English, Bella. "Mothers Wonder: How?" *Boston Globe,* 5 November 1994, 1.

Farrel, Nicholas. "The All-American Conspiracy." *Spectator* (21 June 1997): 16–18.

Farrell, Michael. "Forgo [*sic*] the Monster Test for True Justice. *Los Angeles Times,* 15 January 1998, Column Left, Home edition, B9.

Farrell, Walter C., Jr., and James H. Johnson. "Back to the Future: The Death (Execution) of Jeffrey Dahmer." *New York Voice, Inc.,* 4 January 1995, 15.

Farhi, Paul. "The Monster Hit That Haunts Halloween." *Washington Post,* 30 October 1999, C1.

Fauteux, Kevin. "Fear and Trembling at the Movies." *Pastoral Psychology* 36, no. 2 (1987): 84–87.

Fields-Meyer, Thomas. "Up Front: Odyssey of Violence. All His Adult Life, Richard Davis Was a One-Man Crime Wave. Why Was He Free to Kill Polly Klaas?" *People* (13 May 1996): 44–49.

Fineman, Howard. "The Counterattack." *Newsweek* (9 February 1998): 22–32.

———. "Extreme Measures." *Newsweek* (4 March 1996): 20–24.

Fournier, Ron. "Buchanan Announces White House Bid." AP Headlines, 2 March 2000.

Fowler, Joanne. "One Good Man," *People* (11 August 1997): 54–57.

Fox, Kara. "Reform Party: Pat Buchanan." *Washington Blade* (20 October 2000): 25.

Frazier, Rodney R. "Oklahoma City Bombers Don't Deserve to Live." Letter to the editor. *USA Today,* 30 December 1997, A12.

Fotheringham, Alan. "Children of a Monster Society." *Maclean's* (13 December 1993): 64.

Freeman, Diane. "JonBenet Ramsey's Parents Deny Role in Her Murder." Reuters news service, 1 May 1997.

Fulford, Benjamin. "Monster Mash." *Forbes* (26 July 1999): 54–55.

Gaiter, Leonce. "American Mantra: Blame the Black Man." *New York Times,* 12 November 1994, A21.

Gaumer, Tom. "Prosecutor Adding to People's Contempt." Letter to the editor, *Denver Rocky Mountain News,* 7 March 1998, 59A.

Gibbs, Nancy. "Death and Deceit." *Time* (14 November 1994): 42–48.

———. "We, the Jury." *Time* (21 September 1998): 27–33.

Gibbs, Nancy, and Timothy Roche. "The Columbine Tapes." *Time* (20 December 1999): 40–51.

Gillespie, Nick. "Fuhrer Furor." *Reason Magazine* 31, no. 2 (June 1999): 5–6.

Gold, Sylviane. "One Place Sex Is Seldom Taken Seriously." *New York Times,* 27 June 1999, sec. 2, p. 5.

Grant, Lorrie. "Smith Jury to Hear Testimony in Penalty Phase of Trial." Reuters news service, 23 July 1995.

Green, Jesse. "Gays and Monsters." *New York Times Magazine* (13 June 1999): 13–14.

Hamill, Pete. "Jeffrey Dahmer Is Dead and We Feel Fine . . . Don't We?" *Newsday,* 30 November 1994, A33.

Hamilton, Arnold, and G. Robert Hillman. "Friend Recalls Difference in McVeigh after Waco." *Dallas Morning News,* 10 June 1997, 1A.

Hanna, Janan. "Judge Hears 2 Portraits of Hanover Park Killer." *Chicago Tribune,* 17 September 1999, D edition, 1.

Harrell, Ken. "Little Beauty Tortured to Death." *Globe* (21 January 1997): 24–36.

Heba, Gary. "Everyday Nightmares: The Rhetoric of Social Horror in the *Nightmare on Elm Street* Series." *Journal of Popular Film and Television* (1 September 1995): 106–10.

Hendrie, Caroline. "Sex with Students: When Employees Cross the Line." *Education Week* 18, no. 14 (2 December 1998): 1, 12–14.

———. "Abuse by Women Raises Its Own Set of Problems." *Education Week* 18, no. 14 (2 December 1998): 1, 14–15, 17.

Herman, Jan. "Making Monsters Matter; Film: A Brea author reminds us that the director of 'Frankenstein' was first in giving us creatures to care about." *Los Angeles Times,* 1 August 1998, F1.

Hewitt, Bill. "Sorrow and Outrage." *People* (3 May 1999): 94–102.

———. "Stalemate Eleven Weeks and Counting." *People* (24 March 1997): 108–14.

———. "Terms of Hate, Terms of Pity." *People* (13 March 1995): 76–80.

Hickey, Cardinal James. *Washington Catholic Standard* (13 November 1997): 5.

Hoffman, Merle. "Fatal Denial?" *On the Issues* (1 March 1997): 3–5.

Holston, Noel. "Just When You Thought TV Couldn't Squeeze In Another Talk Show." *Star Tribune,* 18 September 1995, 1E

Howlett, Debbie. "The Cunanan Case: Still a Mystery; Suicide leaves many unanswered questions. *USA Today,* 25 July 1997, A10.

Hughes, Candice. "Pope Denounces Gay Pride Parade." AP Online, 7 July 2000.

Hulbert, Ann. "Home Repairs: Parents, Work, and the Durability of the Family." *New Republic* (16 August 1993): 26–32.

Indiana, Gary. "Summer Psychopath." *Village Voice* (25 June 1996): 18.

Innerst, Carol. "The Bewitching of David Brock," *Washington Times,* 27 October 1996, 31.

Ivie, Robert. "Speaking 'Common Sense' about the Soviet Threat: Reagan's Rhetorical Stance." *Western Journal of Speech Communication* 48, no. 1 (winter 1984): 39–50.

Johnson, Bill. "Student's Death Holds Lesson for US." *Rocky Mountain (Denver) News,* 14 October 1998, 6A.

Johnson, Diane. "My Blue Heaven." *New York Review of Books* (16 July 1998): 15, 18–20.

Johnson, Jeff. "Looking to Stop Child Killing." *Cleveland Call and Post,* 8 May 1997, 4.

Johnson, Kevin. "Invoking McVeigh at the Nichols Trial Carries Some Risks." *USA Today,* 10 November 1997, A10.

———. "Strategy May Save Nichols' Life." *USA Today,* 24 December 1997, 3A.

Johnson, Norris. "Moral Panics: The Social Construction of Deviance." *Social Forces* (1 June 1997): 1514–15.

Johnson, Paul. "Block That Metaphor and Detribalise Yourself, You Flying Pig!" *Spectator* (9 January 1999): 21.

Johnson, Peter, and Alan Bash. "Child-Death Case Grabs Talk Shows, Newsmags." *USA Today,* 7 November 1994, 3.

Johnson, Rheta Grimsley. "May We Never Come to Expect Worst of Mothers." *Atlanta Journal-Constitution,* 6 November 1994, C1.

———. "Martha's Helping Us Do Without Tackiness." *Atlanta Journal-Constitution,* 17 November 1999, Home edition, C2.

Judis, John B. "Washington Possessed." *New Republic* (25 January 1999): 15–17.

Kamen, Al. "Navy's Columbia Roast." *Washington Post,* 28 September 1998, A23.

———. "The Asked, He Told." *Washington Post,* 3 February 1999, A15.

Kaminer, Wendy. "Simpson vs. Smith: Double Standards." *USA Today,* 19 April 1995, A13.

Kavanaugh, P. J. "Monsters and Dragons." *Spectator* (16 Oct 1999): 56–57.

Keen, Lisa. "Fairfax Library Board to Hold Hearing on *Blade* Distribution." *Washington Blade* (19 February 1993): 8.

Kempton, Murray. "A Mother's Shame." *Newsday,* 28 June 1995, A15.

Kenny, Mary. "The Only Disability to Fear Is a Closed Mind." Review. *Sunday Telegraph,* 24 December 1995, 2.

King, Colbert I. "How Monsters Are Born." *Washington Post,* 20 February 1999, A19.

Kitman, Marvin. "The Criminal Cunanan Coverage." *Newsday,* 3 August 1997, The Marvin Kitman Sunday Show, C39.

Klebnikov, Peter. "Encounters with a Monster." *Playboy* (October 1999): 50, 150.

Knight, Robert, and Peter LaBarbera. "Calculated to Provoke: Gay Cultural Warriors Threaten Church." *Washington Times,* 2 August 2000, A21.

Kurtz, Howard. "Larry Flynt: Investigative Pornographer." *Washington Post,* 19 December 1998, C1.

———. "Larry Flynt and the Barers of Bad News." *Washington Post,* 20 December 1998, F1.

Lacayo, Richard. "Anatomy of an Acquittal." *Time* (11 May 1992): 31–32.

———. "Tagged for Murder: The Strange Life and Gaudy Times of Andrew Cunanan and How He Came to Be the Most Wanted Man in America." *Time* (28 July 1997): 28–35.

———. "What Makes Clinton a Survivor?" *Time* (21 September 1998): 74–75.

Laliberte, Richard. "Missing Children: The Truth, the Hype, and What You Must Know." *Redbook* (1 February 1998): 77–79, 110.

Lamar, Hal. "They Don't Have to Kill Children." *Atlanta Inquirer,* 22 July 1995, 4.

Langton, James. "Did Versace and Cunanan Die in Mafia Conspiracy?" *Sunday Telegraph,* 27 July 1997, 24.

Larrubia, Evelyn. "Death Penalty Recommended for Rogers; Court: Jurors took a week to decide the fate of an alleged serial killer, convicted in the 1995 death of a woman he met in a Van Nuys bar." *Los Angeles Times,* 7 July 1999, Valley edition, 1.

Larson, Ruth. "Helms Takes Aim at Pro-Gay Programs." *Washington Times,* 30 January 1995, 4.

L.E.E. "The Invisible Woman." *The Ladder* (June 1965): 1.

Leo, John. "Why Ruin a Good Story?" *US News and World Report* (5 May 1997): 17.

Leonard, John. "The New Puritanism: Who's Afraid of Lolita? (We Are)." *Nation* (24 November, 1997): 11–15.

Levenson, Michael. "The Nayman of Noland." *New Republic* (6 July 1987): 34–37.

Lichfield, John. "Buchanan: The Nightmare Scenario." *Independent,* 22 February 1996, 17.

Livesey, Margot. "Surprise, Surprise." *Times Literary Supplement* (31 October 1997): 25.

Longino, Miriam. "The End of INNOCENCE." *Atlanta Journal-Constitution,* 9 July 1995, M1.

Lopez, Steve. "In Snow, in Ice, in Rain, One Mother's Trip." *Time* (8 February 1999): 45.

Lowry, Brian. "ABC Planning Film on Alleged Serial Killer; Television: Network has made a deal with Avenue Pictures to develop a script for a made-for-TV movie about Andrew Cunanan." *Los Angeles Times,* 30 July 1997, D1, 6.

———. "The Campaign Speech You Will Never Hear." *Los Angeles Times,* 7 December 1999, 1.

Marty, Martin E. "Beauty and Terror: Rapture in Art and the Sacred." *Image,* no. 17 (fall 1997): 72–82.

McCormick, John, and Evan Thomas. "A Lethal Road Trip." *Newsweek* (19 May 1997): 52–53.

McCue, Claudia. "Pay Back Monsters." Letter to the editor. *Atlanta Journal-Constitution,* 28 Sept 1999, Final edition, A19.

McFadden, Cynthia, Diane Sawyer, and Sam Donaldson. "The Secret Tapes." *ABC PrimeTime Live* (19 November 1997).

McGrory, Mary. "More Missile Madness." *Washington Post,* 22 June 2000, A3.

McMillen, Liz. "The Importance of Storytelling: A New Emphasis by Law Scholars." *Chronicle of Higher Education,* 26 July 1996, A10.

Mehren, Elizabeth. "Ex-Priest Gets 18-Year Term for Sex Abuse at 5 Parishes." *Los Angeles Times,* 7 December 1993, A1, 31.

Methvin, Eugene H. "The Face of Evil." *National Review* (23 January 1995): 34–44.

Milton, Edith. "Inside the Creepily Logical Mind of a Monster." *Boston Globe,* 6 June 1999, City edition, N6.

Mones, Paul. "Life and Death and Susan Smith." *New York Times,* 28 July 1995, A27.

Moore, Terence. "Can't Coach 'Em Like They Used To." *Atlanta Journal-Constitution,* 24 August 1999, F3.

Morello, Carol. "School Shooting Trial to Begin." *USA Today,* 9 June 1998, 2A.

Morganthau, Tom. "Will They Kill Susan Smith?" *Newsweek* (31 July 1995): 65.

———. "Condemned to Life." *Newsweek* (7 August 1995): 19–23.

Murphy, Dean E. "Pinning Demerit Badge on Chief Boy Scout; S. Africa: Blacks seek amends for founder Baden-Powell's alleged misdeeds a century ago." *Los Angeles Times,* 24 July 1999, Home edition, 1.

Nichols, Peter M. "It Was a Dark and Stormy . . . " *New York Times,* 8 October 1999, E31.

Oates, Joyce Carol. " 'I Had No Other Thrill or Happiness.' " *New York Review of Books* (24 March 1994): 52–59.

O'Connor, John J. "'Tales from the Crypt' Raises Ratings for HBO," *New York Times,* 26 June 1991.

O'Connor, Patricia E. "Discourse of Violence." *Discourse and Society* 6, no. 3 (July 1995): 309–18.

O'Donnell, Paul. "Another Suspect Plays Victim." *Newsweek* (14 November 1994): 30.

O'Driscoll, Patrick. "Emotions Still High in Shepard Case." *USA Today,* 5 April 1999, 1A, and online, <www.usatoday.com>.

Olcott, Anthony. "No Regrets, Comrades." Review of *The Autobiography of Joseph Stalin,* by Richard Lourie. *Washington Post,* 18 July 1999, X13.

Orth, Maureen. "The Versace Murder: On the Trail of the Gay Serial Killer." *Vanity Fair* (September 1997): 268–75, 329–36.

Schippers, David. "Perspectives." *Newsweek* (21 December 1998): 15.

Pianko, Katey. "Yes, He's a Monster." "Perspectives." *Newsweek* (23 August 1999): 17.

Pawelczak, Andy. "Death and the Maiden." *Films in Review* 46, nos. 5–6 (July 1995): 54–55.

Perry, Tony. "Fugitive a Surprising Suspect; Crime: To acquaintances of a man known in San Diego's gay community as a charming 'party boy,' news that he is being sought in connection with four brutal killings comes as a shock." *Los Angeles Times,* 16 May 1997, Home edition, A3.

Perry, Tony, and Judy Pasternak. "Cunanan Doesn't Fit Serial Killer Mold." *Los Angeles Times,* 20 July 1997, A1.

Peyser, Marc, and Ginny Carroll. "Southern Gothic on Trial." *Newsweek* (17 July 1995): 29.

Phillips, Andrew. "The Cunanan Enigma: Versace's Killer Takes His Own Life and Leaves a Mystery." *Maclean's* (4 August 1997): 32–33.

Phillips, Andrew, et al. "Murder in Miami: Police Accuse a Gay Gigolo of Killing Designer Gianni Versace." *Maclean's* (28 July 1997): 22–27.

Podhoretz, Norman. "A Willful Blindness." *Wall Street Journal,* 8 Nov 1999, A51.

Poniewozik, James. "We Like to Watch." *Time* (26 June 2000): 56–62.

Pooley, Eric. "High Crimes? Or Just a Sex Cover-Up?" *Time* (21 September 1998): 35–40.

Posner, Gerald. "In Search of the Real Boston Strangler." *Talk* (October 2000): 112–18, 160–63.

Potter, Mark, Ken Kashiwahara, and Chris Wallace. "What It Takes to Catch a Serial Killer." *ABC Nightline* (16 July 1997).

Prud'Homme, Alex. "Milwaukee Murders." *Time* (12 August 1991): 28.

———. "Little Flat of Horrors." *Time* (5 August 1991): 26.

Puente, Maria, and Lori Sharn. "Murder Suspect Eluding Manhunt: 4 Killings in 3 States Thought to be Connected." *USA Today,* 13 May 1997, 3A.

Puig, Claudia. "Hollywood Examines Its Soul: Worried about Censorship, Leaders Debate How to Uncreate a Monster." *USA Today,* 7 June 1999, D1.

Pullella, Philip. "Vatican Newspaper Urges Church Respect for Gays." Reuters news service, 24 April 1997.

Purtell, Tim. "The Shock Troops." *Entertainment Weekly* (4 March 1994): 23.

Recchi, Ray. "The Greatest Pain." *Atlanta Journal-Constitution,* 11 November 1994, A19.

Resnick, Edward L. "Jury Found McVeigh Didn't Act Like a Human." (16 June 1997): 18A.

Rich, Frank. "Beverly Russell's Prayers." *New York Times,* 2 August 1995, A19.

Rich, Frank. "The Mother Next Door." *New York Times,* 13 November, 1994, sec. 4, 15.

Riley, Rochelle. "Case against Killer of JonBenet Must Be Tight," Gannet news service, 5 February 1997, ARC.

Roberts, Steven V. "The Murderer Who Was Too Pathetic to Kill." Outlook, *US News and World Report* (7 August 1995): 8–9.

Rogers, Patrick, Margaret Nelson, et al. "Crime: Blood Trail Fugitive Andrew Cunanan Posed as a Class Act." *People* (7 July 1997): 53–56.

Roundy, Bill. "One Dead, Six Injured in Roanoke Shooting." *Washington Blade* (29 September 2000): 1, 10.

Rudnick, Paul. "Seven Men Living in One Cottage Sounds Like Fire Island to Me." *Newsweek* (22 February 1999): 55.

Salvadore, Maria. "Monster (Review)." *Horn Book Magazine* 76 (Jan./Feb. 2000): 42.

Saul, Stephanie. "Authorities ID Dahmer Killer: Lifer Named in Prison Attack." *Newsday,* 30 November 1994, A4.

———. "Dahmer Slain: A Fellow Inmate Kills a Notorious Serial Killer." *Newsday,* 29 November 1994, A3.

Sawyer, Diane. "The Secret Tapes." *ABC PrimeTime* (19 November 1997).

———. "Starr Speaks Out." *ABC 20/20* (25 November 1998).

Sawyer, Diane, and Sam Donaldson. "Family Matters." *ABC PrimeTime Live* (6 August 1997).

Schaeffer, Michael. "Fun and Frolic, It's Florida!" *U.S. News & World Report* (27 November 2000): 37–40.

Schechter, Harold. Cited in Robert Koehler, "Murderers Row: The Actors in 'Mass Murder' Give Voice to the Minds of Such Serial Killers as Jeffrey Dahmer, Ted Bundy and the Night Stalker," *Los Angeles Times,* 3 May 1992, Calendar section, 49.

Schmich, Mary. "Cunanan's Death Keeps Us in His Grip a Little Longer." *Chicago Tribune,* 25 July 1997, 10.

Schneider, Craig. "The Versace Slaying: Fatal Designs." *Atlanta Journal-Constitution,* 16 July 1997, A7.

Sennott, Charles. "Southern Secrets." *Boston Globe,* 28 December 1994, 1.

Shales, Tom. "'Party Monster': A Wild Ride with the Devil." *Washington Post,* 18 June 1998, C1.

Shea, Christopher. "Americans More United in Social Views." *Chronicle of Higher Education,* 17 January 1997, A17.

Sherman, Betsy. "'Party,' 'Raw Images' Challenge Senses, Spirit." *Boston Globe,* 16 July 1999, C6.

Sherman, Betsy. "Pastel to Gothic, a Must-Catch for the Pokemon Set." *Boston Globe,* 10 November 1999, F1.

Simon, Scott. "Murders Tear at Our Hearts, Rightfully So, Says Simon." Weekend Edition, National Public Radio, 5 November 1994.

Smith, Abbe, and Sally Greenberg. "The Law vs. Women." *Boston Globe,* 27 February 1995, 15.

Smith, Lynn, and Elizabeth Mehren. "Why Does a Mother Kill Her Child?" *Los Angeles Times,* 5 November 1994, A1.

Smith, Rhonda. "Phelps Announces Plans." *Washington Blade* (14 April 2000): 18.

Solotaroff, Ivan. "Charlie Manson Saves the Whales." *Esquire* (February 1992): 78+.

Stancavish, Don. "Neighbors See Planned Senior Home as 'Monster.' *(Bergen, N.J.) Record,* 11 November 1998, <www.bergen.com>.

Star, Jack. "The Sad, 'Gay' Life." *Look* (10 January 1967).

Starks, Steven. "Perry Mason Meets Sonny Crocket: The History of Lawyers and Police as Television Heroes." 42 U. Miami Law Rev. (1987).

Stasio, Marilyn. "Night of the Living, and Unliving, Dead." *New York Times,* 31 October 1999, A4.

Steinfels, Peter. "Defining the Sacred and the Profane," *New York Times,* 16 May 1998.

Stone, Andrea. "Ex-Priest's Victims 'Dismayed,' Sentence Called 'Not Enough.'" *USA Today,* 7 December 1993, A3.

———. "Ex-Priest Gets Prison in Child Abuse." *USA Today,* 7 December 1993, 1A.

Strand, Wilson. Letter to the editor. *Newsweek* (1 June 1998): 8H.

Taylor, John. "Murder, the Ultimate Art Form." *Esquire* (1 September 1994): 76–82.

Teepen, Tom. "Gingrich Chooses God as His New Political Ally." *Atlanta Journal-Constitution,* 18 May 1999, A11.

Thernstrom, Melanie. "The Murder: The Crucifixion of Matthew Shepard." *Vanity Fair* (March 1999): 209–14, 267–75.

Thomas, Evan. "End of the Road," *Newsweek* (4 August 1997): 22–27.

Thomas, Evan. "Facing Death." *Newsweek* (28 July 1997): 20–29.

Toufexis, Anastasia. "Dances with Werewolves." *Time* (4 April 1994): 64–66.

Tracy, Carol. E. "Help the Women Drug Users." *Philadelphia Inquirer,* 14 September 1990, 21A.

Transcript. *ABC Day One* (18 April 1993).

Transcript. All Things Considered, National Public Radio, 24 July 1997.

Transcript. "South Carolina Murders Still Stun the Nation." All Things Considered, National Public Radio, 4 November 1994.

Trounstine, Philip. J. "The Starr Report." *San Jose Mercury News,* 13 September 1998, insert, 1–12.

Van Biema, David. "Parents Who Kill." *Time* (14 November 1994): 50.

———. "Death at Every Stop." *Time* (19 May 1997): 40.

Vargas, Elizabeth. "Family Recollections of Andrew Cunanan. *ABC Good Morning America* (7 August 1997).

Vaughan, Kevin. "Suspect 'Flipped Out,' Beat Shepard, Letters Say." *Denver Rocky Mountain News,* 7 April 1999, <insidedenver.com>.

Von Fremd, Mike, Ted Koppel. "Two Different and Extraordinary Views of Cunanan." *ABC Nightline* (24 July 1997).

Welkos, Robert W. "Cunanan's Father Plans Documentary on Son's Life." *Los Angeles Times,* 19 September 1997, F2.

Wentworth, Richard L. "New Battle at Rome Colosseum." *Christian Science Monitor,* 3 July 2000, 6.

West, Woody. "Unforgiven." *The World and I* (1 September 1995).

White, Norma Jean. Letter to the editor. *St. Louis Post-Dispatch,* 21 June 1997, 36.

Whyte, Kemerie A. "Susan Smith: Inconsistent coverage." Letters. *Atlanta Journal-Constitution,* 12 July 1995, A12.

Wickham, Dewayne. "Helms' Wish to Punish AIDS Sufferers Is Irrational." Gannett news service, 6 July 1995.

Willis, Ellen. "Down with Compassion." *New Yorker* (30 September 1996): 4–10.

Wills, Garry. "It's His Party." *New York Times Magazine* (11 August 1996): section 6: 30–37, 52, 55–59.

———. "A Tale of Two Cities." *New York Review of Books* (3 October 1996): 16–22.

———. "The Tragic Pope." *New York Review of Books* (22 December 1994): 4–7.

Wilkes, Paul. "Unholy Acts." *New Yorker* (7 June 1993): 62–79.

Wilson, Tracy. "Parents Go on Trial in Death of Toddler." *Los Angeles Times,* 18 November 1997, Ventura County edition, 1.

Wolf, Leonard. "In Horror Movies, Some Things Are Sacred." *New York Times,* 4 April 1976, sec. 2, 1, 19.

Young, Charles M. "Geraldo Rivera." *Rolling Stone* (18 September 1997): 88–95.

Youngblood, Courtney. Review of *Monsters in the Closet: Homosexuality and the Horror Film,* by Harry M. Benshoff. *American Studies International* 37, no. 2 (June 1999): 116.

Zabarenko, Deborah. "Sleaze Takes Precedence over Impeachment Pomp." Reuters news service, 12 January 1999, from <dailynews.yahoo.com>

Zoglin, Richard. "Manson Family Values." *Time* (21 March 1994): 77.

Online

Adolf Eichmann's Final Plea: "In His Own Words." <www.remember.org/eichmann/ownwords.htm>.

Anonymous. "A History of Hatred: Suspect in Gay Slaying Known for Hostility." *Times Herald Record,* 6 March 1999, <www.th-record.com>.

Anonymous. "Anti-Gay Phelps to Protest at Shepard Funeral." *Casper Star Tribune,* 13 October 1998, <www.trib.com/CST>.

Anonymous. "Anti-Gay Group Plans to Protest Funeral," *Casper Star Tribune,* 13 October 1998, <www.trib.com/CST>.

Anonymous. "Did Shepard's Accused Killers Attack Before?" Channel 3000 (Madison) News (13 October 1998): <www.channel3000.com>.

Anonymous. "Gay Student Clings to Life after Savage Beating." CNN Interactive (10 October 1998): <www.cnn.com/US>.

Anonymous. "Northern CA High School Student Beaten in Apparent Hate Crime." *GLAADLines* (16 February 1999): <www.glaad.org>.

Anonymous. "Parents Alert: Tinky Winky Comes Out of the Closet." *National Liberty Journal* (February): <www.liberty.edu/chancellor/nlj/feb99/politics2.htm>.

Anonymous. "Revelations Prompt Morris Resignation as Clinton Adviser." CIS Congressional Universe. *National Journal's CongressDaily,* 29 August 1996.

Anonymous [Newsplanet Staff]. "Shepard as Cause Celebre." *PlanetOut* (13 October 1998): <www.planetout.com/news/article.html?1998/10/13/2>.

Anonymous. "Special GLAADLINES Edition on the Death of Matthew Shepard." *GLAADLines* (12 October 1998): <www.glaad.org>.

Anonymous. "Target for Homophobes." Editorial. *PlanetOut* (13 October 1998): <www.planetout.com/news/article.html?1998/10/13/2>.

Anonymous. "Victim of Anti-Gay Attack in Wyoming Clings to Life." CNN Interactive (11 October 1998): <www.cnn.com/US>.

Aravosis, John. "Anti-Gay Rhetoric Chronicled on New Web Site." Wired Strategies (7 December 1998): <www.wiredstrategies.com/hate.html>.

"Brawley Defamation Suit Goes to Court," *Law Street Journal* (21 November 1997): <www.lawstreet.com>.

Cameron, Paul. "Medical Consequences of What Homosexuals Do." Family Research Institute, <www.biblebelievers.com/Cameron2.html>.

———. "Anti-Gay Quotes from Paul Cameron." Wired Strategies, <www.wiredstrategies.com/cameron.html>.

———. "The Religious Right and Anti-Gay Speech: In Their Own Words," under "Dr. Paul Cameron." Wired Strategies, <www.wiredstrategies.com/hate.html>.

Cornelius, Coleman. "In Face of Hate, a Call for Peace." *Denver Post,* 17 October 1998, <www.denverpost.com>.

Davila, Robert D. "Schools Losing Tolerance for AntiGgay Harassment." *Sacramento Bee,* 10 September 1998, <www.sacbee.com>.

Delsohn, Gary, and Sam Stanton. "I'm Guilty of Obeying the Laws of the Creator." *Salon.com* (8 November 1999): <www.salon.com>.

Falzarano, Anthony, PFOX. "Satan uses homosexuals as pawns" quotation. Cited in Wired Strategies, <www.wiredstrategies.com/exgay.html>.

Gurnon, Emily. "Specter of Hate in 2 Assaults on Youths." *San Francisco Examiner,* 14 February 1999, <www.sfgate.com>.

Hill, Michael S. "Wyoming Death Has National, Local Impact." *Auburn Plainsman via U-WIRE,* 23 October 1998, <www.uwire.com>.

Knight, Robert. Quoted in "Anti-Gay Quotes from the Family Research Council." Wired Strategies, <www.wiredstrategies.com/frc. html>.

Lott, Trent. Associated Press, 15 June 1998. Cited in Wired Strategies, <www.wired strategies.com/claremont.html>; also <www.wiredstrategies.com/hate.html>.

Miller, Arthur. Editorial, "Our Bloodless Coup." *Nation* (11 January 1999):<www .thenation.com>.

"Monster Definition." Simon and Schuster Inc. 1998. <www.elibrary.com/search>.

Pearlman, John. "At Full Blast." *CNN Sports Illustrated Online* (23 December 1999): <sportsillustrated.cnn.com>.

People for the American Way, <www.pfaw.org>.

Perry, Troy. Referred to in "Anti-Gay Quotes from the Family Research Council." Wired Strategies, <www.wiredstrategies.com/frc.html>.

Phelps, Fred. "Anti-Gay Quotes from Baptist Rev. Fred Phelps" (Westboro Baptist Church press release and assorted comments). Wired Strategies, <www.wired strategies.com/phelps.html>.

Postrel, Virginia I., and Nick Gillespie. "The New, New World: Richard Rodriguez on Culture and Assimilation." *Reason Online,* <www.reason.com/Rodri.html>.

Robertson, Pat. "Satanists . . . and homosexuals" quotation. Cited in Wired Strategies, <www.wiredstrategies.com/robertson.html>; and People for the American Way, "Anti-Gay Politics and the Religious Right," <www.pfaw.org/issues/right/ rtvw.antigay.shtml>

Sheldon, Reverend Louis. Cited by Mark E. Pietrzyk, *News-Telegraph,* 10 March 1995. Wired Strategies, <www.wiredstrategies.com/hate.html>; also <www.wired strategies.com/sheldon.html>.

Soraghan, Michael. "Activists, Protesters Trade Views Outside Church." *Denver Post,* 17 October 1998, <www.denverpost.com>.

Spivey, Nigel. "Christ and the Art of Agony." *History Today* (August 1999): on <www .britannica.com>.

"Text of Buchanan's Speech." AP Online, 25 October 1999.

Volle, Paul. "Anti-Gay Quotes from the Christian Coalition of Maine's Paul Volle."

Wired Strategies, <www.wiredstrategies.com/cc.html>; also <www.wiredstrategies.com/hate.html>.

White, Reggie. Interview. *ABC's 20/20* (27 April 1998). Cited in Wired Strategies, <www.wiredstrategies.com/claremont.html>.

TV Vérité

"America's Serial Killer Epidemic." *20th Century* (1994), Mike Wallace. (Ressler quotation, "The Monsters among us do live on.")

"Dahmer: Mystery of the Serial Killer." Arts and Entertainment Network (1993).

"Murder: No Apparent Motive" (1984). (Detective Salerno; Ed Kemper.)

"The Minds of Serial Killers and the Women Who Love Them." *Geraldo* (1993).

INDEX